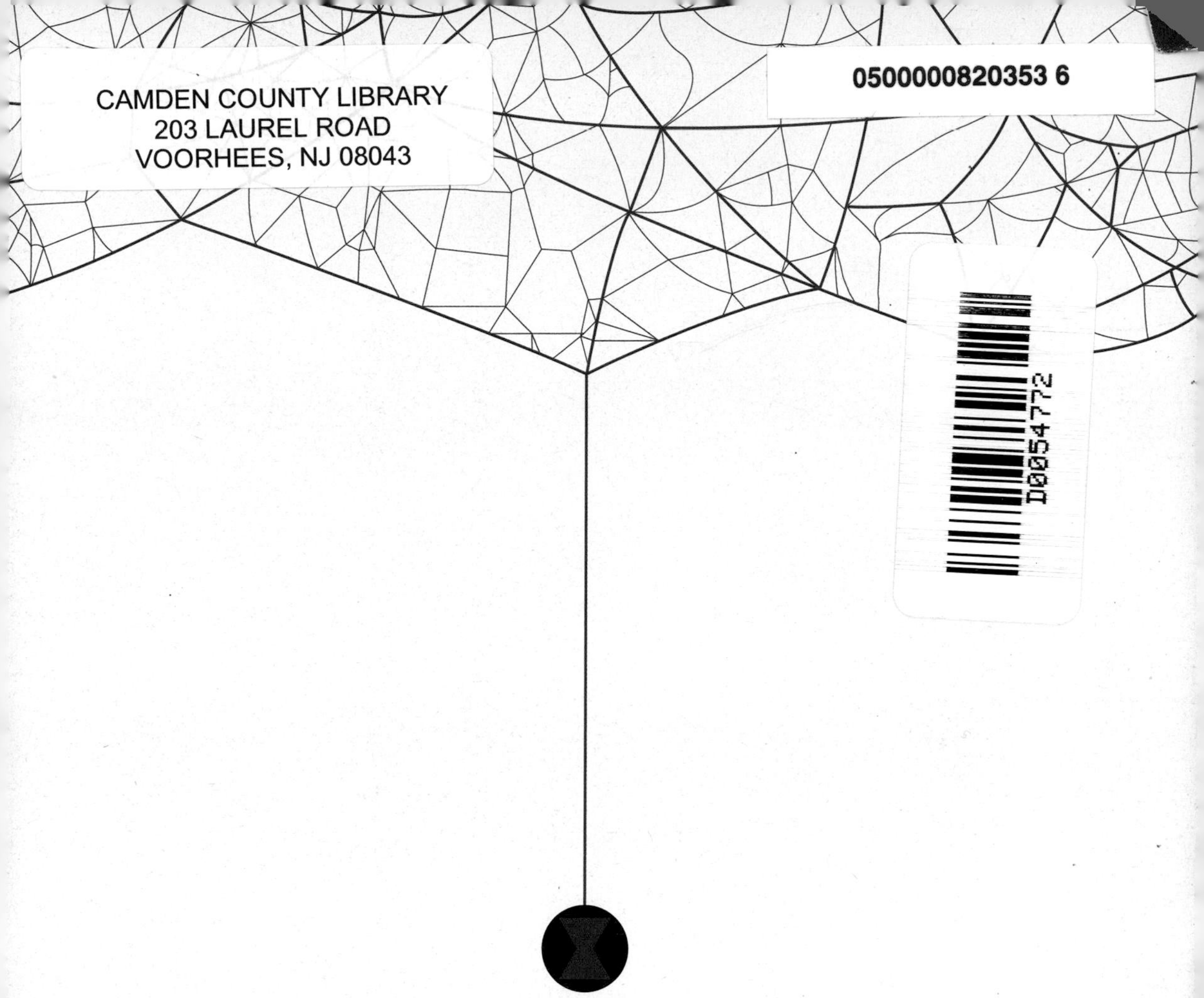

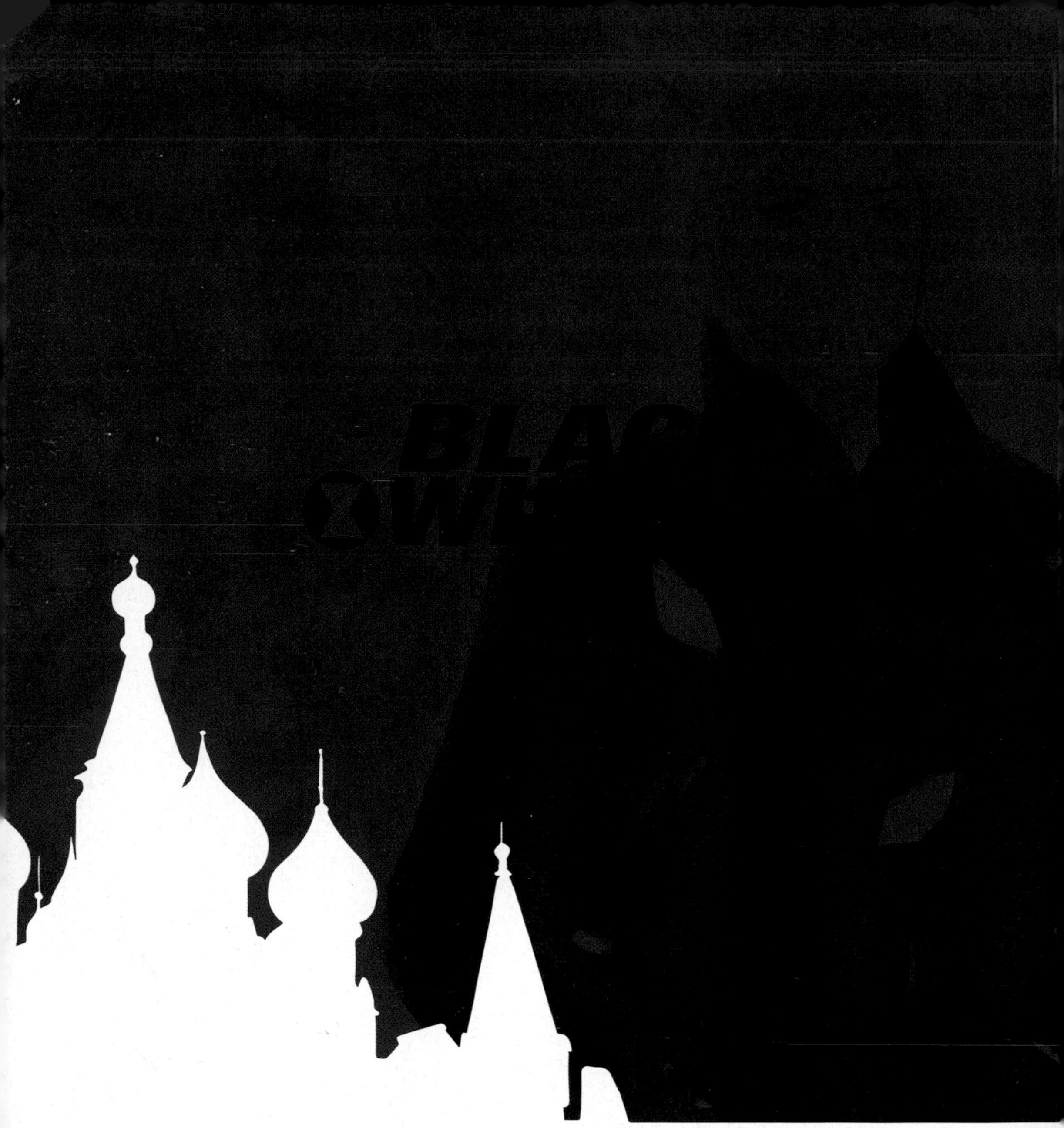

WRITER
NATHAN EDMONDSON

ARTIST/COVER ART
PHIL NOTO

LETTERER
VC'S CLAYTON COWLES

EDITORS
JAKE THOMAS & ELLIE PYLE

Collection Editor: Jennifer Grünwald • Assistant Editor: Sarah Brunstad • Associate Managing Editor: Alex Starbuck • Editor, Special Projects: Mark D. Beazley
Senior Editor, Special Projects: Jeff Youngquist • SVP Print, Sales & Marketing: David Gabriel

Editor in Chief: Axel Alonso • Chief Creative Officer: Joe Quesada • Publisher: Dan Buckley • Executive Producer: Alan Fine

BLACK WIDOW VOL. 3: LAST DAYS. Contains material originally published in magazine form as BLACK WIDOW #13-20. First printing 2015. ISBN# 978-0-7851-9253-4. Published by MARVEL WORLDWIDE, INC.
a subsidiary of MARVEL ENTERTAINMENT, LLC. OFFICE OF PUBLICATION: 135 West 50th Street, New York, NY 10020. Copyright © 2015 MARVEL No similarity between any of the names, characters, persons, and/
or institutions in this magazine with those of any living or dead person or institution is intended, and any such similarity which may exist is purely coincidental. **Printed in the U.S.A.** ALAN FINE, President, Marvel
Entertainment; DAN BUCKLEY, President, TV, Publishing and Brand Management; JOE QUESADA, Chief Creative Officer; TOM BREVOORT, SVP of Publishing; DAVID BOGART, SVP of Operations & Procurement, Publishing;
C.B. CEBULSKI, VP of International Development & Brand Management; DAVID GABRIEL, SVP Print, Sales & Marketing; JIM O'KEEFE, VP of Operations & Logistics; DAN CARR, Executive Director of Publishing Technology;
SUSAN CRESPI, Editorial Operations Manager; ALEX MORALES, Publishing Operations Manager; STAN LEE, Chairman Emeritus. For information regarding advertising in Marvel Comics or on Marvel.com, please contact
Jonathan Rheingold, VP of Custom Solutions & Ad Sales, at jrheingold@marvel.com. For Marvel subscription inquiries, please call 800-217-9158. **Manufactured between 7/31/2015 and 9/7/2015 by HESS PRINT
SOLUTIONS, A DIVISION OF BANG PRINTING, BRIMFIELD, OH, USA.**

10 9 8 7 6 5 4 3 2 1

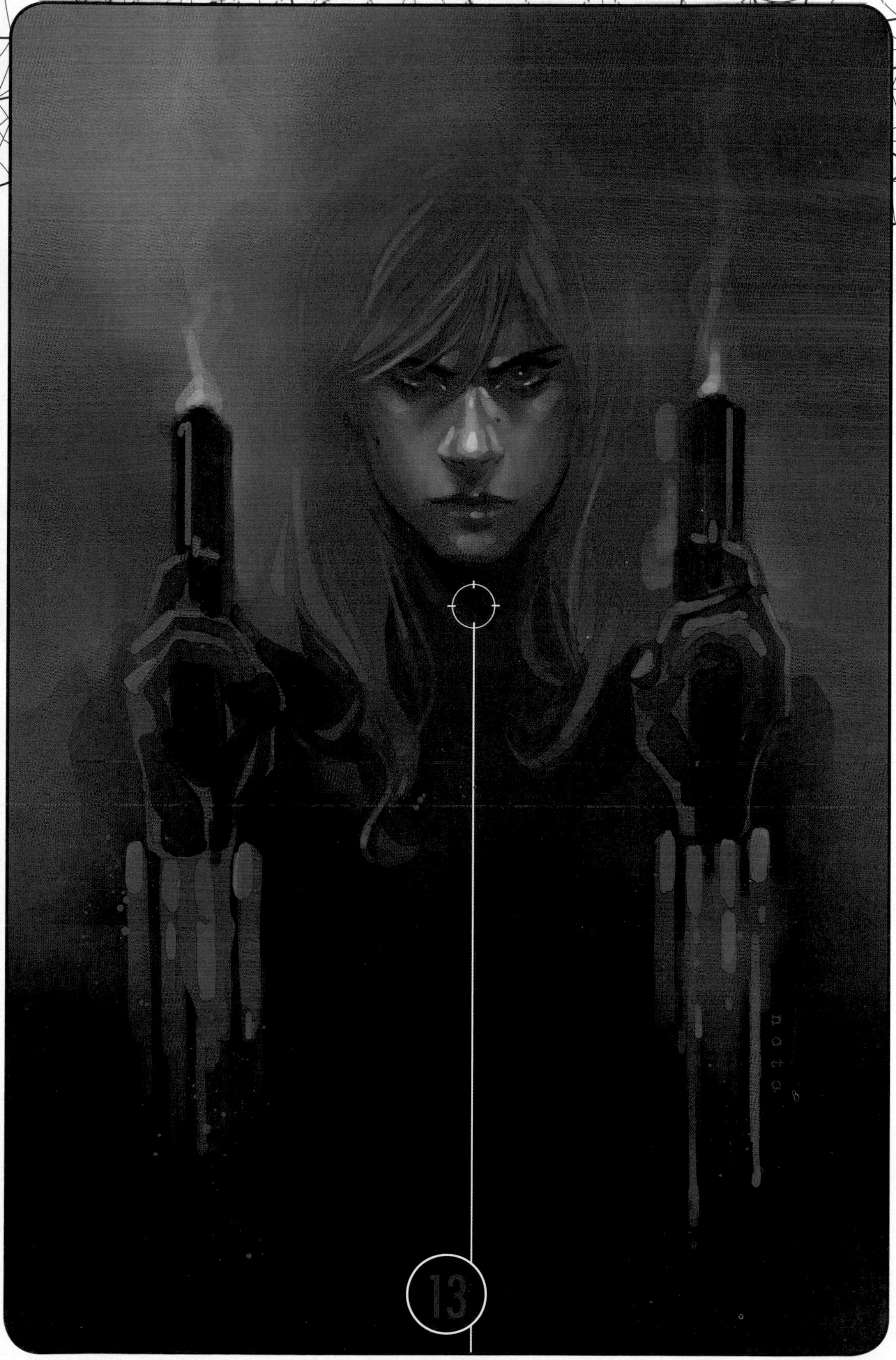
13

AUTUMN

SOCIOPATHY.

DEFINED:

PSYCHOPATHIC.

ANTISOCIAL.

CRIMINAL.

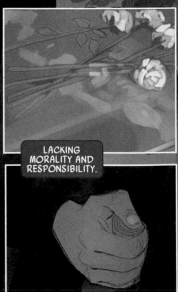

LACKING MORALITY AND RESPONSIBILITY.

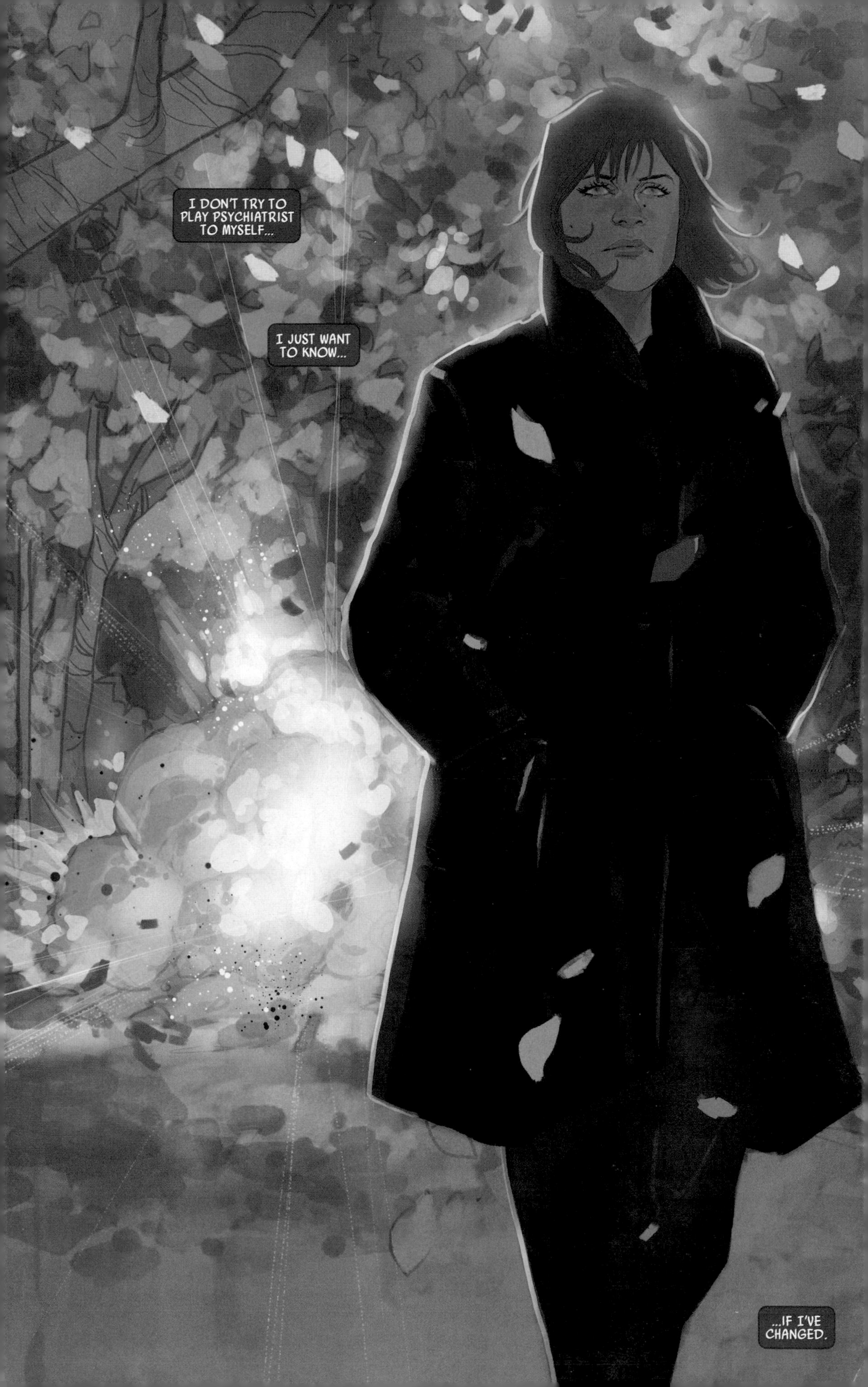
I DON'T TRY TO PLAY PSYCHIATRIST TO MYSELF...
I JUST WANT TO KNOW...
...IF I'VE CHANGED.

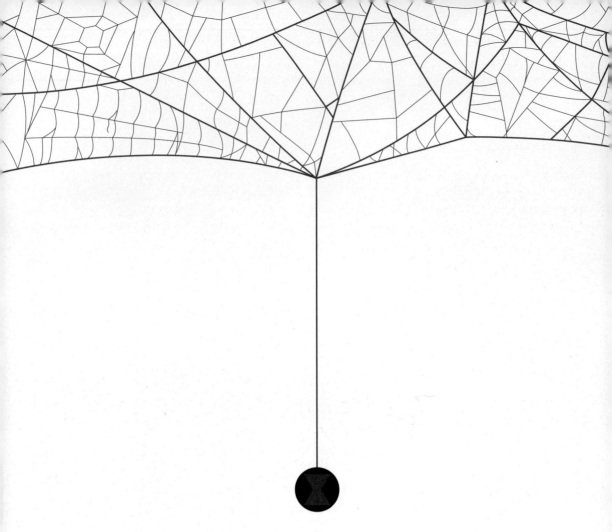

Natasha Romanova is an Avenger, an agent of S.H.I.E.L.D. and an ex-KGB assassin, but on her own time, she uses her unique skill set to atone for her past. She is:

BLACK WIDOW

Natasha has been on the trail of Chaos, a mysterious and destructive organization whose reach seems infinite. While she was on assignment, they shot her attorney. This will not make their lives easier.

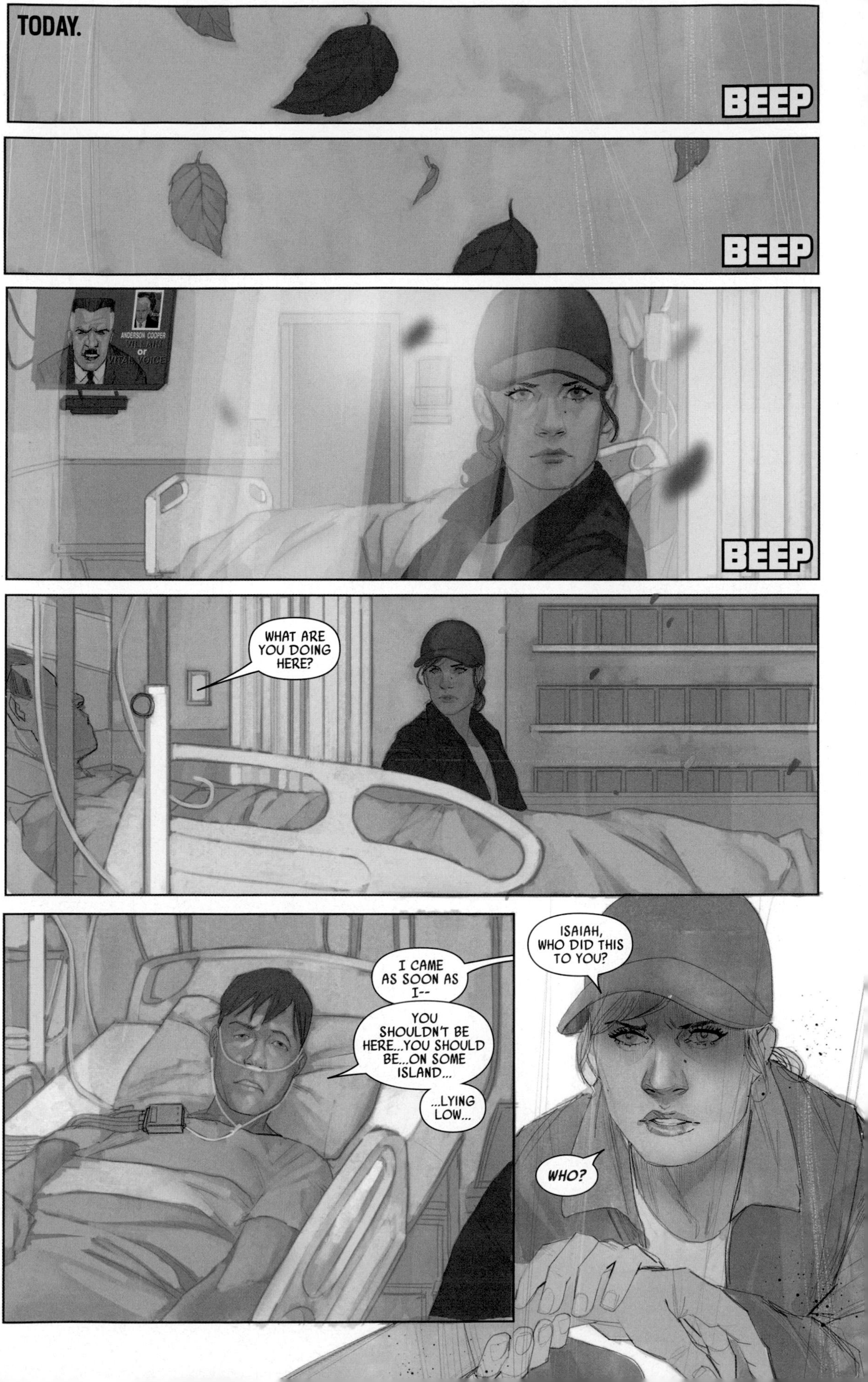
TODAY.
BEEP
BEEP
ANDERSON COOPER
VILLAIN
or
VITAL VOICE
BEEP
WHAT ARE YOU DOING HERE?
I CAME AS SOON AS I--
YOU SHOULDN'T BE HERE...YOU SHOULD BE...ON SOME ISLAND...
...LYING LOW...
ISAIAH, WHO DID THIS TO YOU?
WHO?

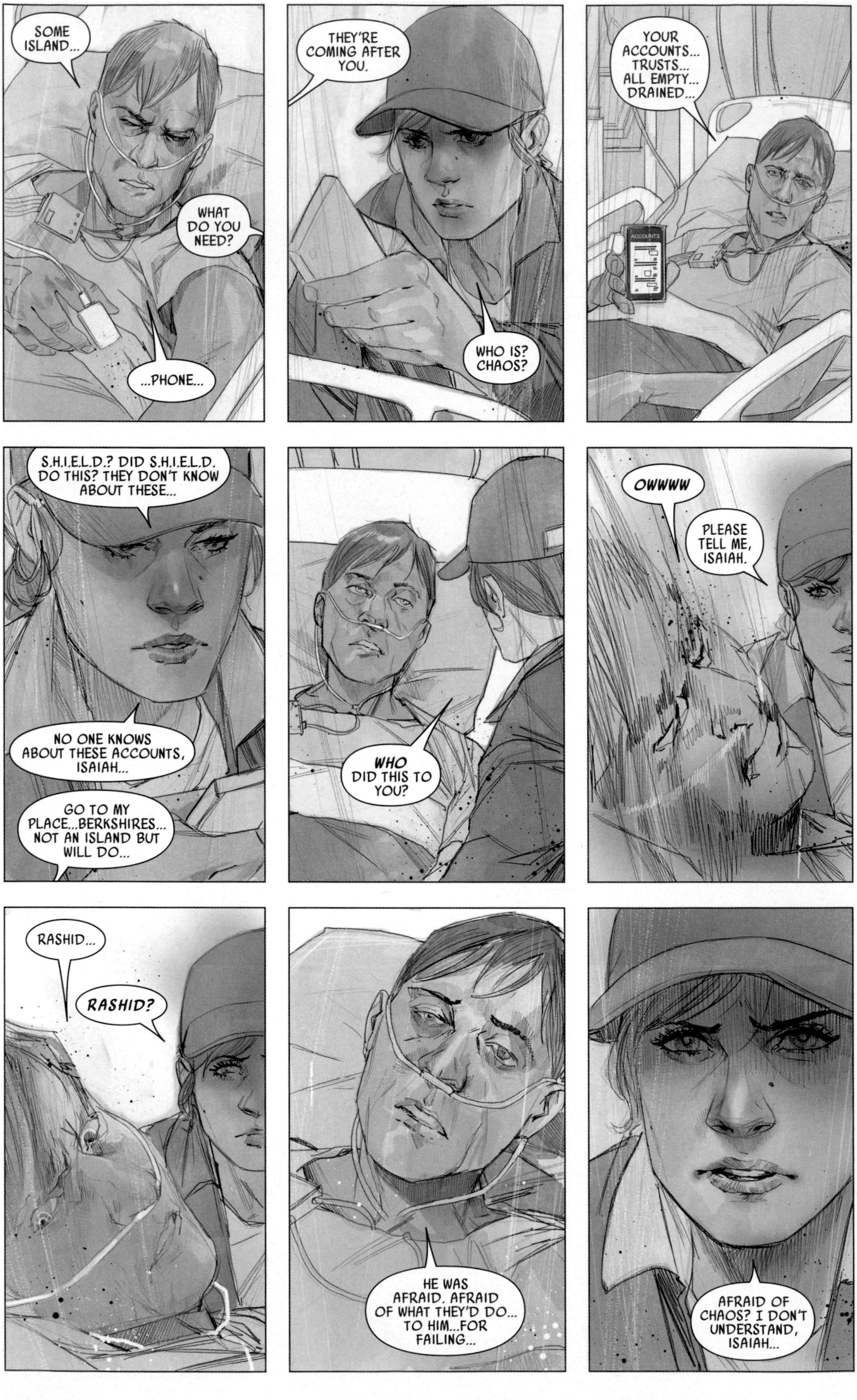

SOME ISLAND...
WHAT DO YOU NEED?
...PHONE...
THEY'RE COMING AFTER YOU.
WHO IS? CHAOS?
YOUR ACCOUNTS... TRUSTS... ALL EMPTY... DRAINED...
ACCOUNTS
S.H.I.E.L.D.? DID S.H.I.E.L.D. DO THIS? THEY DON'T KNOW ABOUT THESE...
NO ONE KNOWS ABOUT THESE ACCOUNTS, ISAIAH...
GO TO MY PLACE...BERKSHIRES... NOT AN ISLAND BUT WILL DO...
WHO DID THIS TO YOU?
OWWWW
PLEASE TELL ME, ISAIAH.
RASHID...
RASHID?
HE WAS AFRAID. AFRAID OF WHAT THEY'D DO... TO HIM...FOR FAILING...
AFRAID OF CHAOS? I DON'T UNDERSTAND, ISAIAH...

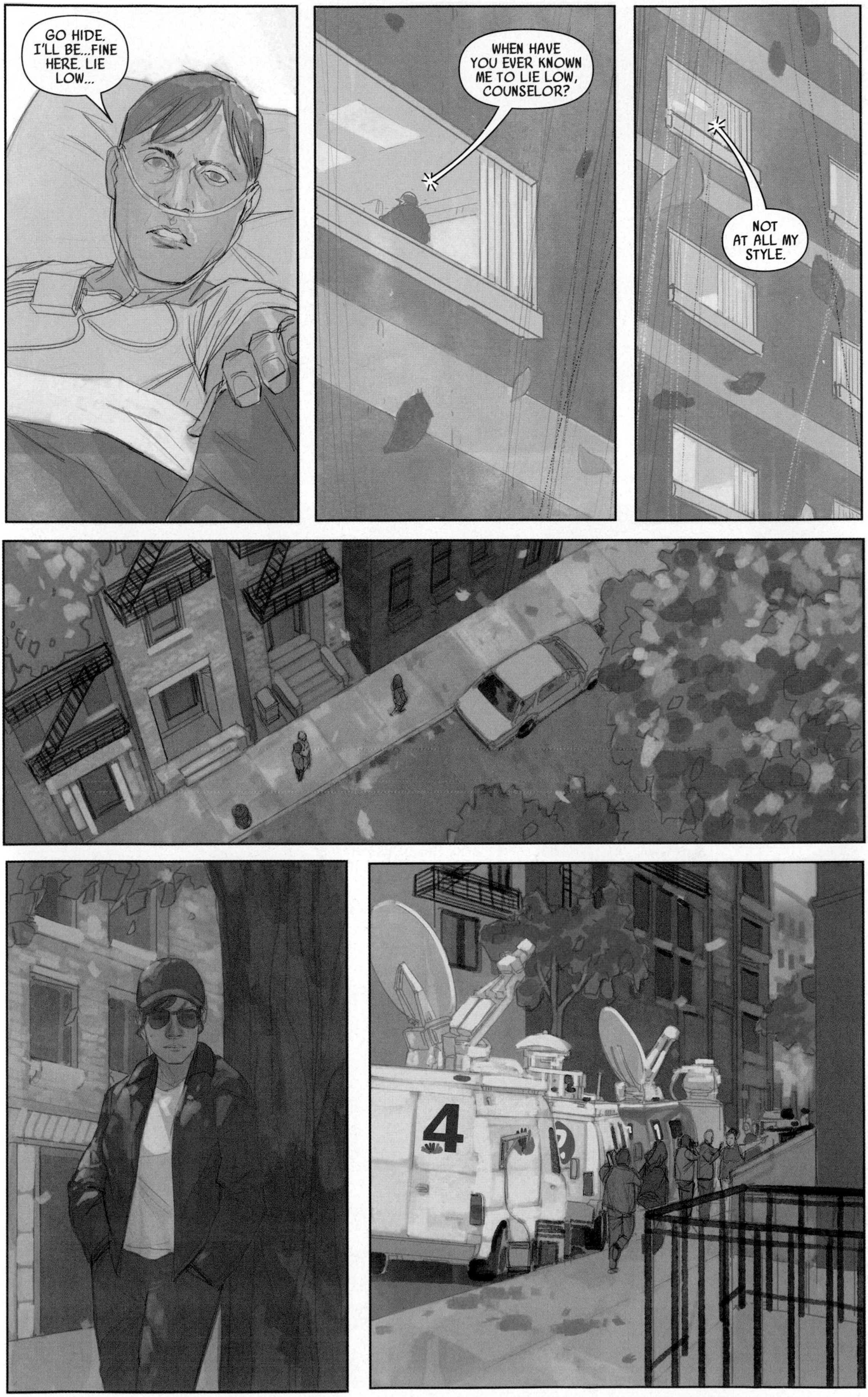
GO HIDE. I'LL BE...FINE HERE. LIE LOW...
WHEN HAVE YOU EVER KNOWN ME TO LIE LOW, COUNSELOR?
NOT AT ALL MY STYLE.
4

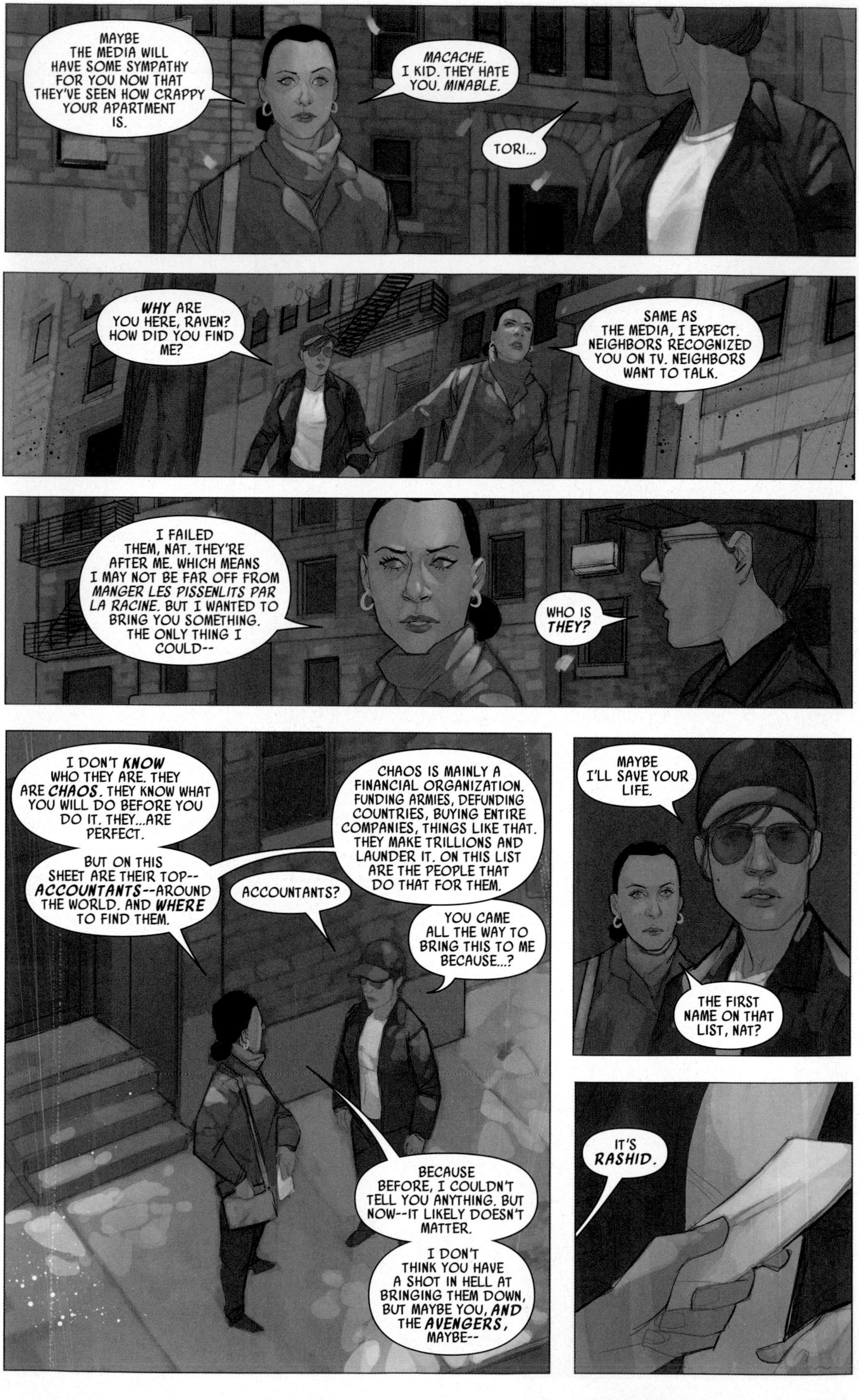
MAYBE THE MEDIA WILL HAVE SOME SYMPATHY FOR YOU NOW THAT THEY'VE SEEN HOW CRAPPY YOUR APARTMENT IS.
MACACHE. I KID. THEY HATE YOU. MINABLE.
TORI...
WHY ARE YOU HERE, RAVEN? HOW DID YOU FIND ME?
SAME AS THE MEDIA, I EXPECT. NEIGHBORS RECOGNIZED YOU ON TV. NEIGHBORS WANT TO TALK.
I FAILED THEM, NAT. THEY'RE AFTER ME. WHICH MEANS I MAY NOT BE FAR OFF FROM MANGER LES PISSENLITS PAR LA RACINE. BUT I WANTED TO BRING YOU SOMETHING. THE ONLY THING I COULD--
WHO IS THEY?
I DON'T KNOW WHO THEY ARE. THEY ARE CHAOS. THEY KNOW WHAT YOU WILL DO BEFORE YOU DO IT. THEY...ARE PERFECT.
BUT ON THIS SHEET ARE THEIR TOP-- ACCOUNTANTS--AROUND THE WORLD. AND WHERE TO FIND THEM.
ACCOUNTANTS?
CHAOS IS MAINLY A FINANCIAL ORGANIZATION. FUNDING ARMIES, DEFUNDING COUNTRIES, BUYING ENTIRE COMPANIES, THINGS LIKE THAT. THEY MAKE TRILLIONS AND LAUNDER IT. ON THIS LIST ARE THE PEOPLE THAT DO THAT FOR THEM.
YOU CAME ALL THE WAY TO BRING THIS TO ME BECAUSE...?
BECAUSE BEFORE, I COULDN'T TELL YOU ANYTHING. BUT NOW--IT LIKELY DOESN'T MATTER.
I DON'T THINK YOU HAVE A SHOT IN HELL AT BRINGING THEM DOWN, BUT MAYBE YOU, AND THE AVENGERS, MAYBE--
MAYBE I'LL SAVE YOUR LIFE.
THE FIRST NAME ON THAT LIST, NAT?
IT'S RASHID.

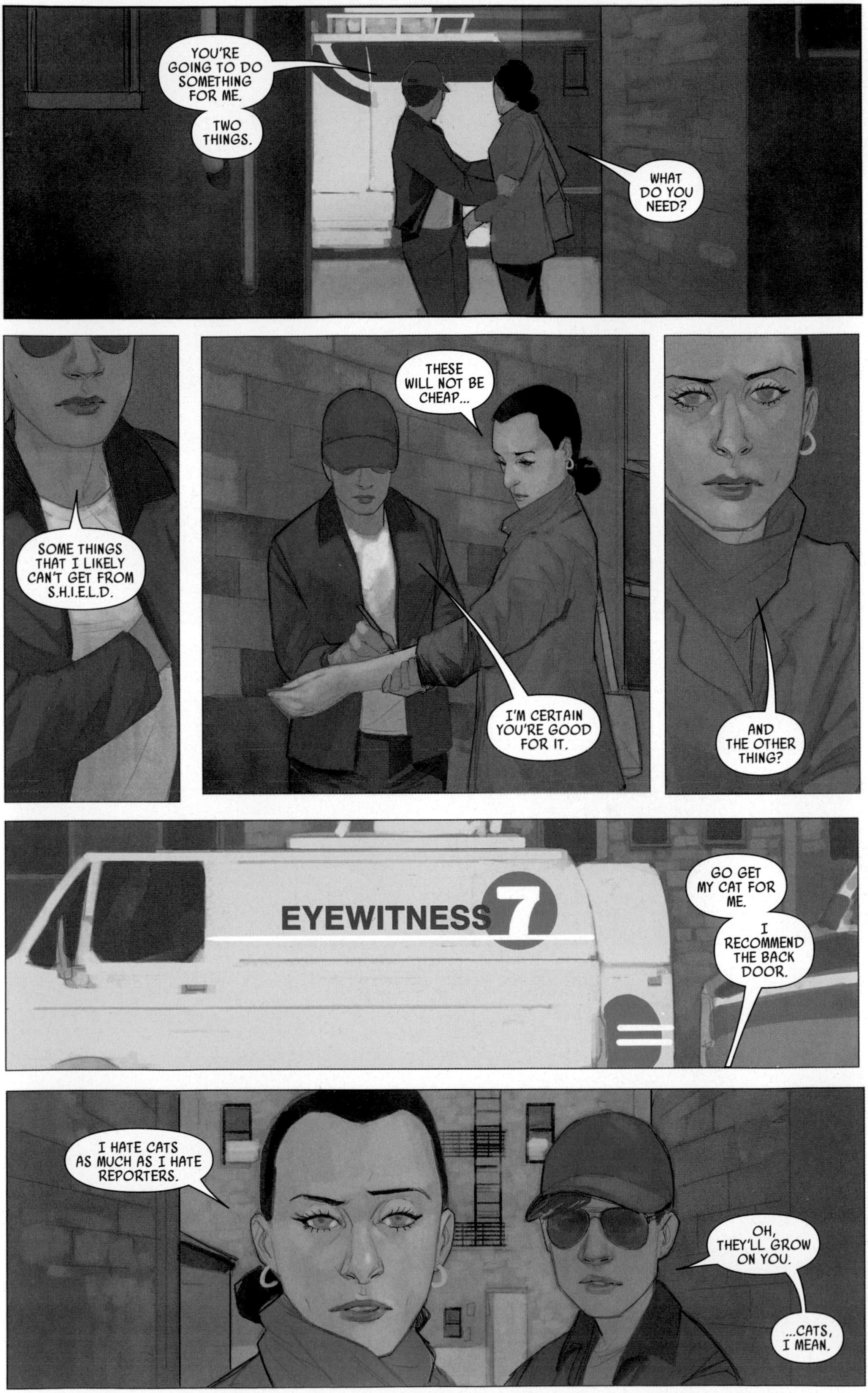

YOU'RE GOING TO DO SOMETHING FOR ME.
TWO THINGS.
WHAT DO YOU NEED?
SOME THINGS THAT I LIKELY CAN'T GET FROM S.H.I.E.L.D.
THESE WILL NOT BE CHEAP...
I'M CERTAIN YOU'RE GOOD FOR IT.
AND THE OTHER THING?
EYEWITNESS 7
GO GET MY CAT FOR ME.
I RECOMMEND THE BACK DOOR.
I HATE CATS AS MUCH AS I HATE REPORTERS.
OH, THEY'LL GROW ON YOU.
...CATS, I MEAN.

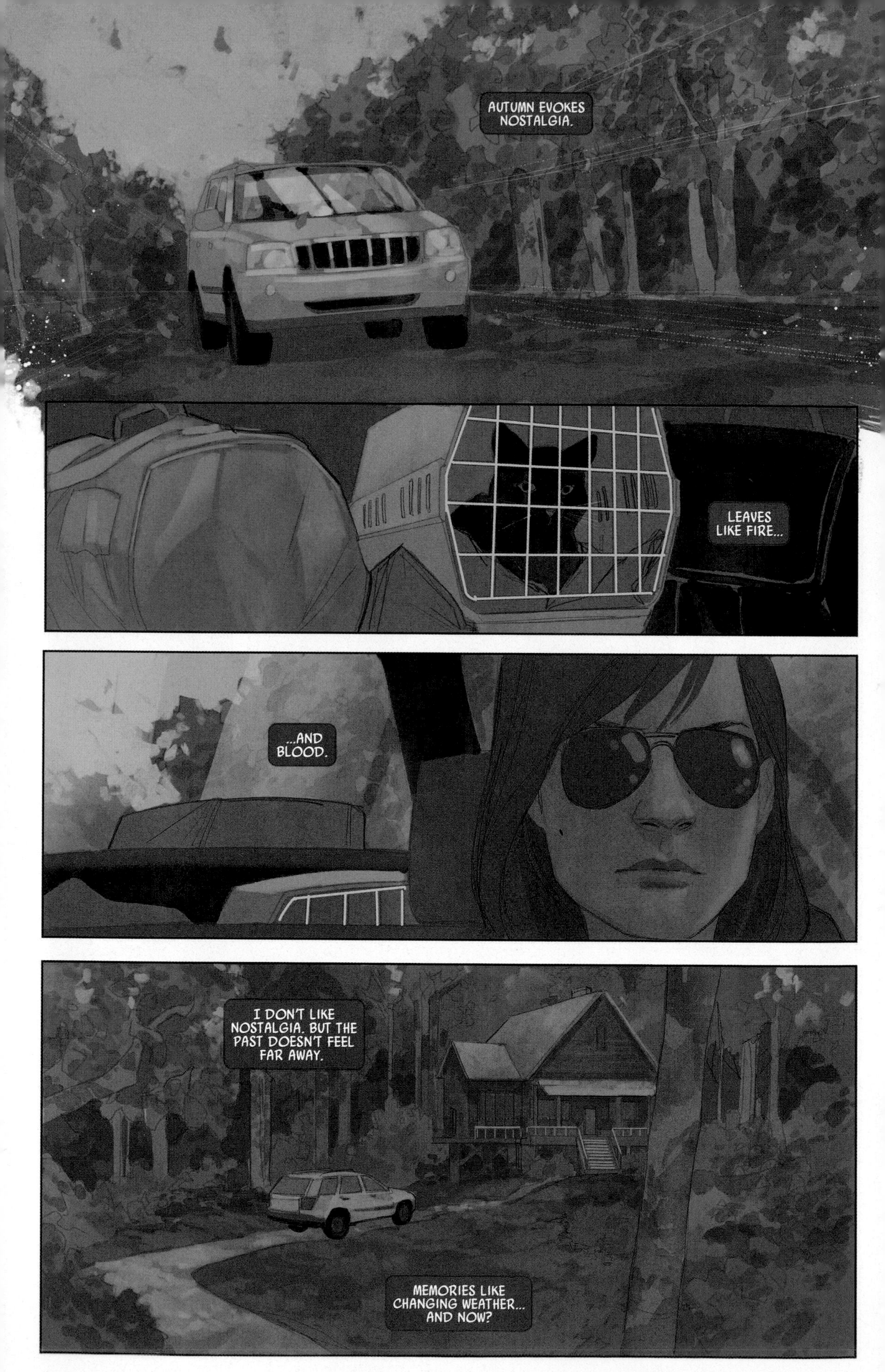
AUTUMN EVOKES NOSTALGIA.
LEAVES LIKE FIRE...
...AND BLOOD.
I DON'T LIKE NOSTALGIA. BUT THE PAST DOESN'T FEEL FAR AWAY.
MEMORIES LIKE CHANGING WEATHER... AND NOW?

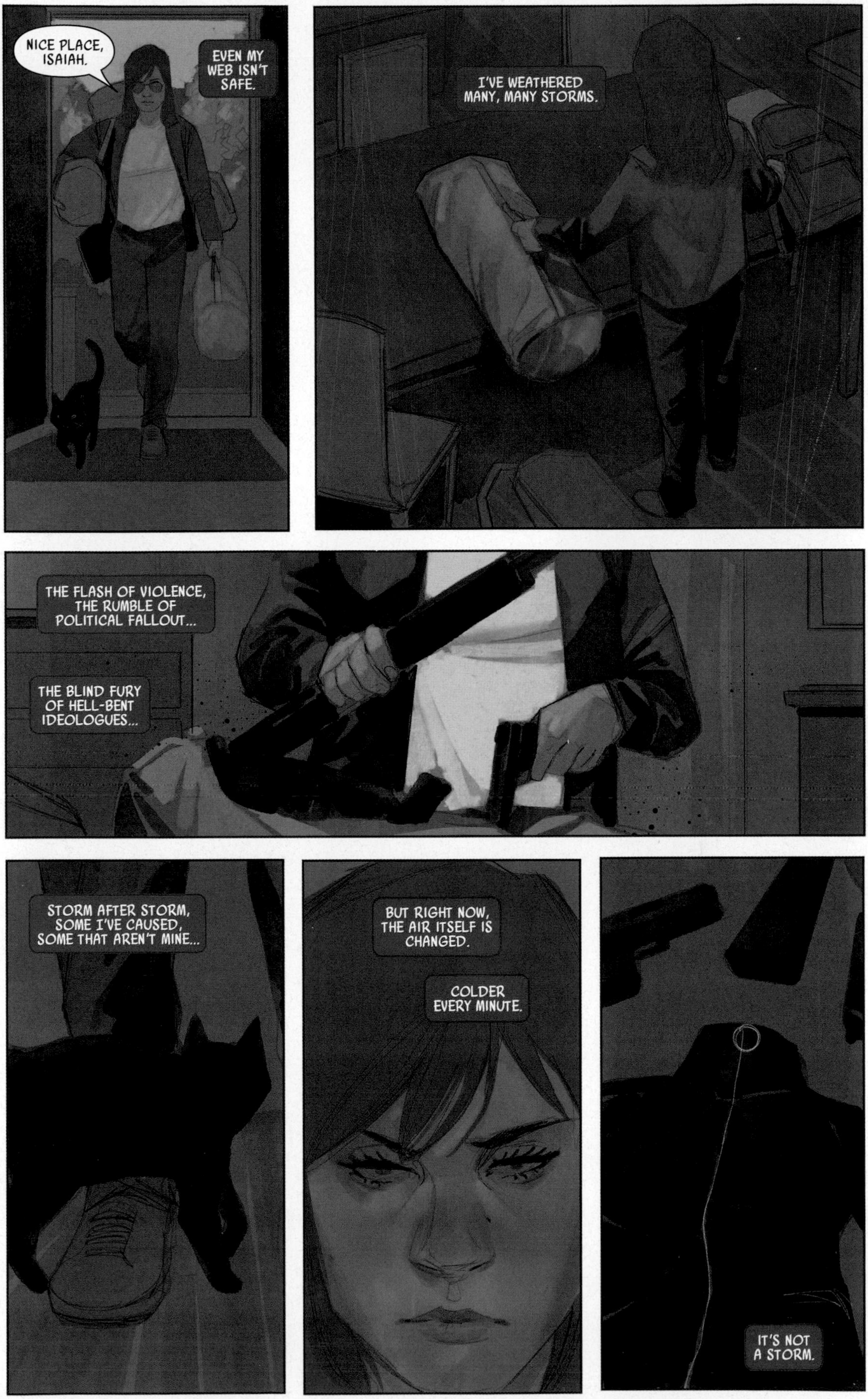
NICE PLACE, ISAIAH.
EVEN MY WEB ISN'T SAFE.
I'VE WEATHERED MANY, MANY STORMS.
THE FLASH OF VIOLENCE, THE RUMBLE OF POLITICAL FALLOUT...
THE BLIND FURY OF HELL-BENT IDEOLOGUES...
STORM AFTER STORM, SOME I'VE CAUSED, SOME THAT AREN'T MINE...
BUT RIGHT NOW, THE AIR ITSELF IS CHANGED.
COLDER EVERY MINUTE.
IT'S NOT A STORM.

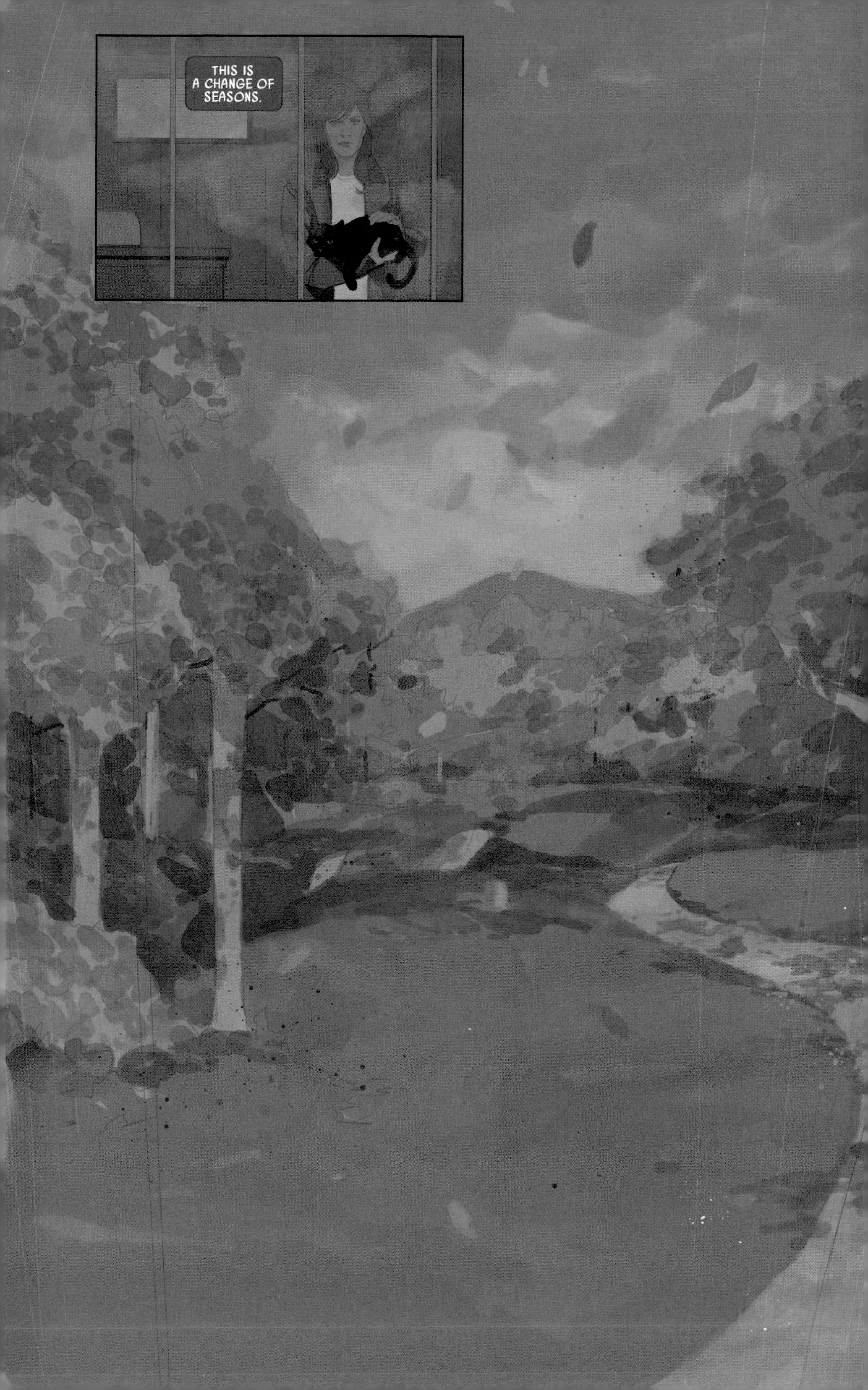
THIS IS A CHANGE OF SEASONS.

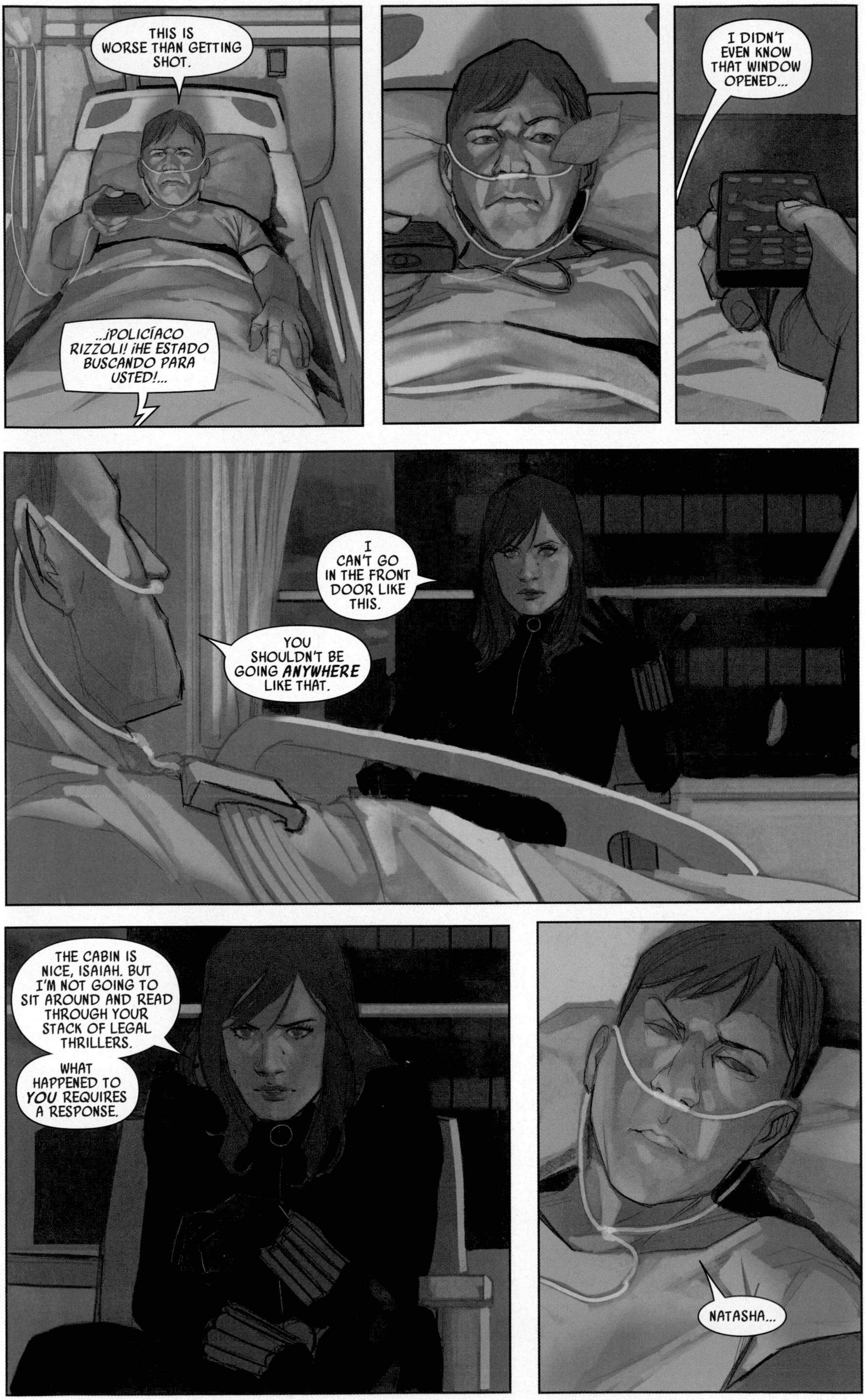

THIS IS WORSE THAN GETTING SHOT.
...¡POLICÍACO RIZZOLI! ¡HE ESTADO BUSCANDO PARA USTED!...
I DIDN'T EVEN KNOW THAT WINDOW OPENED...
I CAN'T GO IN THE FRONT DOOR LIKE THIS.
YOU SHOULDN'T BE GOING ANYWHERE LIKE THAT.
THE CABIN IS NICE, ISAIAH. BUT I'M NOT GOING TO SIT AROUND AND READ THROUGH YOUR STACK OF LEGAL THRILLERS.
WHAT HAPPENED TO YOU REQUIRES A RESPONSE.
NATASHA...

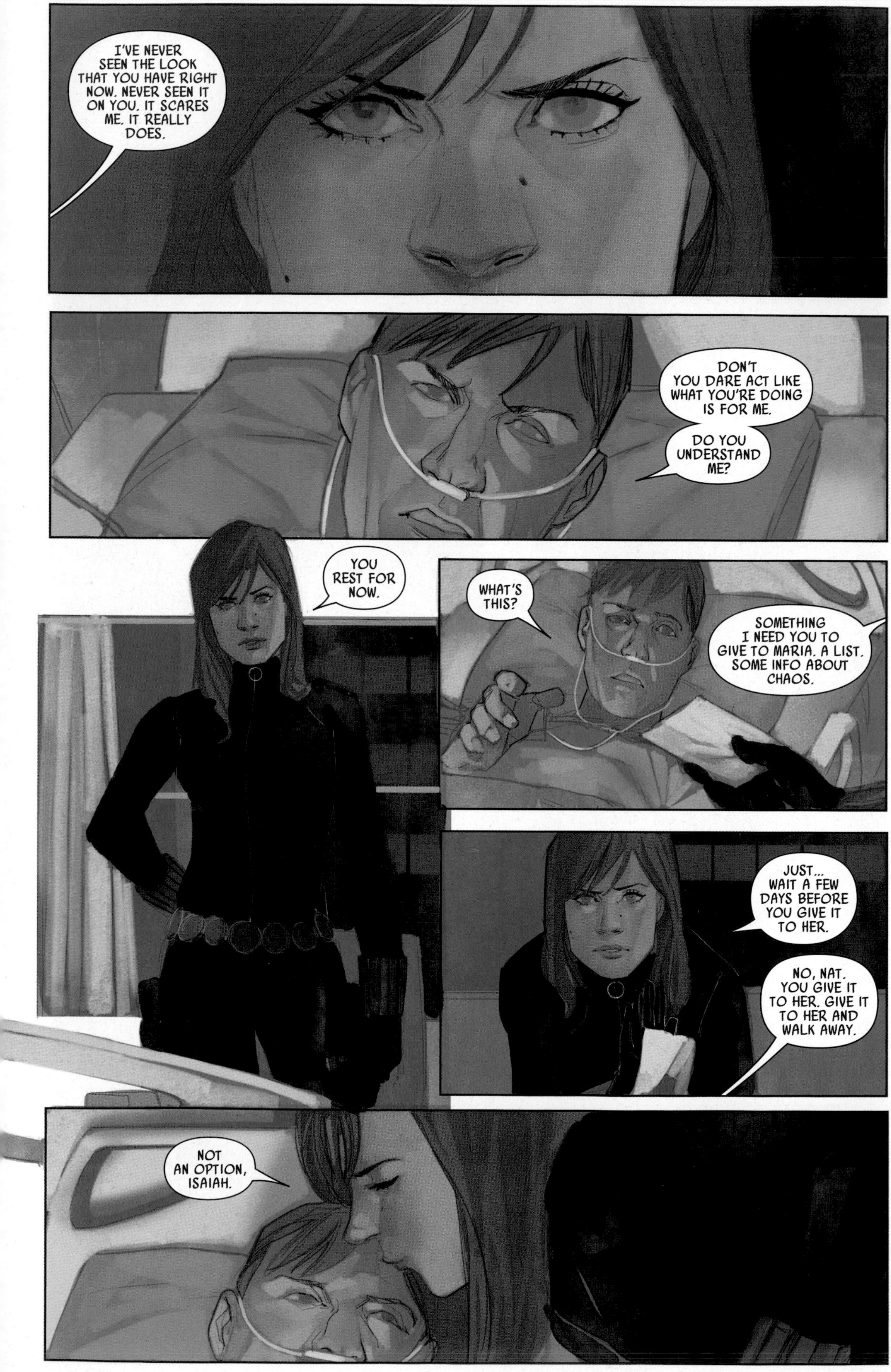
I'VE NEVER SEEN THE LOOK THAT YOU HAVE RIGHT NOW. NEVER SEEN IT ON YOU. IT SCARES ME. IT REALLY DOES.
DON'T YOU DARE ACT LIKE WHAT YOU'RE DOING IS FOR ME.
DO YOU UNDERSTAND ME?
YOU REST FOR NOW.
WHAT'S THIS?
SOMETHING I NEED YOU TO GIVE TO MARIA. A LIST. SOME INFO ABOUT CHAOS.
JUST... WAIT A FEW DAYS BEFORE YOU GIVE IT TO HER.
NO, NAT. YOU GIVE IT TO HER. GIVE IT TO HER AND WALK AWAY.
NOT AN OPTION, ISAIAH.

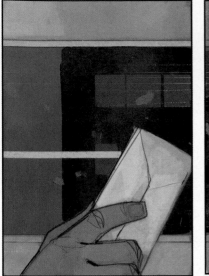

UNITED STATES
OF AMERICA VISA

YUSEF

ANDRADI

JFK
AIR TRAIN

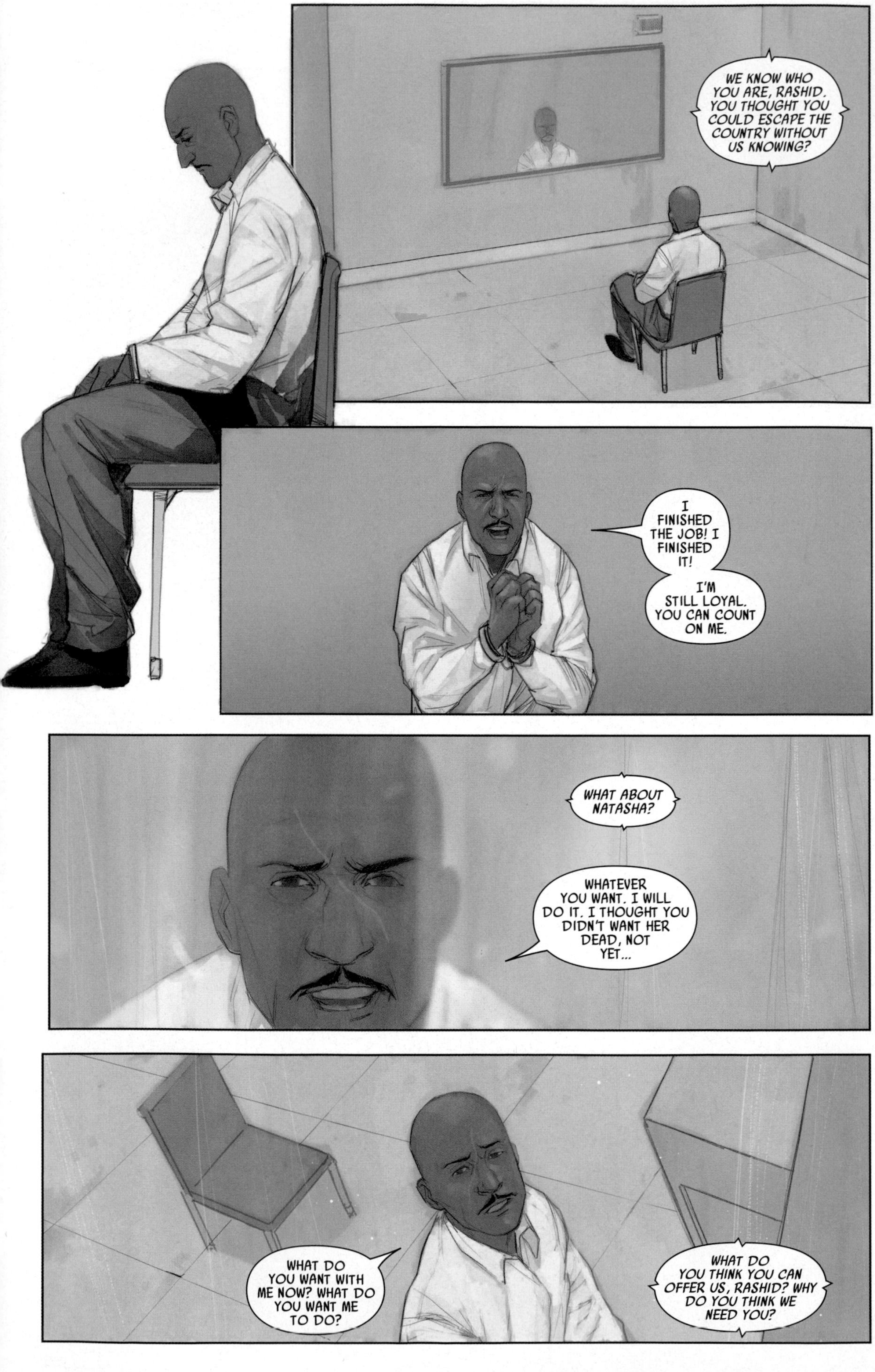
WE KNOW WHO YOU ARE, RASHID. YOU THOUGHT YOU COULD ESCAPE THE COUNTRY WITHOUT US KNOWING?
I FINISHED THE JOB! I FINISHED IT!
I'M STILL LOYAL. YOU CAN COUNT ON ME.
WHAT ABOUT NATASHA?
WHATEVER YOU WANT. I WILL DO IT. I THOUGHT YOU DIDN'T WANT HER DEAD, NOT YET...
WHAT DO YOU WANT WITH ME NOW? WHAT DO YOU WANT ME TO DO?
WHAT DO YOU THINK YOU CAN OFFER US, RASHID? WHY DO YOU THINK WE NEED YOU?

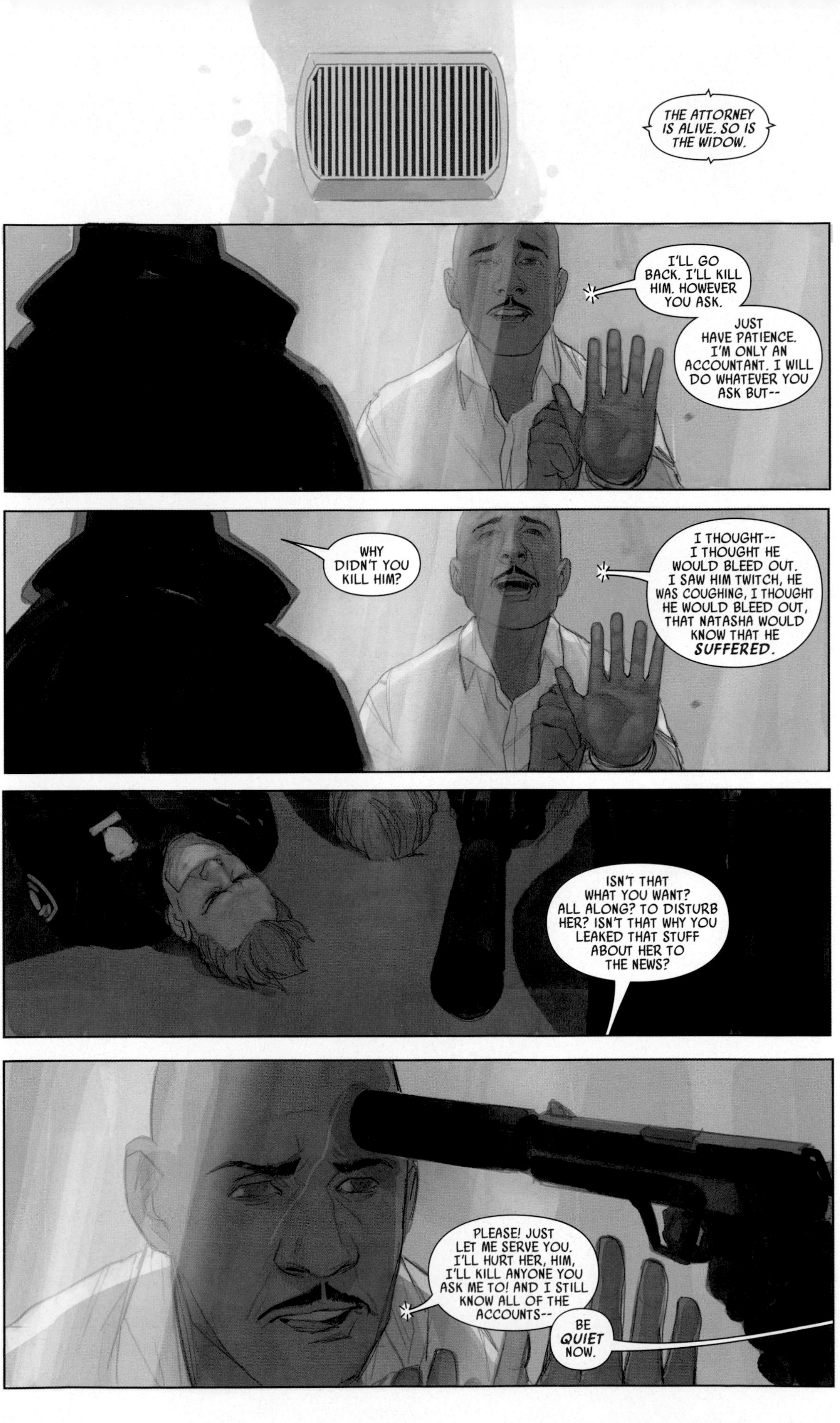
THE ATTORNEY IS ALIVE. SO IS THE WIDOW.
I'LL GO BACK. I'LL KILL HIM. HOWEVER YOU ASK.
JUST HAVE PATIENCE. I'M ONLY AN ACCOUNTANT. I WILL DO WHATEVER YOU ASK BUT--
WHY DIDN'T YOU KILL HIM?
I THOUGHT-- I THOUGHT HE WOULD BLEED OUT. I SAW HIM TWITCH, HE WAS COUGHING, I THOUGHT HE WOULD BLEED OUT, THAT NATASHA WOULD KNOW THAT HE SUFFERED.
ISN'T THAT WHAT YOU WANT? ALL ALONG? TO DISTURB HER? ISN'T THAT WHY YOU LEAKED THAT STUFF ABOUT HER TO THE NEWS?
PLEASE! JUST LET ME SERVE YOU. I'LL HURT HER, HIM, I'LL KILL ANYONE YOU ASK ME TO! AND I STILL KNOW ALL OF THE ACCOUNTS--
BE QUIET NOW.

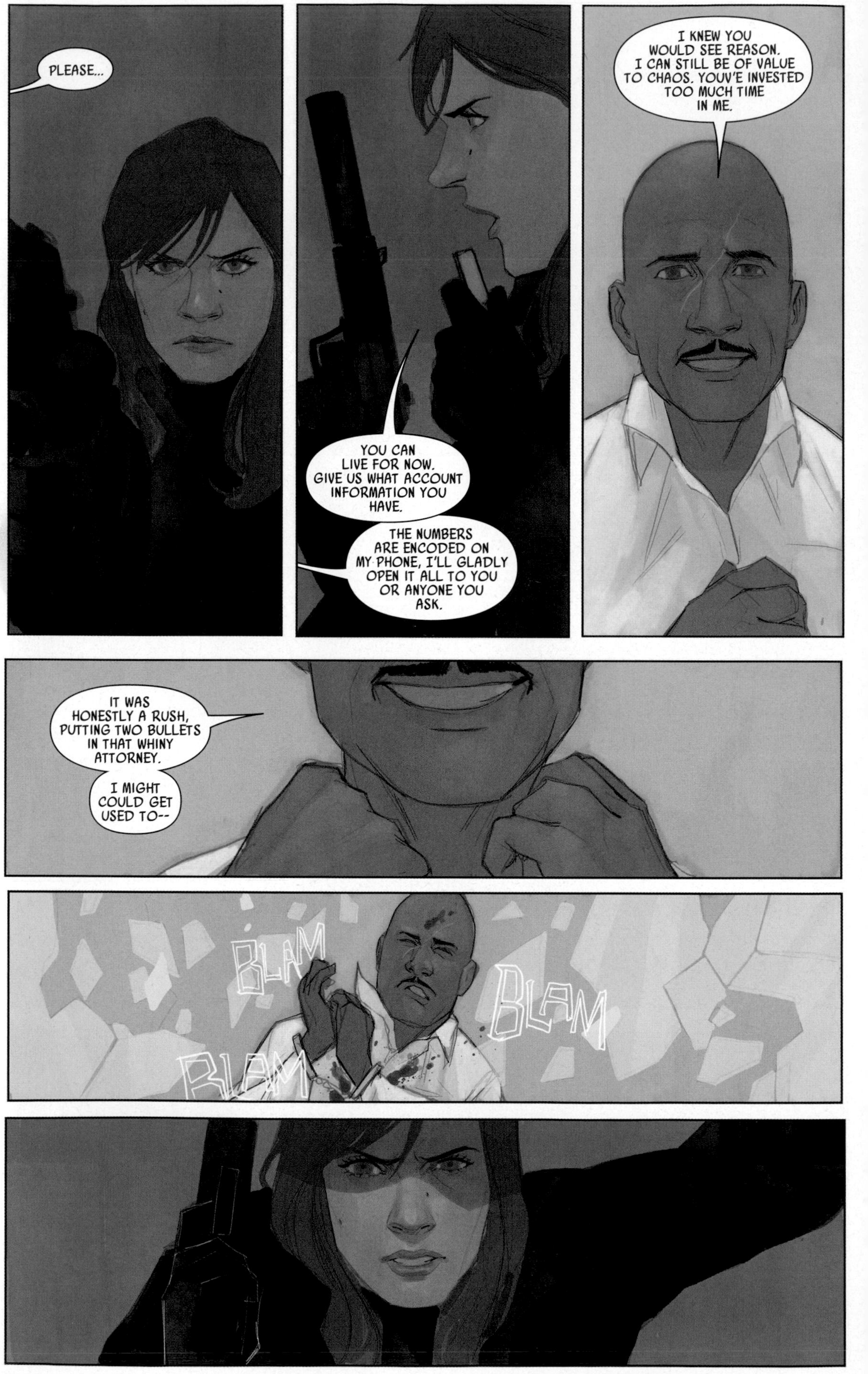
PLEASE...
YOU CAN LIVE FOR NOW. GIVE US WHAT ACCOUNT INFORMATION YOU HAVE.
THE NUMBERS ARE ENCODED ON MY PHONE, I'LL GLADLY OPEN IT ALL TO YOU OR ANYONE YOU ASK.
I KNEW YOU WOULD SEE REASON. I CAN STILL BE OF VALUE TO CHAOS. YOUV'E INVESTED TOO MUCH TIME IN ME.
IT WAS HONESTLY A RUSH, PUTTING TWO BULLETS IN THAT WHINY ATTORNEY.
I MIGHT COULD GET USED TO--
BLAM
BLAM
BLAM

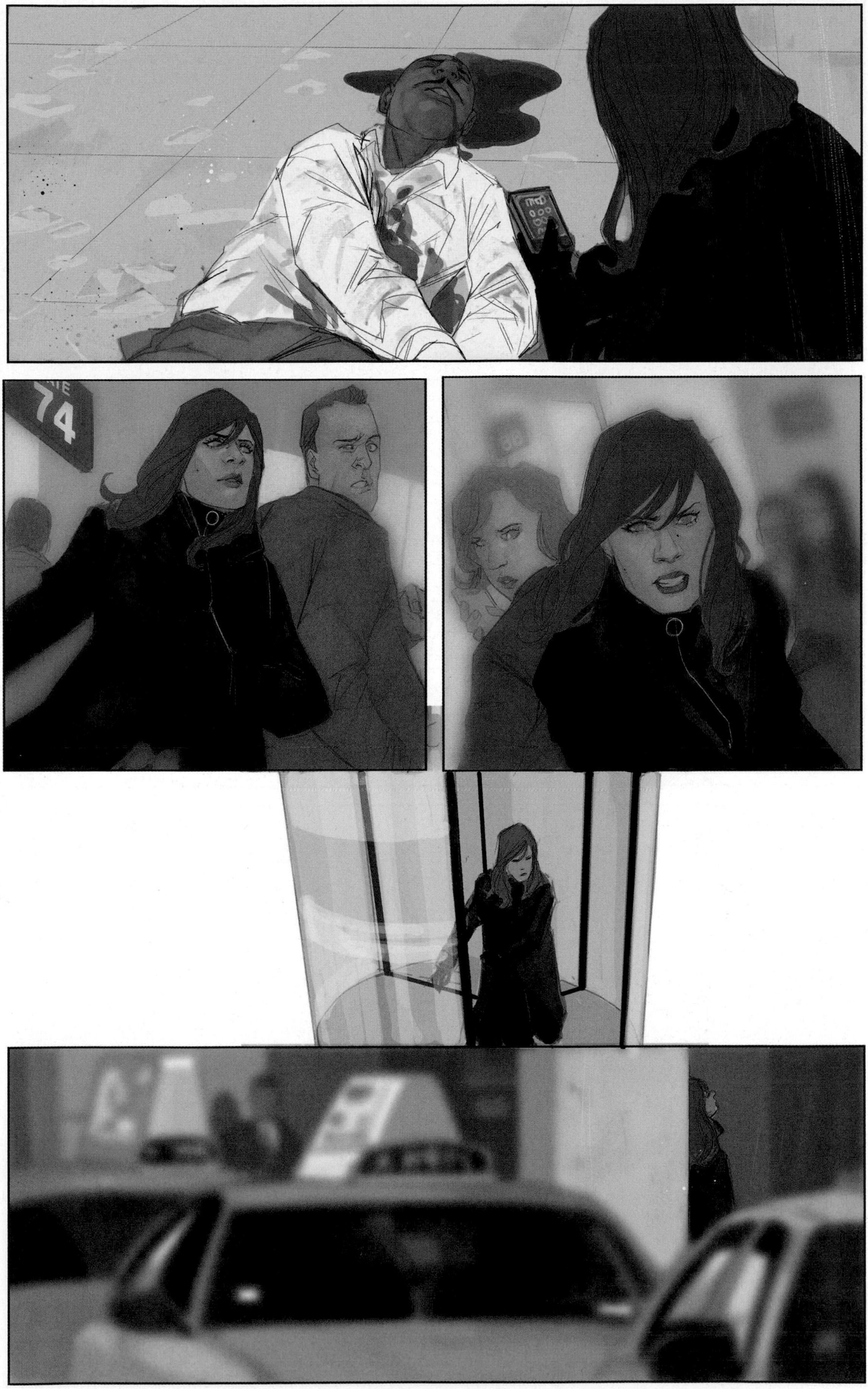
74

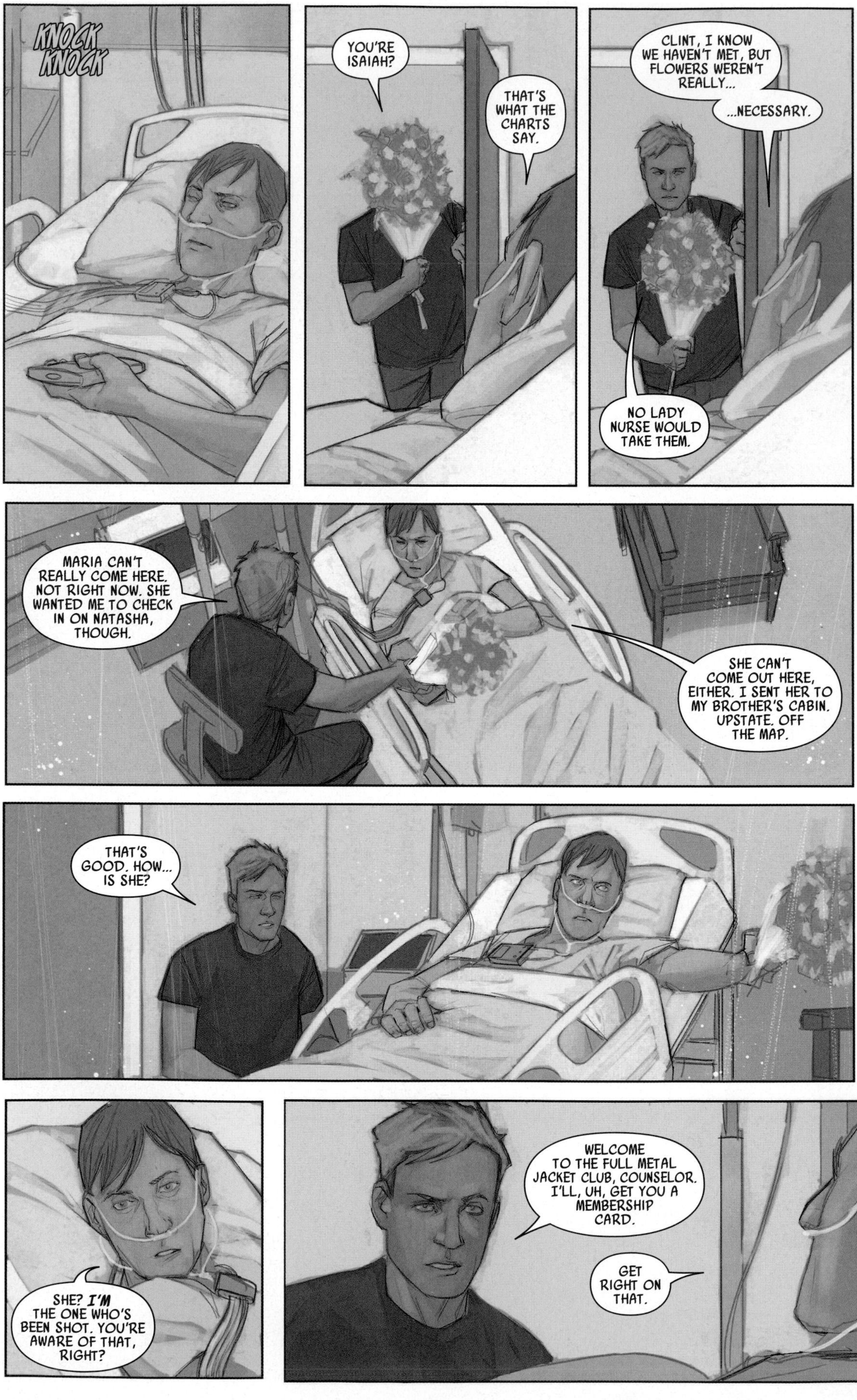
KNOCK KNOCK
YOU'RE ISAIAH?
THAT'S WHAT THE CHARTS SAY.
CLINT, I KNOW WE HAVEN'T MET, BUT FLOWERS WEREN'T REALLY...
...NECESSARY.
NO LADY NURSE WOULD TAKE THEM.
MARIA CAN'T REALLY COME HERE. NOT RIGHT NOW. SHE WANTED ME TO CHECK IN ON NATASHA, THOUGH.
SHE CAN'T COME OUT HERE, EITHER. I SENT HER TO MY BROTHER'S CABIN. UPSTATE. OFF THE MAP.
THAT'S GOOD. HOW... IS SHE?
SHE? *I'M* THE ONE WHO'S BEEN SHOT. YOU'RE AWARE OF THAT, RIGHT?
WELCOME TO THE FULL METAL JACKET CLUB, COUNSELOR. I'LL, UH, GET YOU A MEMBERSHIP CARD.
GET RIGHT ON THAT.

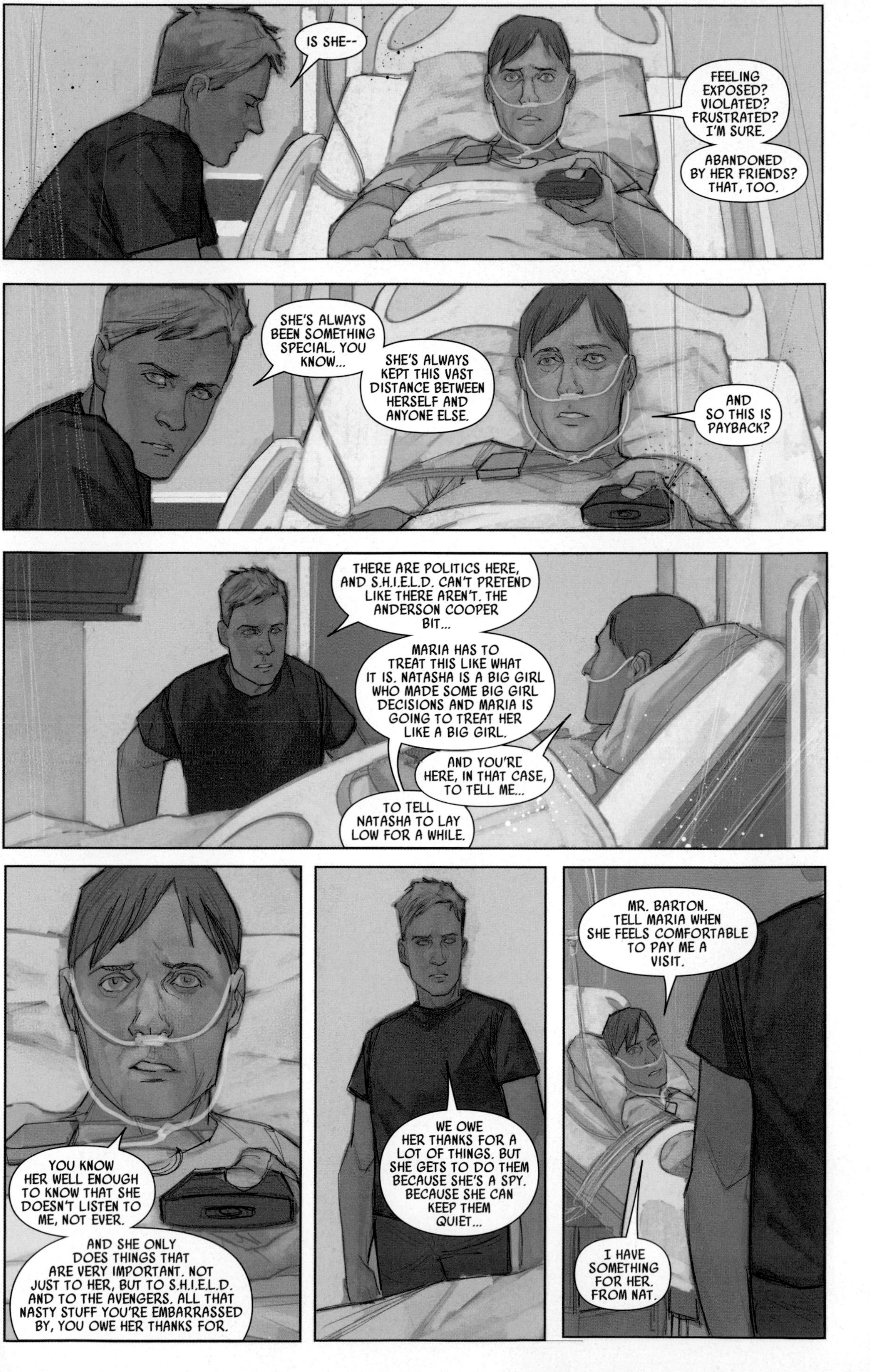

IS SHE--
FEELING EXPOSED? VIOLATED? FRUSTRATED? I'M SURE.
ABANDONED BY HER FRIENDS? THAT, TOO.
SHE'S ALWAYS BEEN SOMETHING SPECIAL. YOU KNOW...
SHE'S ALWAYS KEPT THIS VAST DISTANCE BETWEEN HERSELF AND ANYONE ELSE.
AND SO THIS IS PAYBACK?
THERE ARE POLITICS HERE, AND S.H.I.E.L.D. CAN'T PRETEND LIKE THERE AREN'T. THE ANDERSON COOPER BIT...
MARIA HAS TO TREAT THIS LIKE WHAT IT IS. NATASHA IS A BIG GIRL WHO MADE SOME BIG GIRL DECISIONS AND MARIA IS GOING TO TREAT HER LIKE A BIG GIRL.
AND YOU'RE HERE, IN THAT CASE, TO TELL ME...
TO TELL NATASHA TO LAY LOW FOR A WHILE.
YOU KNOW HER WELL ENOUGH TO KNOW THAT SHE DOESN'T LISTEN TO ME, NOT EVER.
AND SHE ONLY DOES THINGS THAT ARE VERY IMPORTANT. NOT JUST TO HER, BUT TO S.H.I.E.L.D. AND TO THE AVENGERS. ALL THAT NASTY STUFF YOU'RE EMBARRASSED BY, YOU OWE HER THANKS FOR.
WE OWE HER THANKS FOR A LOT OF THINGS. BUT SHE GETS TO DO THEM BECAUSE SHE'S A SPY. BECAUSE SHE CAN KEEP THEM QUIET...
MR. BARTON. TELL MARIA WHEN SHE FEELS COMFORTABLE TO PAY ME A VISIT.
I HAVE SOMETHING FOR HER. FROM NAT.

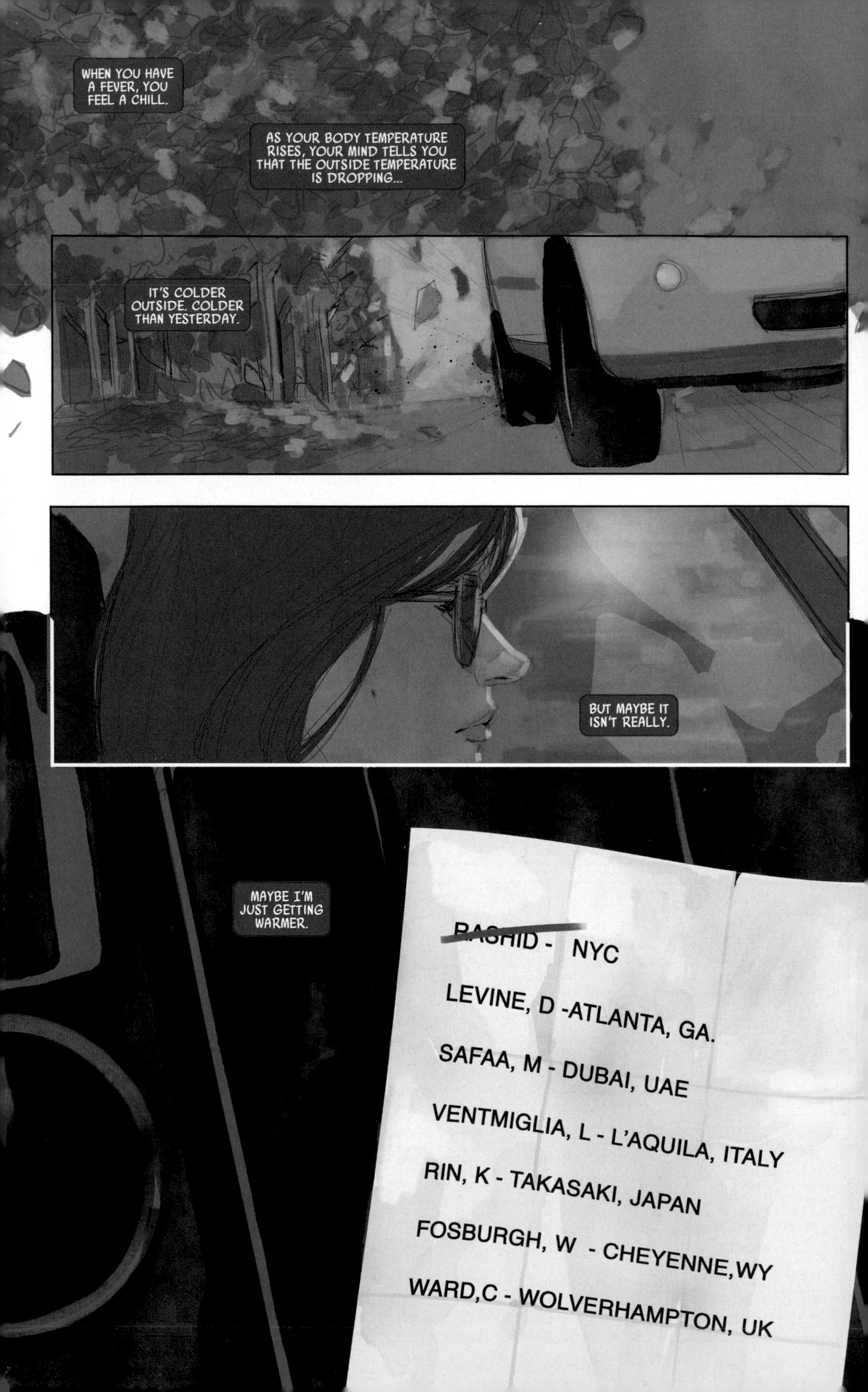
WHEN YOU HAVE A FEVER, YOU FEEL A CHILL.
AS YOUR BODY TEMPERATURE RISES, YOUR MIND TELLS YOU THAT THE OUTSIDE TEMPERATURE IS DROPPING...
IT'S COLDER OUTSIDE. COLDER THAN YESTERDAY.
BUT MAYBE IT ISN'T REALLY.
MAYBE I'M JUST GETTING WARMER.
~~RASHID~~ - NYC
LEVINE, D -ATLANTA, GA.
SAFAA, M - DUBAI, UAE
VENTMIGLIA, L - L'AQUILA, ITALY
RIN, K - TAKASAKI, JAPAN
FOSBURGH, W - CHEYENNE,WY
WARD,C - WOLVERHAMPTON, UK

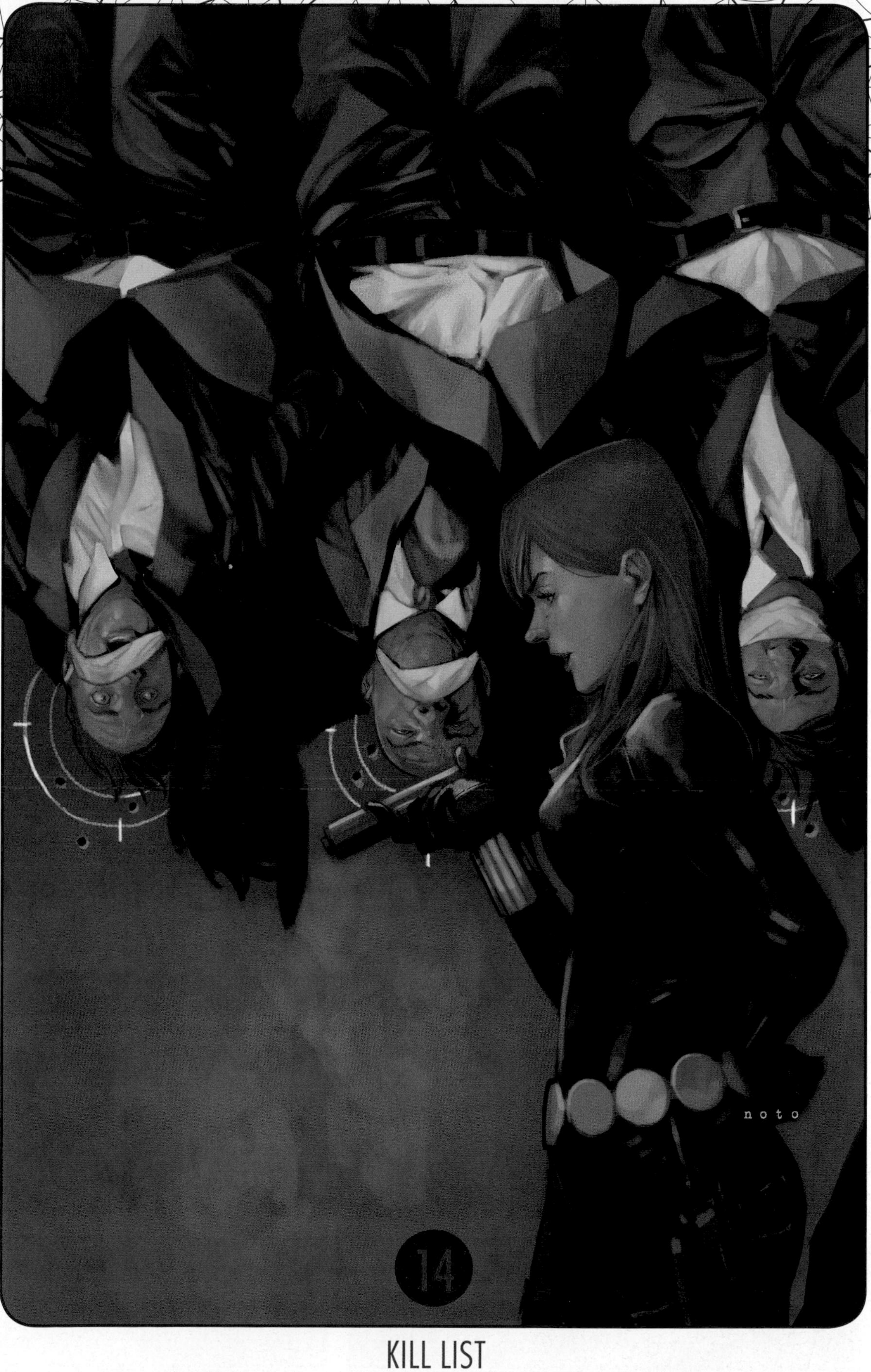
noto
14

KILL LIST

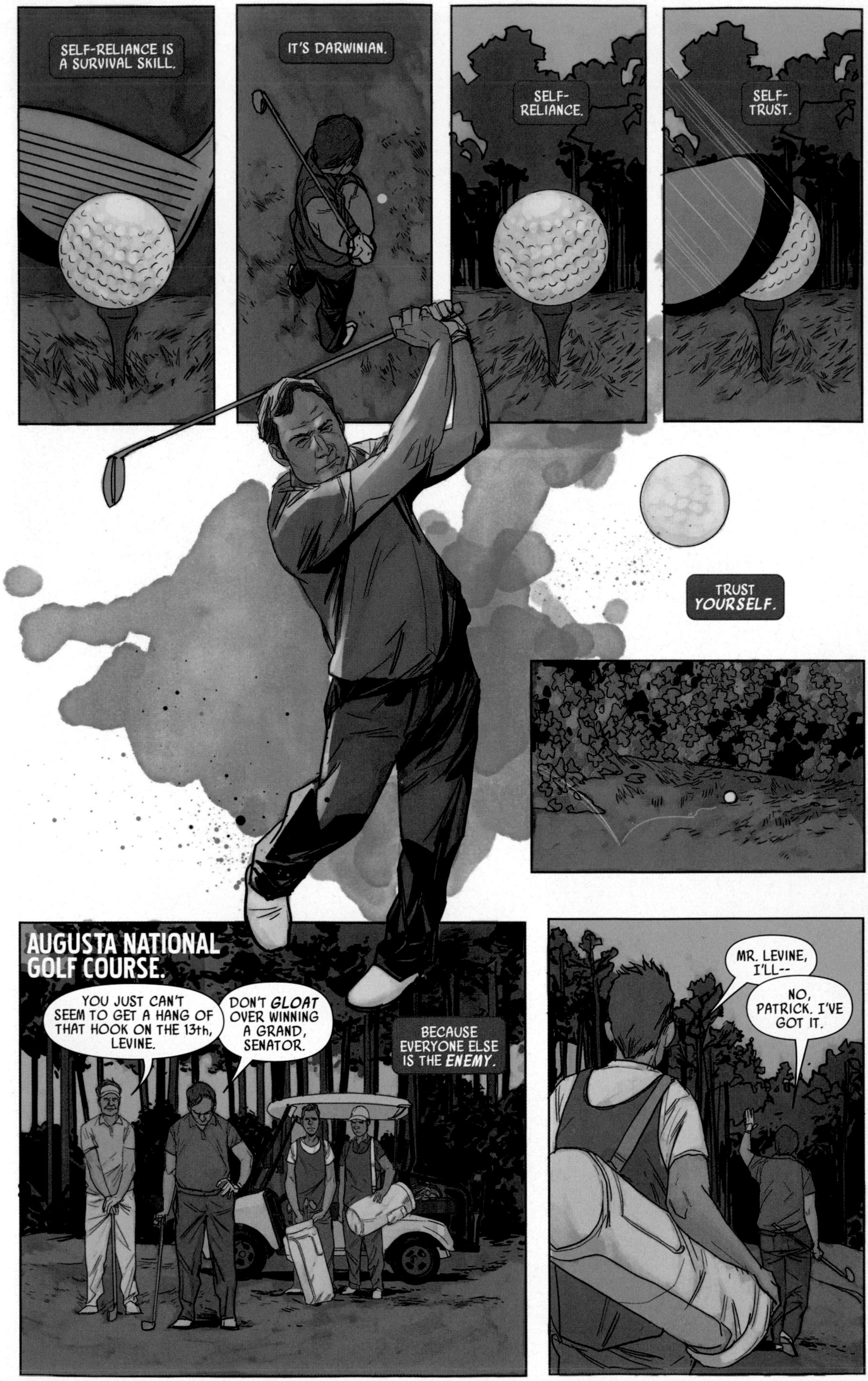
SELF-RELIANCE IS A SURVIVAL SKILL.
IT'S DARWINIAN.
SELF-RELIANCE.
SELF-TRUST.
TRUST YOURSELF.
AUGUSTA NATIONAL GOLF COURSE.
YOU JUST CAN'T SEEM TO GET A HANG OF THAT HOOK ON THE 13th, LEVINE.
DON'T GLOAT OVER WINNING A GRAND, SENATOR.
BECAUSE EVERYONE ELSE IS THE ENEMY.
MR. LEVINE, I'LL--
NO, PATRICK. I'VE GOT IT.

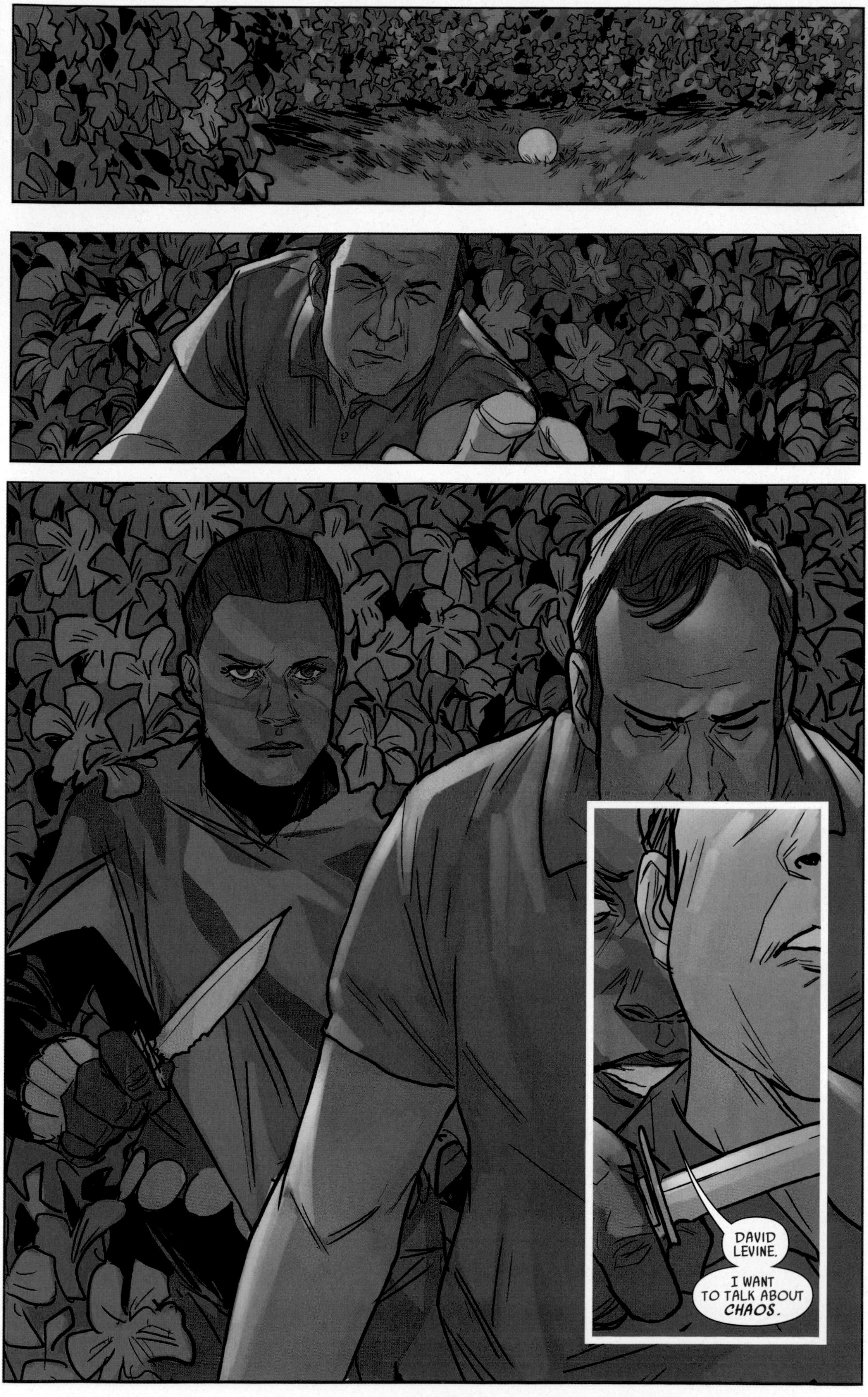
DAVID LEVINE.
I WANT TO TALK ABOUT CHAOS.

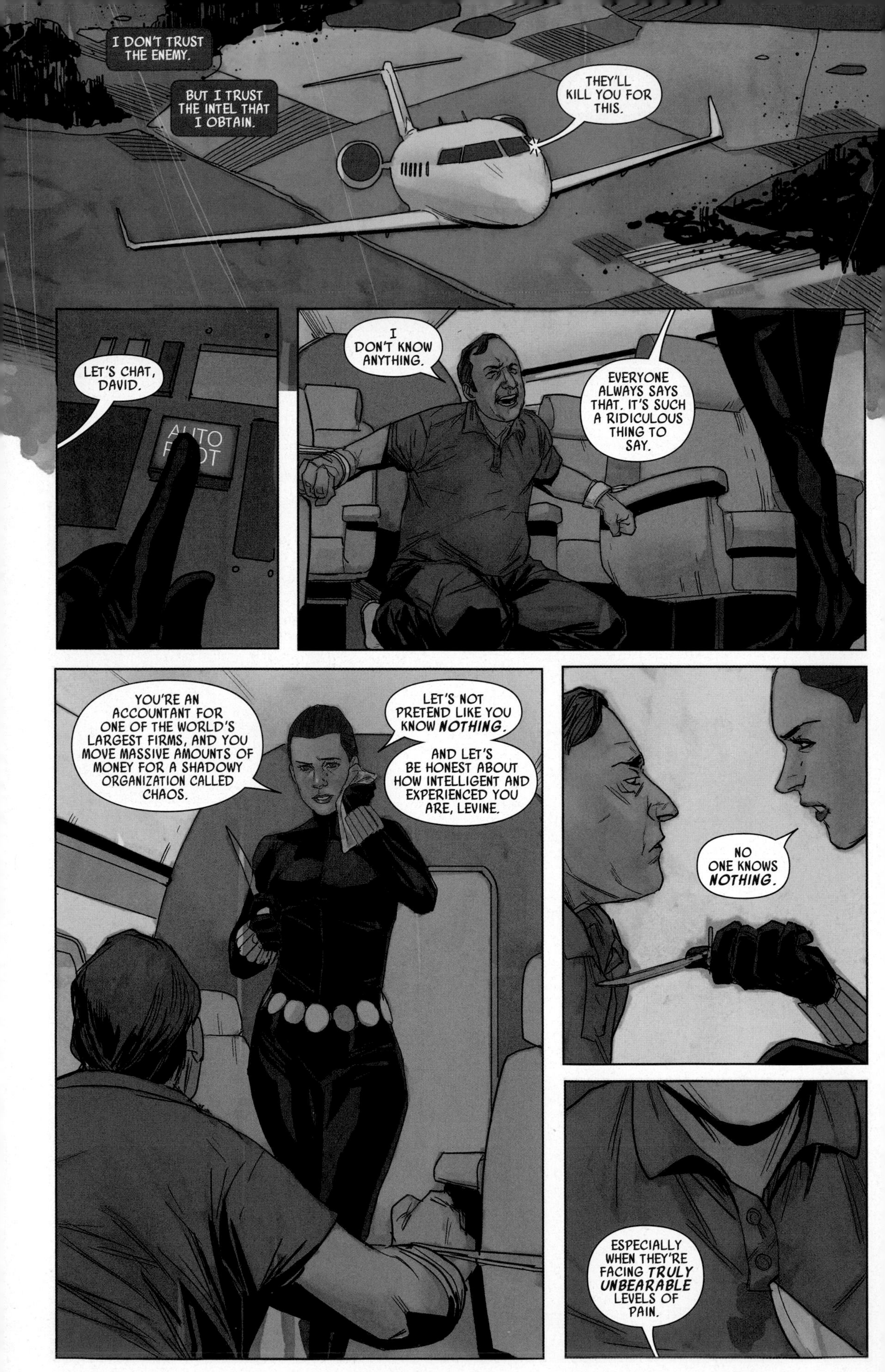
I DON'T TRUST THE ENEMY.
BUT I TRUST THE INTEL THAT I OBTAIN.
THEY'LL KILL YOU FOR THIS.
LET'S CHAT, DAVID.
AUTO PILOT
I DON'T KNOW ANYTHING.
EVERYONE ALWAYS SAYS THAT. IT'S SUCH A RIDICULOUS THING TO SAY.
YOU'RE AN ACCOUNTANT FOR ONE OF THE WORLD'S LARGEST FIRMS, AND YOU MOVE MASSIVE AMOUNTS OF MONEY FOR A SHADOWY ORGANIZATION CALLED CHAOS.
LET'S NOT PRETEND LIKE YOU KNOW NOTHING.
AND LET'S BE HONEST ABOUT HOW INTELLIGENT AND EXPERIENCED YOU ARE, LEVINE.
NO ONE KNOWS NOTHING.
ESPECIALLY WHEN THEY'RE FACING TRULY UNBEARABLE LEVELS OF PAIN.

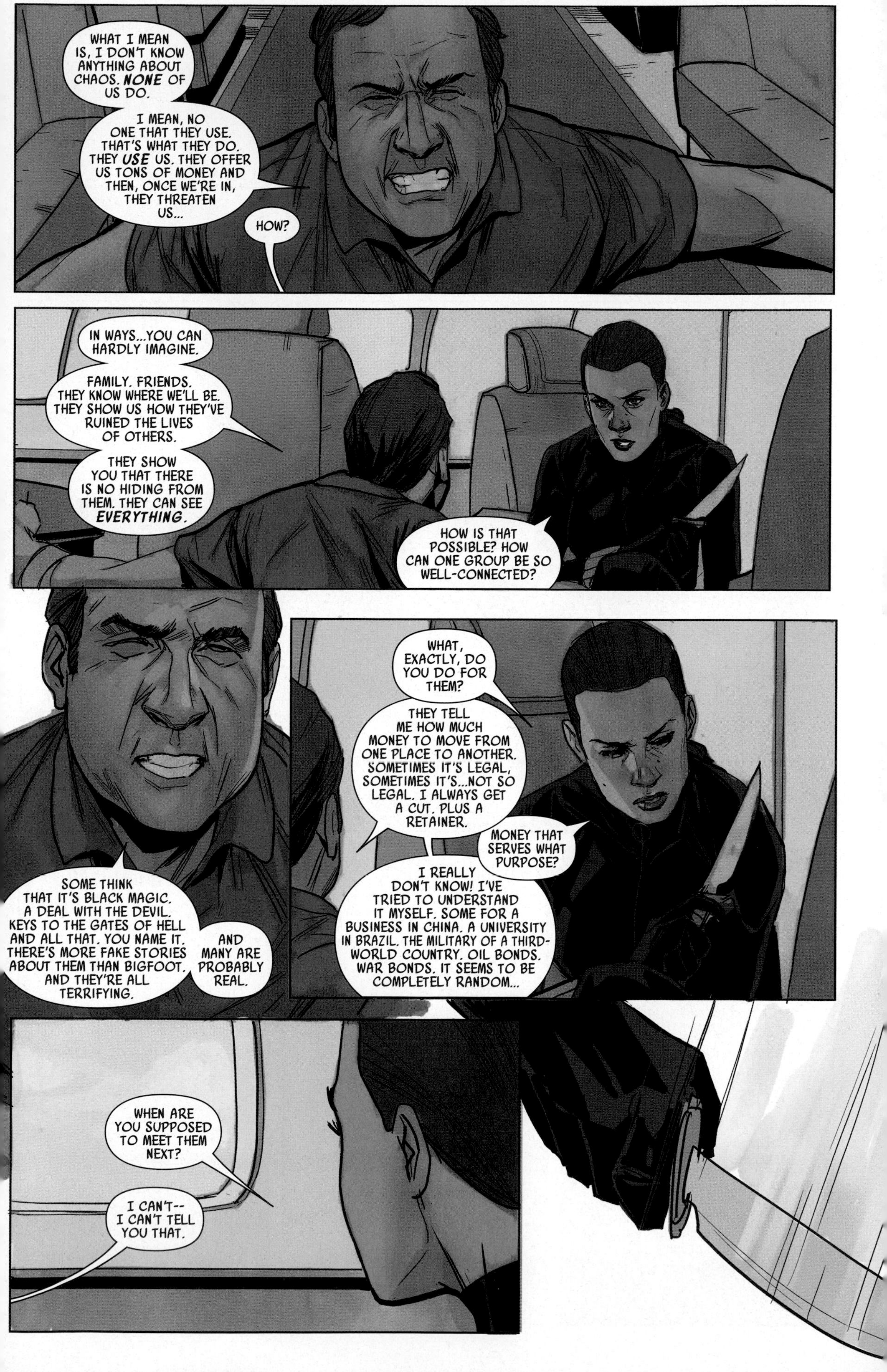
WHAT I MEAN IS, I DON'T KNOW ANYTHING ABOUT CHAOS. NONE OF US DO.
I MEAN, NO ONE THAT THEY USE. THAT'S WHAT THEY DO. THEY USE US. THEY OFFER US TONS OF MONEY AND THEN, ONCE WE'RE IN, THEY THREATEN US...
HOW?
IN WAYS...YOU CAN HARDLY IMAGINE.
FAMILY. FRIENDS. THEY KNOW WHERE WE'LL BE. THEY SHOW US HOW THEY'VE RUINED THE LIVES OF OTHERS.
THEY SHOW YOU THAT THERE IS NO HIDING FROM THEM. THEY CAN SEE EVERYTHING.
HOW IS THAT POSSIBLE? HOW CAN ONE GROUP BE SO WELL-CONNECTED?
SOME THINK THAT IT'S BLACK MAGIC. A DEAL WITH THE DEVIL. KEYS TO THE GATES OF HELL AND ALL THAT. YOU NAME IT. THERE'S MORE FAKE STORIES ABOUT THEM THAN BIGFOOT. AND THEY'RE ALL TERRIFYING.
AND MANY ARE PROBABLY REAL.
WHAT, EXACTLY, DO YOU DO FOR THEM?
THEY TELL ME HOW MUCH MONEY TO MOVE FROM ONE PLACE TO ANOTHER. SOMETIMES IT'S LEGAL, SOMETIMES IT'S...NOT SO LEGAL. I ALWAYS GET A CUT. PLUS A RETAINER.
MONEY THAT SERVES WHAT PURPOSE?
I REALLY DON'T KNOW! I'VE TRIED TO UNDERSTAND IT MYSELF. SOME FOR A BUSINESS IN CHINA. A UNIVERSITY IN BRAZIL. THE MILITARY OF A THIRD-WORLD COUNTRY. OIL BONDS. WAR BONDS. IT SEEMS TO BE COMPLETELY RANDOM...
WHEN ARE YOU SUPPOSED TO MEET THEM NEXT?
I CAN'T-- I CAN'T TELL YOU THAT.

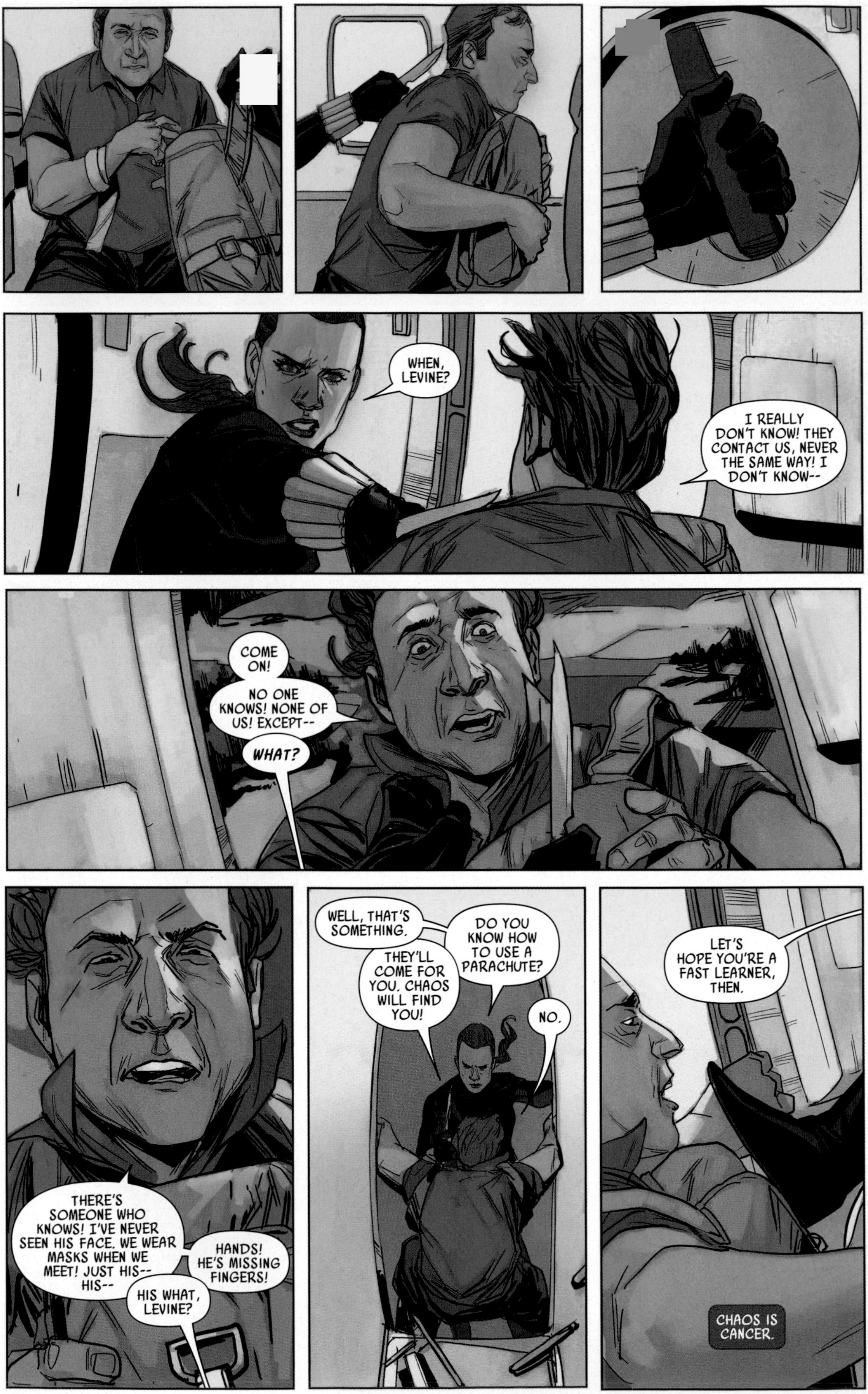
WHEN, LEVINE?
I REALLY DON'T KNOW! THEY CONTACT US, NEVER THE SAME WAY! I DON'T KNOW--
COME ON!
NO ONE KNOWS! NONE OF US! EXCEPT--
WHAT?
THERE'S SOMEONE WHO KNOWS! I'VE NEVER SEEN HIS FACE. WE WEAR MASKS WHEN WE MEET! JUST HIS-- HIS--
HIS WHAT, LEVINE?
HANDS! HE'S MISSING FINGERS!
WELL, THAT'S SOMETHING.
THEY'LL COME FOR YOU. CHAOS WILL FIND YOU!
DO YOU KNOW HOW TO USE A PARACHUTE?
NO.
LET'S HOPE YOU'RE A FAST LEARNER, THEN.
CHAOS IS CANCER.

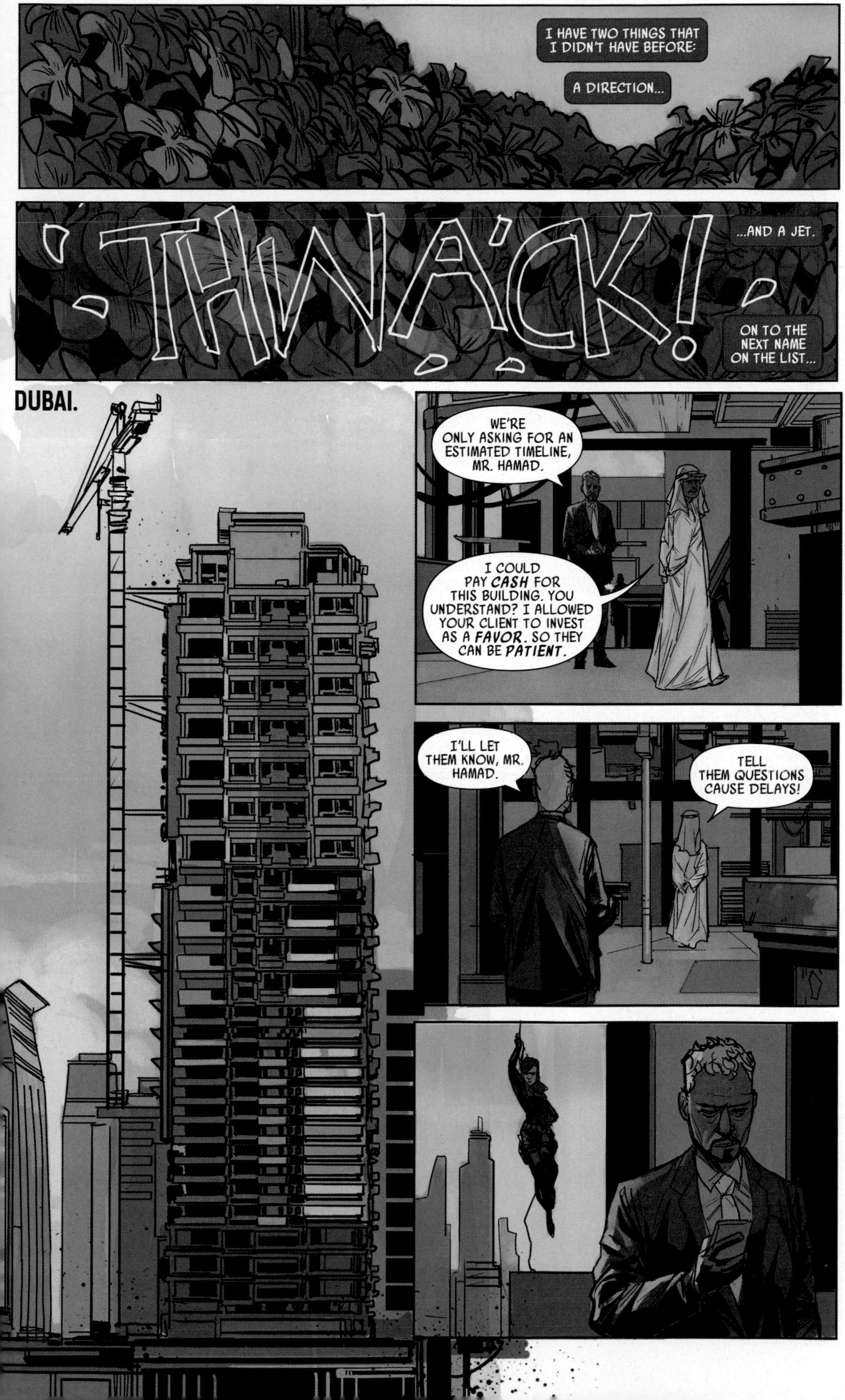
I HAVE TWO THINGS THAT I DIDN'T HAVE BEFORE:
A DIRECTION...
'THWACK!'
...AND A JET.
ON TO THE NEXT NAME ON THE LIST...
DUBAI.
WE'RE ONLY ASKING FOR AN ESTIMATED TIMELINE, MR. HAMAD.
I COULD PAY CASH FOR THIS BUILDING. YOU UNDERSTAND? I ALLOWED YOUR CLIENT TO INVEST AS A FAVOR. SO THEY CAN BE PATIENT.
I'LL LET THEM KNOW, MR. HAMAD.
TELL THEM QUESTIONS CAUSE DELAYS!

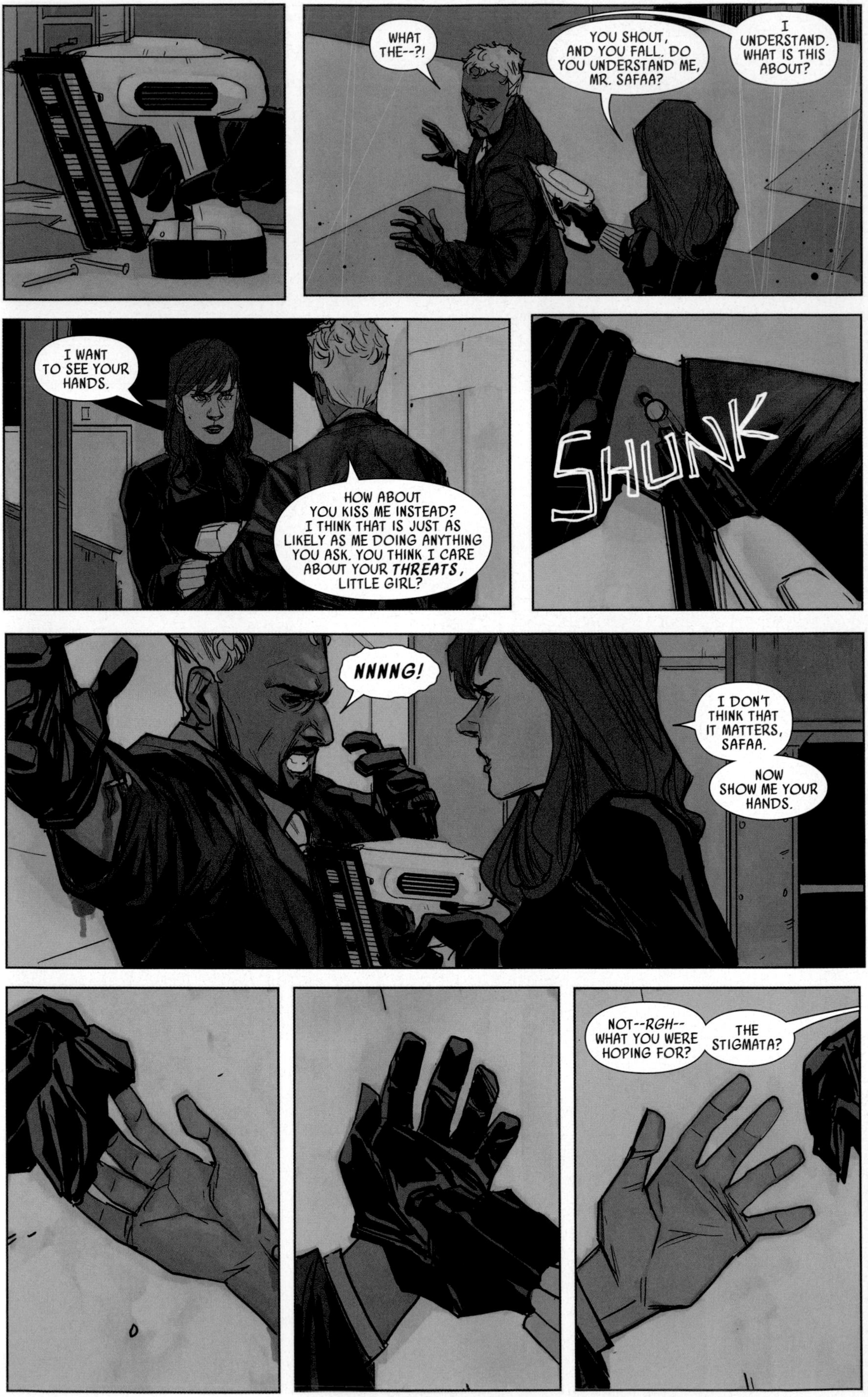
WHAT THE--?!
YOU SHOUT, AND YOU FALL. DO YOU UNDERSTAND ME, MR. SAFAA?
I UNDERSTAND. WHAT IS THIS ABOUT?
I WANT TO SEE YOUR HANDS.
HOW ABOUT YOU KISS ME INSTEAD? I THINK THAT IS JUST AS LIKELY AS ME DOING ANYTHING YOU ASK. YOU THINK I CARE ABOUT YOUR *THREATS*, LITTLE GIRL?
SHUNK
NNNNG!
I DON'T THINK THAT IT MATTERS, SAFAA.
NOW SHOW ME YOUR HANDS.
NOT--*RGH*--WHAT YOU WERE HOPING FOR?
THE STIGMATA?

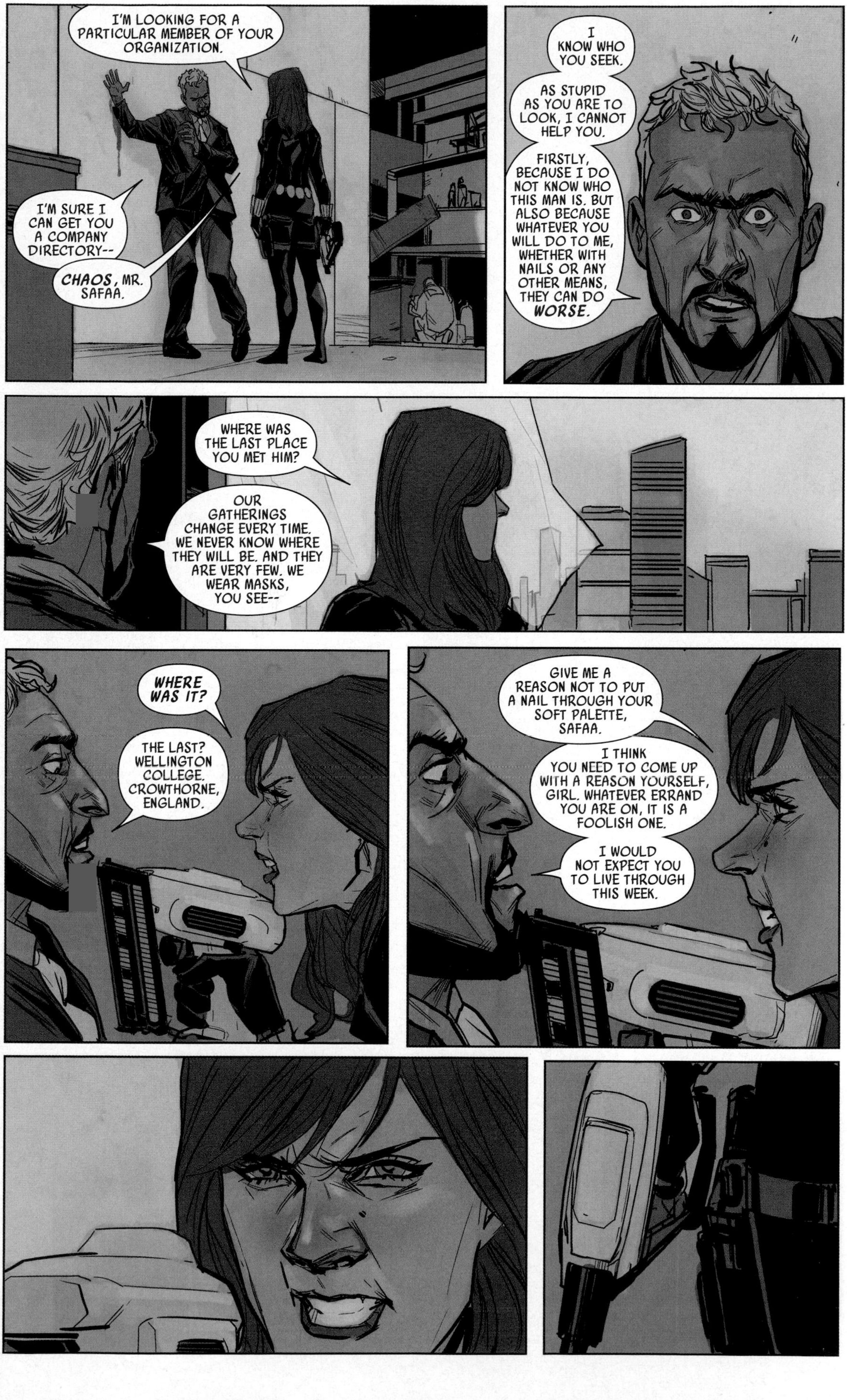
I'M LOOKING FOR A PARTICULAR MEMBER OF YOUR ORGANIZATION.
I'M SURE I CAN GET YOU A COMPANY DIRECTORY--
CHAOS, MR. SAFAA.
I KNOW WHO YOU SEEK.
AS STUPID AS YOU ARE TO LOOK, I CANNOT HELP YOU.
FIRSTLY, BECAUSE I DO NOT KNOW WHO THIS MAN IS. BUT ALSO BECAUSE WHATEVER YOU WILL DO TO ME, WHETHER WITH NAILS OR ANY OTHER MEANS, THEY CAN DO WORSE.
WHERE WAS THE LAST PLACE YOU MET HIM?
OUR GATHERINGS CHANGE EVERY TIME. WE NEVER KNOW WHERE THEY WILL BE. AND THEY ARE VERY FEW. WE WEAR MASKS, YOU SEE--
WHERE WAS IT?
THE LAST? WELLINGTON COLLEGE. CROWTHORNE, ENGLAND.
GIVE ME A REASON NOT TO PUT A NAIL THROUGH YOUR SOFT PALETTE, SAFAA.
I THINK YOU NEED TO COME UP WITH A REASON YOURSELF, GIRL. WHATEVER ERRAND YOU ARE ON, IT IS A FOOLISH ONE.
I WOULD NOT EXPECT YOU TO LIVE THROUGH THIS WEEK.

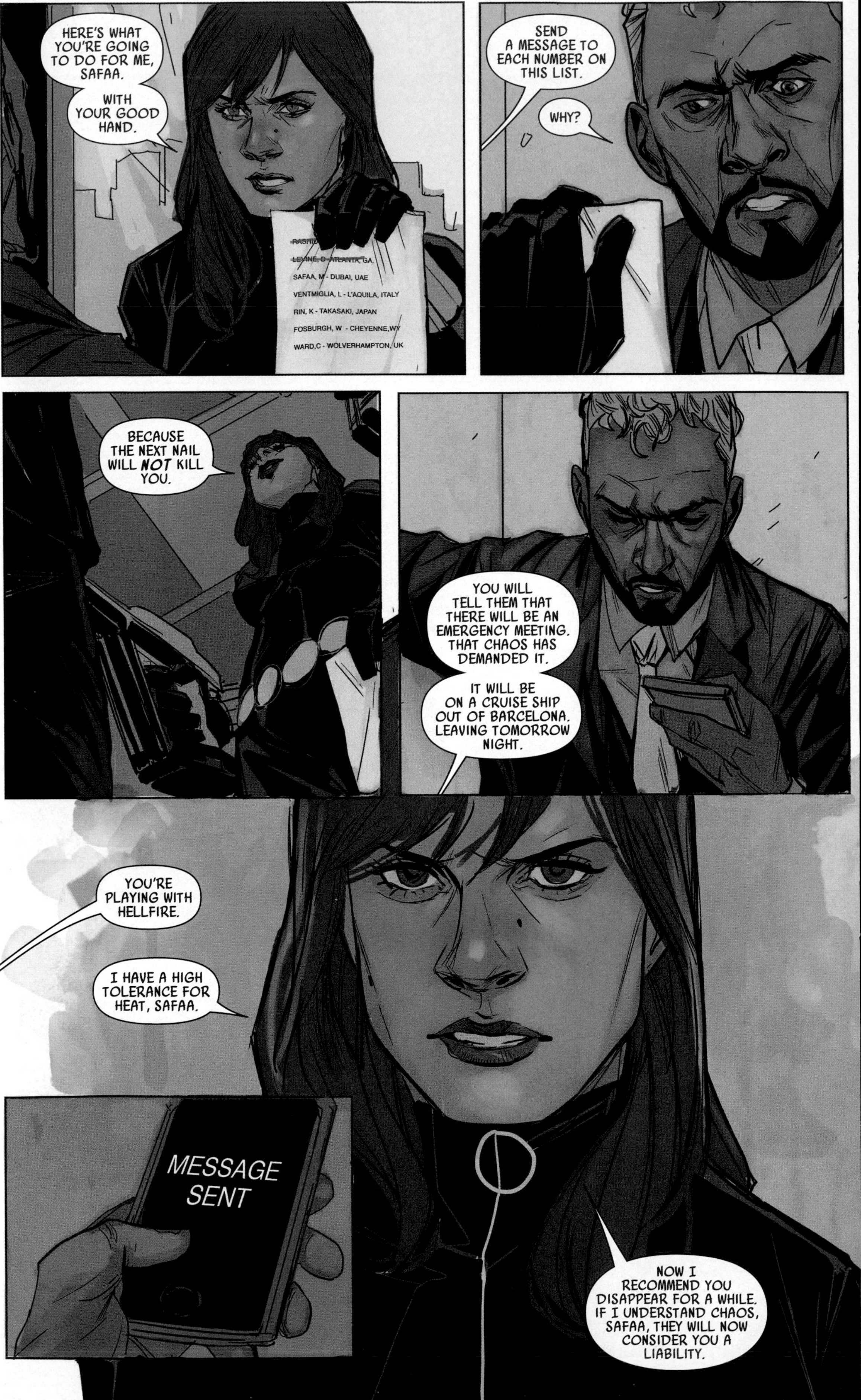
HERE'S WHAT YOU'RE GOING TO DO FOR ME, SAFAA.
WITH YOUR GOOD HAND.
LEVINE, D - ATLANTA, GA.
SAFAA, M - DUBAI, UAE
VENTMIGLIA, L - L'AQUILA, ITALY
RIN, K - TAKASAKI, JAPAN
FOSBURGH, W - CHEYENNE, WY
WARD, C - WOLVERHAMPTON, UK
SEND A MESSAGE TO EACH NUMBER ON THIS LIST.
WHY?
BECAUSE THE NEXT NAIL WILL ***NOT*** KILL YOU.
YOU WILL TELL THEM THAT THERE WILL BE AN EMERGENCY MEETING. THAT CHAOS HAS DEMANDED IT.
IT WILL BE ON A CRUISE SHIP OUT OF BARCELONA. LEAVING TOMORROW NIGHT.
YOU'RE PLAYING WITH HELLFIRE.
I HAVE A HIGH TOLERANCE FOR HEAT, SAFAA.
MESSAGE SENT
NOW I RECOMMEND YOU DISAPPEAR FOR A WHILE. IF I UNDERSTAND CHAOS, SAFAA, THEY WILL NOW CONSIDER YOU A LIABILITY.

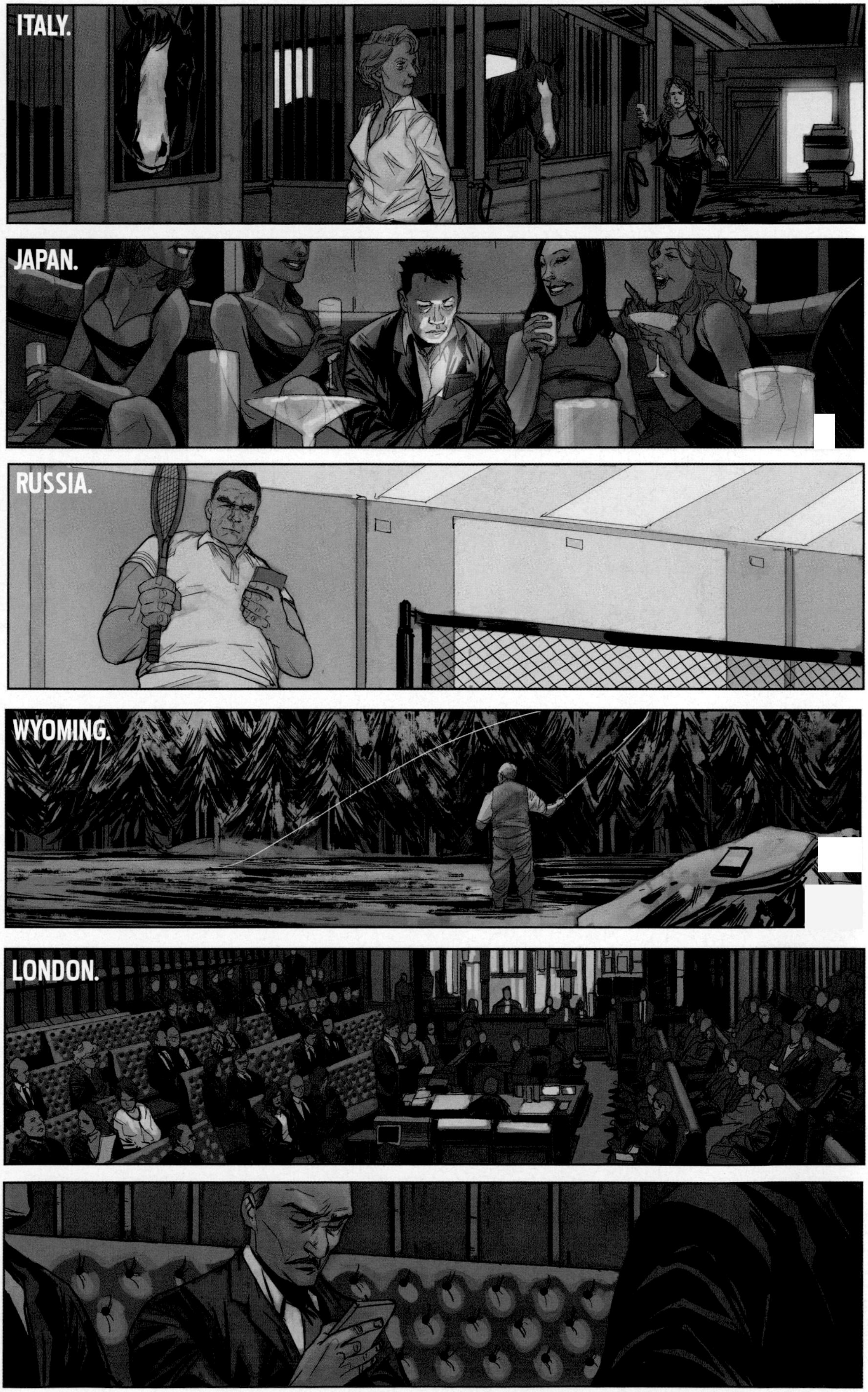
ITALY.
JAPAN.
RUSSIA.
WYOMING.
LONDON.

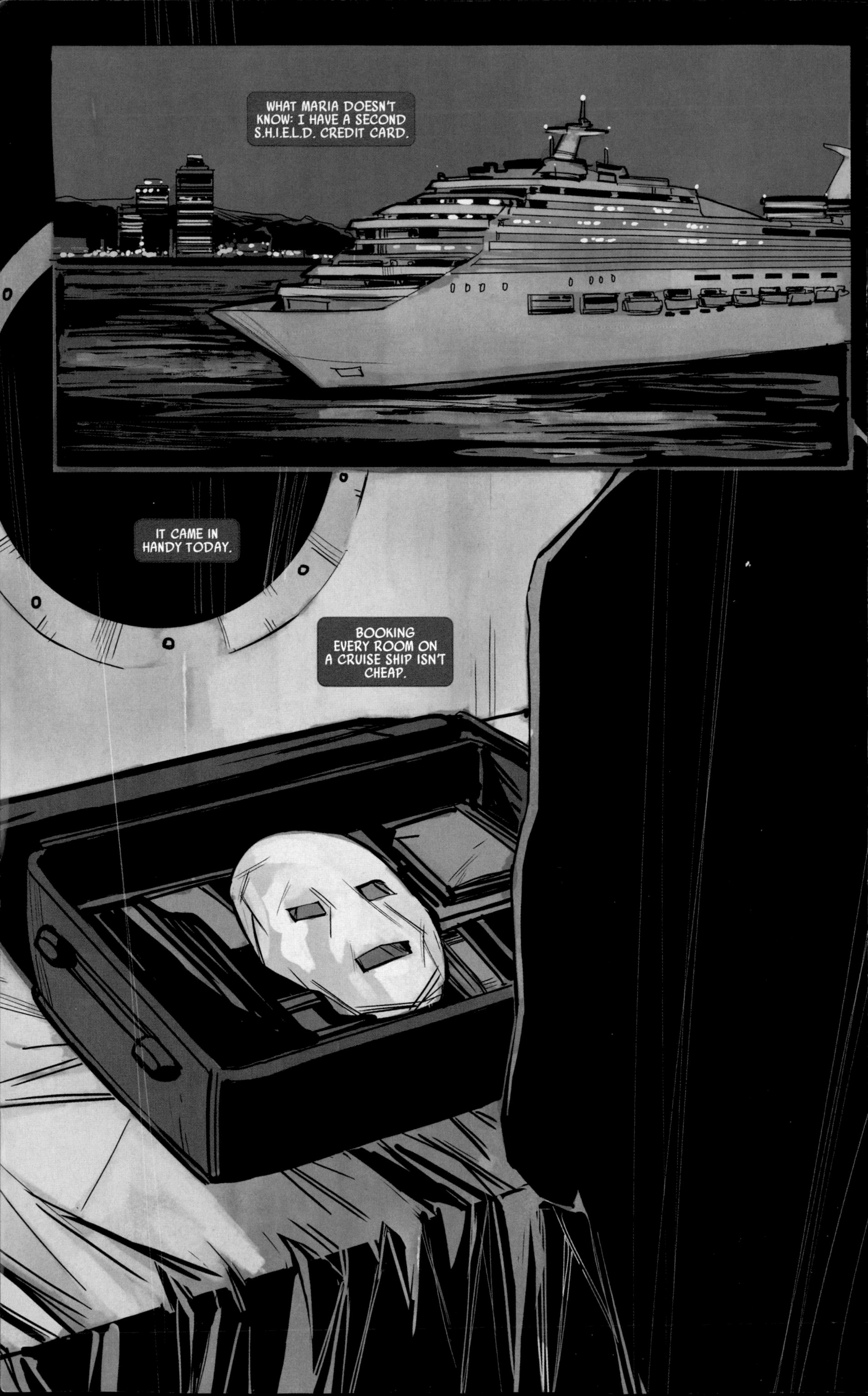
WHAT MARIA DOESN'T KNOW: I HAVE A SECOND S.H.I.E.L.D. CREDIT CARD.
IT CAME IN HANDY TODAY.
BOOKING EVERY ROOM ON A CRUISE SHIP ISN'T CHEAP.

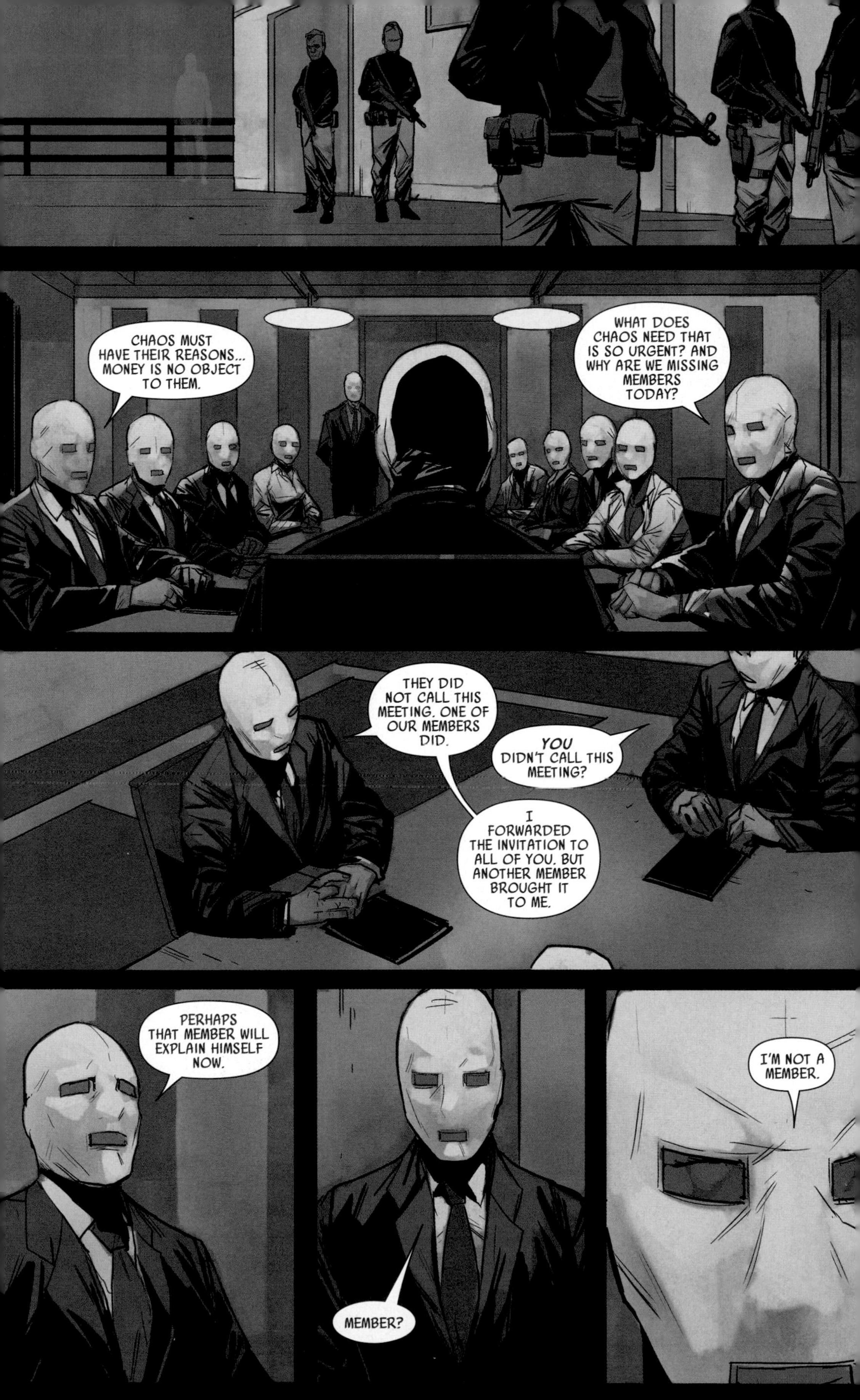
CHAOS MUST HAVE THEIR REASONS... MONEY IS NO OBJECT TO THEM.
WHAT DOES CHAOS NEED THAT IS SO URGENT? AND WHY ARE WE MISSING MEMBERS TODAY?
THEY DID NOT CALL THIS MEETING. ONE OF OUR MEMBERS DID.
YOU DIDN'T CALL THIS MEETING?
I FORWARDED THE INVITATION TO ALL OF YOU. BUT ANOTHER MEMBER BROUGHT IT TO ME.
PERHAPS THAT MEMBER WILL EXPLAIN HIMSELF NOW.
MEMBER?
I'M NOT A MEMBER.

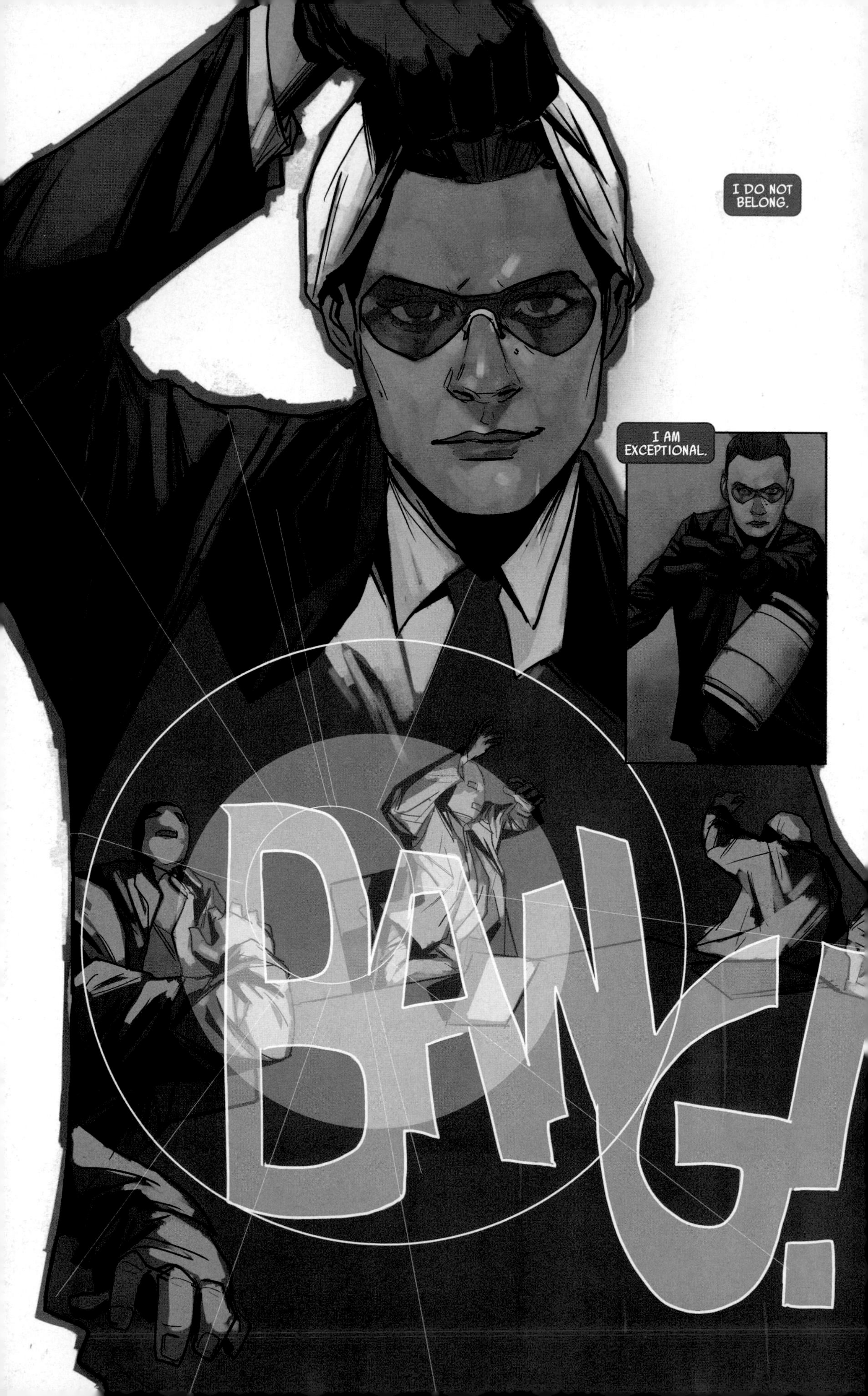
I DO NOT BELONG.
I AM EXCEPTIONAL.
BANG!

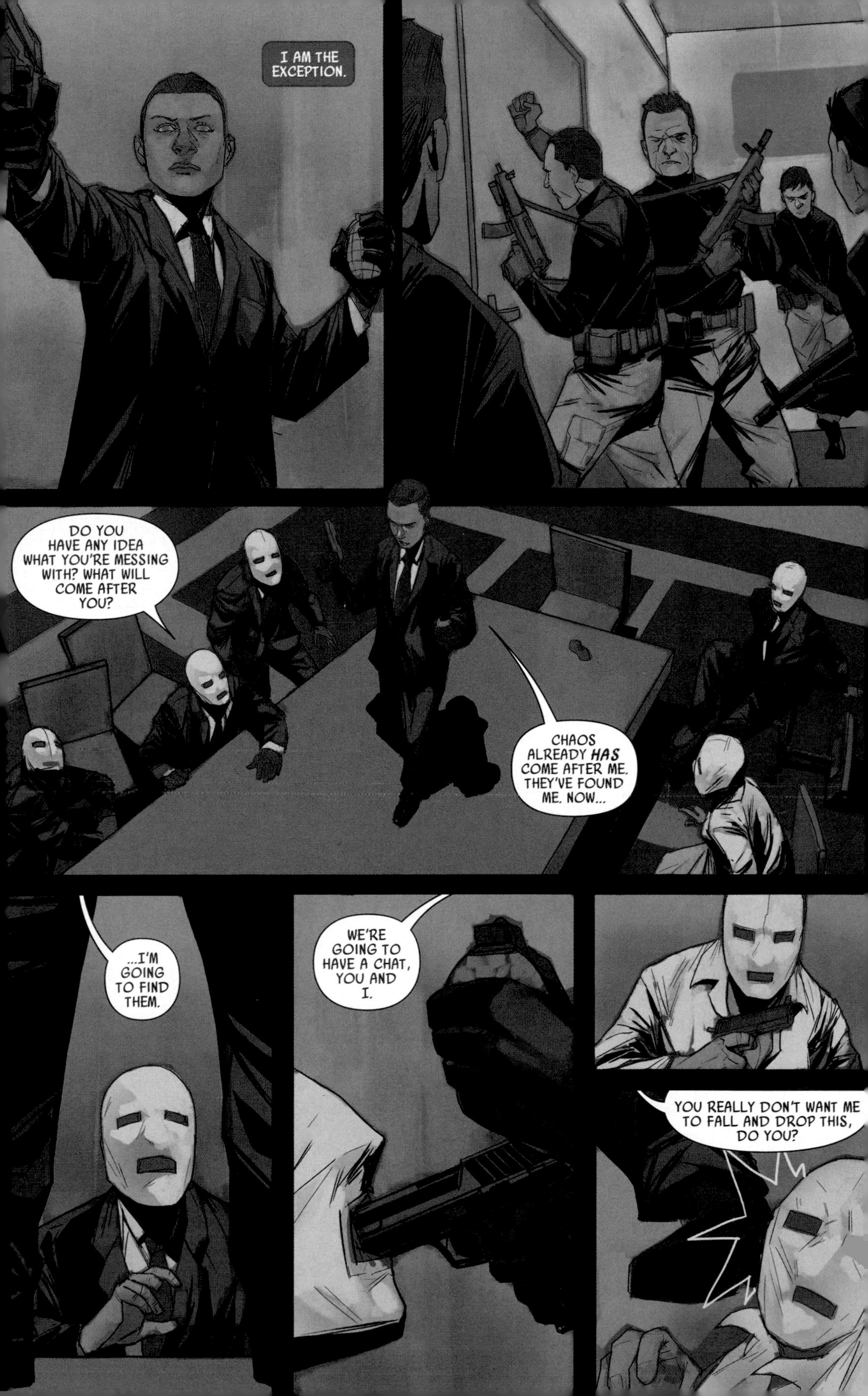
I AM THE EXCEPTION.
DO YOU HAVE ANY IDEA WHAT YOU'RE MESSING WITH? WHAT WILL COME AFTER YOU?
CHAOS ALREADY **HAS** COME AFTER ME. THEY'VE FOUND ME. NOW...
...I'M GOING TO FIND THEM.
WE'RE GOING TO HAVE A CHAT, YOU AND I.
YOU REALLY DON'T WANT ME TO FALL AND DROP THIS, DO YOU?

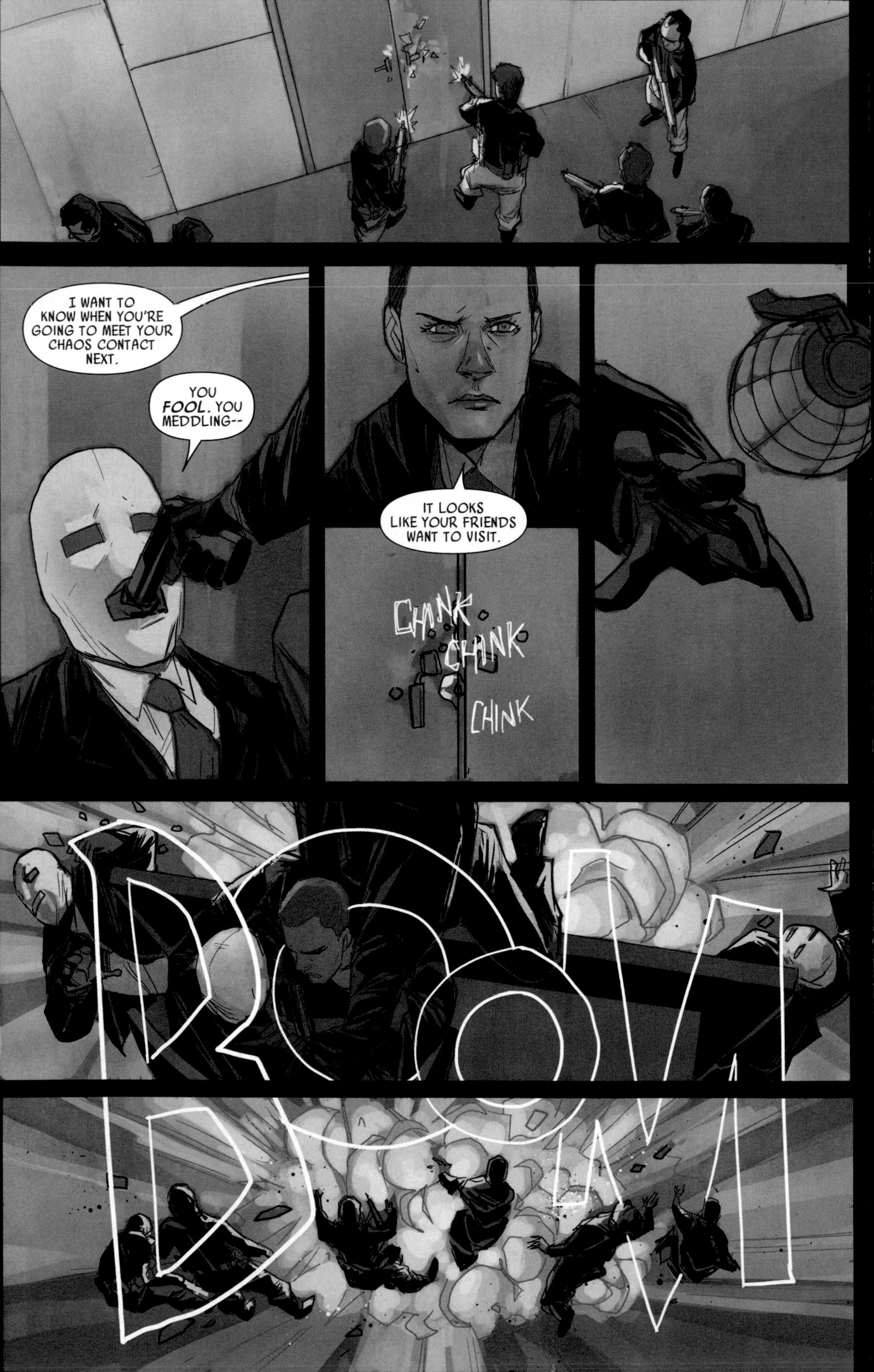
I WANT TO KNOW WHEN YOU'RE GOING TO MEET YOUR CHAOS CONTACT NEXT.
YOU FOOL. YOU MEDDLING--
IT LOOKS LIKE YOUR FRIENDS WANT TO VISIT.
CHINK CHINK
CHINK
BOOM
BOOM

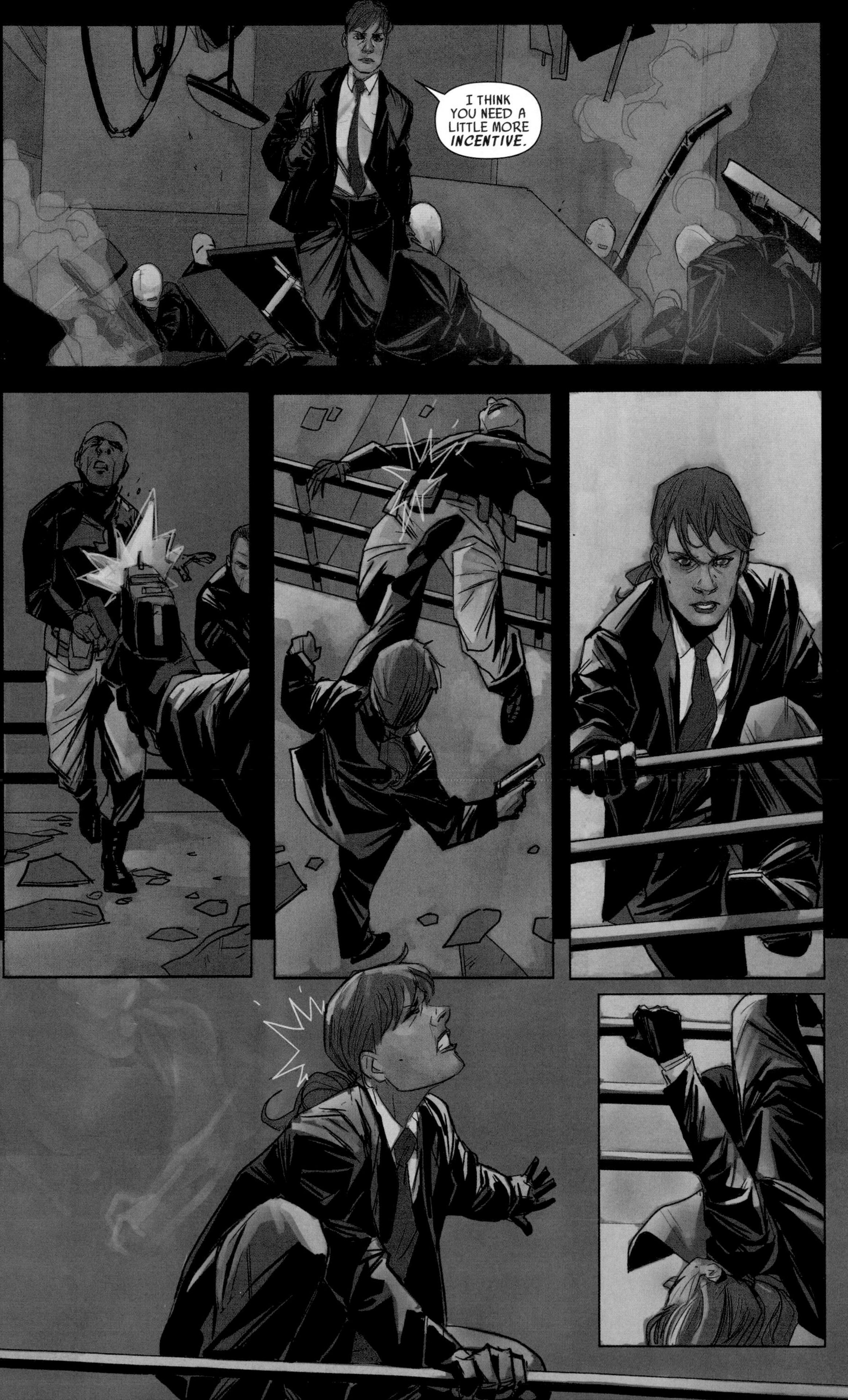
I THINK YOU NEED A LITTLE MORE INCENTIVE.

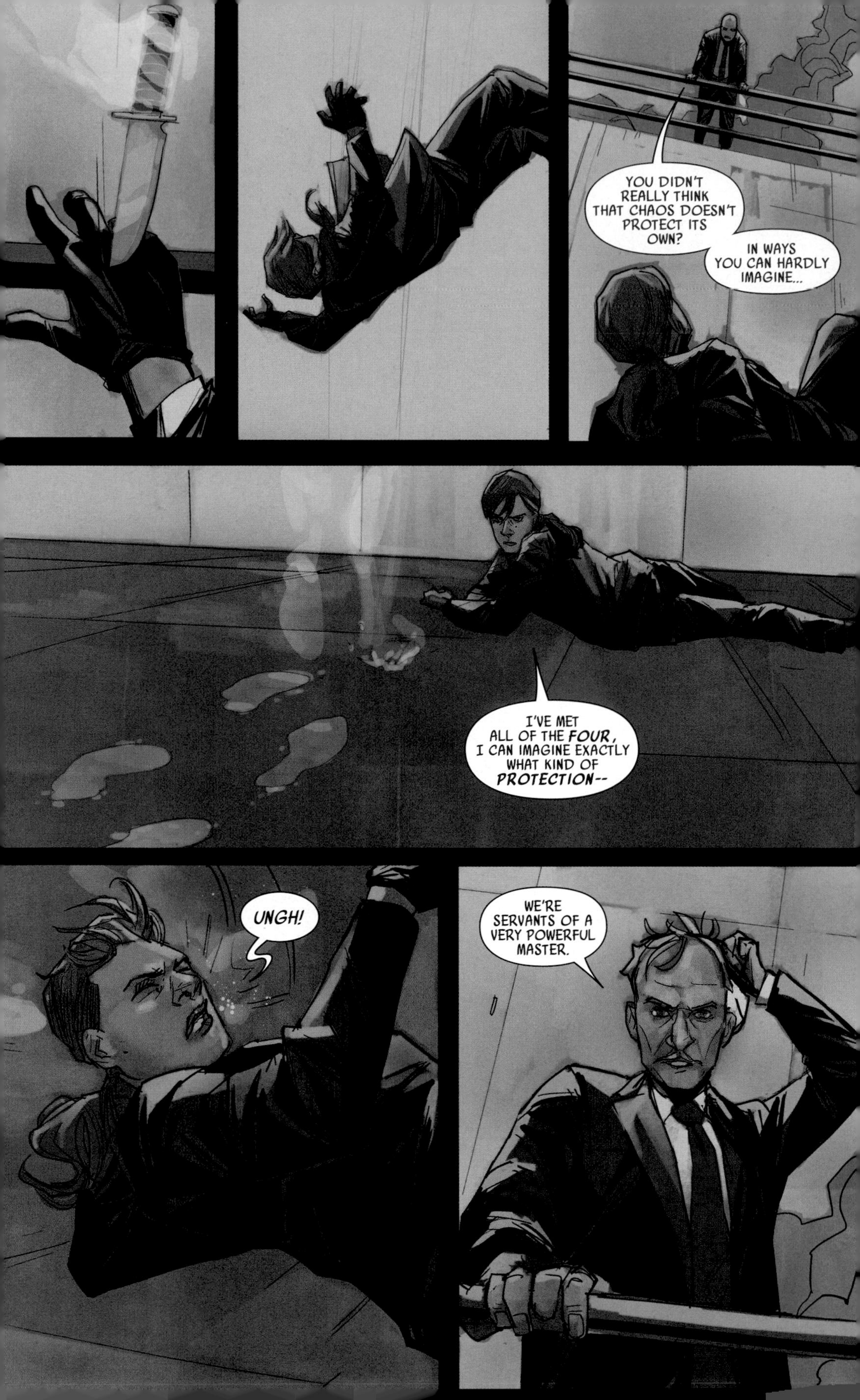
YOU DIDN'T REALLY THINK THAT CHAOS DOESN'T PROTECT ITS OWN?
IN WAYS YOU CAN HARDLY IMAGINE...
I'VE MET ALL OF THE FOUR, I CAN IMAGINE EXACTLY WHAT KIND OF PROTECTION--
UNGH!
WE'RE SERVANTS OF A VERY POWERFUL MASTER.

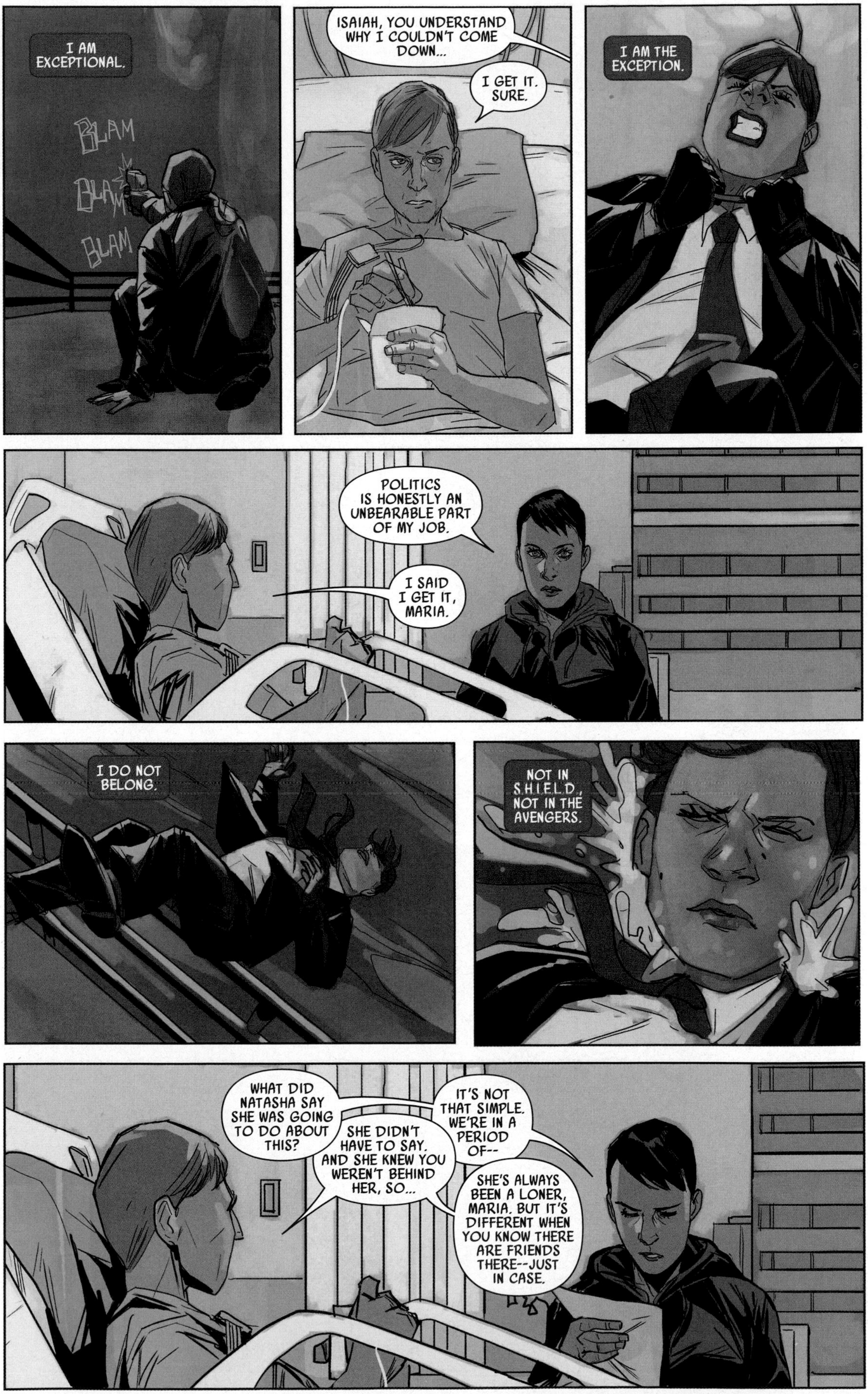

I AM EXCEPTIONAL.
BLAM
BLAM
BLAM
ISAIAH, YOU UNDERSTAND WHY I COULDN'T COME DOWN...
I GET IT. SURE.
I AM THE EXCEPTION.
POLITICS IS HONESTLY AN UNBEARABLE PART OF MY JOB.
I SAID I GET IT, MARIA.
I DO NOT BELONG.
NOT IN S.H.I.E.L.D., NOT IN THE AVENGERS.
WHAT DID NATASHA SAY SHE WAS GOING TO DO ABOUT THIS?
IT'S NOT THAT SIMPLE. WE'RE IN A PERIOD OF--
SHE DIDN'T HAVE TO SAY. AND SHE KNEW YOU WEREN'T BEHIND HER, SO...
SHE'S ALWAYS BEEN A LONER, MARIA. BUT IT'S DIFFERENT WHEN YOU KNOW THERE ARE FRIENDS THERE--JUST IN CASE.

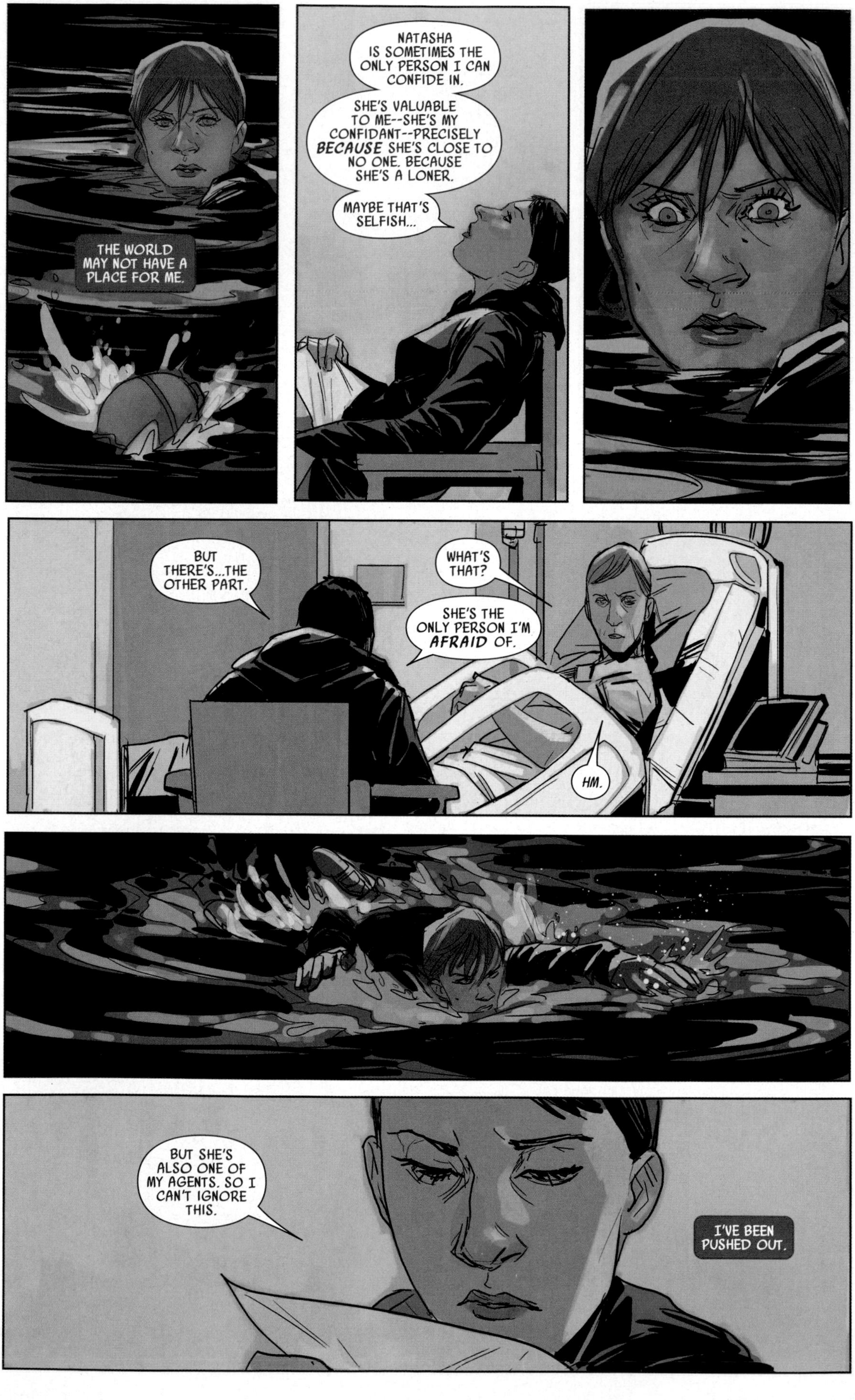
THE WORLD MAY NOT HAVE A PLACE FOR ME.
NATASHA IS SOMETIMES THE ONLY PERSON I CAN CONFIDE IN.
SHE'S VALUABLE TO ME--SHE'S MY CONFIDANT--PRECISELY *BECAUSE* SHE'S CLOSE TO NO ONE. BECAUSE SHE'S A LONER.
MAYBE THAT'S SELFISH...
BUT THERE'S...THE OTHER PART.
WHAT'S THAT?
SHE'S THE ONLY PERSON I'M *AFRAID* OF.
HM.
BUT SHE'S ALSO ONE OF MY AGENTS. SO I CAN'T IGNORE THIS.
I'VE BEEN PUSHED OUT.

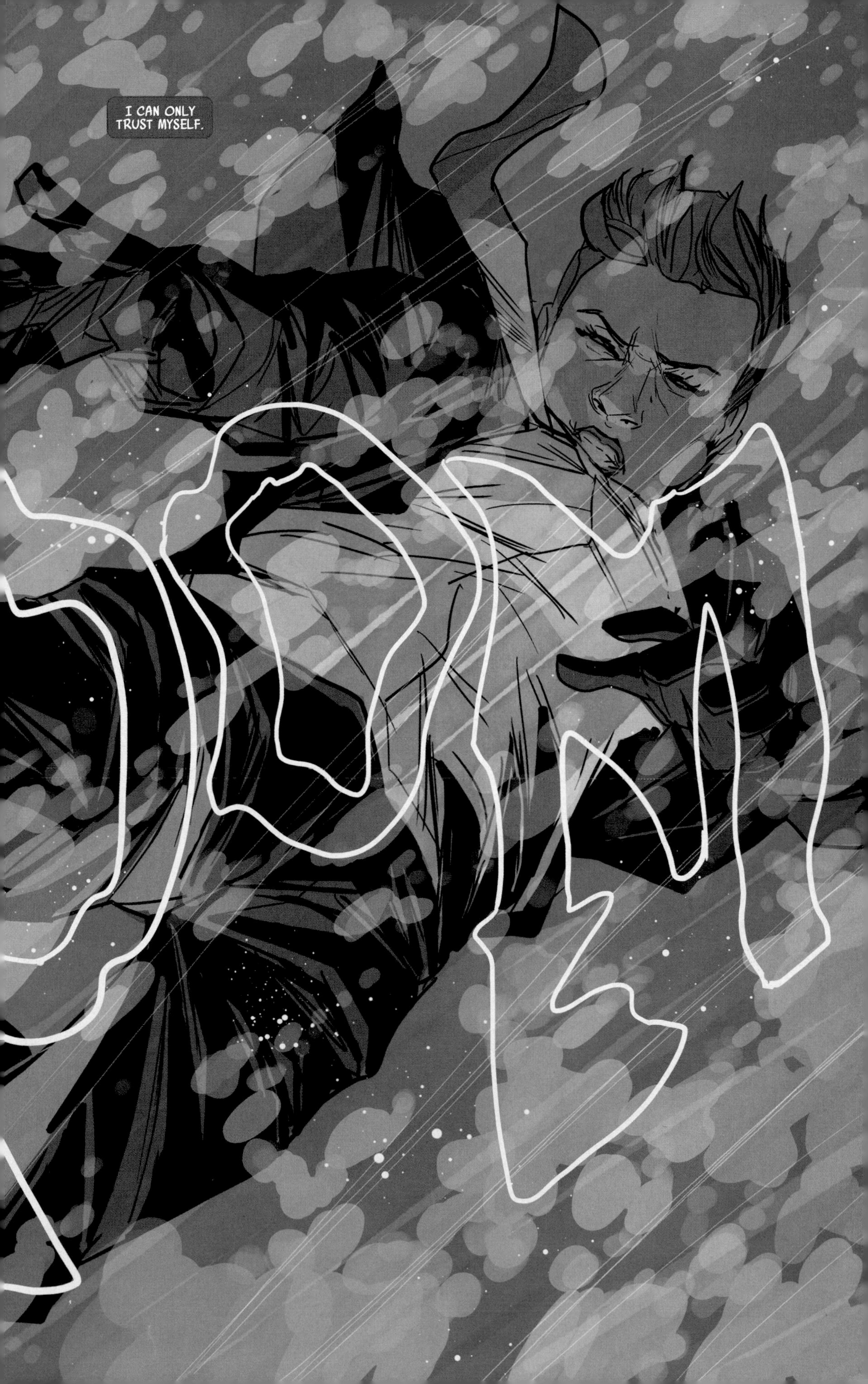
I CAN ONLY TRUST MYSELF.

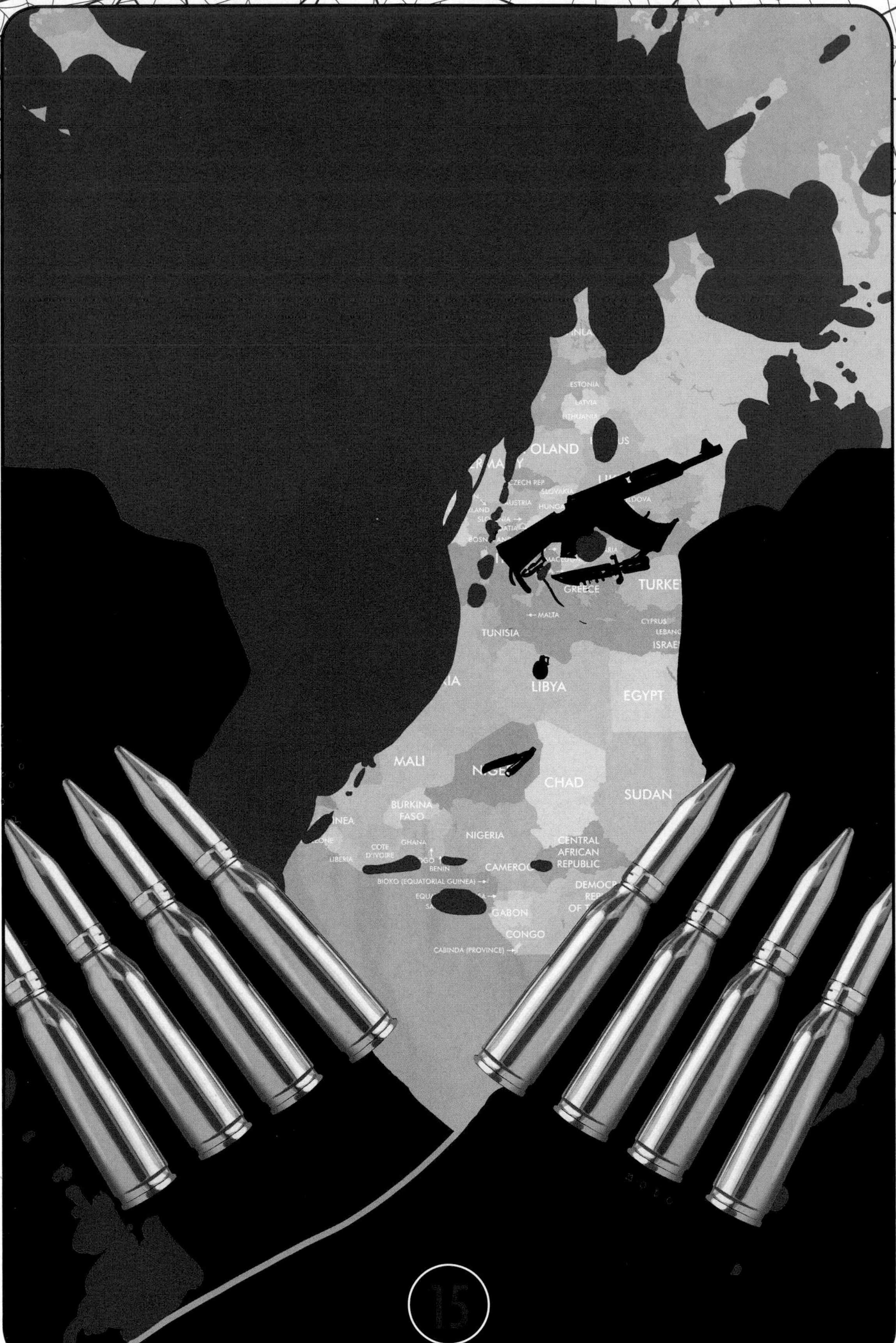
ESTONIA
LATVIA
CZECH REP
SLOVAKIA
AUSTRIA
GREECE
MALTA
TUNISIA
CYPRUS
LIBYA
EGYPT
MALI
CHAD
SUDAN
BURKINA FASO
NIGERIA
CENTRAL AFRICAN REPUBLIC
GHANA
COTE D'IVOIRE
LIBERIA
BENIN
BIOKO (EQUATORIAL GUINEA)
GABON
CONGO
CABINDA (PROVINCE)
15

AN ENEMY REVEALED

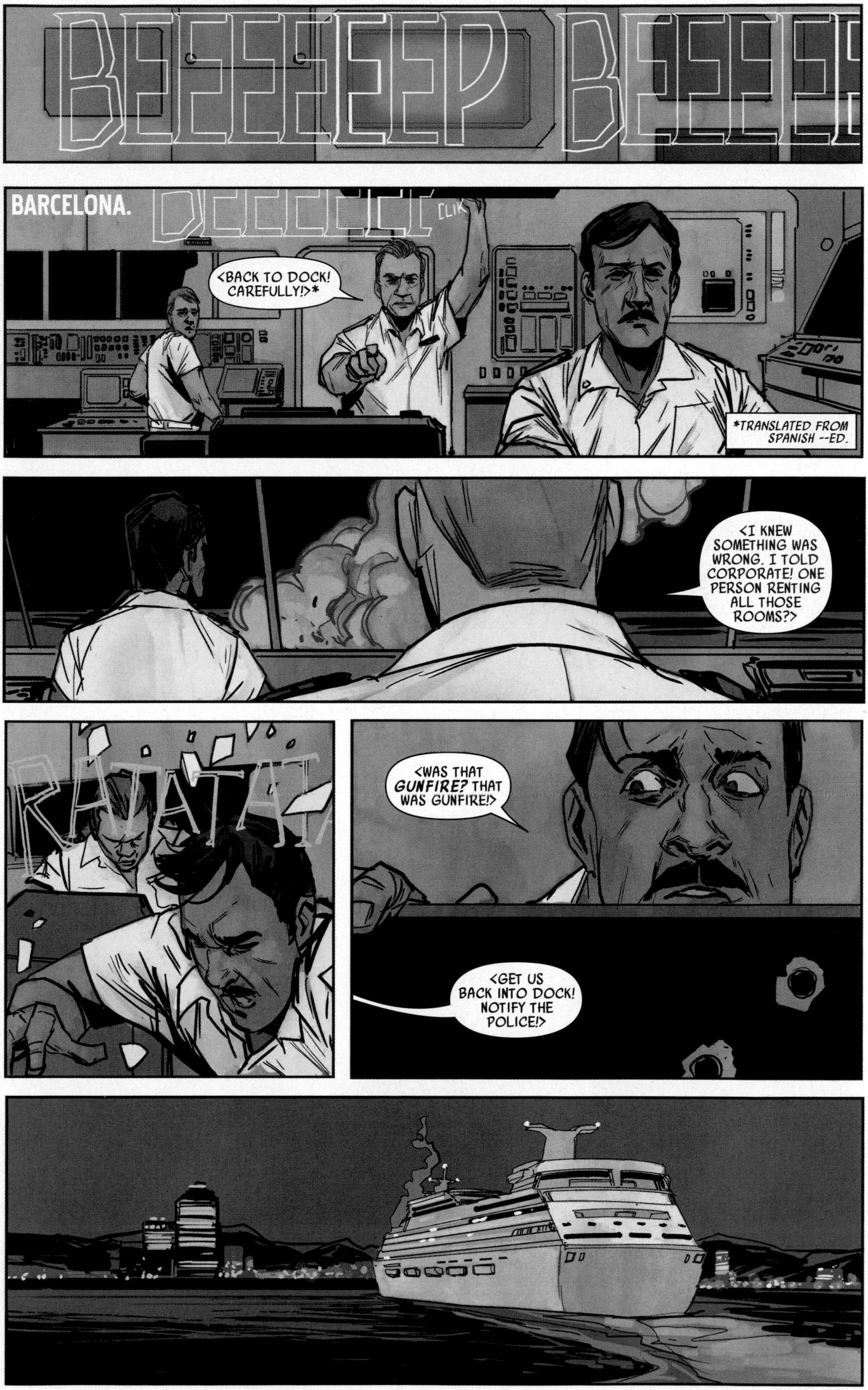
BEEEEEEP BEEEE
BARCELONA.
BEEEEEE
CLIK
<BACK TO DOCK! CAREFULLY!>*
*TRANSLATED FROM SPANISH --ED.
<I KNEW SOMETHING WAS WRONG. I TOLD CORPORATE! ONE PERSON RENTING ALL THOSE ROOMS?>
RATATATA
<WAS THAT GUNFIRE? THAT WAS GUNFIRE!>
<GET US BACK INTO DOCK! NOTIFY THE POLICE!>

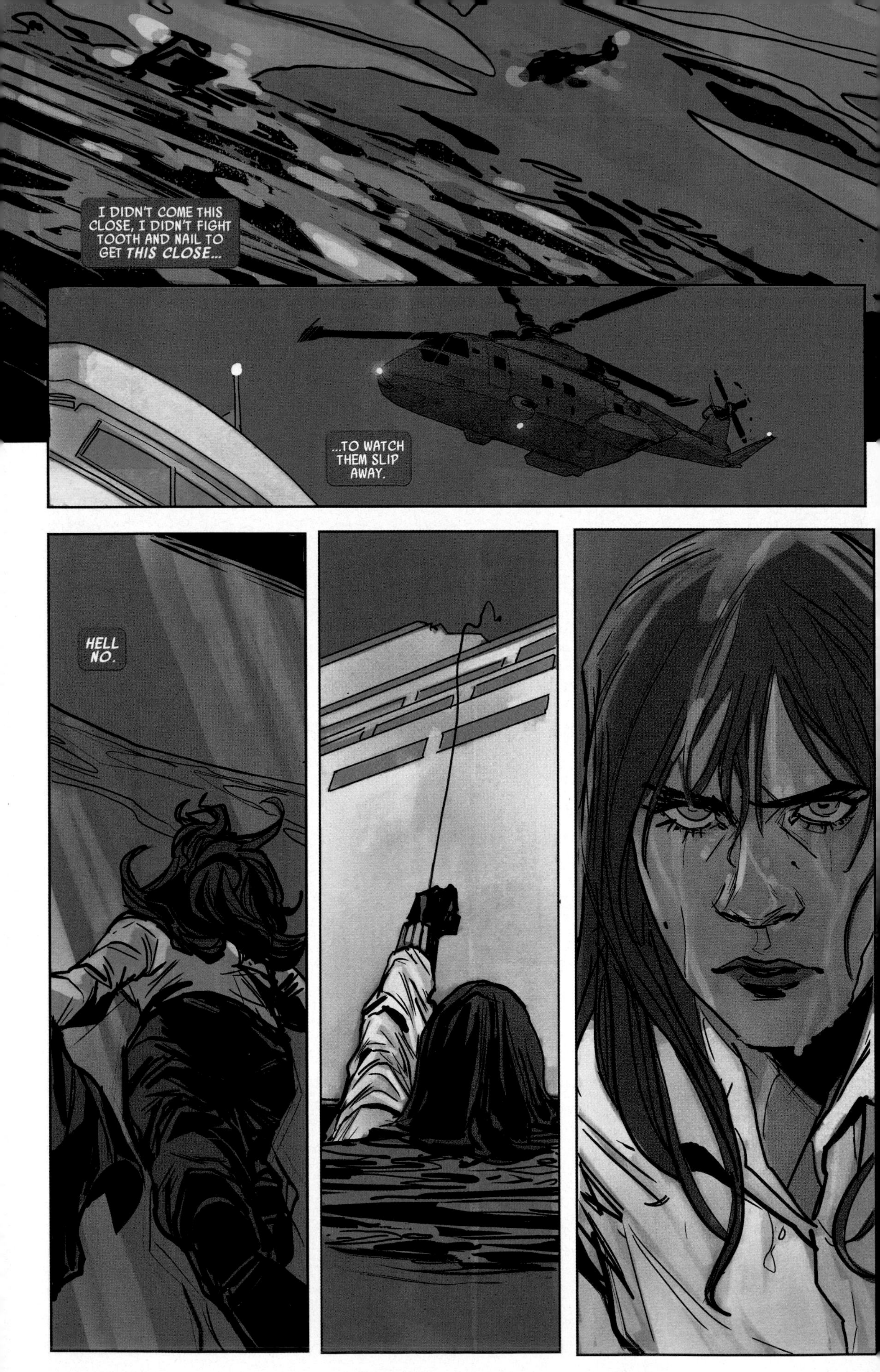
I DIDN'T COME THIS CLOSE, I DIDN'T FIGHT TOOTH AND NAIL TO GET THIS CLOSE...
...TO WATCH THEM SLIP AWAY.
HELL NO.

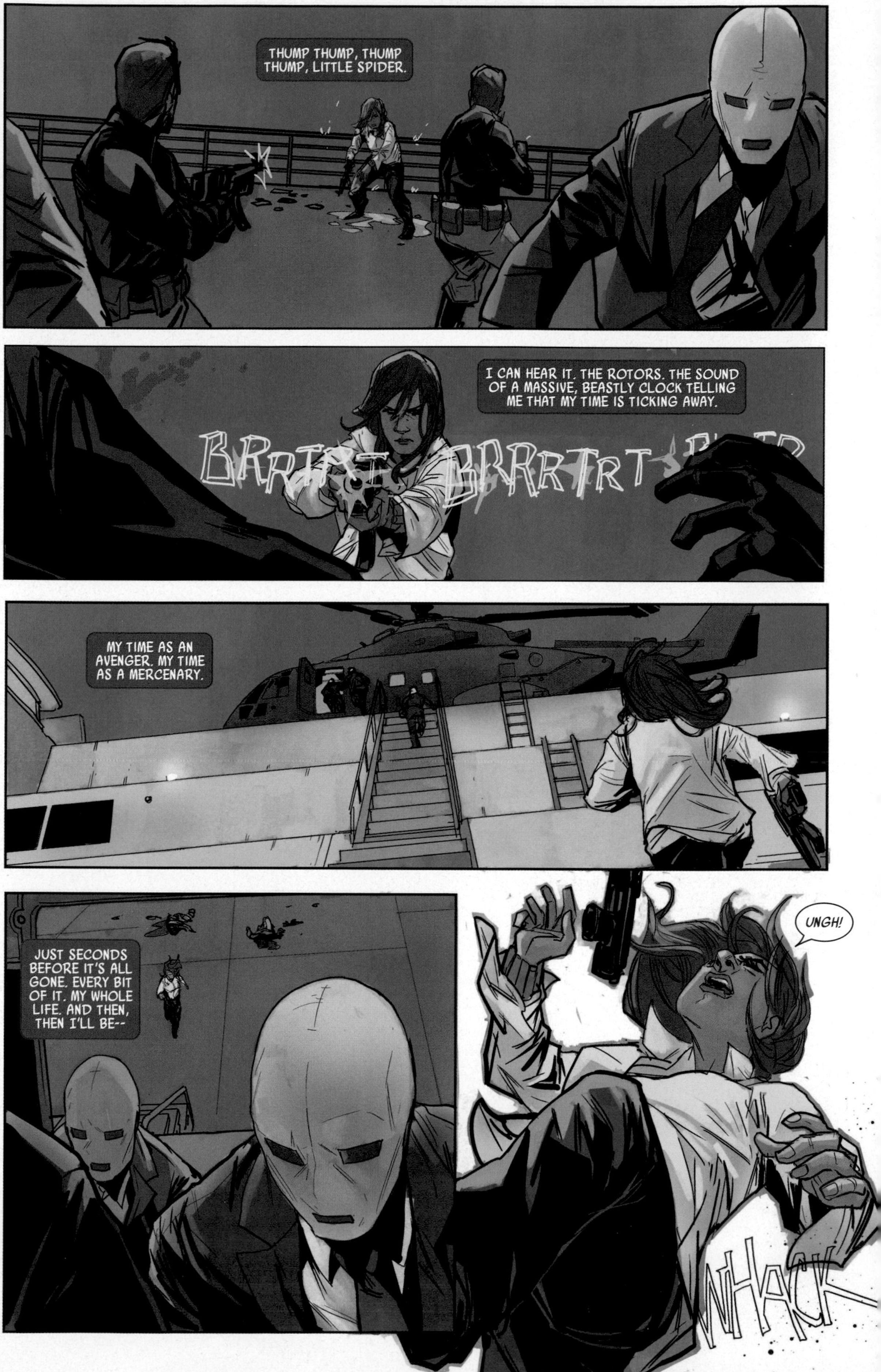
THUMP THUMP, THUMP THUMP, LITTLE SPIDER.
I CAN HEAR IT. THE ROTORS. THE SOUND OF A MASSIVE, BEASTLY CLOCK TELLING ME THAT MY TIME IS TICKING AWAY.
BRRTRT
BRRRRTRT
MY TIME AS AN AVENGER. MY TIME AS A MERCENARY.
JUST SECONDS BEFORE IT'S ALL GONE. EVERY BIT OF IT. MY WHOLE LIFE. AND THEN, THEN I'LL BE--
UNGH!
WHACK

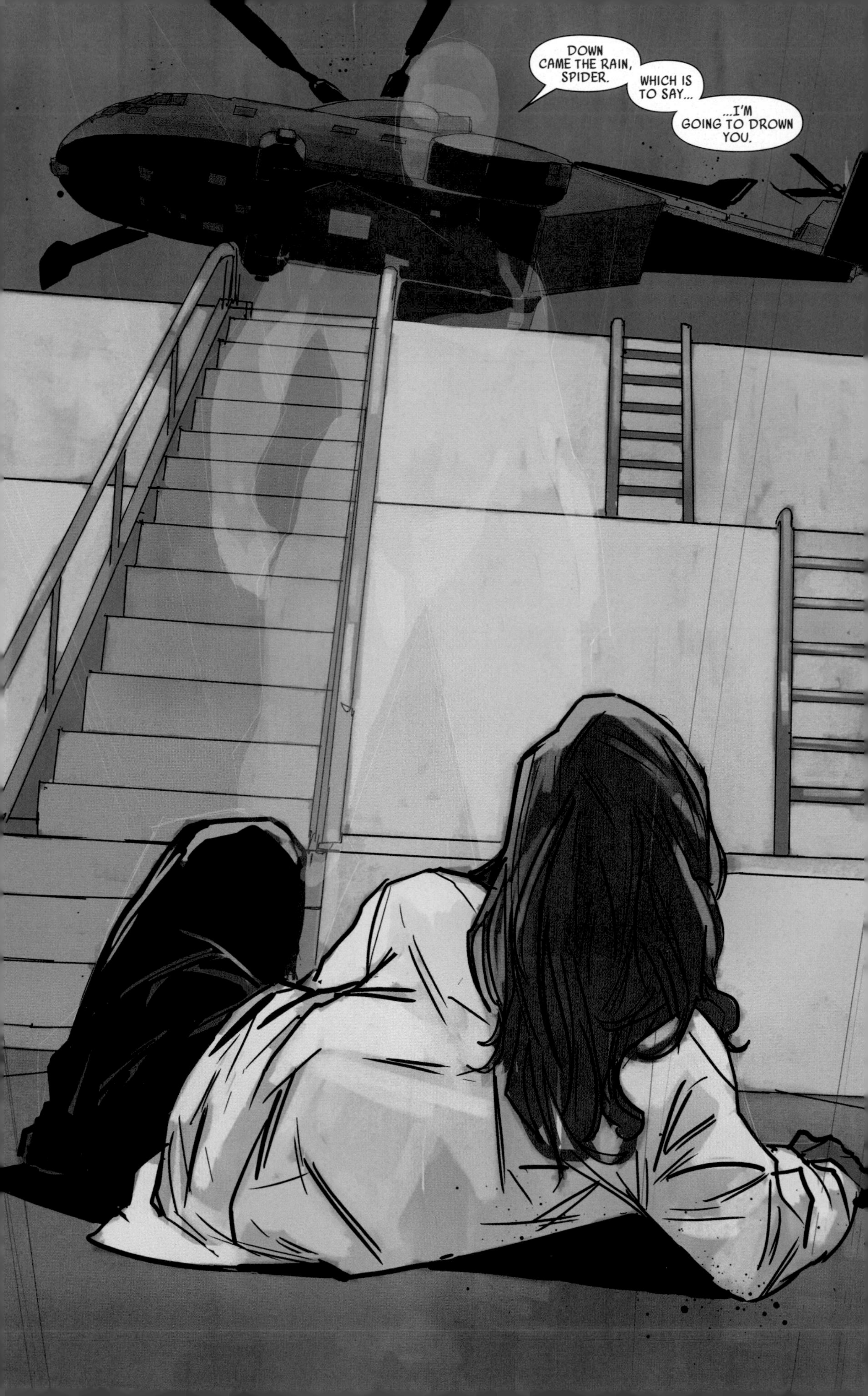
DOWN CAME THE RAIN, SPIDER.
WHICH IS TO SAY...
...I'M GOING TO DROWN YOU.

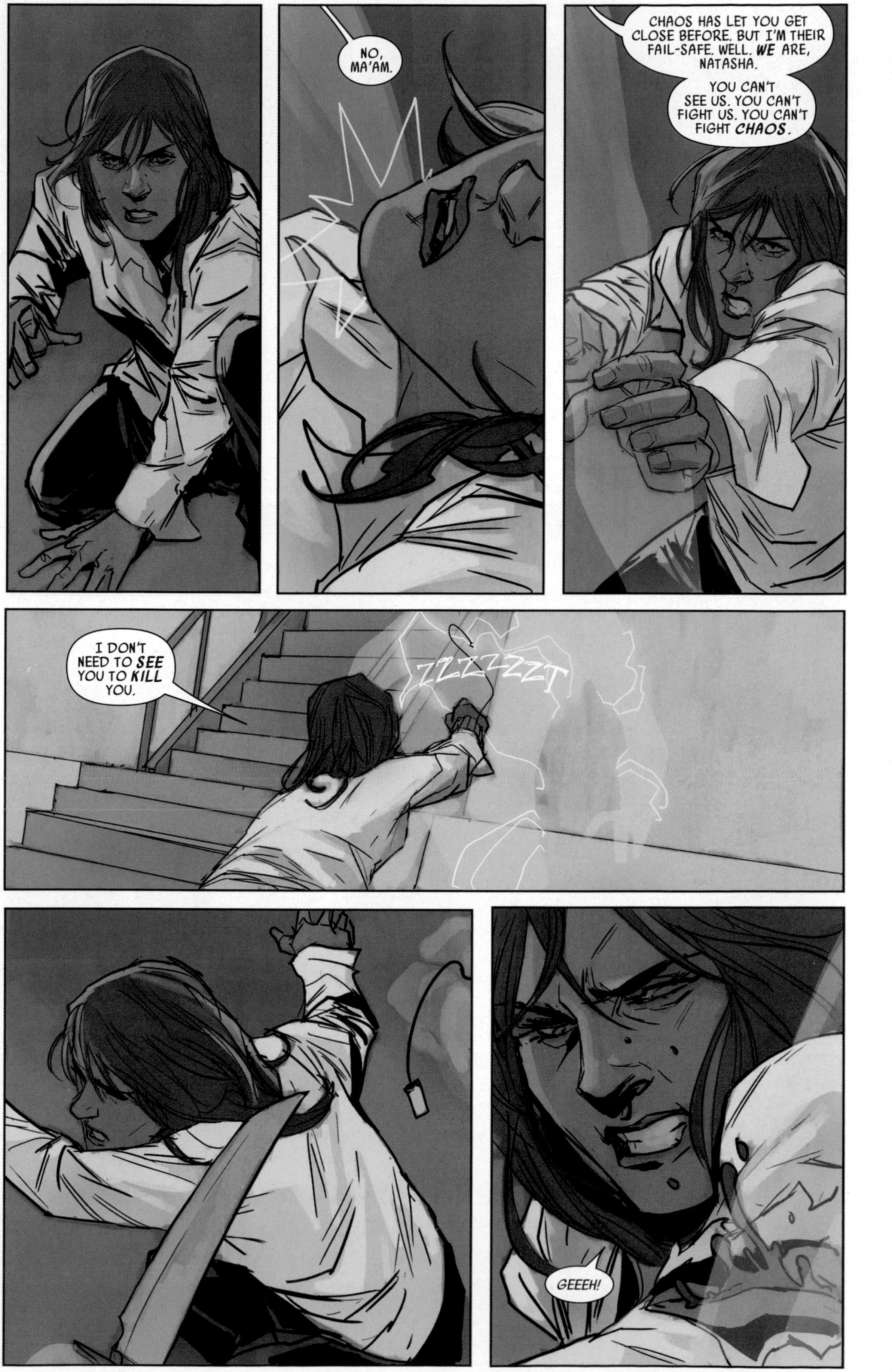
NO, MA'AM.
CHAOS HAS LET YOU GET CLOSE BEFORE. BUT I'M THEIR FAIL-SAFE. WELL. WE ARE, NATASHA.
YOU CAN'T SEE US. YOU CAN'T FIGHT US. YOU CAN'T FIGHT CHAOS.
I DON'T NEED TO SEE YOU TO KILL YOU.
ZZZZZZZT
GEEEH!

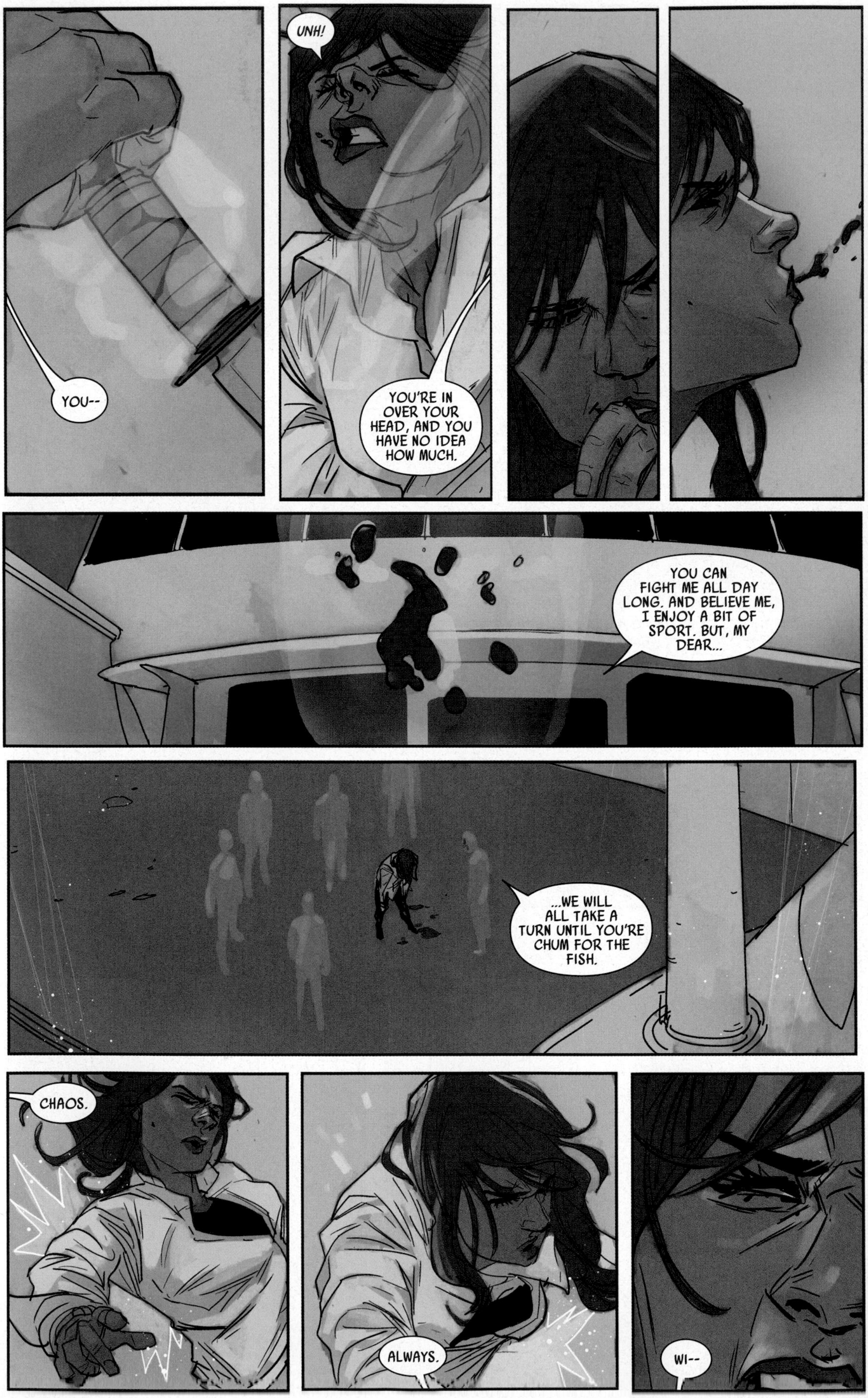
YOU--
UNH!
YOU'RE IN OVER YOUR HEAD, AND YOU HAVE NO IDEA HOW MUCH.
YOU CAN FIGHT ME ALL DAY LONG. AND BELIEVE ME, I ENJOY A BIT OF SPORT. BUT, MY DEAR...
...WE WILL ALL TAKE A TURN UNTIL YOU'RE CHUM FOR THE FISH.
CHAOS.
ALWAYS.
WI--

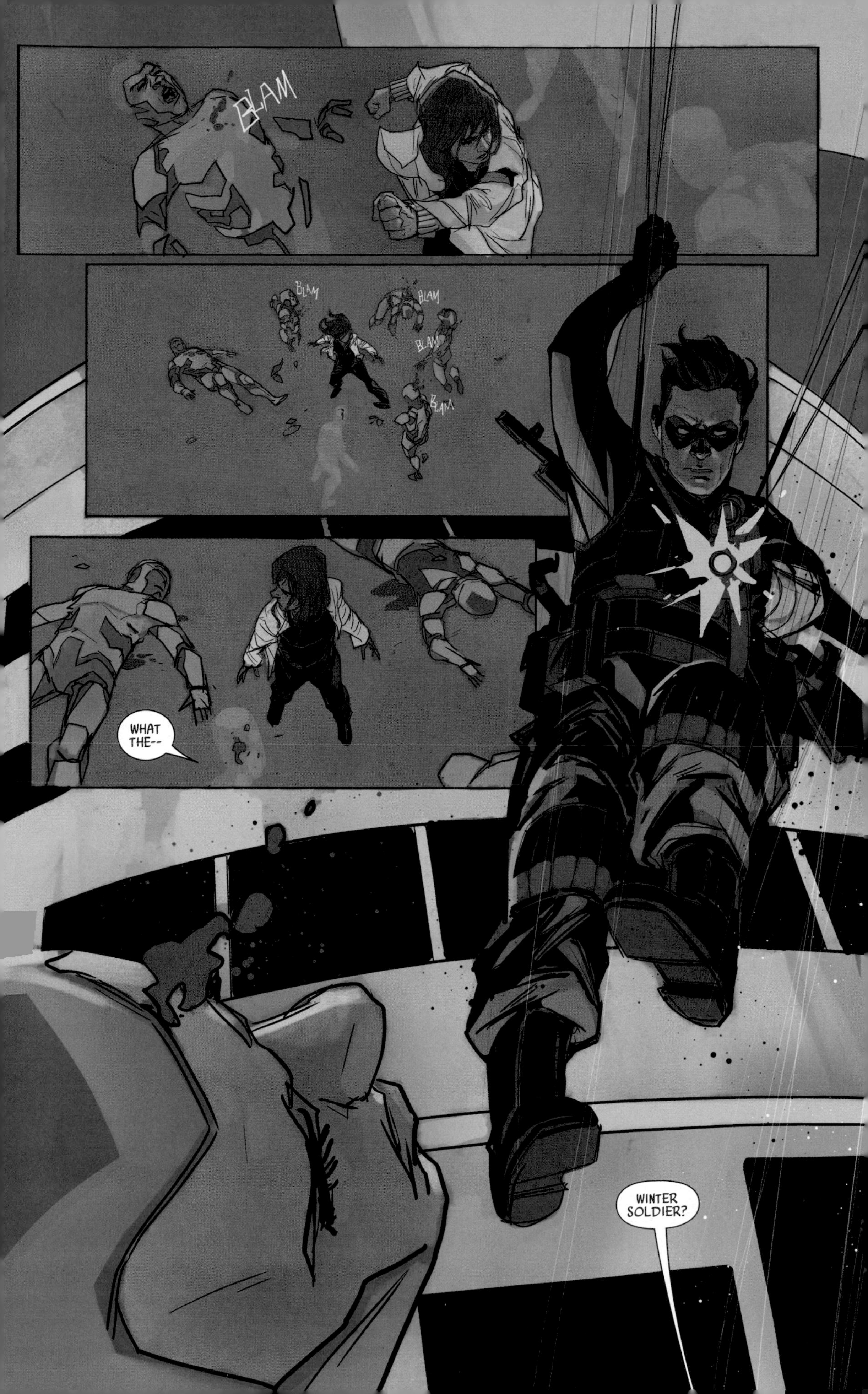
BLAM
BLAM
BLAM
BLAM
BLAM
WHAT THE--
WINTER SOLDIER?

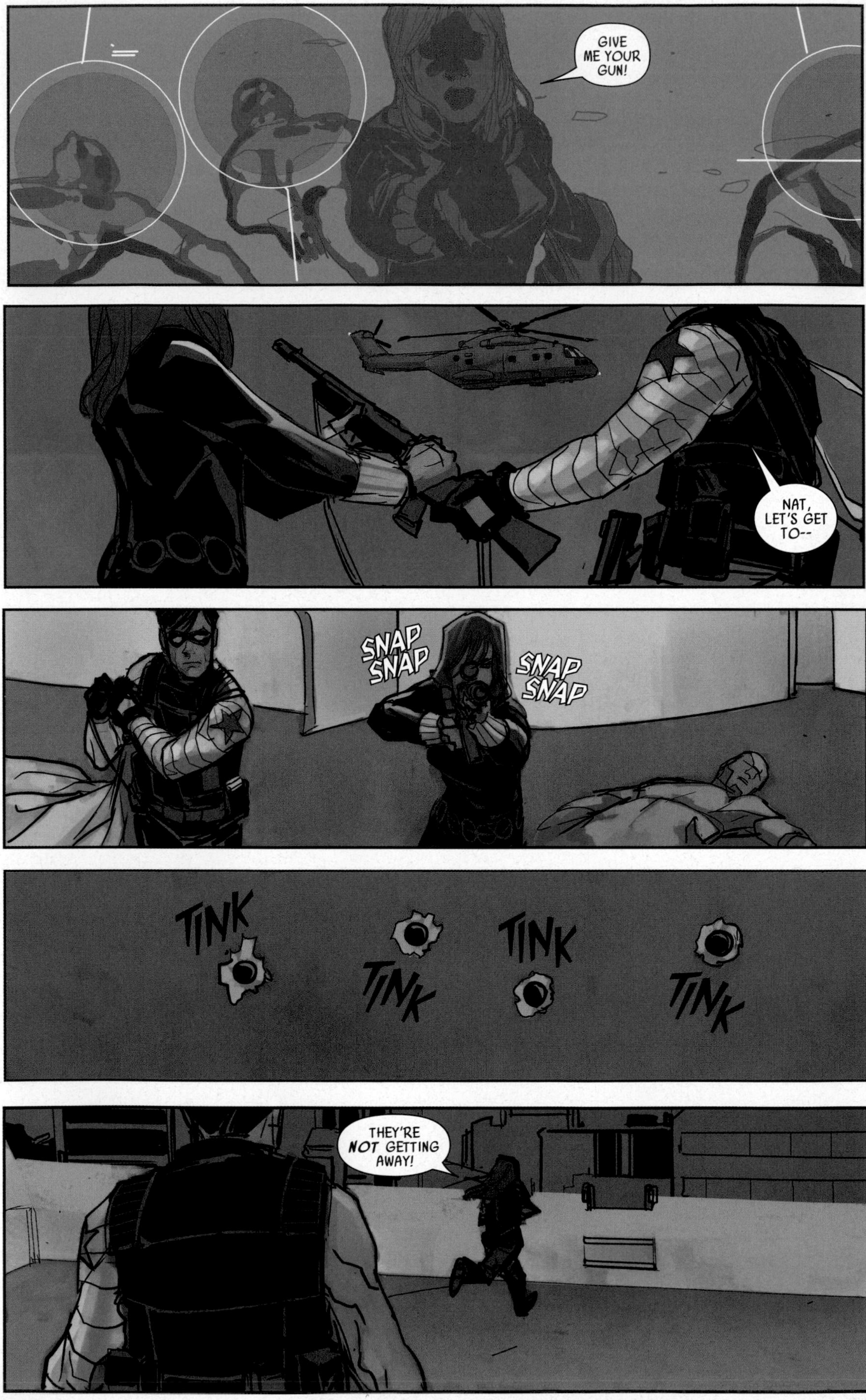
GIVE ME YOUR GUN!
NAT, LET'S GET TO--
SNAP SNAP
SNAP SNAP
TINK
TINK
TINK
TINK
THEY'RE *NOT* GETTING AWAY!

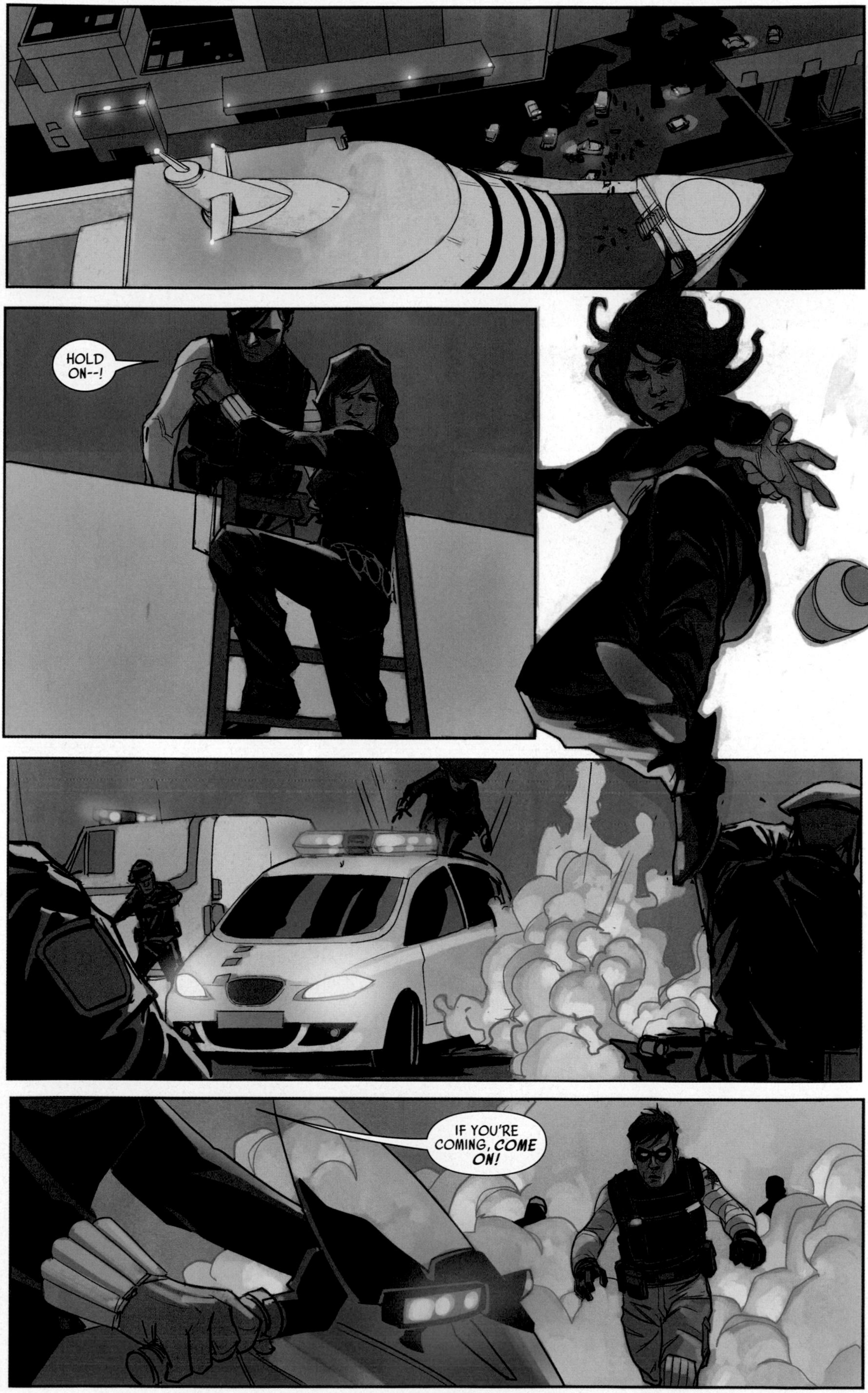
HOLD ON--!
IF YOU'RE COMING, COME ON!

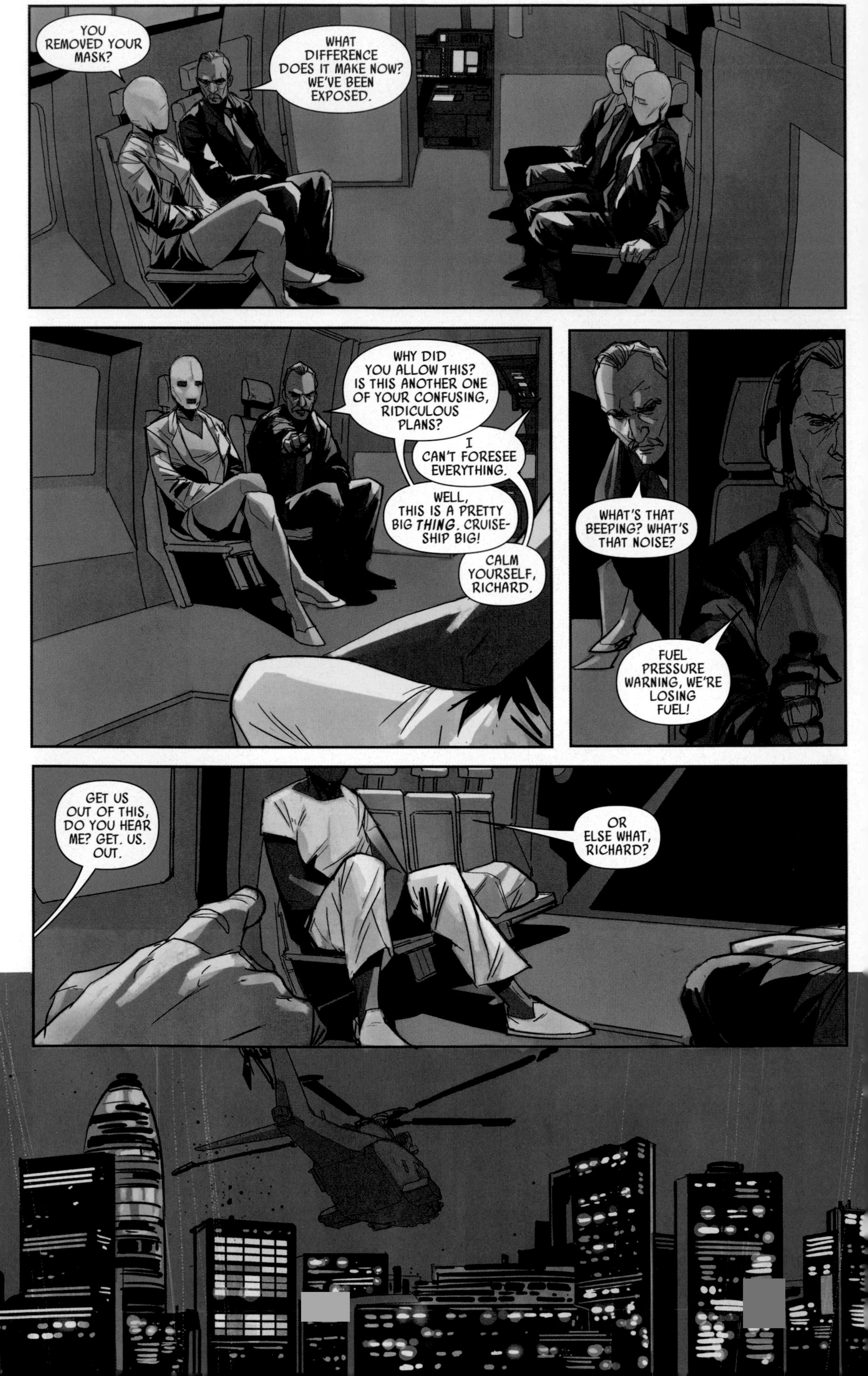
YOU REMOVED YOUR MASK?
WHAT DIFFERENCE DOES IT MAKE NOW? WE'VE BEEN EXPOSED.
WHY DID YOU ALLOW THIS? IS THIS ANOTHER ONE OF YOUR CONFUSING, RIDICULOUS PLANS?
I CAN'T FORESEE EVERYTHING.
WELL, THIS IS A PRETTY BIG *THING*. CRUISE-SHIP BIG!
CALM YOURSELF, RICHARD.
WHAT'S THAT BEEPING? WHAT'S THAT NOISE?
FUEL PRESSURE WARNING, WE'RE LOSING FUEL!
GET US OUT OF THIS, DO YOU HEAR ME? GET. US. OUT.
OR ELSE WHAT, RICHARD?

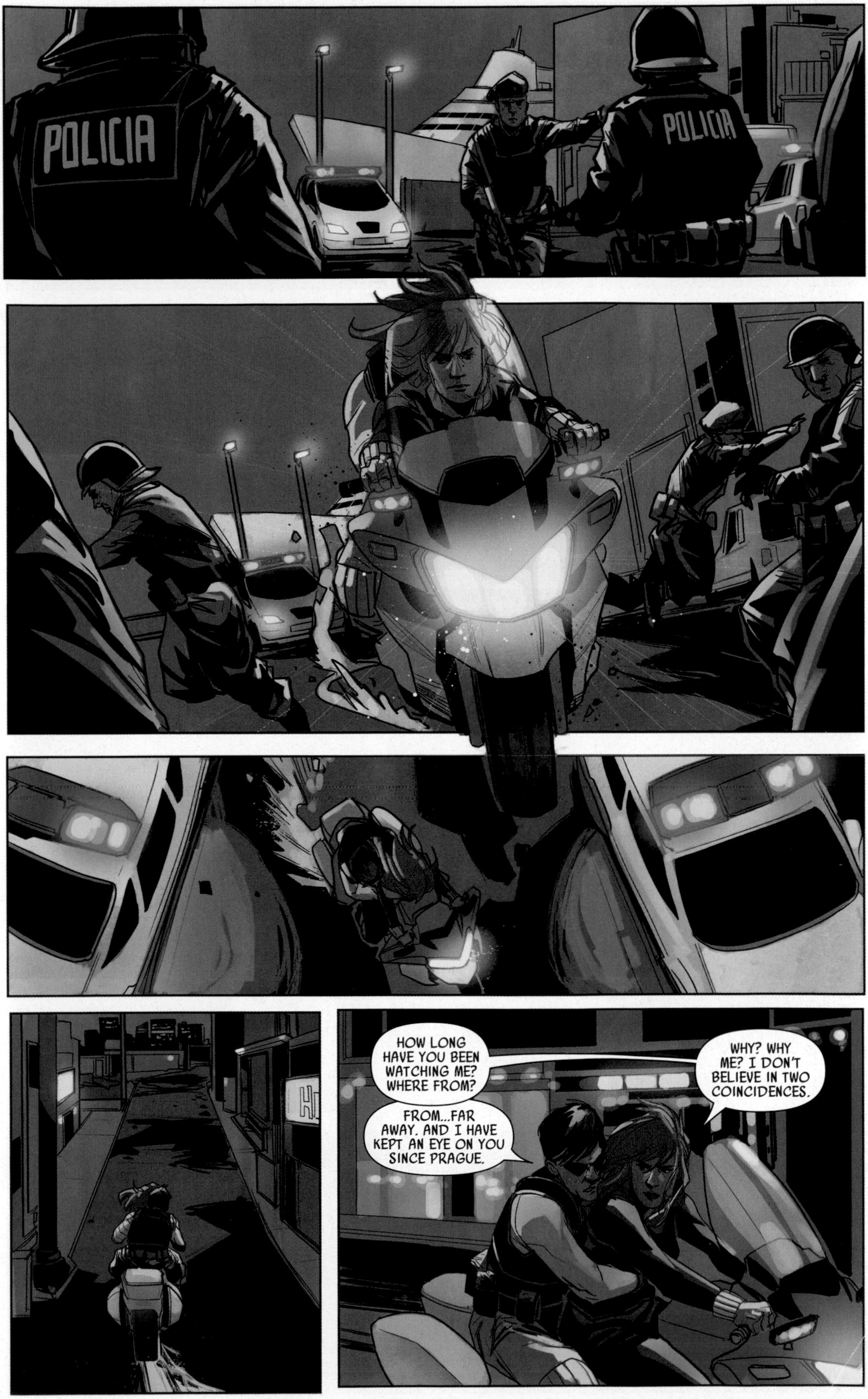
POLICIA
POLICIA
HOW LONG HAVE YOU BEEN WATCHING ME? WHERE FROM?
FROM...FAR AWAY. AND I HAVE KEPT AN EYE ON YOU SINCE PRAGUE.
WHY? WHY ME? I DON'T BELIEVE IN TWO COINCIDENCES.

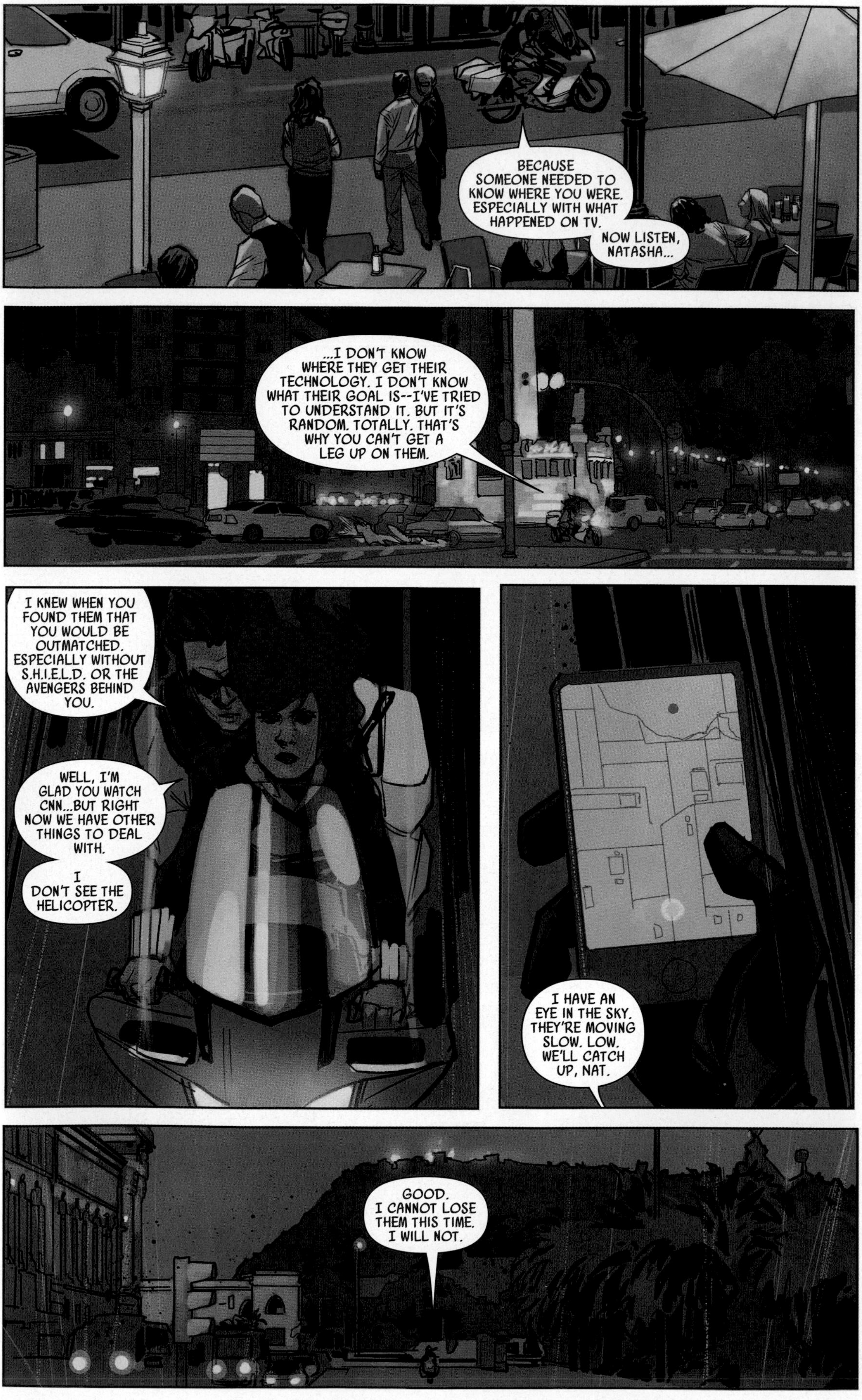
BECAUSE SOMEONE NEEDED TO KNOW WHERE YOU WERE. ESPECIALLY WITH WHAT HAPPENED ON TV.
NOW LISTEN, NATASHA...
...I DON'T KNOW WHERE THEY GET THEIR TECHNOLOGY. I DON'T KNOW WHAT THEIR GOAL IS--I'VE TRIED TO UNDERSTAND IT. BUT IT'S RANDOM. TOTALLY. THAT'S WHY YOU CAN'T GET A LEG UP ON THEM.
I KNEW WHEN YOU FOUND THEM THAT YOU WOULD BE OUTMATCHED. ESPECIALLY WITHOUT S.H.I.E.L.D. OR THE AVENGERS BEHIND YOU.
WELL, I'M GLAD YOU WATCH CNN...BUT RIGHT NOW WE HAVE OTHER THINGS TO DEAL WITH.
I DON'T SEE THE HELICOPTER.
I HAVE AN EYE IN THE SKY. THEY'RE MOVING SLOW. LOW. WE'LL CATCH UP, NAT.
GOOD. I CANNOT LOSE THEM THIS TIME. I WILL NOT.

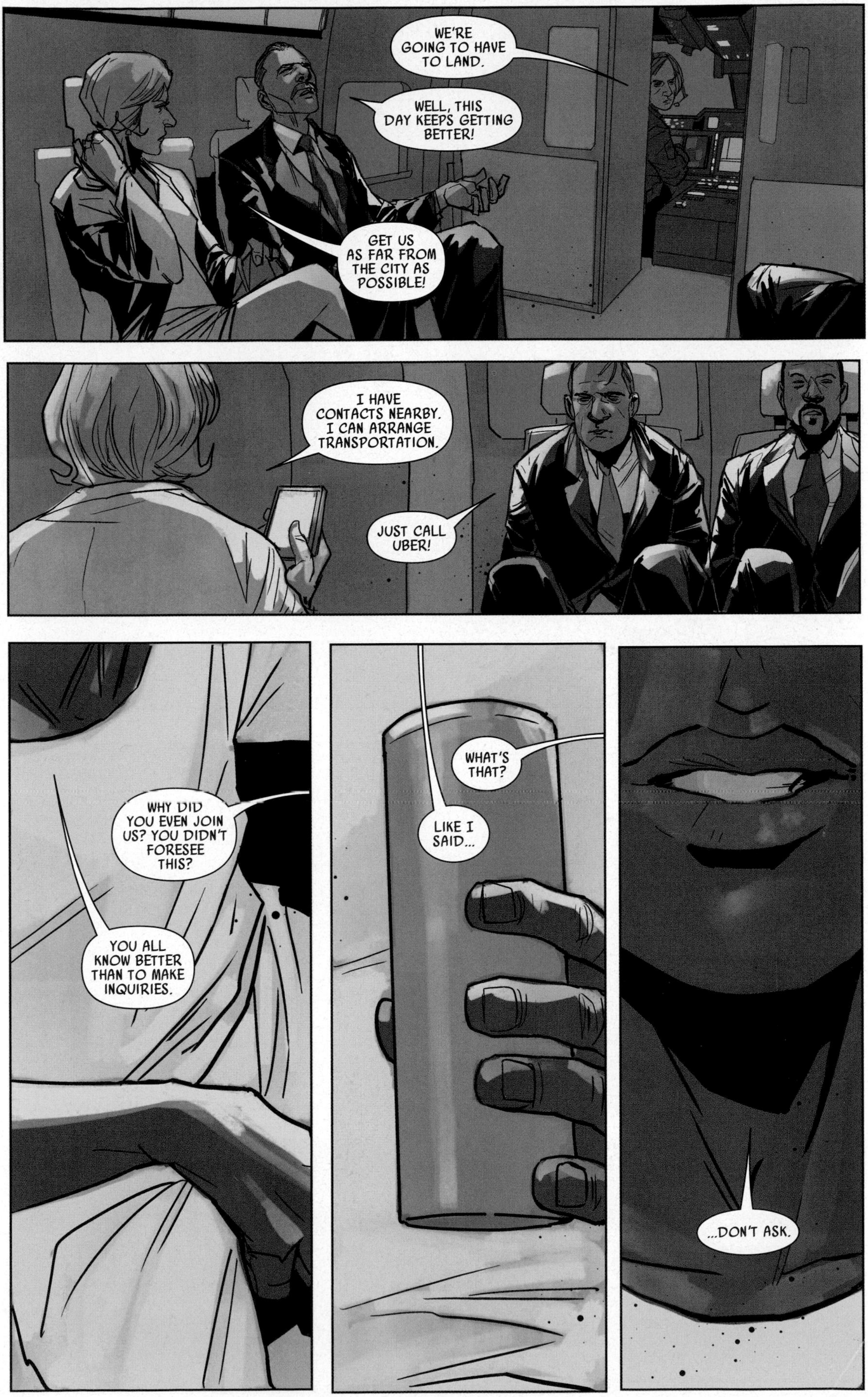
WE'RE GOING TO HAVE TO LAND.
WELL, THIS DAY KEEPS GETTING BETTER!
GET US AS FAR FROM THE CITY AS POSSIBLE!
I HAVE CONTACTS NEARBY. I CAN ARRANGE TRANSPORTATION.
JUST CALL UBER!
WHY DID YOU EVEN JOIN US? YOU DIDN'T FORESEE THIS?
YOU ALL KNOW BETTER THAN TO MAKE INQUIRIES.
WHAT'S THAT?
LIKE I SAID...
...DON'T ASK.

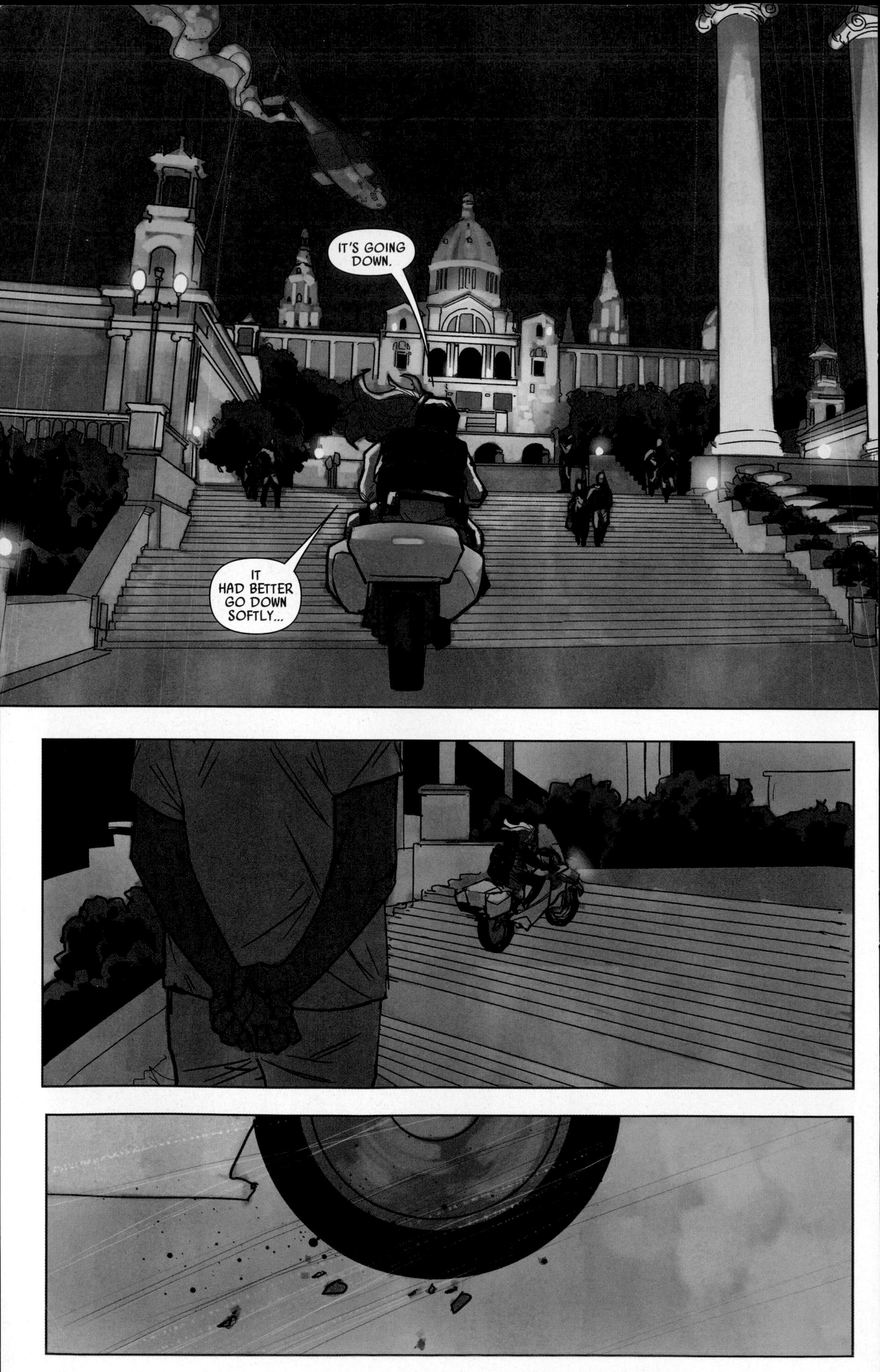
IT'S GOING DOWN.
IT HAD BETTER GO DOWN SOFTLY...

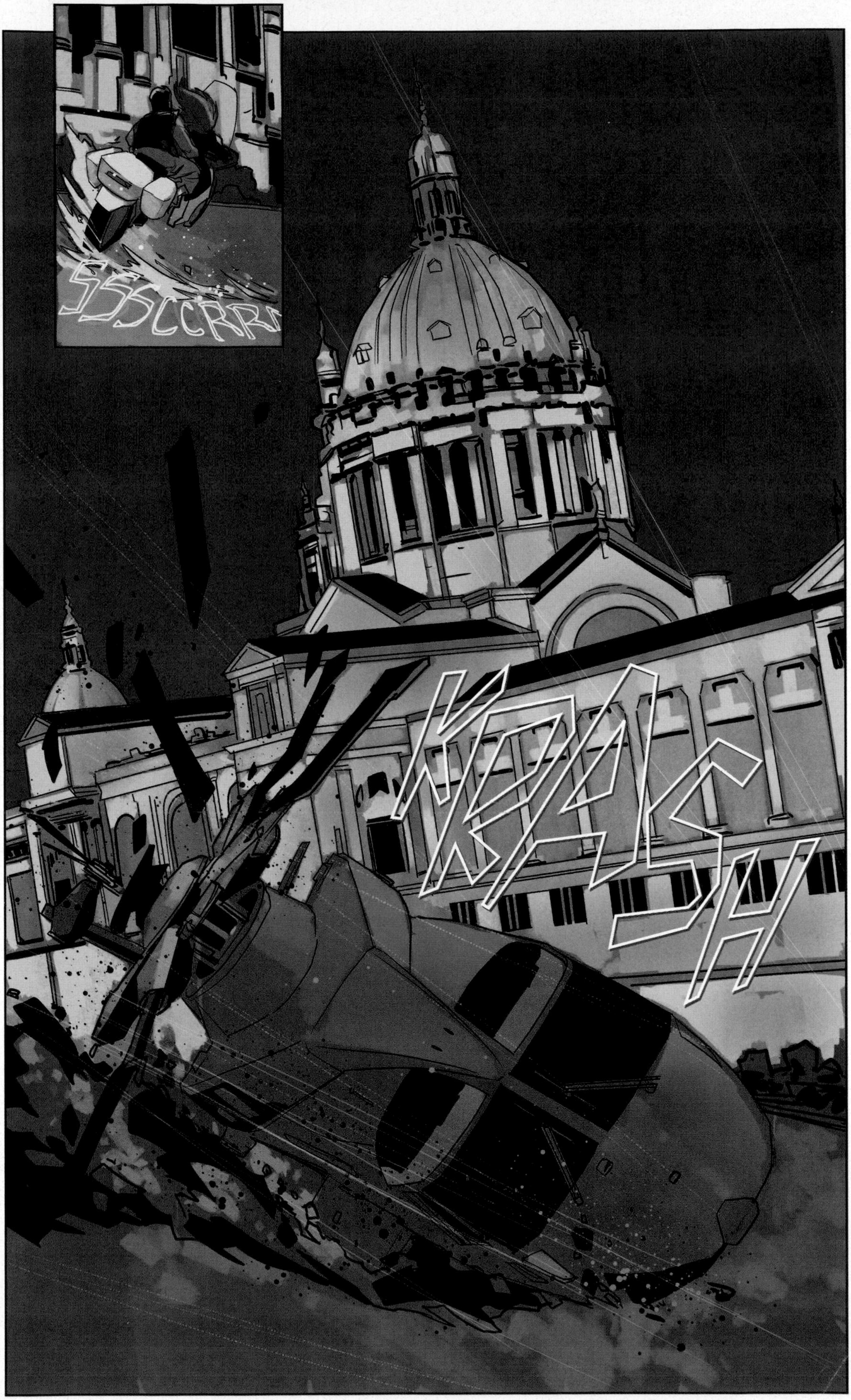
SSSCCRRR
KRASH

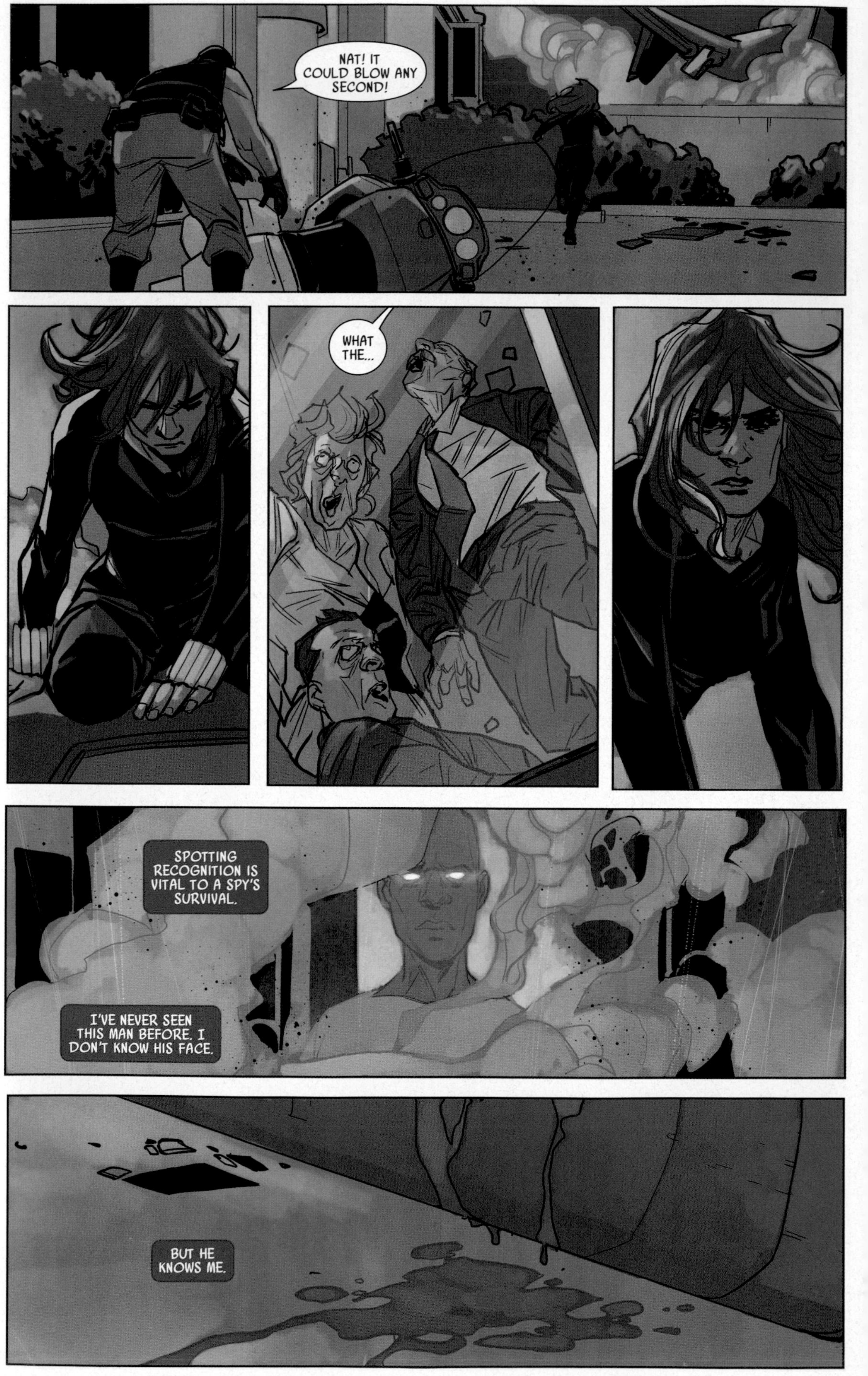
NAT! IT COULD BLOW ANY SECOND!
WHAT THE...
SPOTTING RECOGNITION IS VITAL TO A SPY'S SURVIVAL.
I'VE NEVER SEEN THIS MAN BEFORE. I DON'T KNOW HIS FACE.
BUT HE KNOWS ME.

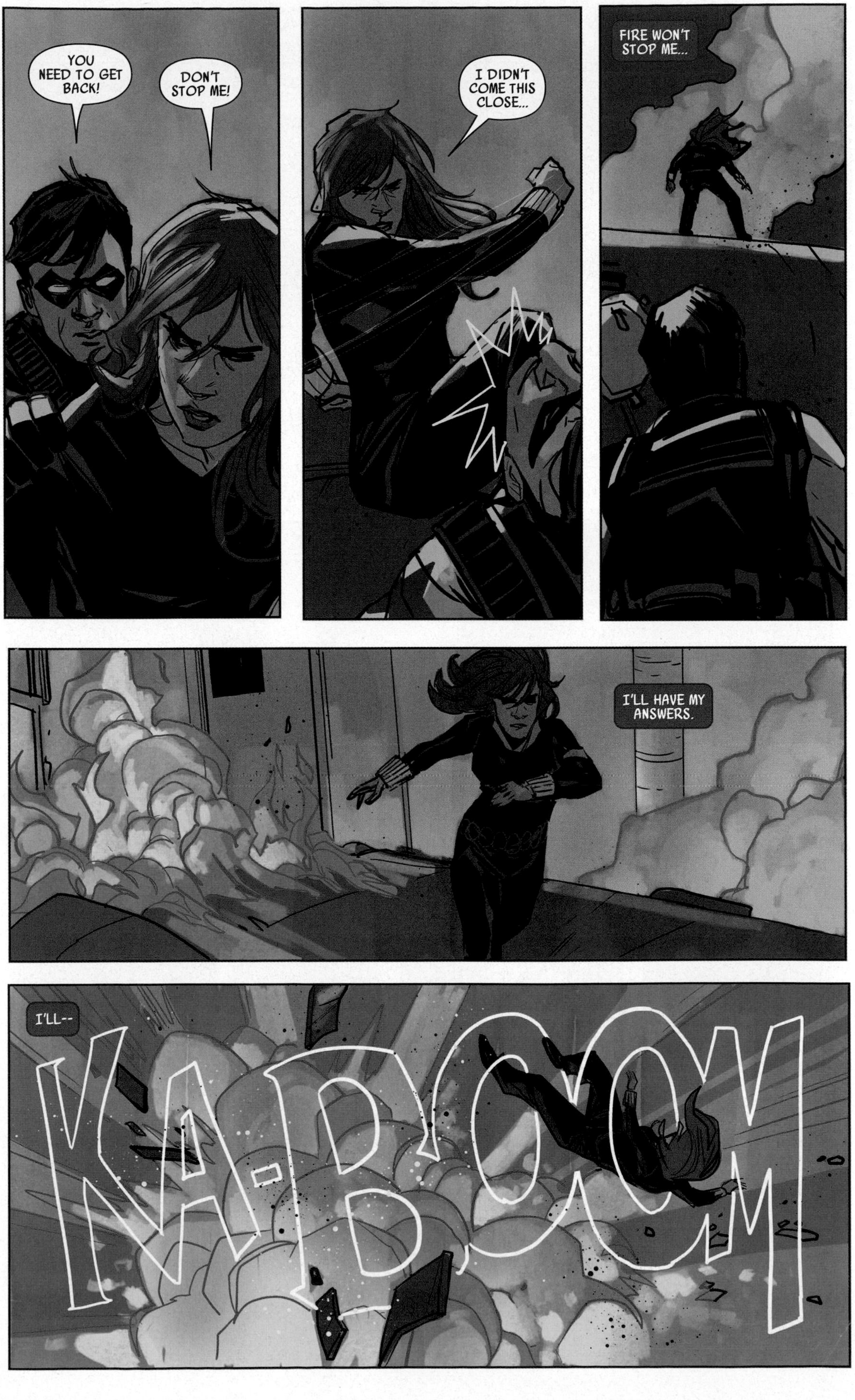
YOU NEED TO GET BACK!
DON'T STOP ME!
I DIDN'T COME THIS CLOSE...
FIRE WON'T STOP ME...
I'LL HAVE MY ANSWERS.
I'LL--
KA-BOOM

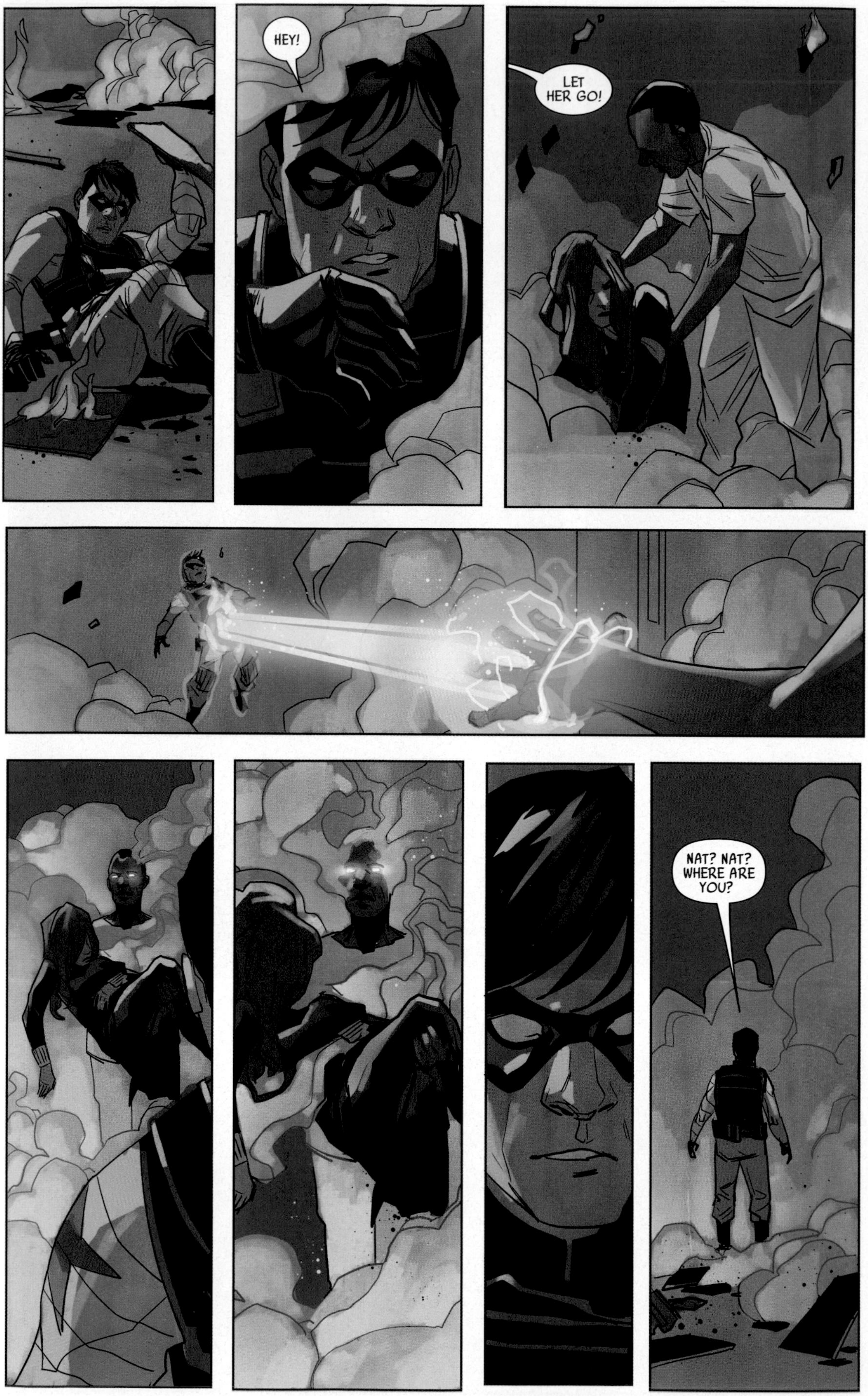
HEY!
LET HER GO!
NAT? NAT? WHERE ARE YOU?

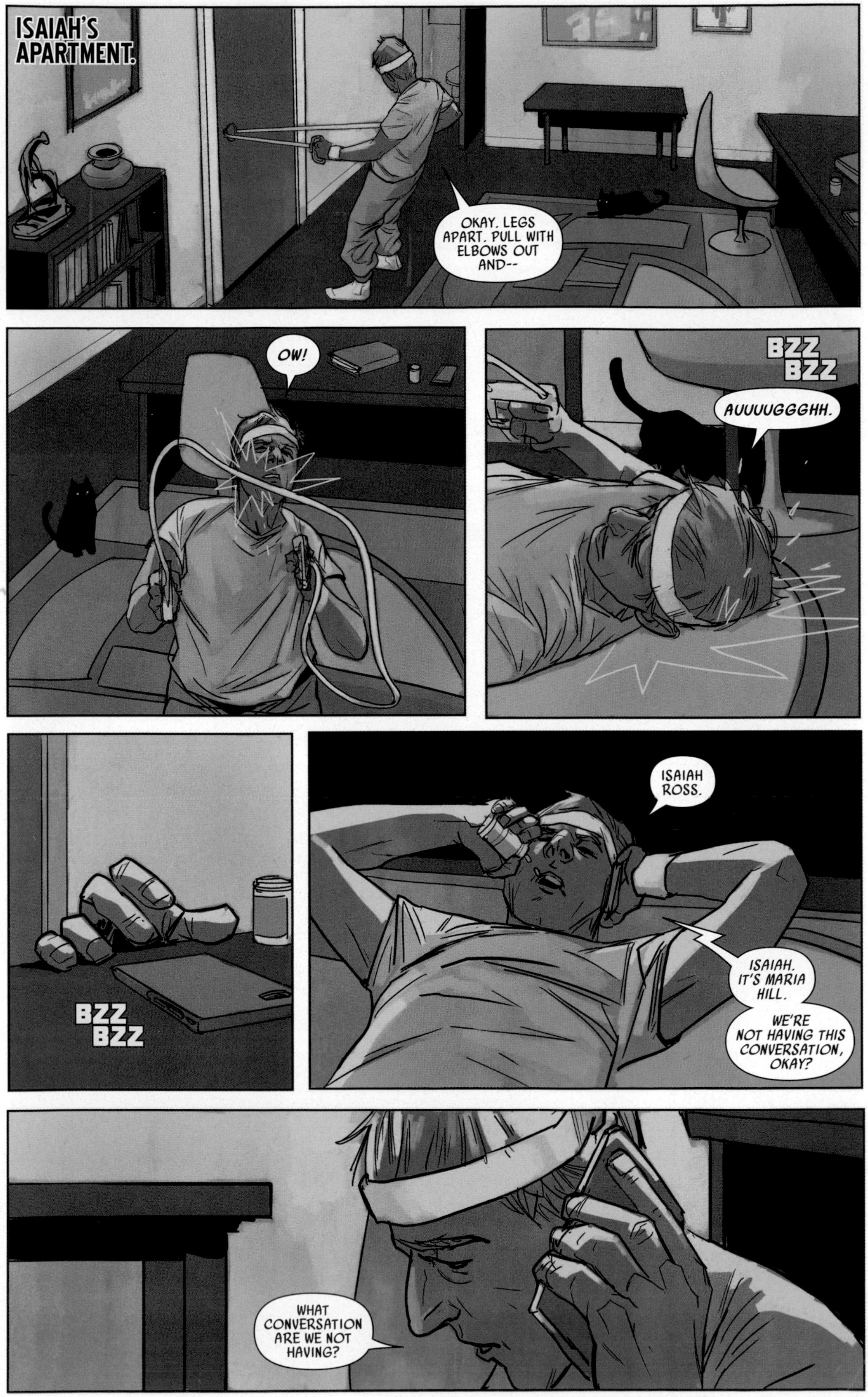
ISAIAH'S APARTMENT.
OKAY. LEGS APART. PULL WITH ELBOWS OUT AND--
OW!
BZZ BZZ
AUUUUGGGHH.
BZZ BZZ
ISAIAH ROSS.
ISAIAH. IT'S MARIA HILL.
WE'RE NOT HAVING THIS CONVERSATION, OKAY?
WHAT CONVERSATION ARE WE NOT HAVING?

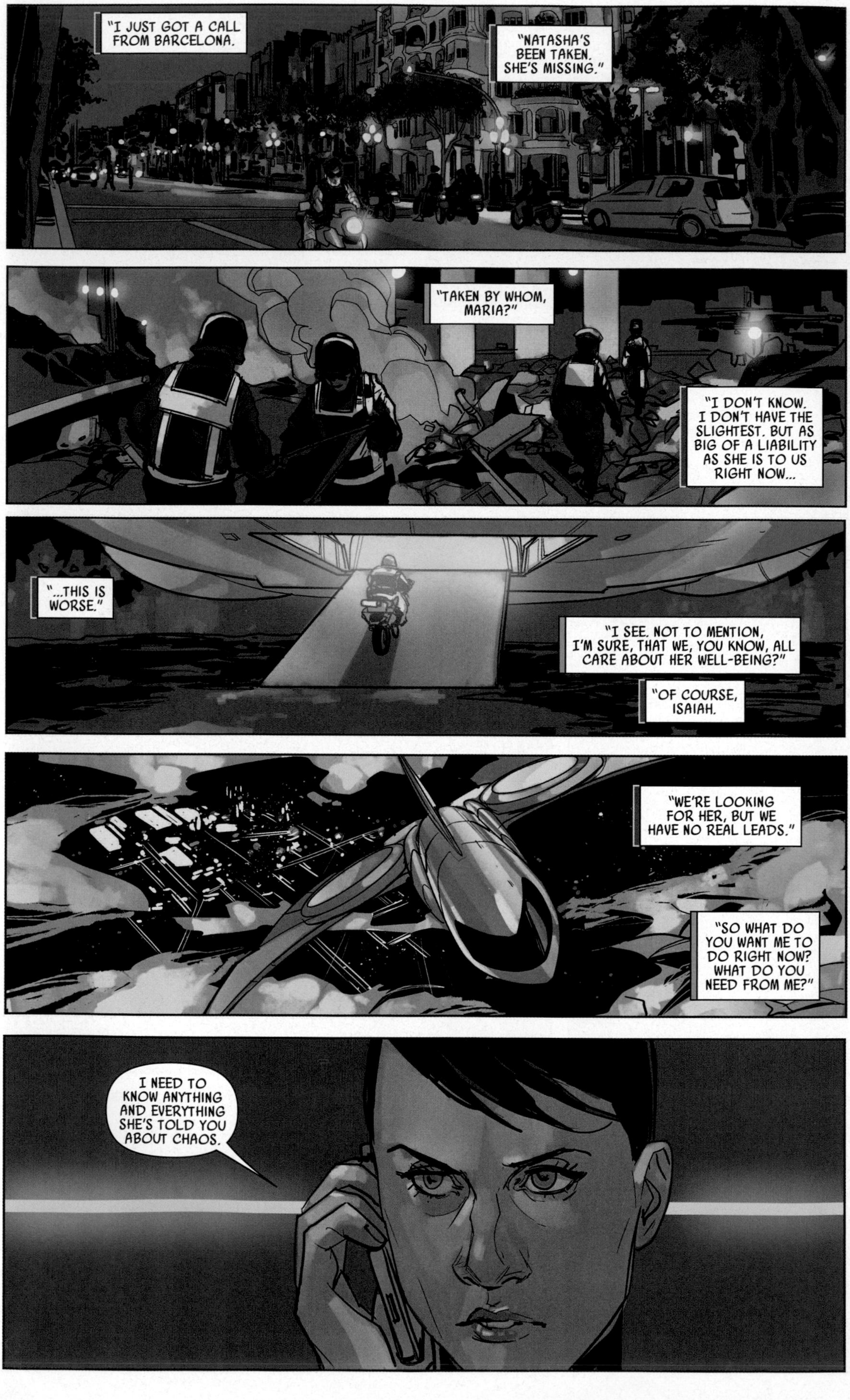
"I JUST GOT A CALL FROM BARCELONA.
"NATASHA'S BEEN TAKEN. SHE'S MISSING."
"TAKEN BY WHOM, MARIA?"
"I DON'T KNOW. I DON'T HAVE THE SLIGHTEST. BUT AS BIG OF A LIABILITY AS SHE IS TO US RIGHT NOW...
"...THIS IS WORSE."
"I SEE. NOT TO MENTION, I'M SURE, THAT WE, YOU KNOW, ALL CARE ABOUT HER WELL-BEING?"
"OF COURSE, ISAIAH.
"WE'RE LOOKING FOR HER, BUT WE HAVE NO REAL LEADS."
"SO WHAT DO YOU WANT ME TO DO RIGHT NOW? WHAT DO YOU NEED FROM ME?"
I NEED TO KNOW ANYTHING AND EVERYTHING SHE'S TOLD YOU ABOUT CHAOS.

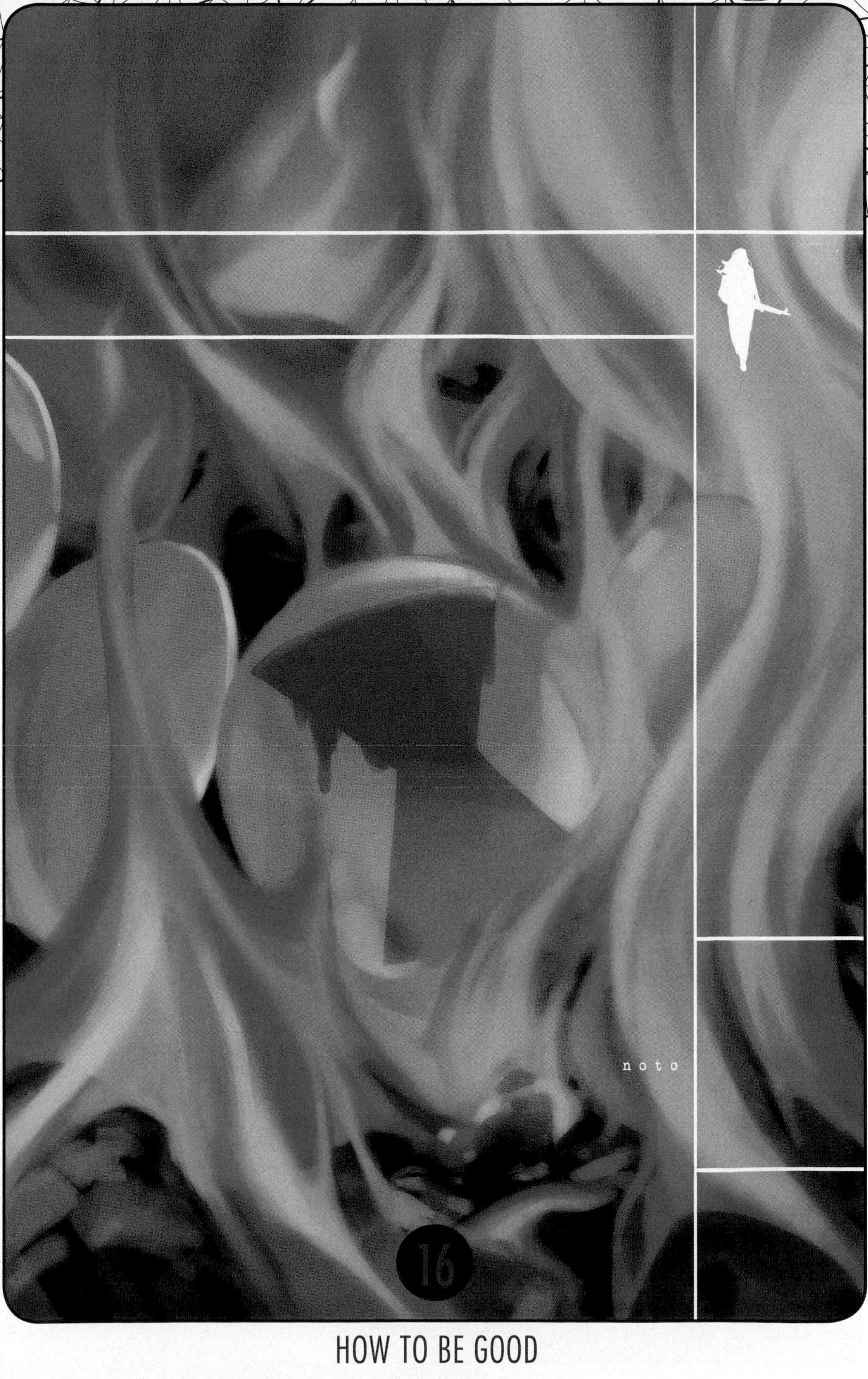
noto
16

HOW TO BE GOOD

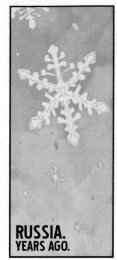

RUSSIA.
YEARS AGO.

I'LL BE LIKE THAT ONE DAY.

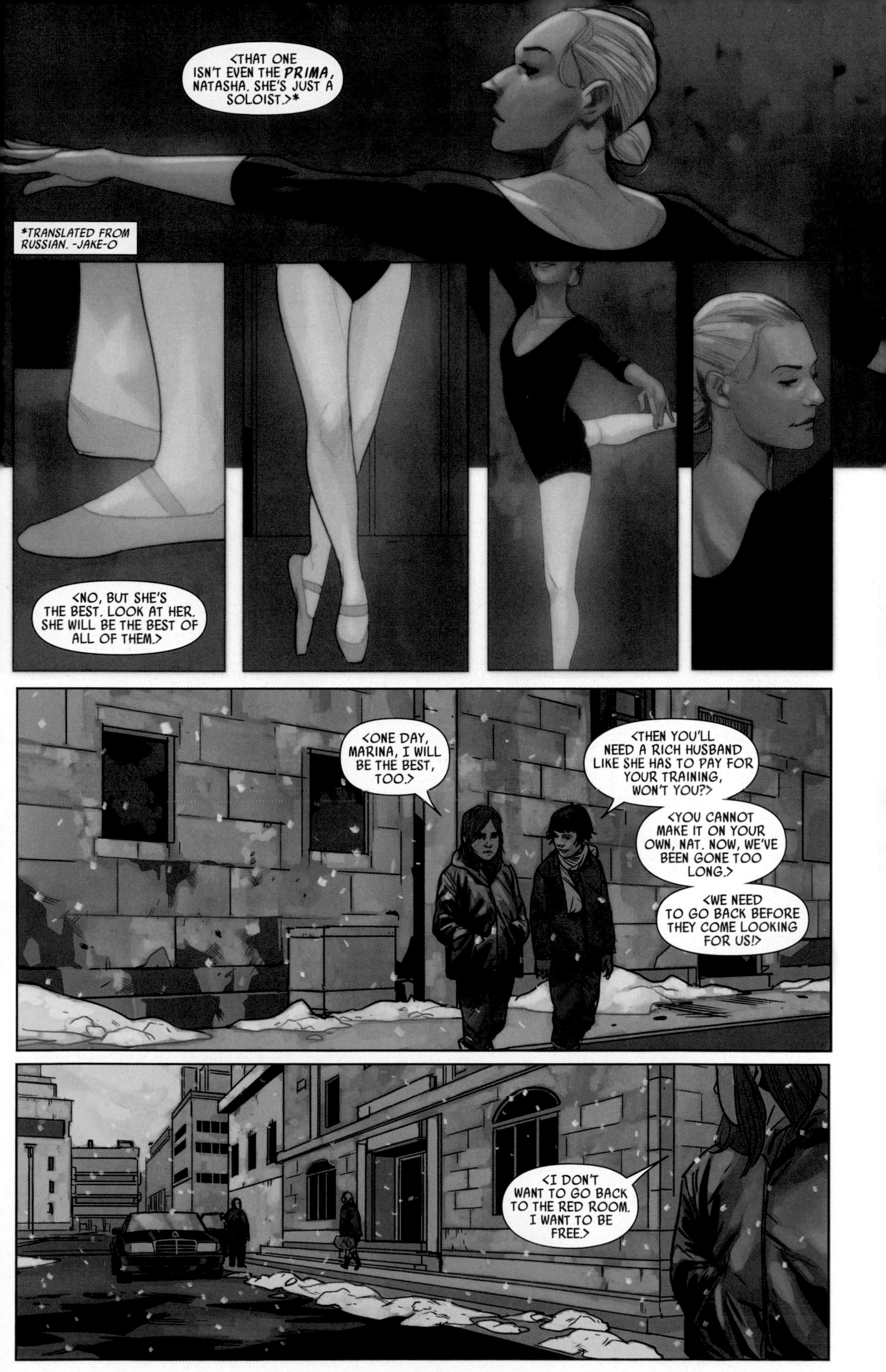
<THAT ONE ISN'T EVEN THE PRIMA, NATASHA. SHE'S JUST A SOLOIST.>*
*TRANSLATED FROM RUSSIAN. -JAKE-O
<NO, BUT SHE'S THE BEST. LOOK AT HER. SHE WILL BE THE BEST OF ALL OF THEM.>
<ONE DAY, MARINA, I WILL BE THE BEST, TOO.>
<THEN YOU'LL NEED A RICH HUSBAND LIKE SHE HAS TO PAY FOR YOUR TRAINING, WON'T YOU?>
<YOU CANNOT MAKE IT ON YOUR OWN, NAT. NOW, WE'VE BEEN GONE TOO LONG.>
<WE NEED TO GO BACK BEFORE THEY COME LOOKING FOR US!>
<I DON'T WANT TO GO BACK TO THE RED ROOM. I WANT TO BE FREE.>

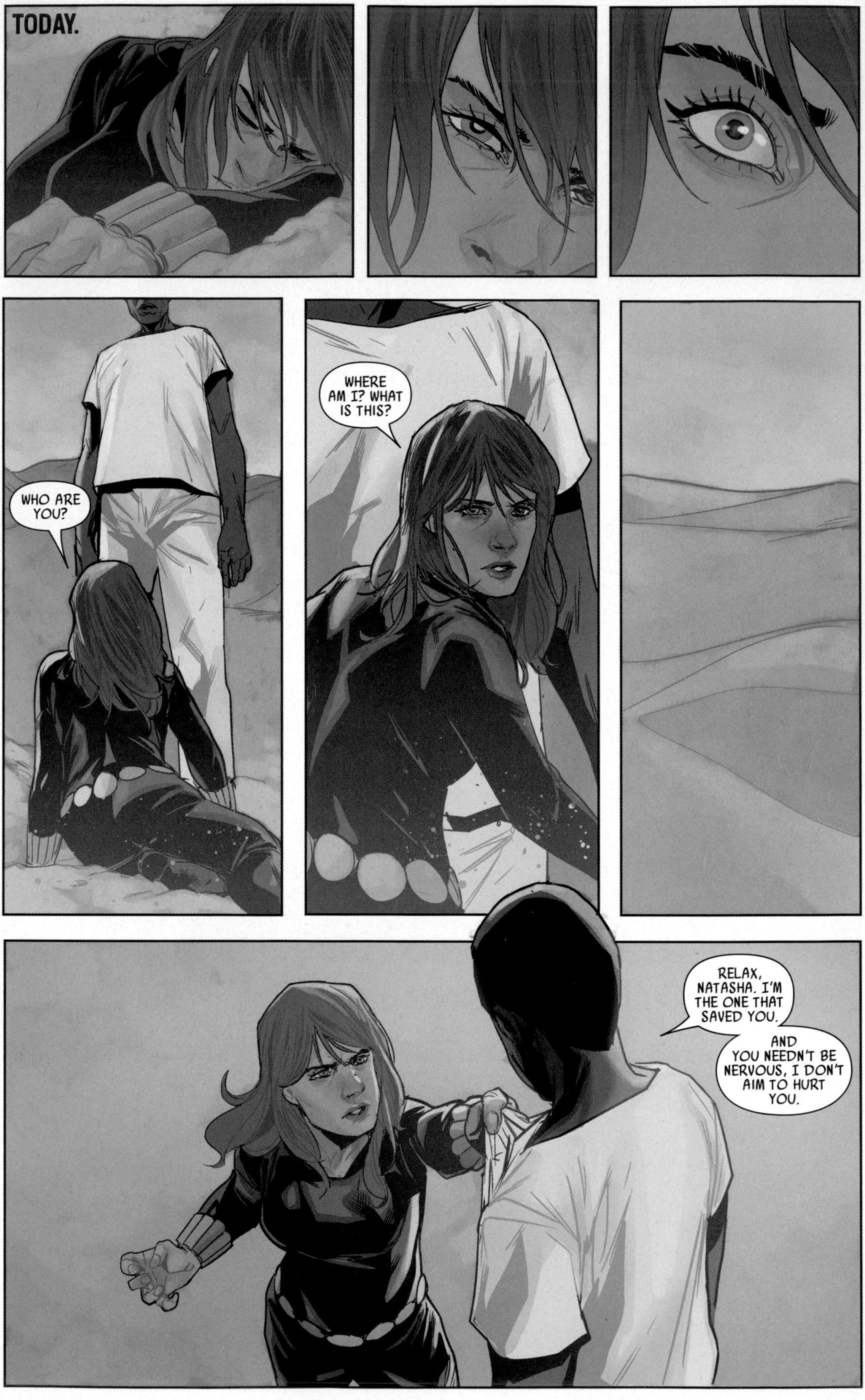
TODAY.
WHO ARE YOU?
WHERE AM I? WHAT IS THIS?
RELAX, NATASHA. I'M THE ONE THAT SAVED YOU.
AND YOU NEEDN'T BE NERVOUS, I DON'T AIM TO HURT YOU.

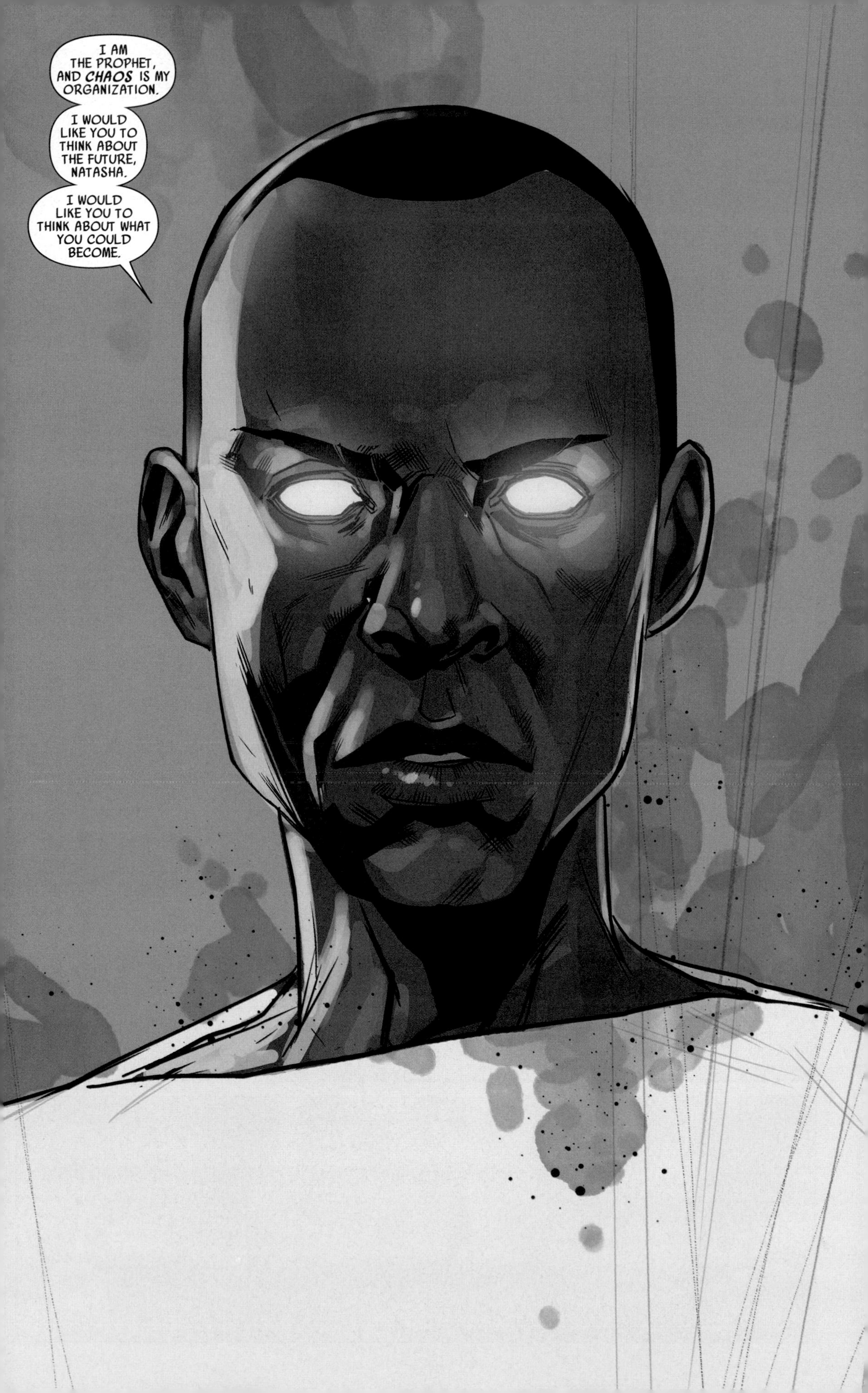
I AM THE PROPHET, AND *CHAOS* IS MY ORGANIZATION.
I WOULD LIKE YOU TO THINK ABOUT THE FUTURE, NATASHA.
I WOULD LIKE YOU TO THINK ABOUT WHAT YOU COULD BECOME.

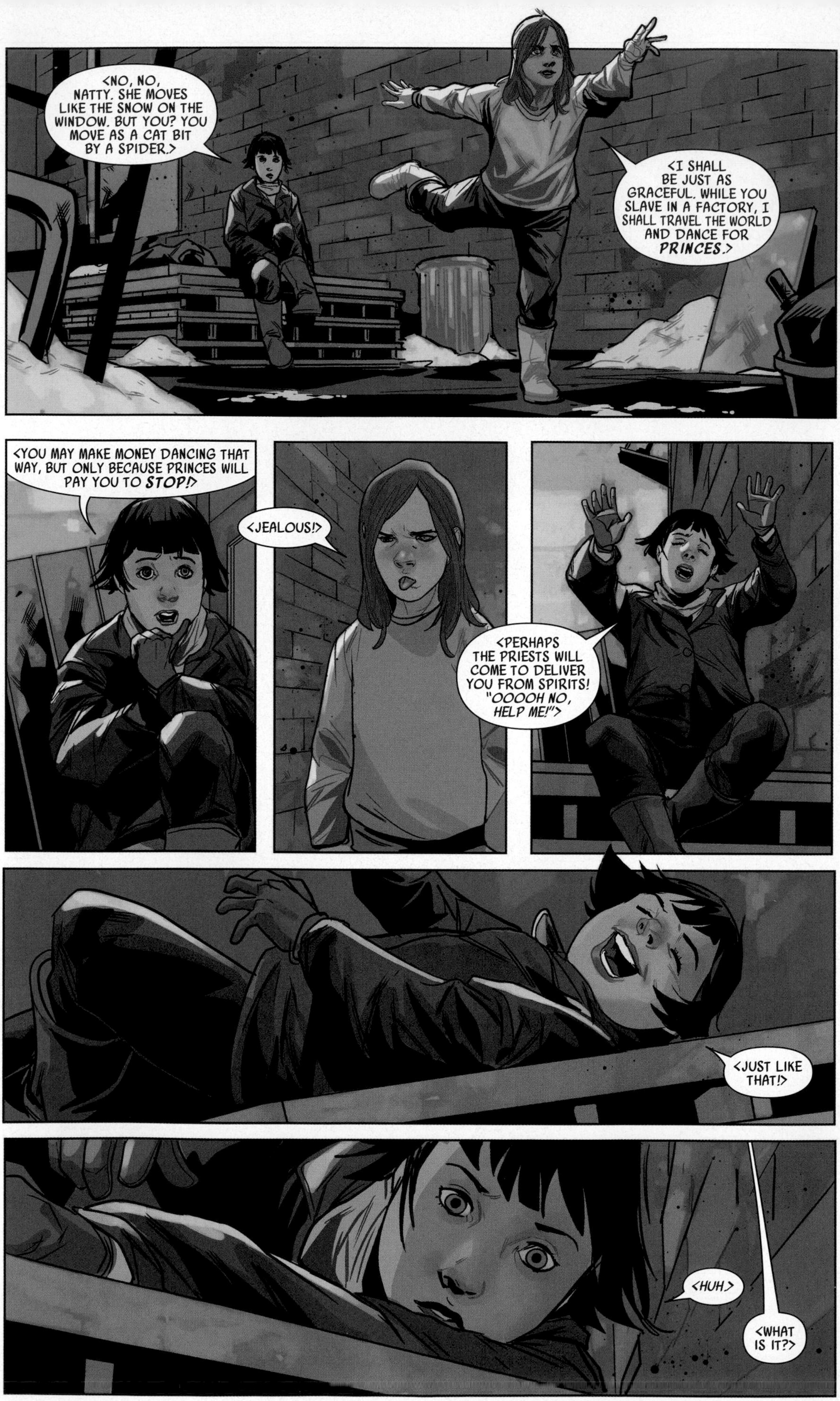
<NO, NO, NATTY. SHE MOVES LIKE THE SNOW ON THE WINDOW. BUT YOU? YOU MOVE AS A CAT BIT BY A SPIDER.>
<I SHALL BE JUST AS GRACEFUL. WHILE YOU SLAVE IN A FACTORY, I SHALL TRAVEL THE WORLD AND DANCE FOR PRINCES.>
<YOU MAY MAKE MONEY DANCING THAT WAY, BUT ONLY BECAUSE PRINCES WILL PAY YOU TO STOP!>
<JEALOUS!>
<PERHAPS THE PRIESTS WILL COME TO DELIVER YOU FROM SPIRITS! "OOOOH NO, HELP ME!">
<JUST LIKE THAT!>
<HUH.>
<WHAT IS IT?>

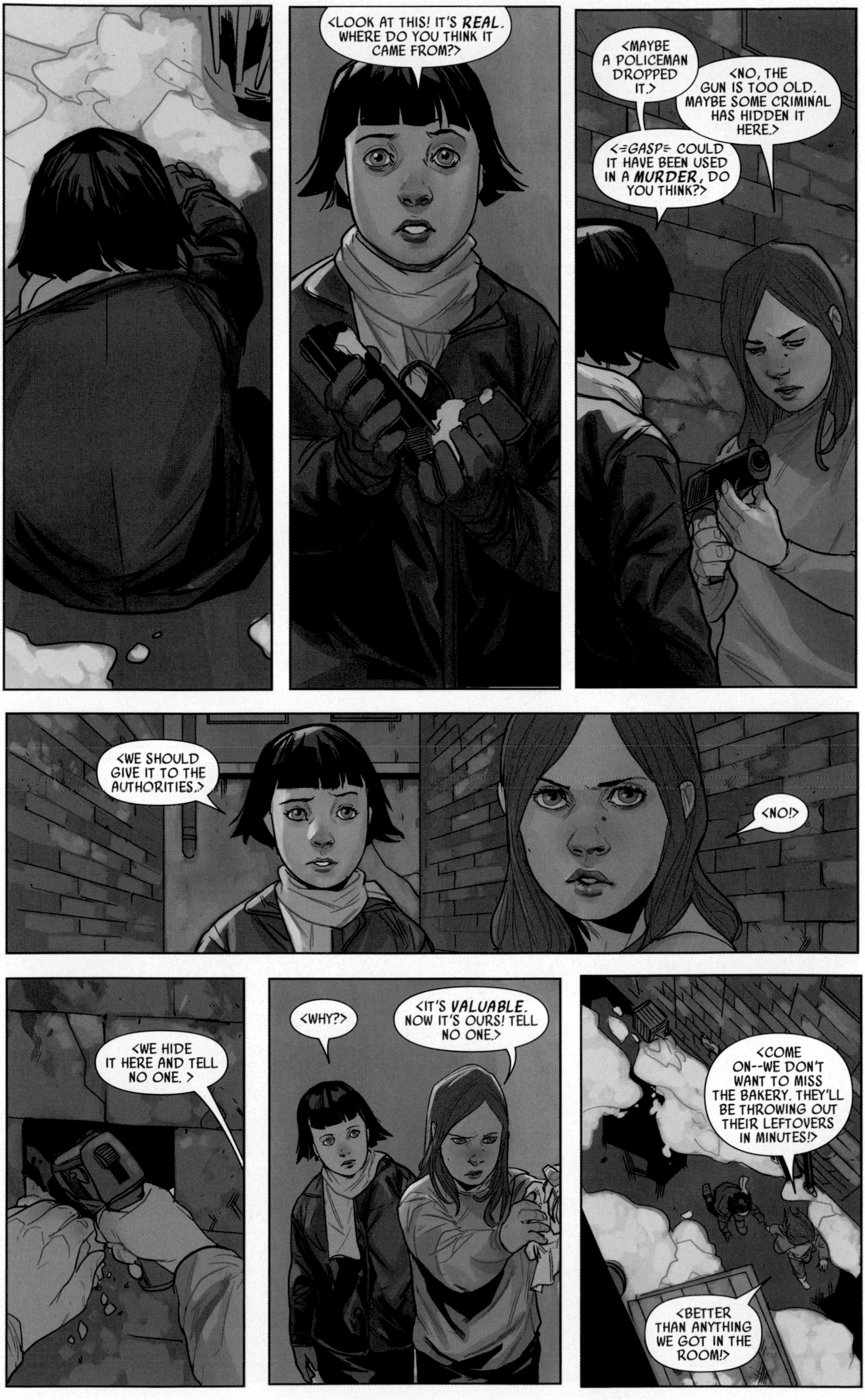
<LOOK AT THIS! IT'S REAL. WHERE DO YOU THINK IT CAME FROM?>
<MAYBE A POLICEMAN DROPPED IT.>
<NO, THE GUN IS TOO OLD. MAYBE SOME CRIMINAL HAS HIDDEN IT HERE.>
<=GASP= COULD IT HAVE BEEN USED IN A MURDER, DO YOU THINK?>
<WE SHOULD GIVE IT TO THE AUTHORITIES.>
<NO!>
<WE HIDE IT HERE AND TELL NO ONE. >
<WHY?>
<IT'S VALUABLE. NOW IT'S OURS! TELL NO ONE.>
<COME ON--WE DON'T WANT TO MISS THE BAKERY. THEY'LL BE THROWING OUT THEIR LEFTOVERS IN MINUTES!>
<BETTER THAN ANYTHING WE GOT IN THE ROOM!>

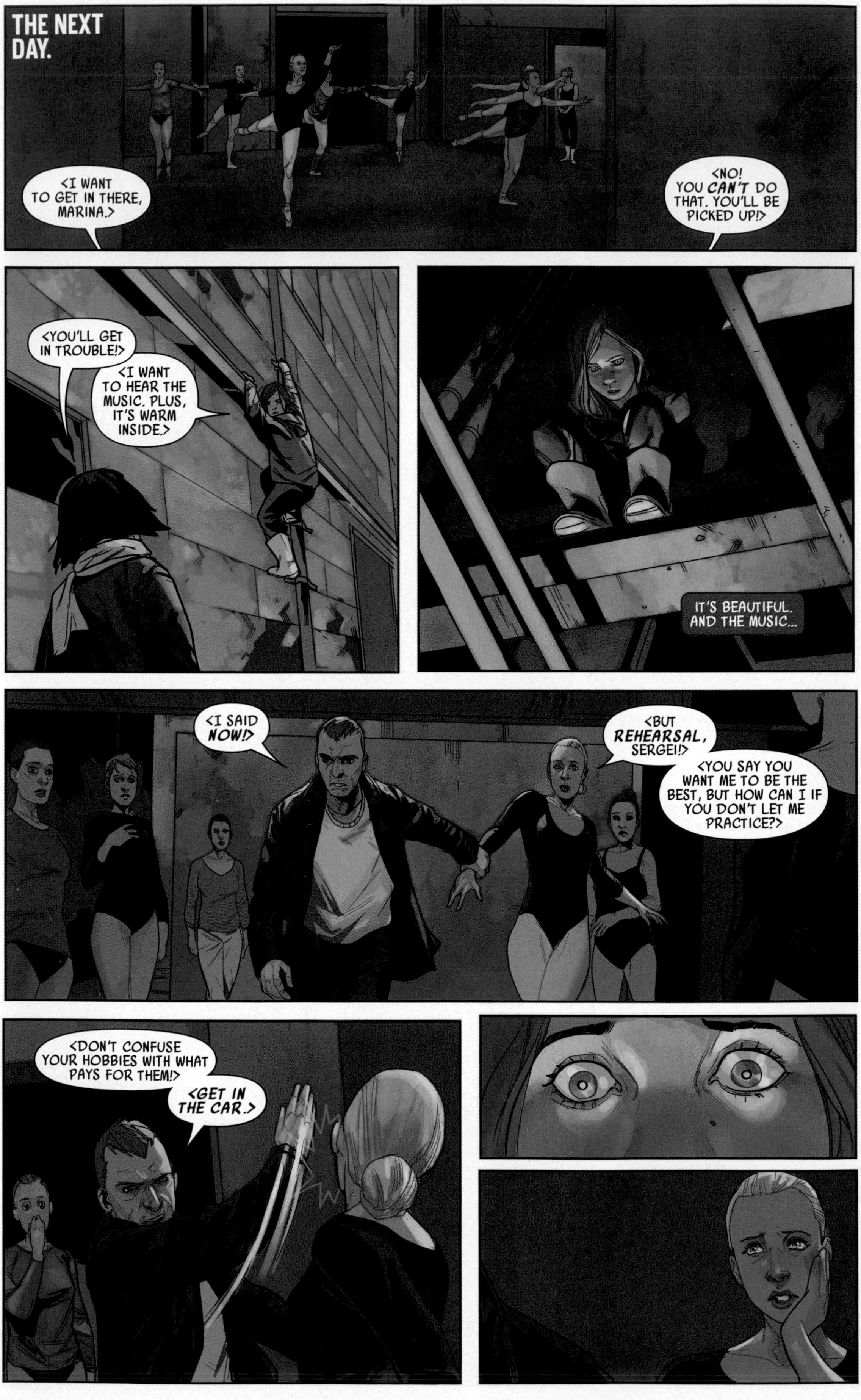
THE NEXT DAY.
<I WANT TO GET IN THERE, MARINA.>
<NO! YOU CAN'T DO THAT. YOU'LL BE PICKED UP!>
<YOU'LL GET IN TROUBLE!>
<I WANT TO HEAR THE MUSIC. PLUS, IT'S WARM INSIDE.>
IT'S BEAUTIFUL. AND THE MUSIC...
<I SAID NOW!>
<BUT REHEARSAL, SERGEI!>
<YOU SAY YOU WANT ME TO BE THE BEST, BUT HOW CAN I IF YOU DON'T LET ME PRACTICE?>
<DON'T CONFUSE YOUR HOBBIES WITH WHAT PAYS FOR THEM!>
<GET IN THE CAR.>

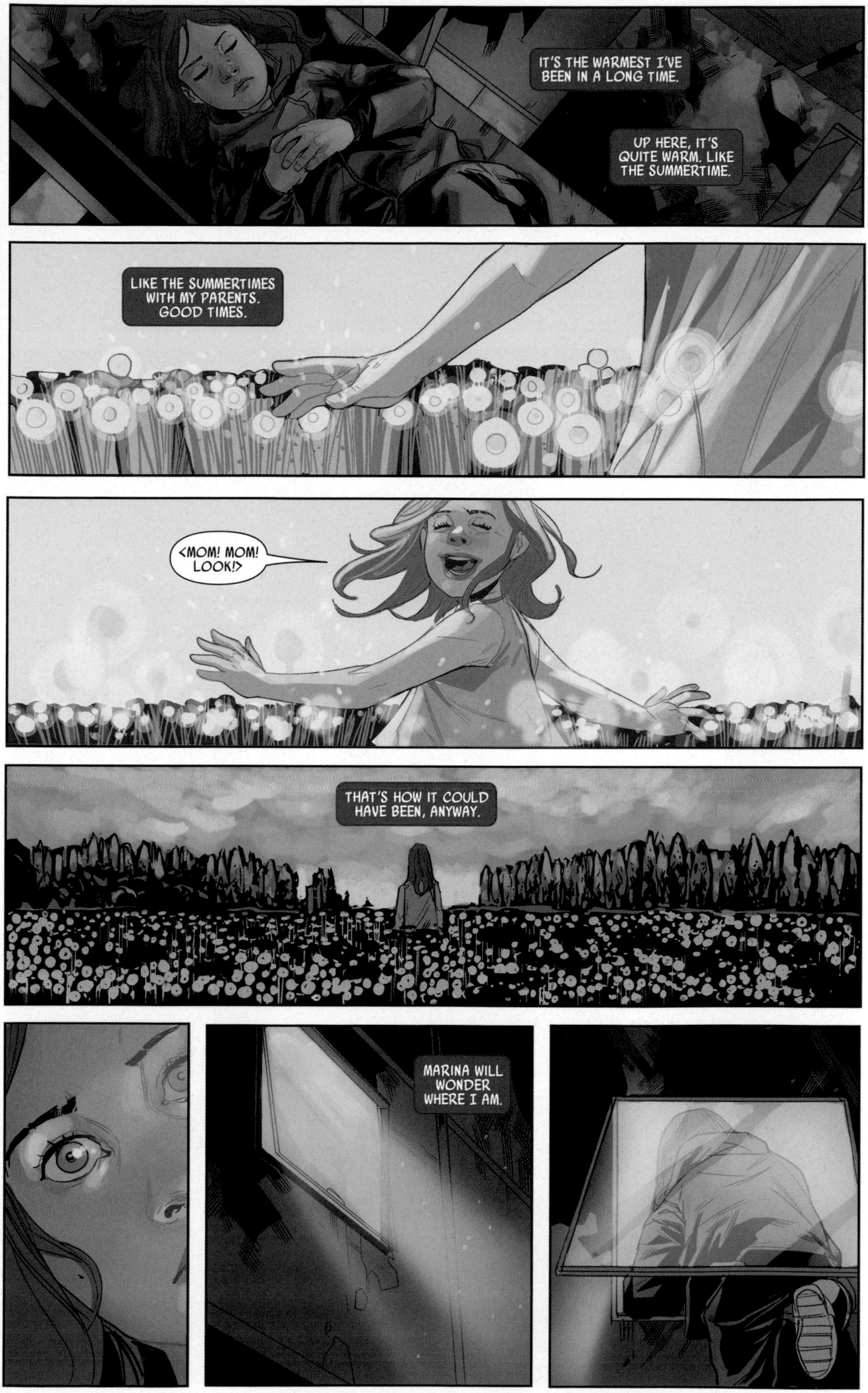
IT'S THE WARMEST I'VE BEEN IN A LONG TIME.
UP HERE, IT'S QUITE WARM. LIKE THE SUMMERTIME.
LIKE THE SUMMERTIMES WITH MY PARENTS. GOOD TIMES.
<MOM! MOM! LOOK!>
THAT'S HOW IT COULD HAVE BEEN, ANYWAY.
MARINA WILL WONDER WHERE I AM.

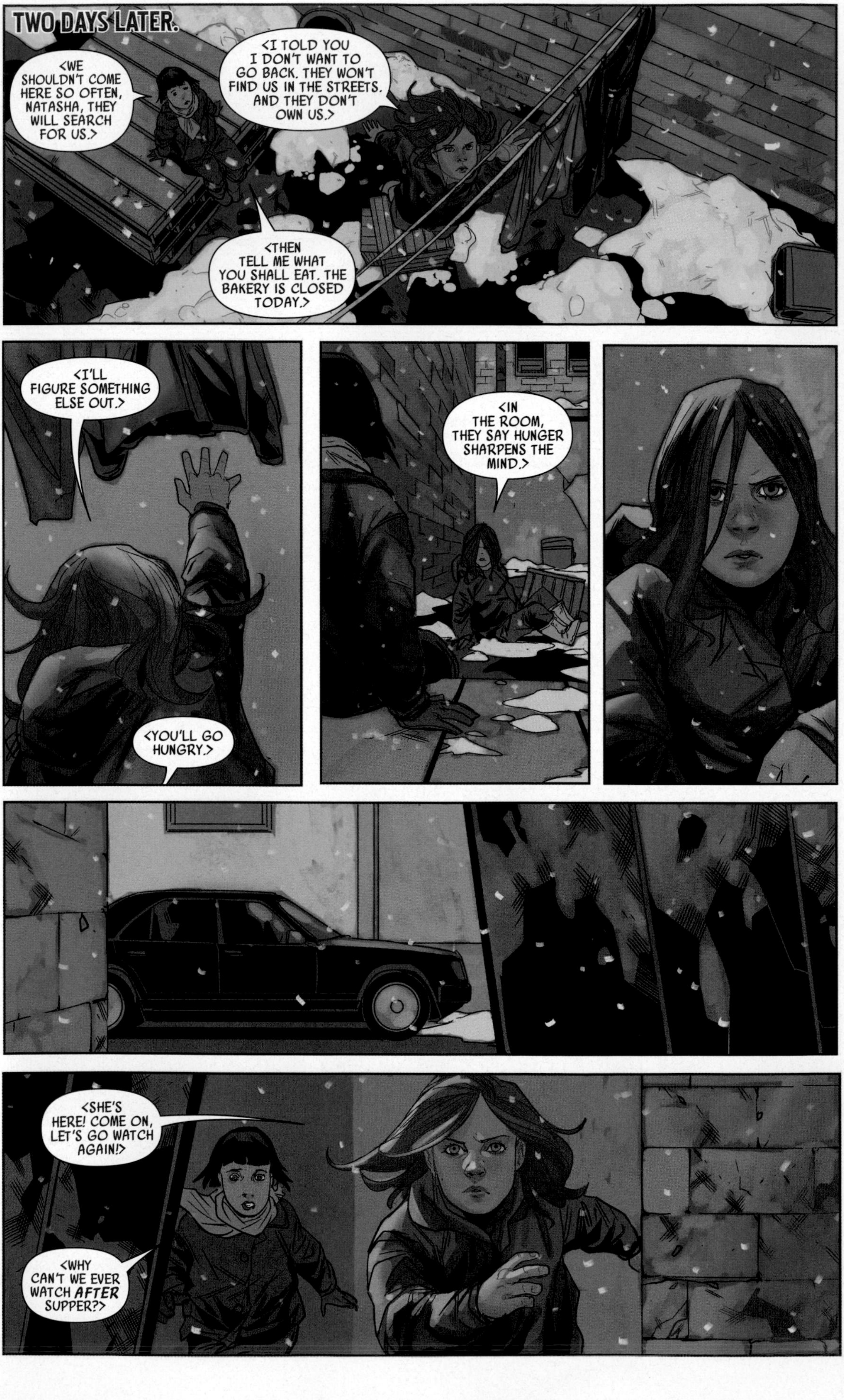
TWO DAYS LATER.
<WE SHOULDN'T COME HERE SO OFTEN, NATASHA, THEY WILL SEARCH FOR US.>
<I TOLD YOU I DON'T WANT TO GO BACK. THEY WON'T FIND US IN THE STREETS. AND THEY DON'T OWN US.>
<THEN TELL ME WHAT YOU SHALL EAT. THE BAKERY IS CLOSED TODAY.>
<I'LL FIGURE SOMETHING ELSE OUT.>
<YOU'LL GO HUNGRY.>
<IN THE ROOM, THEY SAY HUNGER SHARPENS THE MIND.>
<SHE'S HERE! COME ON, LET'S GO WATCH AGAIN!>
<WHY CAN'T WE EVER WATCH AFTER SUPPER?>

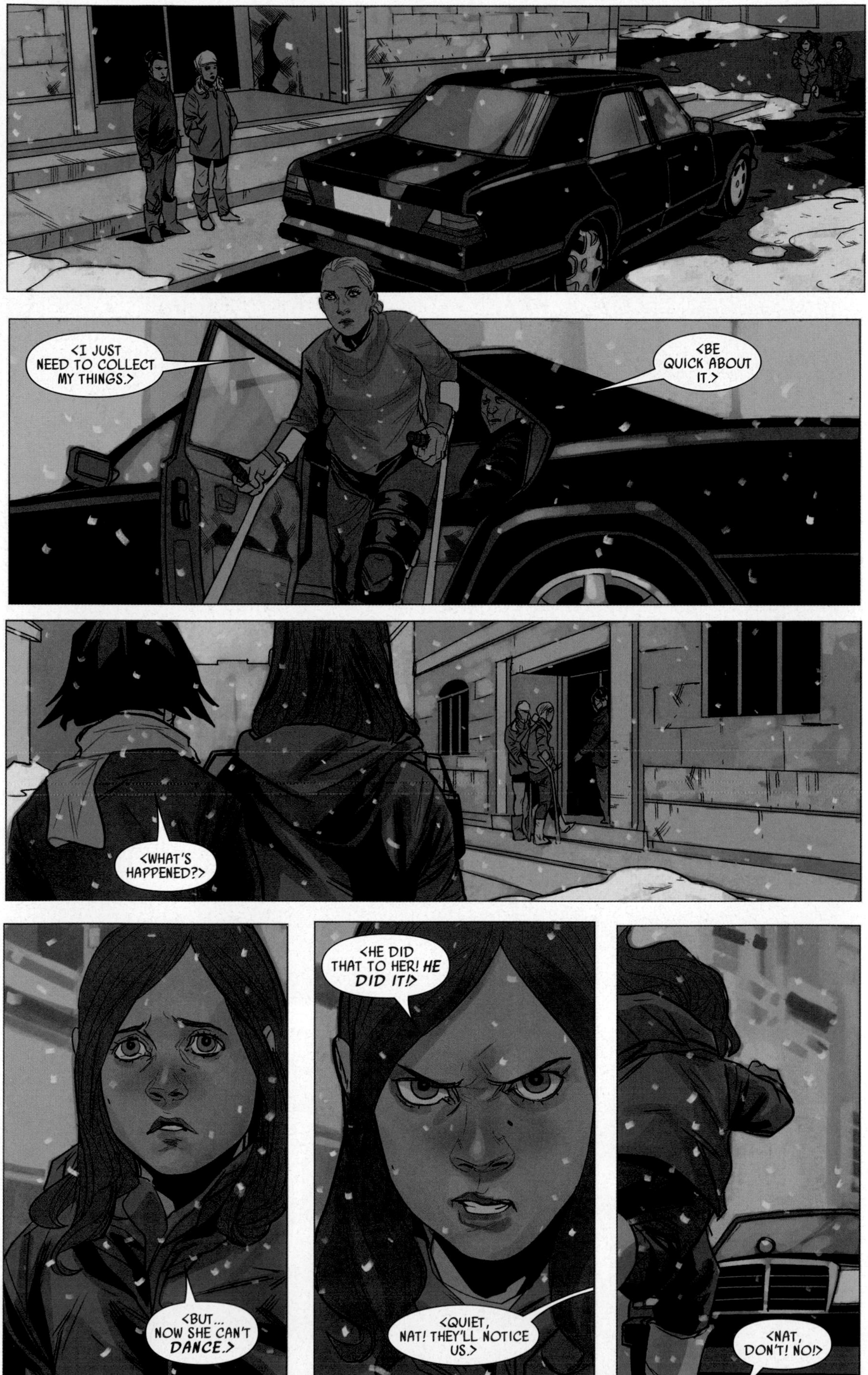
<I JUST NEED TO COLLECT MY THINGS.>
<BE QUICK ABOUT IT.>
<WHAT'S HAPPENED?>
<BUT... NOW SHE CAN'T *DANCE*.>
<HE DID THAT TO HER! *HE DID IT!*>
<QUIET, NAT! THEY'LL NOTICE US.>
<NAT, DON'T! NO!>

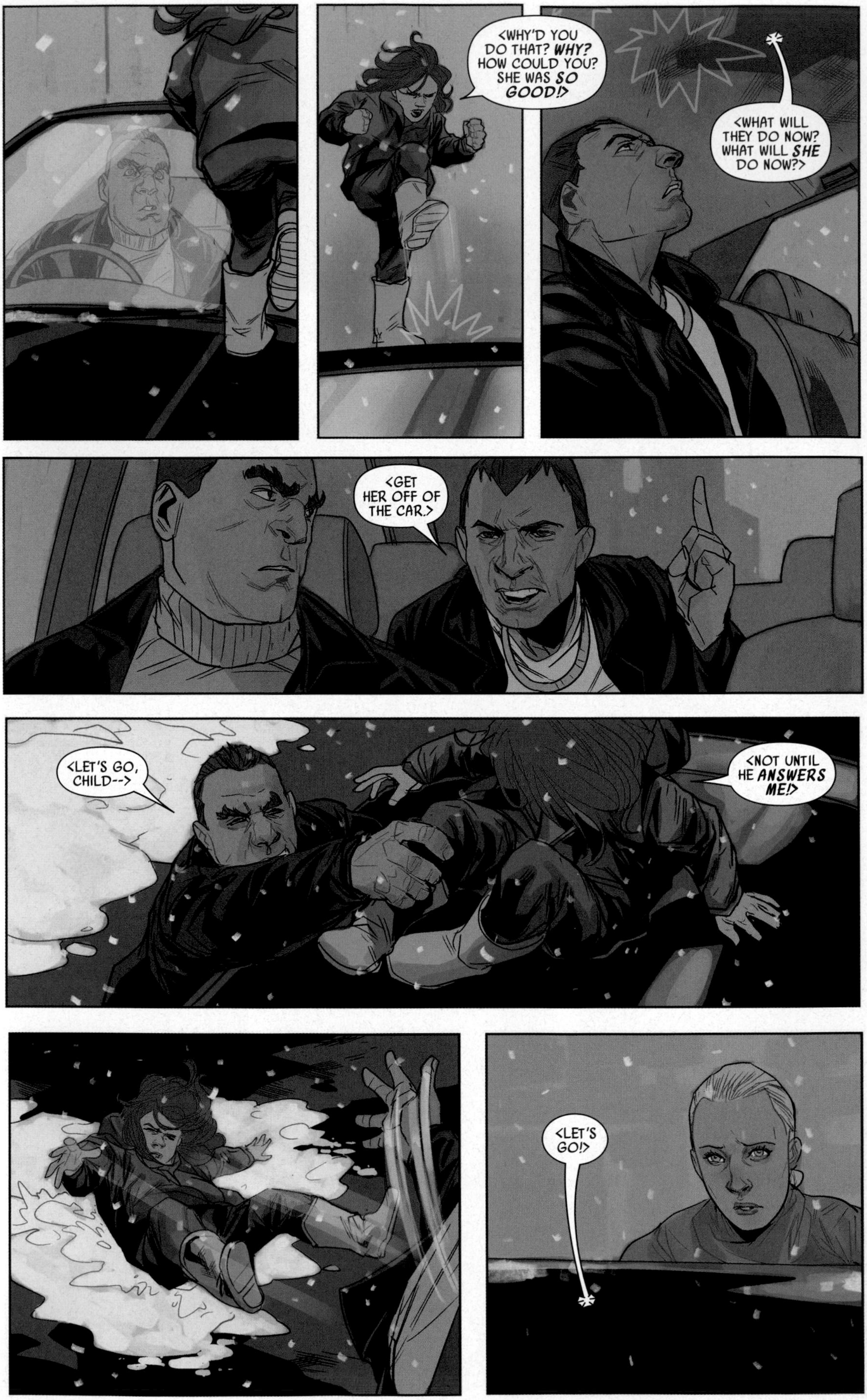
<WHY'D YOU DO THAT? WHY? HOW COULD YOU? SHE WAS SO GOOD!>
<WHAT WILL THEY DO NOW? WHAT WILL SHE DO NOW?>
<GET HER OFF OF THE CAR.>
<LET'S GO, CHILD-->
<NOT UNTIL HE ANSWERS ME!>
<LET'S GO!>

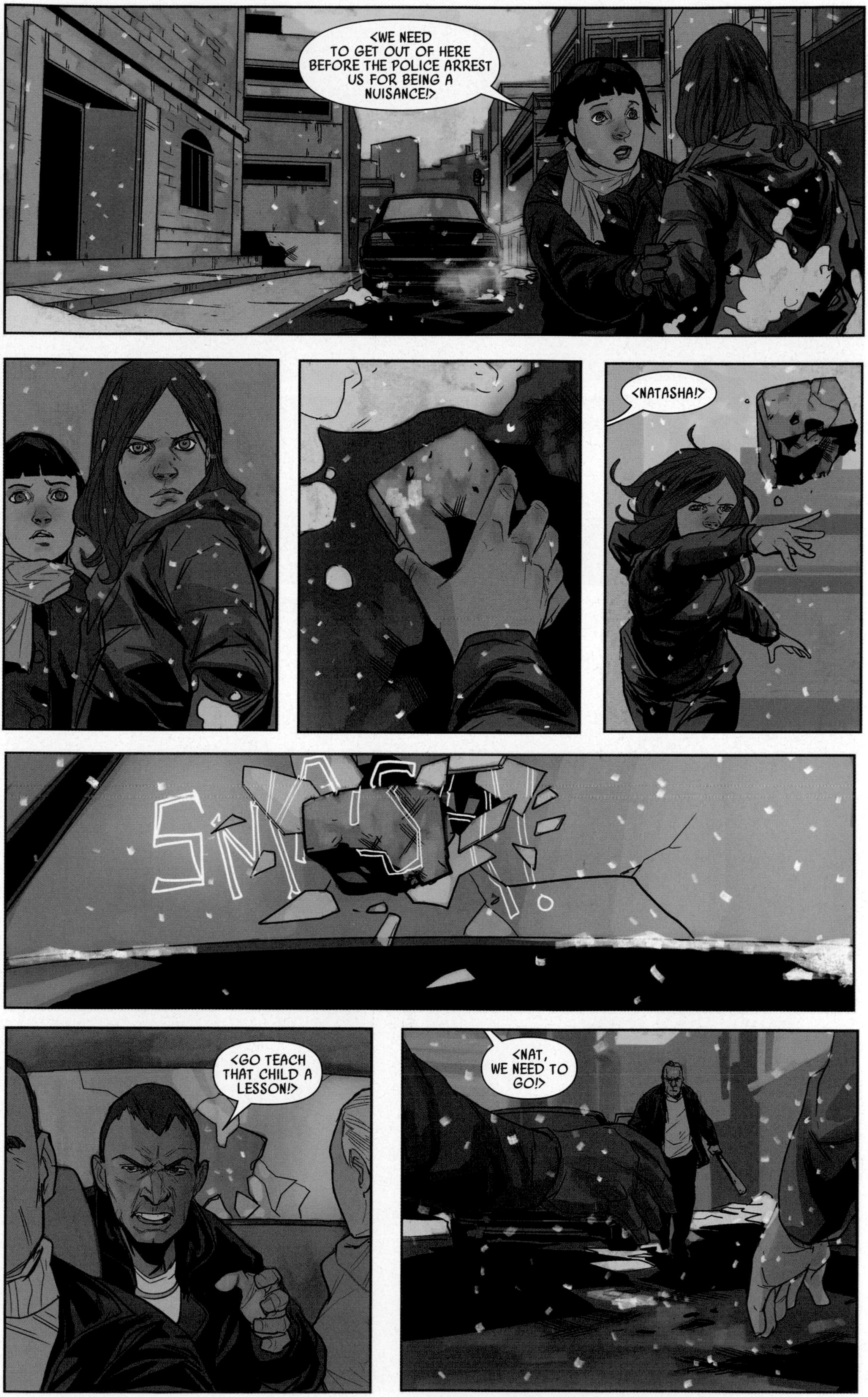
<WE NEED TO GET OUT OF HERE BEFORE THE POLICE ARREST US FOR BEING A NUISANCE!>
<NATASHA!>
SMASH!
<GO TEACH THAT CHILD A LESSON!>
<NAT, WE NEED TO GO!>

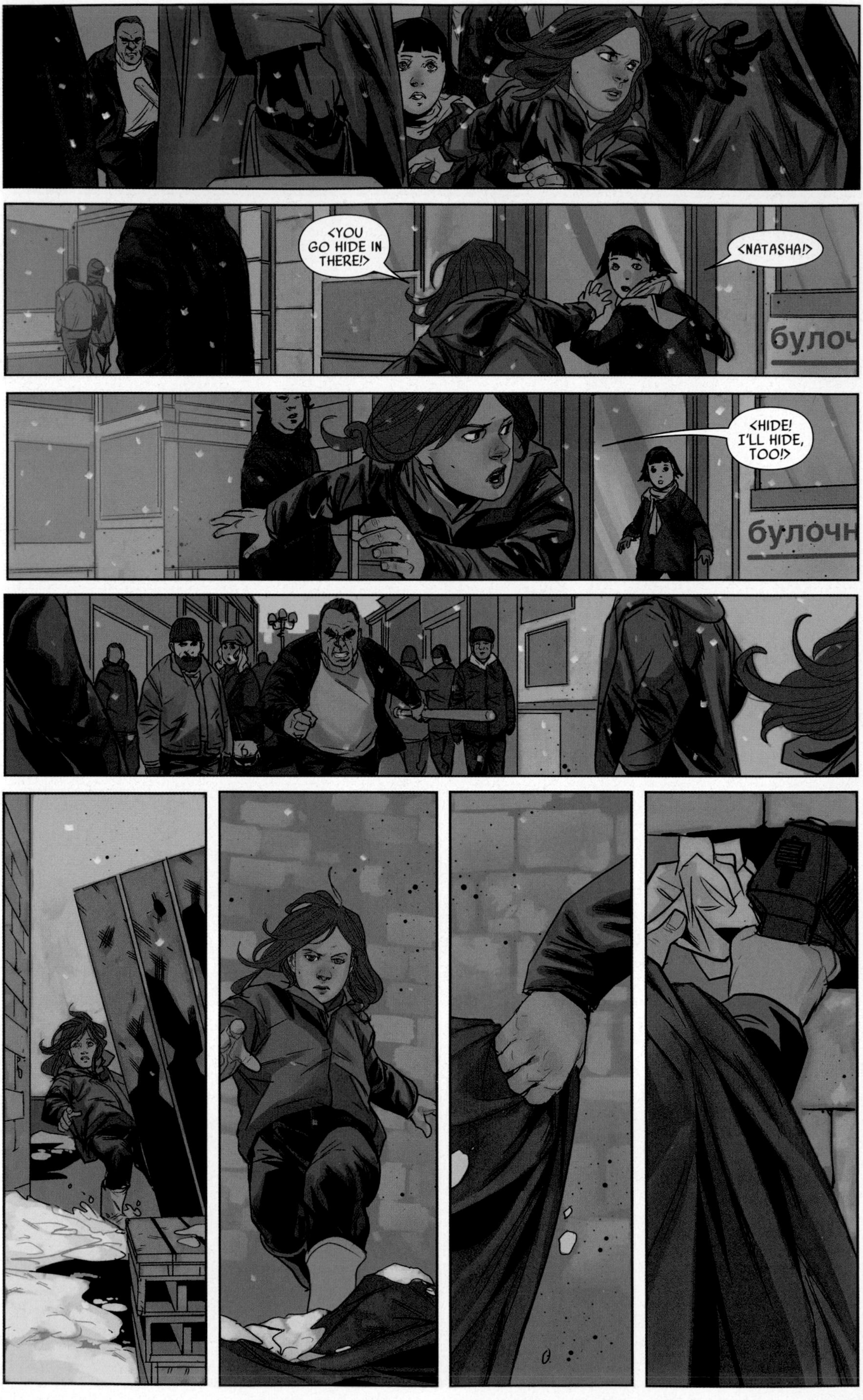
<YOU GO HIDE IN THERE!>
<NATASHA!>
булочн
<HIDE! I'LL HIDE, TOO!>
булочн

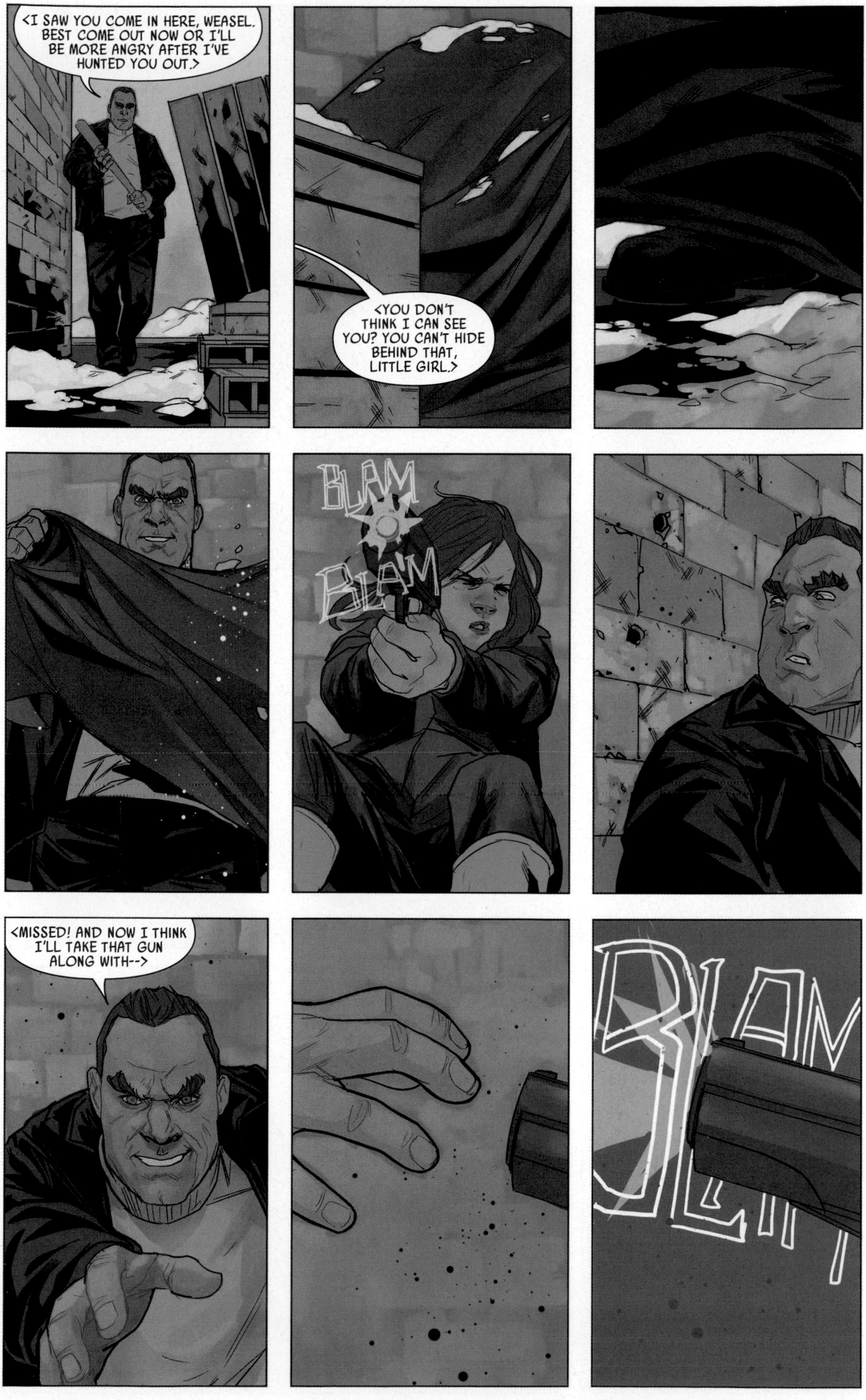
<I SAW YOU COME IN HERE, WEASEL. BEST COME OUT NOW OR I'LL BE MORE ANGRY AFTER I'VE HUNTED YOU OUT.>
<YOU DON'T THINK I CAN SEE YOU? YOU CAN'T HIDE BEHIND THAT, LITTLE GIRL.>
BLAM
BLAM
<MISSED! AND NOW I THINK I'LL TAKE THAT GUN ALONG WITH-->
BLAM

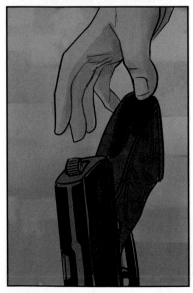

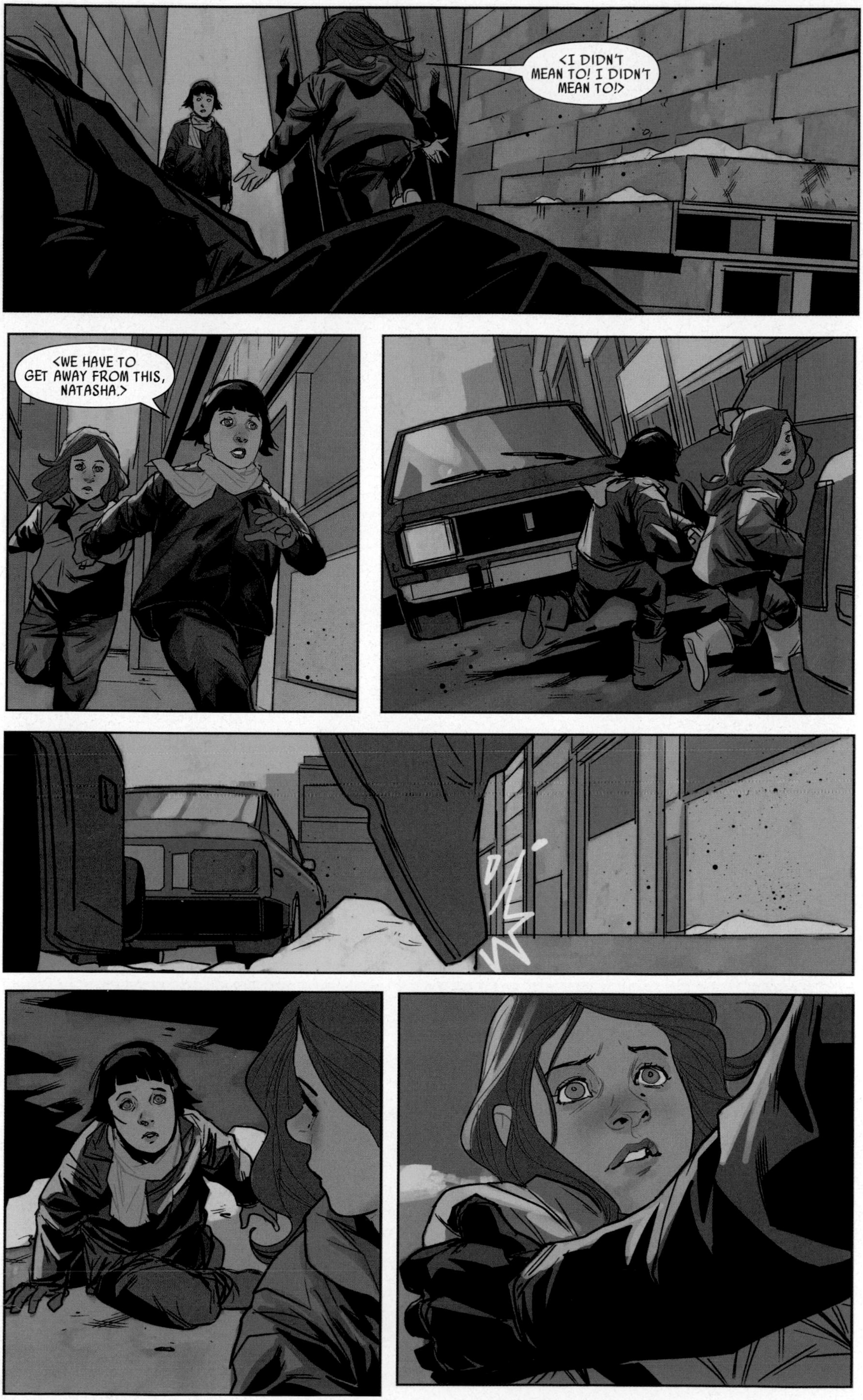
<I DIDN'T MEAN TO! I DIDN'T MEAN TO!>
<WE HAVE TO GET AWAY FROM THIS, NATASHA.>

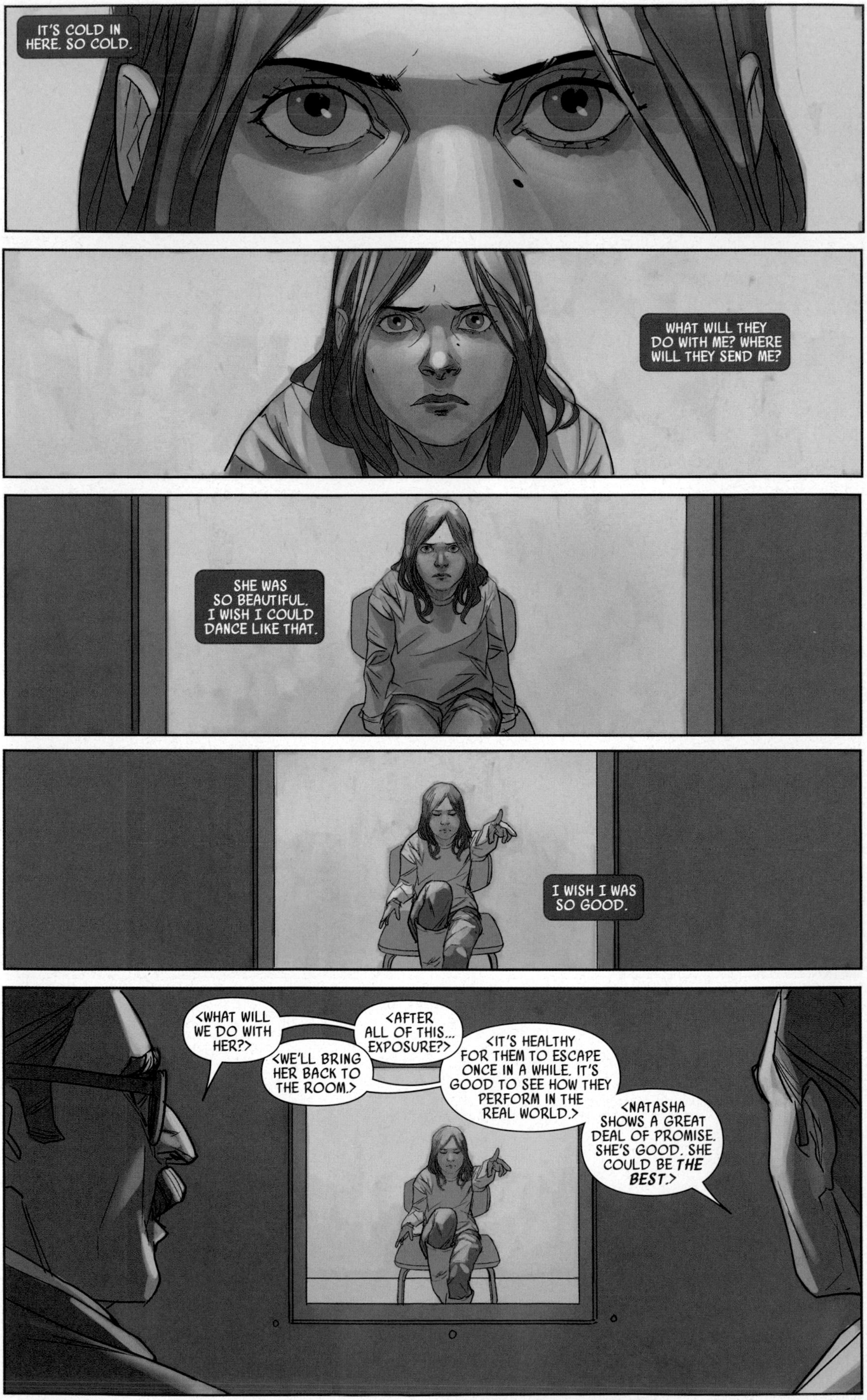
IT'S COLD IN HERE. SO COLD.
WHAT WILL THEY DO WITH ME? WHERE WILL THEY SEND ME?
SHE WAS SO BEAUTIFUL. I WISH I COULD DANCE LIKE THAT.
I WISH I WAS SO GOOD.
<WHAT WILL WE DO WITH HER?>
<AFTER ALL OF THIS... EXPOSURE?>
<WE'LL BRING HER BACK TO THE ROOM.>
<IT'S HEALTHY FOR THEM TO ESCAPE ONCE IN A WHILE. IT'S GOOD TO SEE HOW THEY PERFORM IN THE REAL WORLD.>
<NATASHA SHOWS A GREAT DEAL OF PROMISE. SHE'S GOOD. SHE COULD BE *THE BEST*.>

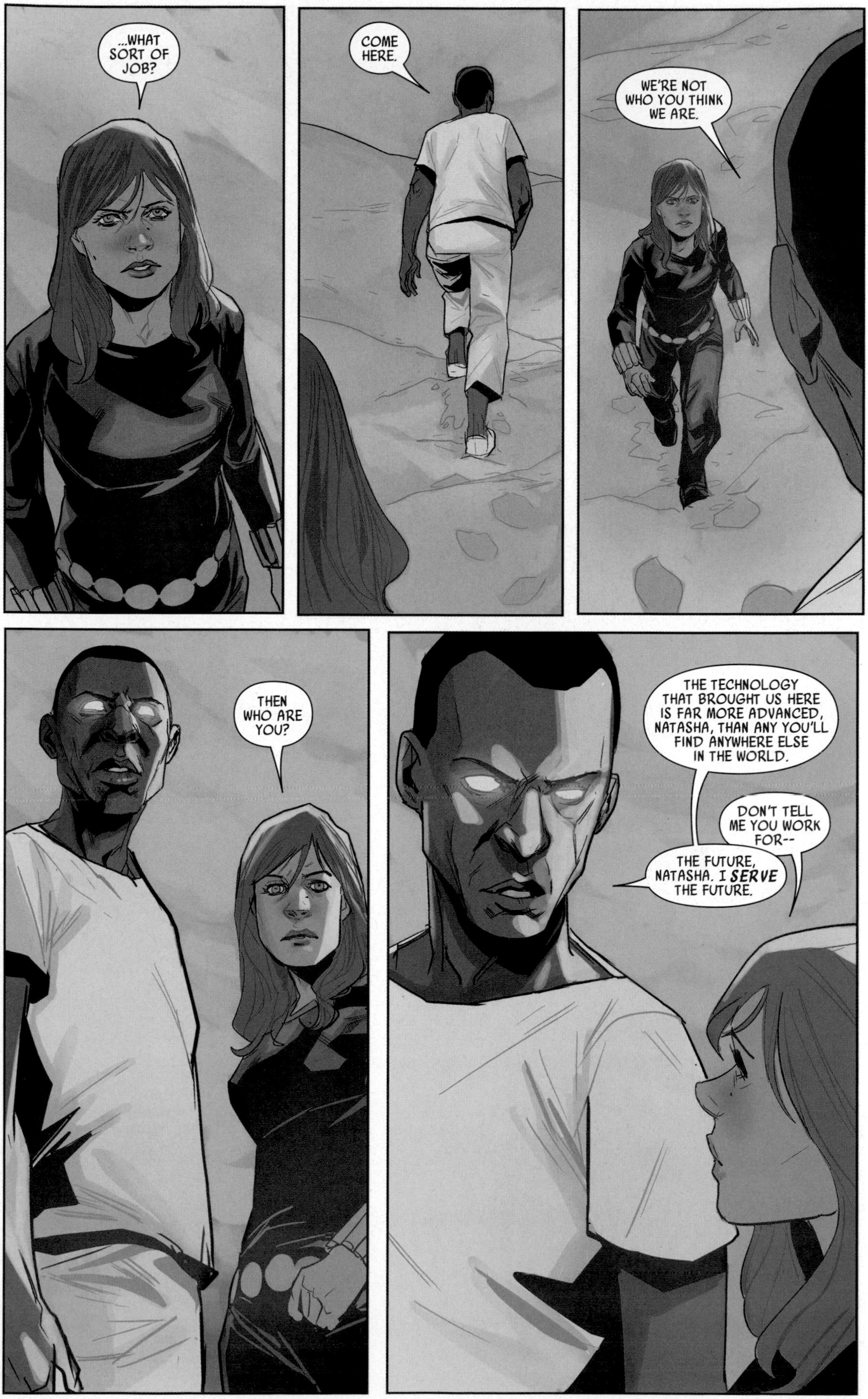

...WHAT SORT OF JOB?
COME HERE.
WE'RE NOT WHO YOU THINK WE ARE.
THEN WHO ARE YOU?
THE TECHNOLOGY THAT BROUGHT US HERE IS FAR MORE ADVANCED, NATASHA, THAN ANY YOU'LL FIND ANYWHERE ELSE IN THE WORLD.
DON'T TELL ME YOU WORK FOR--
THE FUTURE, NATASHA. I SERVE THE FUTURE.

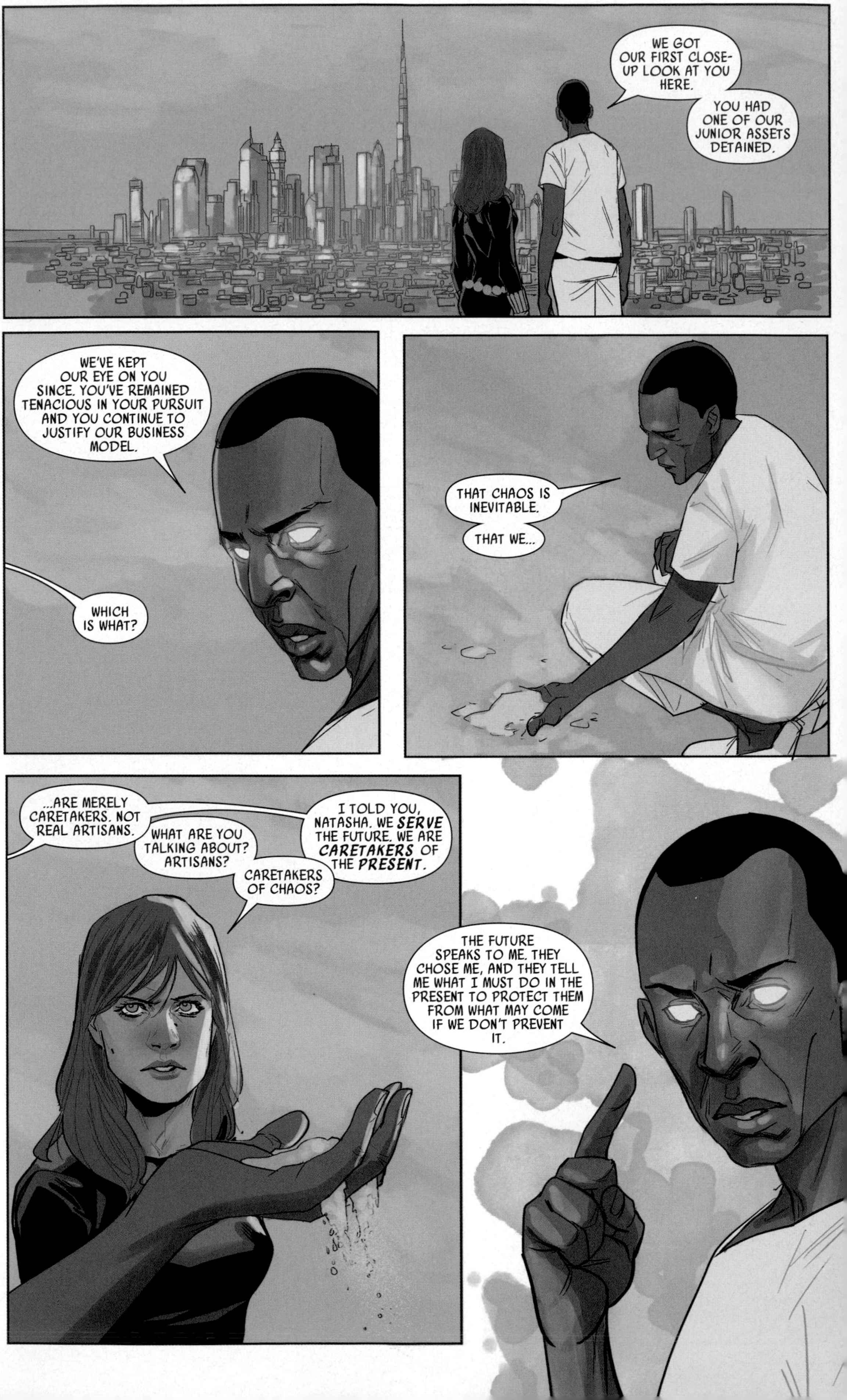

WE GOT OUR FIRST CLOSE-UP LOOK AT YOU HERE.
YOU HAD ONE OF OUR JUNIOR ASSETS DETAINED.
WE'VE KEPT OUR EYE ON YOU SINCE. YOU'VE REMAINED TENACIOUS IN YOUR PURSUIT AND YOU CONTINUE TO JUSTIFY OUR BUSINESS MODEL.
WHICH IS WHAT?
THAT CHAOS IS INEVITABLE.
THAT WE...
...ARE MERELY CARETAKERS. NOT REAL ARTISANS.
WHAT ARE YOU TALKING ABOUT? ARTISANS?
CARETAKERS OF CHAOS?
I TOLD YOU, NATASHA. WE SERVE THE FUTURE. WE ARE CARETAKERS OF THE PRESENT.
THE FUTURE SPEAKS TO ME. THEY CHOSE ME, AND THEY TELL ME WHAT I MUST DO IN THE PRESENT TO PROTECT THEM FROM WHAT MAY COME IF WE DON'T PREVENT IT.

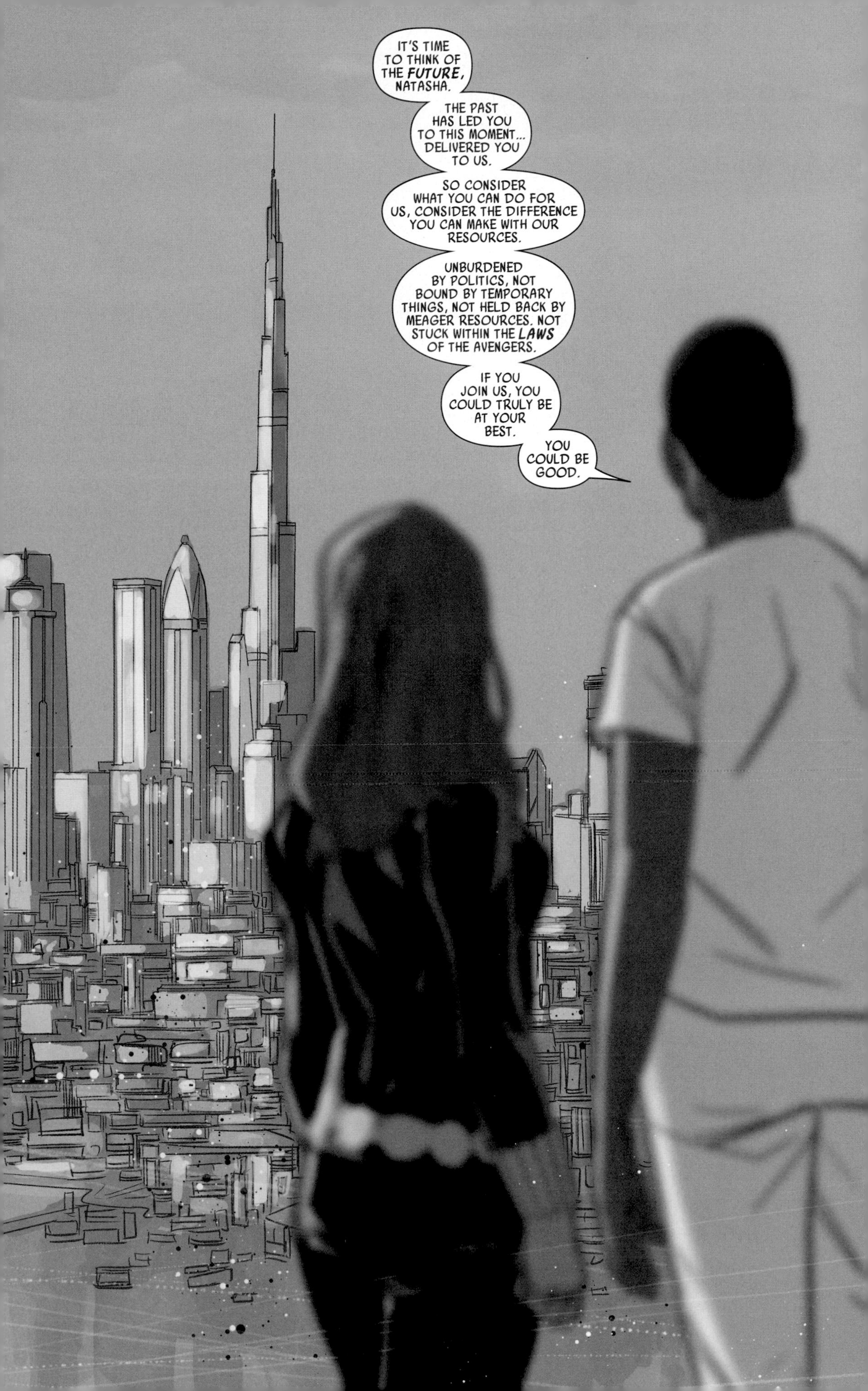
IT'S TIME TO THINK OF THE FUTURE, NATASHA.
THE PAST HAS LED YOU TO THIS MOMENT... DELIVERED YOU TO US.
SO CONSIDER WHAT YOU CAN DO FOR US, CONSIDER THE DIFFERENCE YOU CAN MAKE WITH OUR RESOURCES.
UNBURDENED BY POLITICS, NOT BOUND BY TEMPORARY THINGS, NOT HELD BACK BY MEAGER RESOURCES. NOT STUCK WITHIN THE LAWS OF THE AVENGERS.
IF YOU JOIN US, YOU COULD TRULY BE AT YOUR BEST.
YOU COULD BE GOOD.

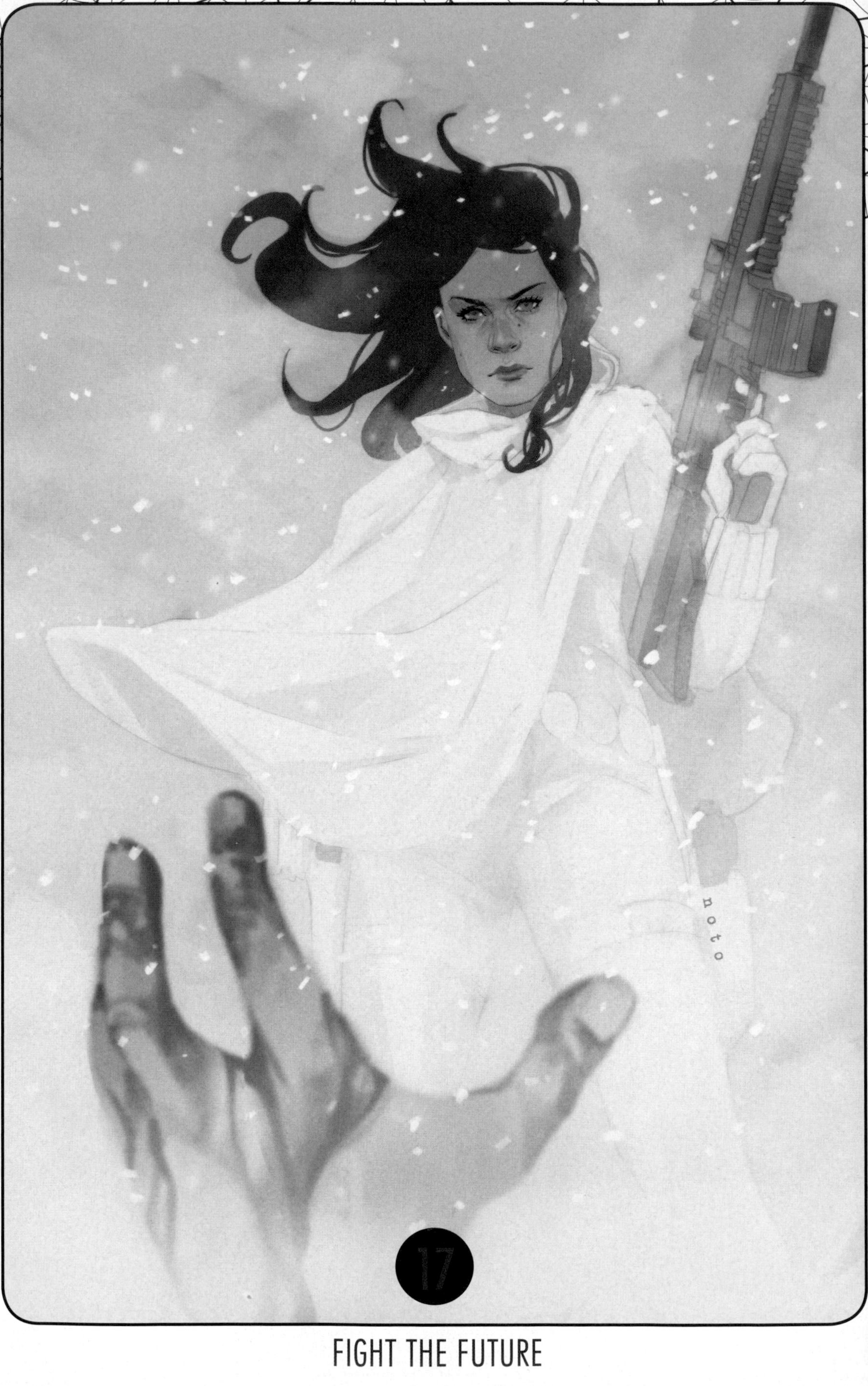
17
noto

FIGHT THE FUTURE

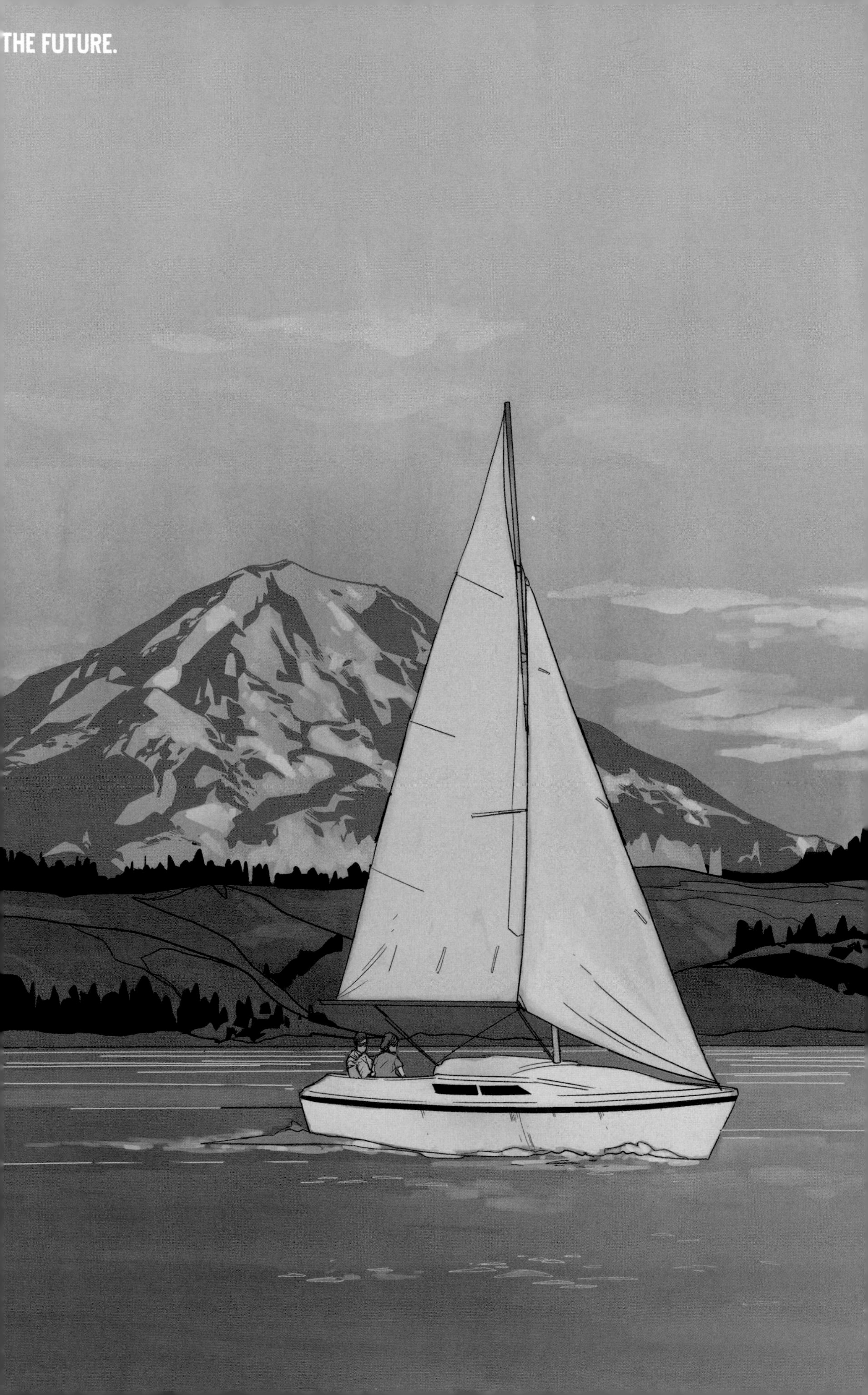
THE FUTURE.

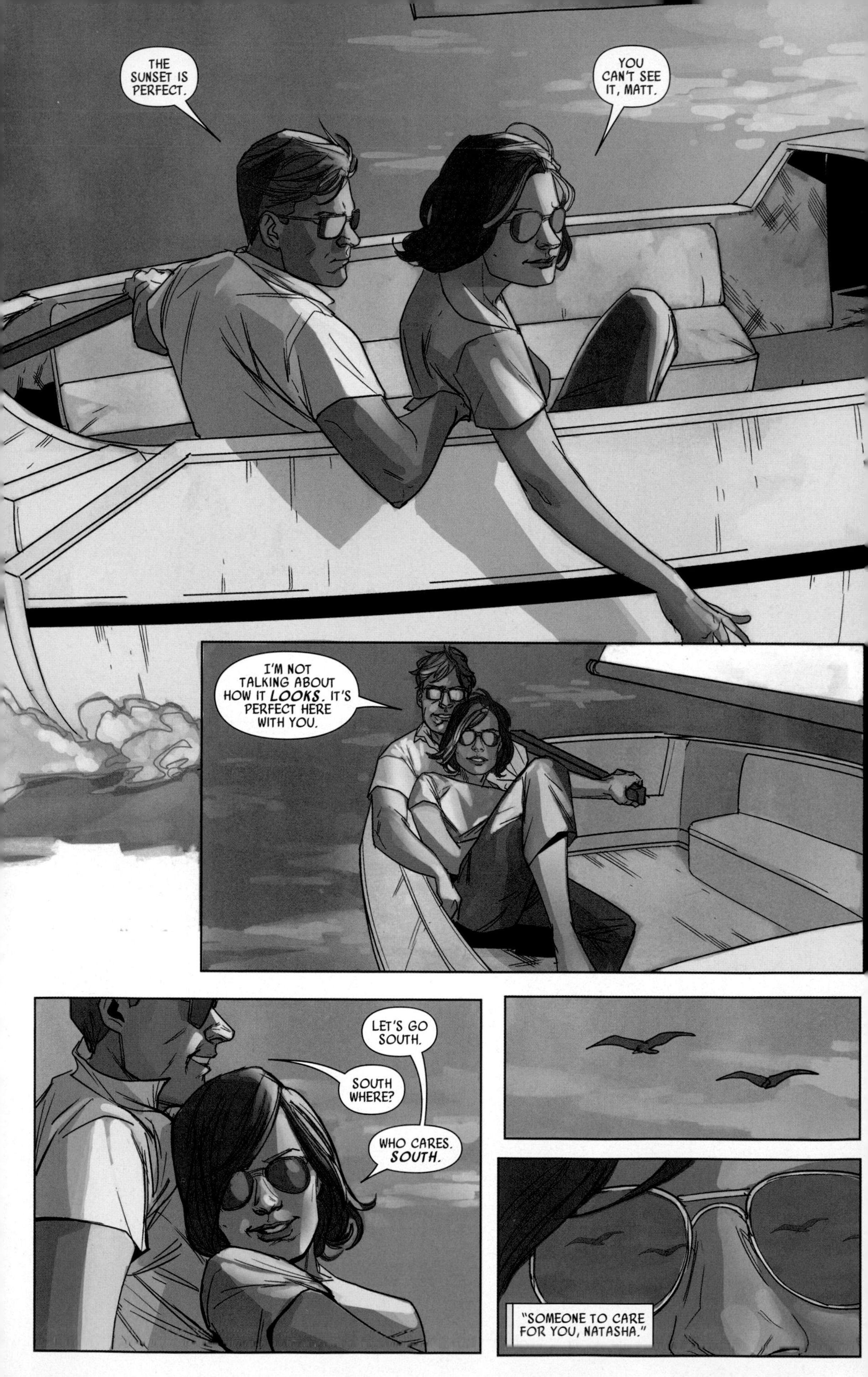
THE SUNSET IS PERFECT.
YOU CAN'T SEE IT, MATT.
I'M NOT TALKING ABOUT HOW IT LOOKS. IT'S PERFECT HERE WITH YOU.
LET'S GO SOUTH.
SOUTH WHERE?
WHO CARES. SOUTH.
"SOMEONE TO CARE FOR YOU, NATASHA."

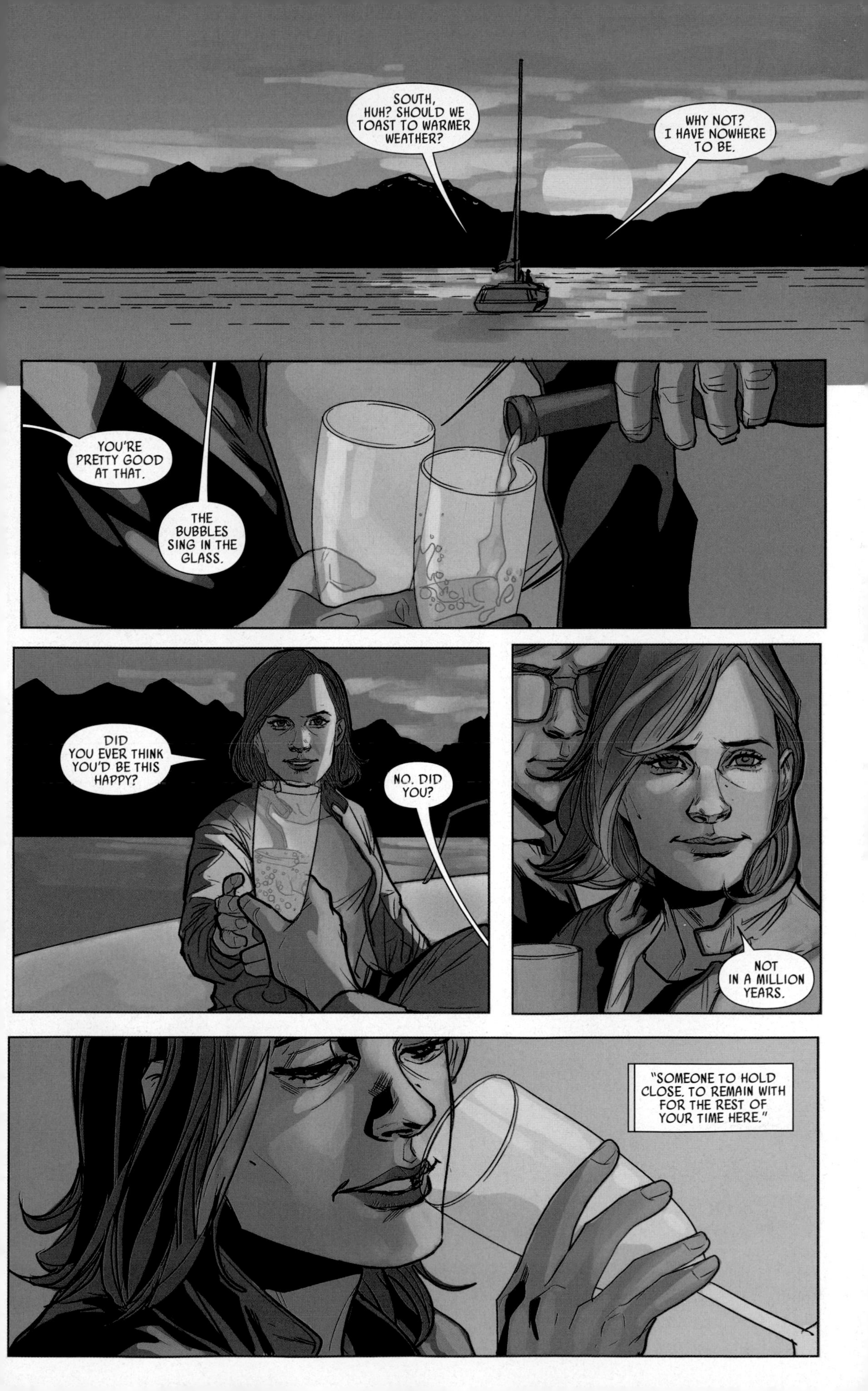
SOUTH, HUH? SHOULD WE TOAST TO WARMER WEATHER?
WHY NOT? I HAVE NOWHERE TO BE.
YOU'RE PRETTY GOOD AT THAT.
THE BUBBLES SING IN THE GLASS.
DID YOU EVER THINK YOU'D BE THIS HAPPY?
NO. DID YOU?
NOT IN A MILLION YEARS.
"SOMEONE TO HOLD CLOSE. TO REMAIN WITH FOR THE REST OF YOUR TIME HERE."

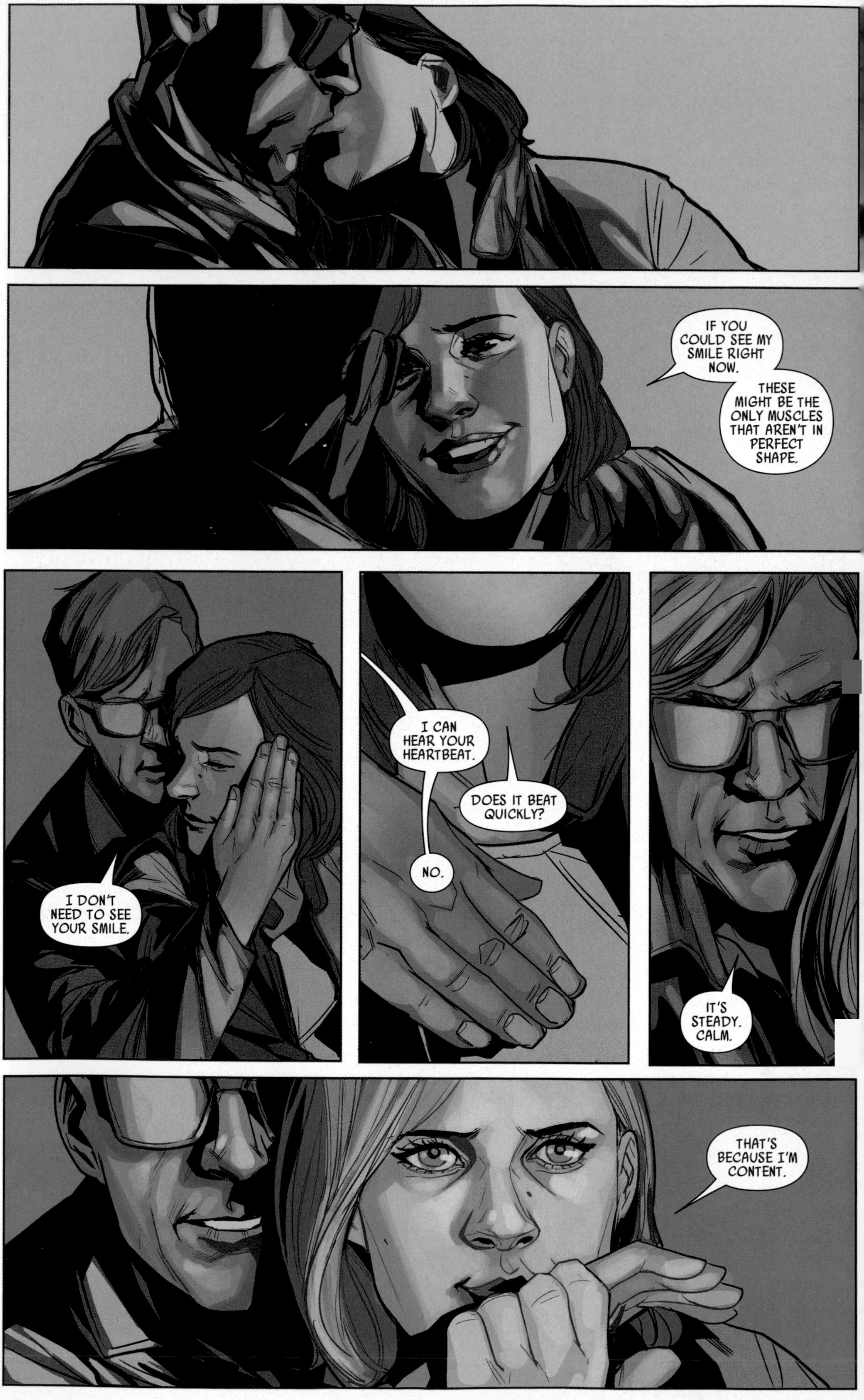
IF YOU COULD SEE MY SMILE RIGHT NOW.
THESE MIGHT BE THE ONLY MUSCLES THAT AREN'T IN PERFECT SHAPE.
I DON'T NEED TO SEE YOUR SMILE.
I CAN HEAR YOUR HEARTBEAT.
DOES IT BEAT QUICKLY?
NO.
IT'S STEADY. CALM.
THAT'S BECAUSE I'M CONTENT.

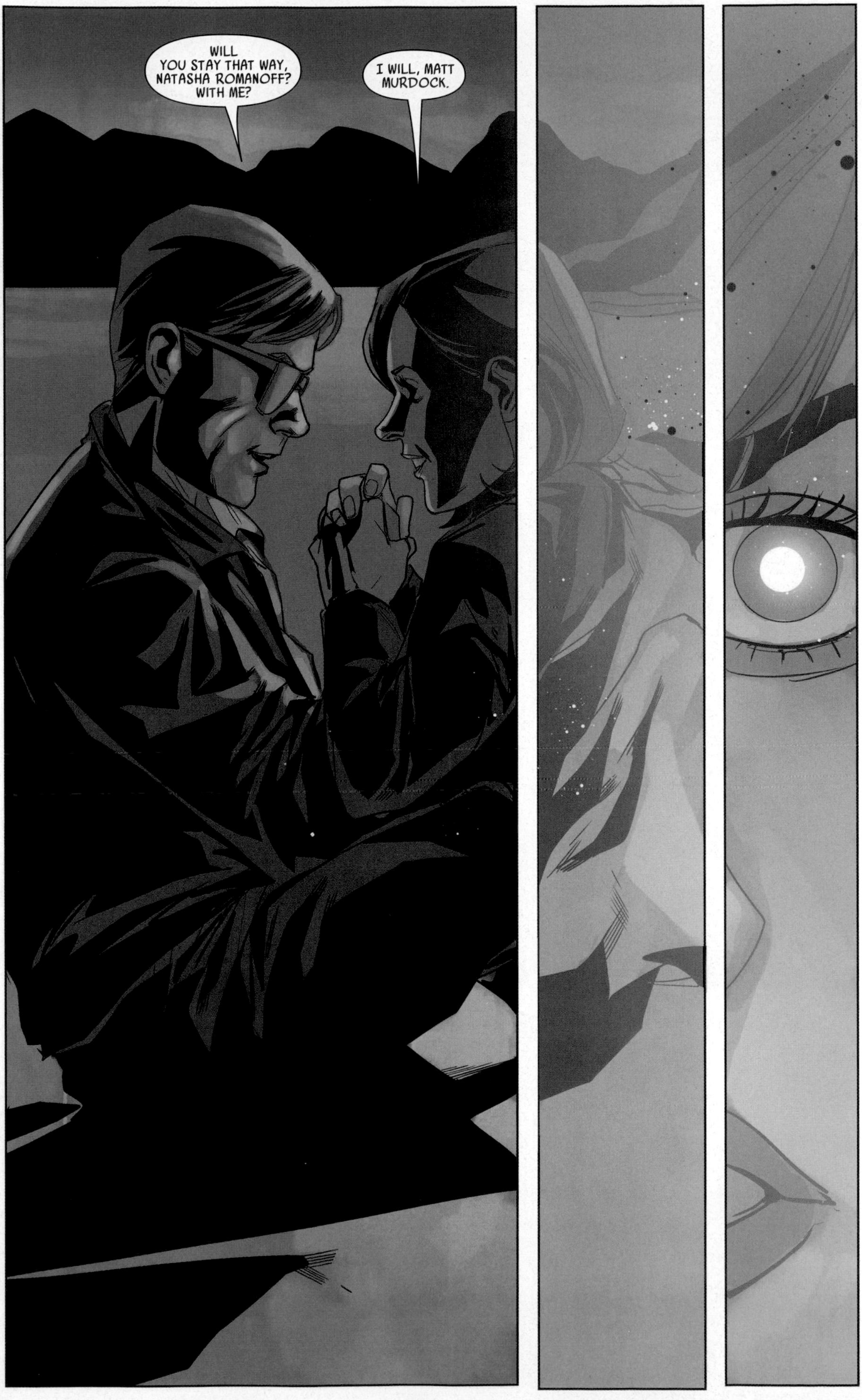
WILL YOU STAY THAT WAY, NATASHA ROMANOFF? WITH ME?
I WILL, MATT MURDOCK.

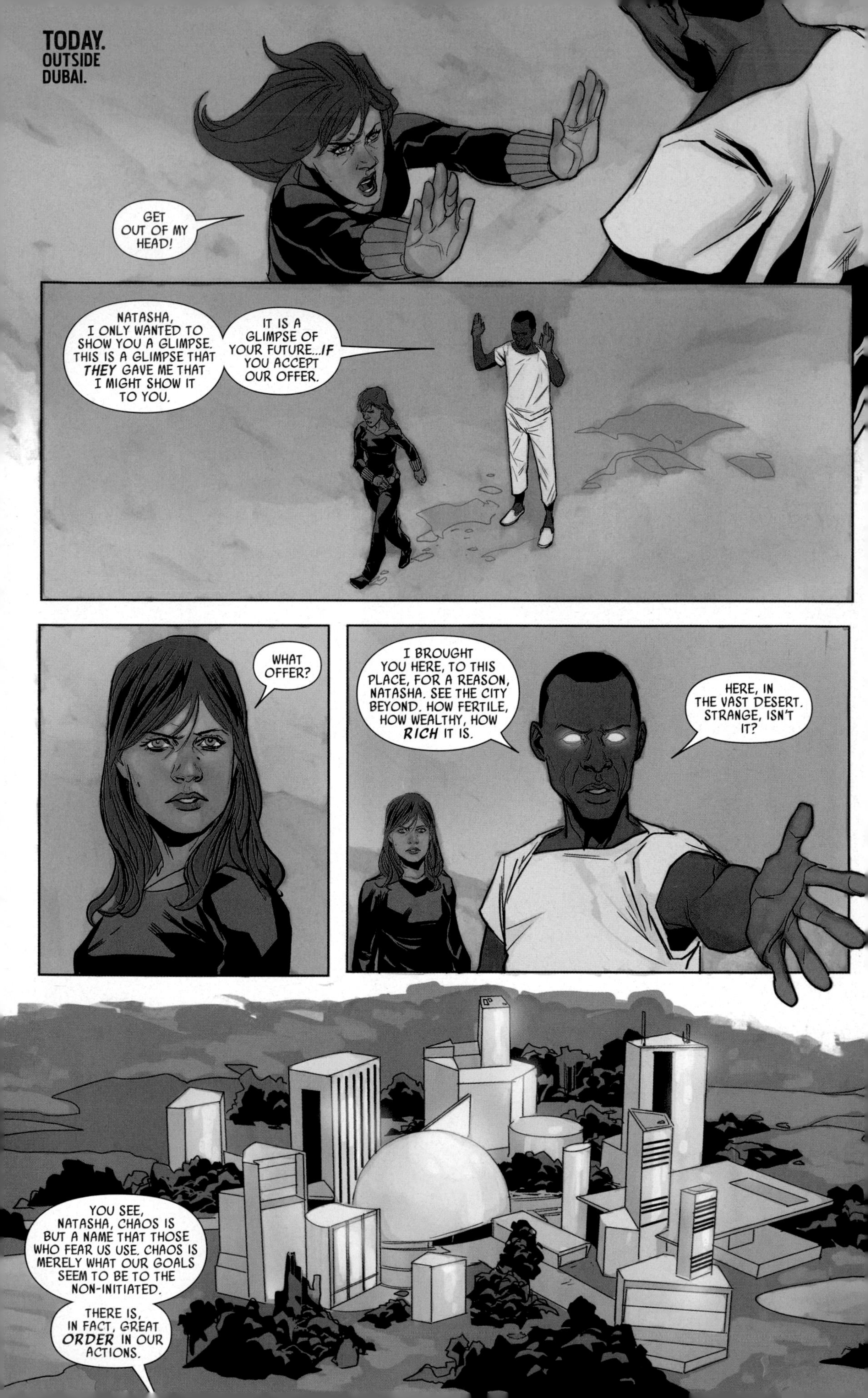
TODAY. OUTSIDE DUBAI.
GET OUT OF MY HEAD!
NATASHA, I ONLY WANTED TO SHOW YOU A GLIMPSE. THIS IS A GLIMPSE THAT THEY GAVE ME THAT I MIGHT SHOW IT TO YOU.
IT IS A GLIMPSE OF YOUR FUTURE...IF YOU ACCEPT OUR OFFER.
WHAT OFFER?
I BROUGHT YOU HERE, TO THIS PLACE, FOR A REASON, NATASHA. SEE THE CITY BEYOND. HOW FERTILE, HOW WEALTHY, HOW RICH IT IS.
HERE, IN THE VAST DESERT. STRANGE, ISN'T IT?
YOU SEE, NATASHA, CHAOS IS BUT A NAME THAT THOSE WHO FEAR US USE. CHAOS IS MERELY WHAT OUR GOALS SEEM TO BE TO THE NON-INITIATED.
THERE IS, IN FACT, GREAT ORDER IN OUR ACTIONS.

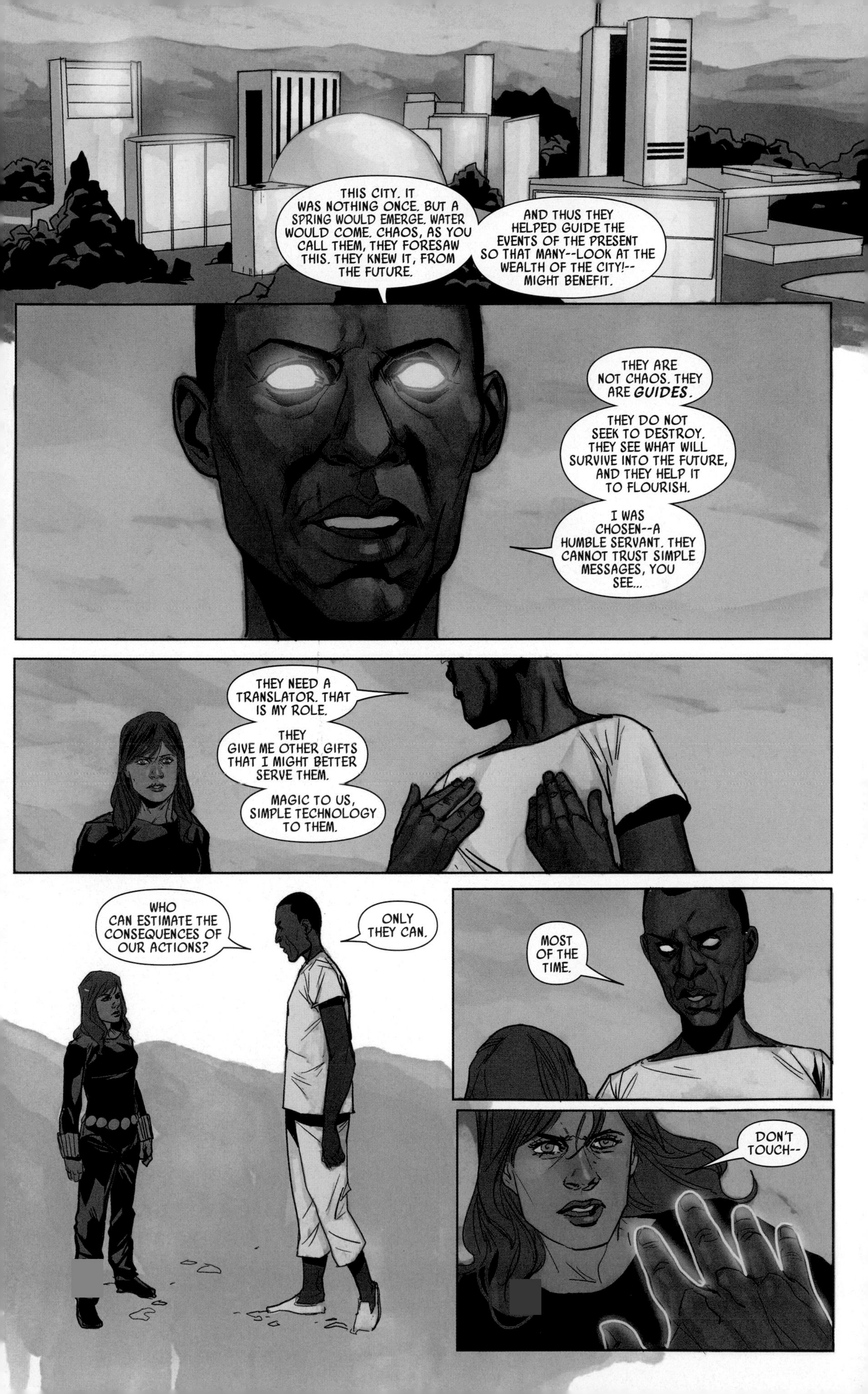
THIS CITY. IT WAS NOTHING ONCE. BUT A SPRING WOULD EMERGE. WATER WOULD COME. CHAOS, AS YOU CALL THEM, THEY FORESAW THIS. THEY KNEW IT, FROM THE FUTURE.
AND THUS THEY HELPED GUIDE THE EVENTS OF THE PRESENT SO THAT MANY--LOOK AT THE WEALTH OF THE CITY!--MIGHT BENEFIT.
THEY ARE NOT CHAOS. THEY ARE **GUIDES**.
THEY DO NOT SEEK TO DESTROY. THEY SEE WHAT WILL SURVIVE INTO THE FUTURE, AND THEY HELP IT TO FLOURISH.
I WAS CHOSEN--A HUMBLE SERVANT. THEY CANNOT TRUST SIMPLE MESSAGES, YOU SEE...
THEY NEED A TRANSLATOR. THAT IS MY ROLE.
THEY GIVE ME OTHER GIFTS THAT I MIGHT BETTER SERVE THEM.
MAGIC TO US, SIMPLE TECHNOLOGY TO THEM.
WHO CAN ESTIMATE THE CONSEQUENCES OF OUR ACTIONS?
ONLY THEY CAN.
MOST OF THE TIME.
DON'T TOUCH--

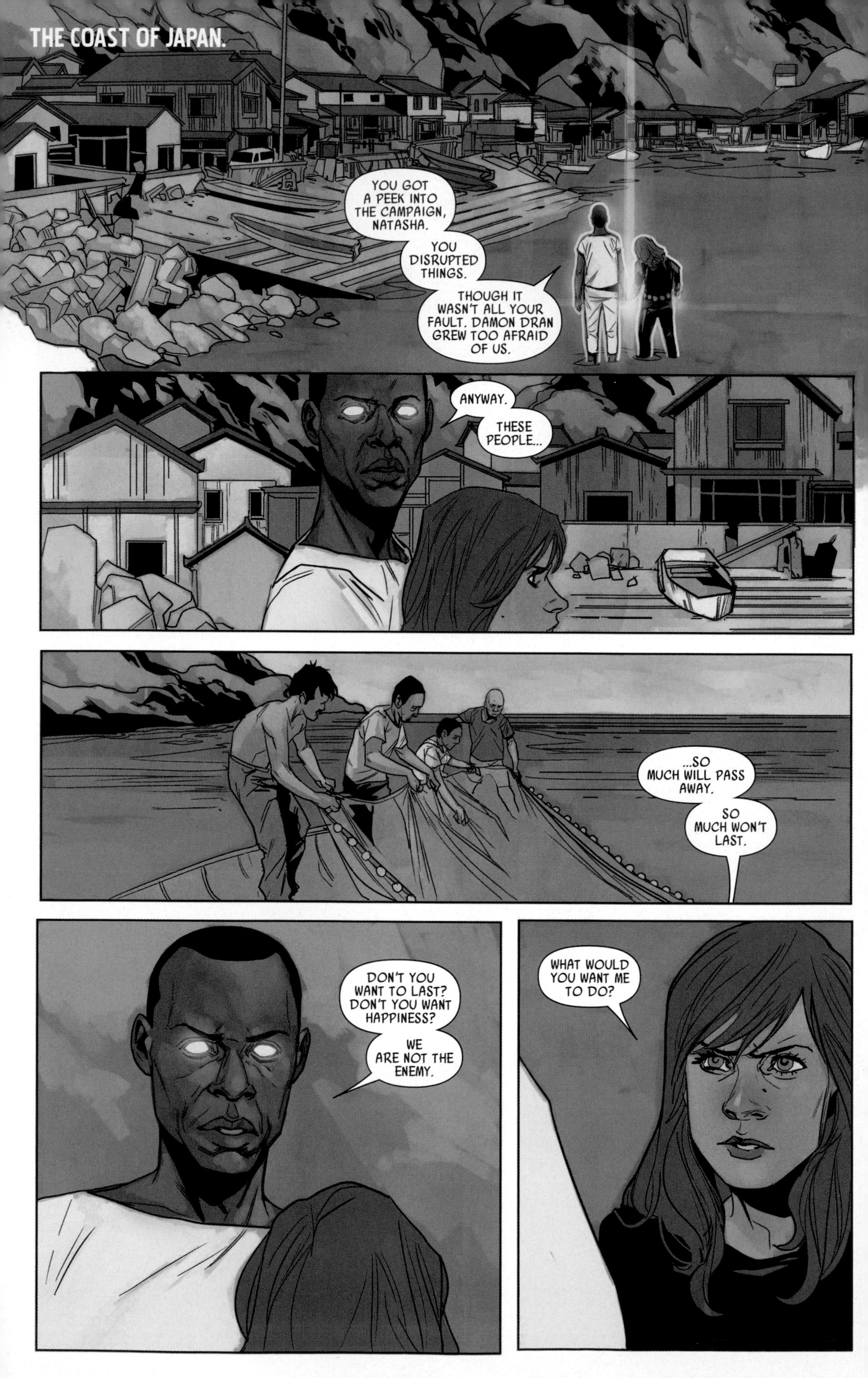
THE COAST OF JAPAN.
YOU GOT A PEEK INTO THE CAMPAIGN, NATASHA.
YOU DISRUPTED THINGS.
THOUGH IT WASN'T ALL YOUR FAULT. DAMON DRAN GREW TOO AFRAID OF US.
ANYWAY.
THESE PEOPLE...
...SO MUCH WILL PASS AWAY.
SO MUCH WON'T LAST.
DON'T YOU WANT TO LAST? DON'T YOU WANT HAPPINESS?
WE ARE NOT THE ENEMY.
WHAT WOULD YOU WANT ME TO DO?

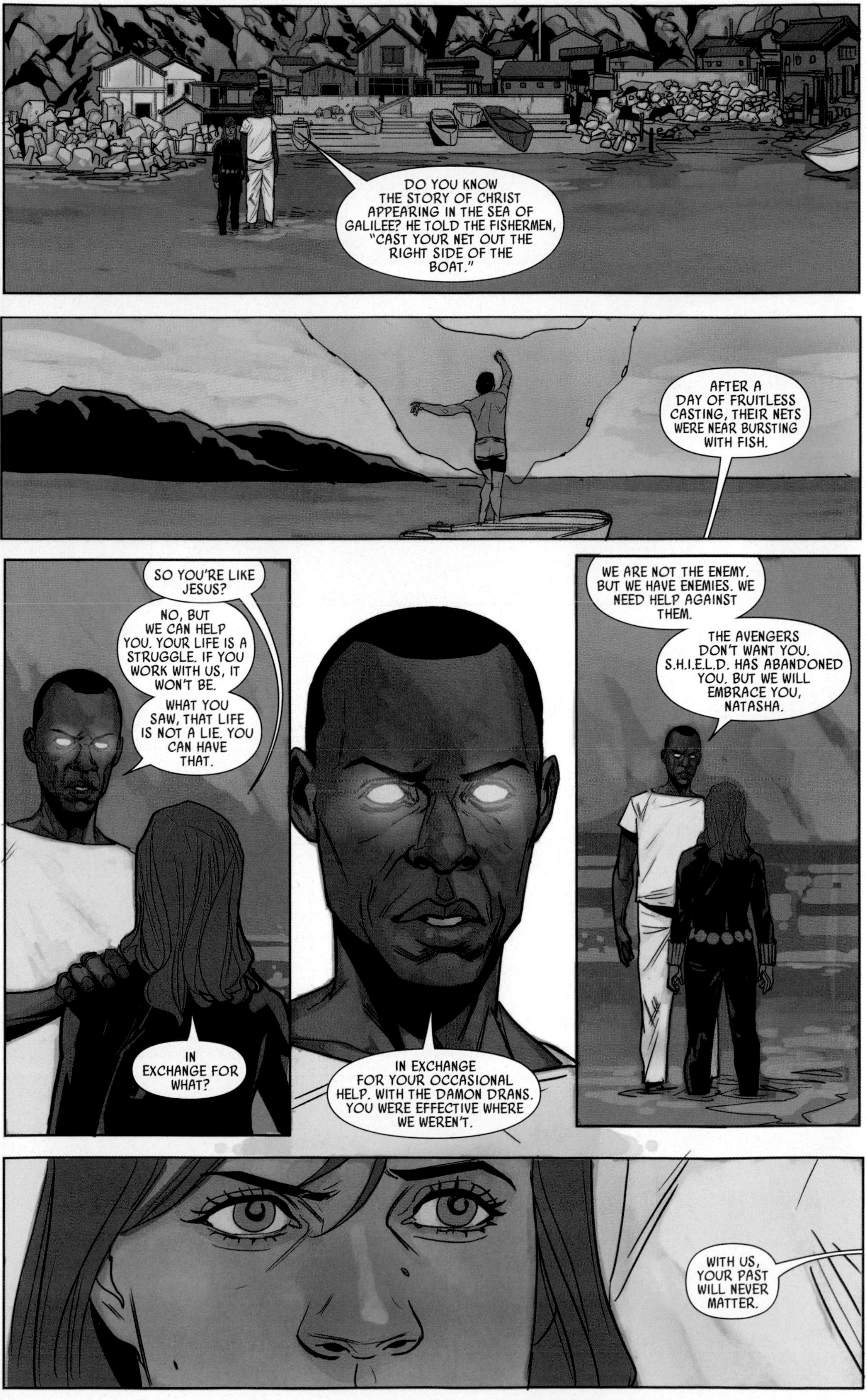
DO YOU KNOW THE STORY OF CHRIST APPEARING IN THE SEA OF GALILEE? HE TOLD THE FISHERMEN, "CAST YOUR NET OUT THE RIGHT SIDE OF THE BOAT."
AFTER A DAY OF FRUITLESS CASTING, THEIR NETS WERE NEAR BURSTING WITH FISH.
SO YOU'RE LIKE JESUS?
NO, BUT WE CAN HELP YOU. YOUR LIFE IS A STRUGGLE. IF YOU WORK WITH US, IT WON'T BE.
WHAT YOU SAW, THAT LIFE IS NOT A LIE. YOU CAN HAVE THAT.
IN EXCHANGE FOR WHAT?
IN EXCHANGE FOR YOUR OCCASIONAL HELP. WITH THE DAMON DRANS. YOU WERE EFFECTIVE WHERE WE WEREN'T.
WE ARE NOT THE ENEMY. BUT WE HAVE ENEMIES. WE NEED HELP AGAINST THEM.
THE AVENGERS DON'T WANT YOU. S.H.I.E.L.D. HAS ABANDONED YOU. BUT WE WILL EMBRACE YOU, NATASHA.
WITH US, YOUR PAST WILL NEVER MATTER.

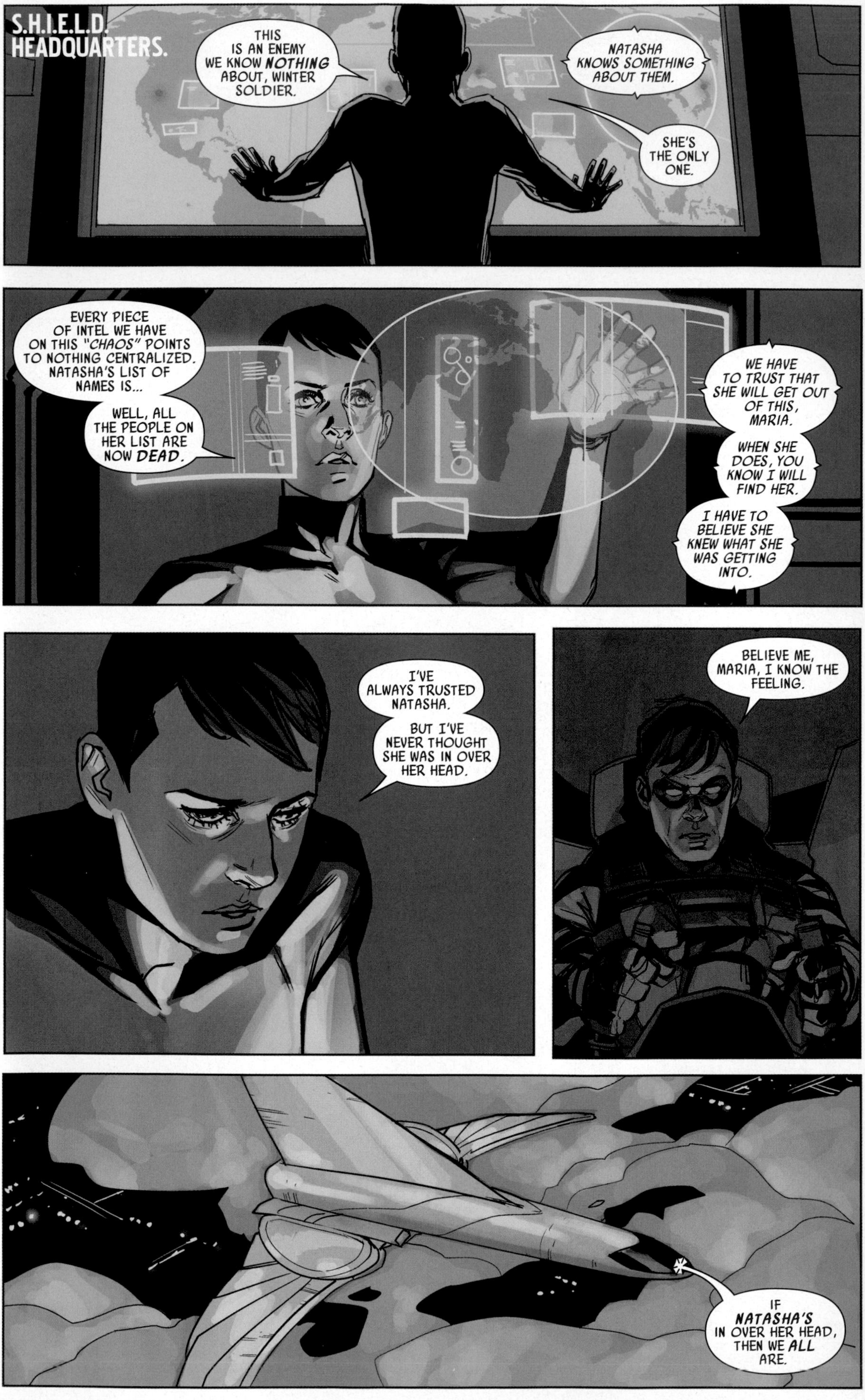
S.H.I.E.L.D. HEADQUARTERS.
THIS IS AN ENEMY WE KNOW NOTHING ABOUT, WINTER SOLDIER.
NATASHA KNOWS SOMETHING ABOUT THEM.
SHE'S THE ONLY ONE.
EVERY PIECE OF INTEL WE HAVE ON THIS "CHAOS" POINTS TO NOTHING CENTRALIZED. NATASHA'S LIST OF NAMES IS...
WELL, ALL THE PEOPLE ON HER LIST ARE NOW DEAD.
WE HAVE TO TRUST THAT SHE WILL GET OUT OF THIS, MARIA.
WHEN SHE DOES, YOU KNOW I WILL FIND HER.
I HAVE TO BELIEVE SHE KNEW WHAT SHE WAS GETTING INTO.
I'VE ALWAYS TRUSTED NATASHA.
BUT I'VE NEVER THOUGHT SHE WAS IN OVER HER HEAD.
BELIEVE ME, MARIA, I KNOW THE FEELING.
IF NATASHA'S IN OVER HER HEAD, THEN WE ALL ARE.

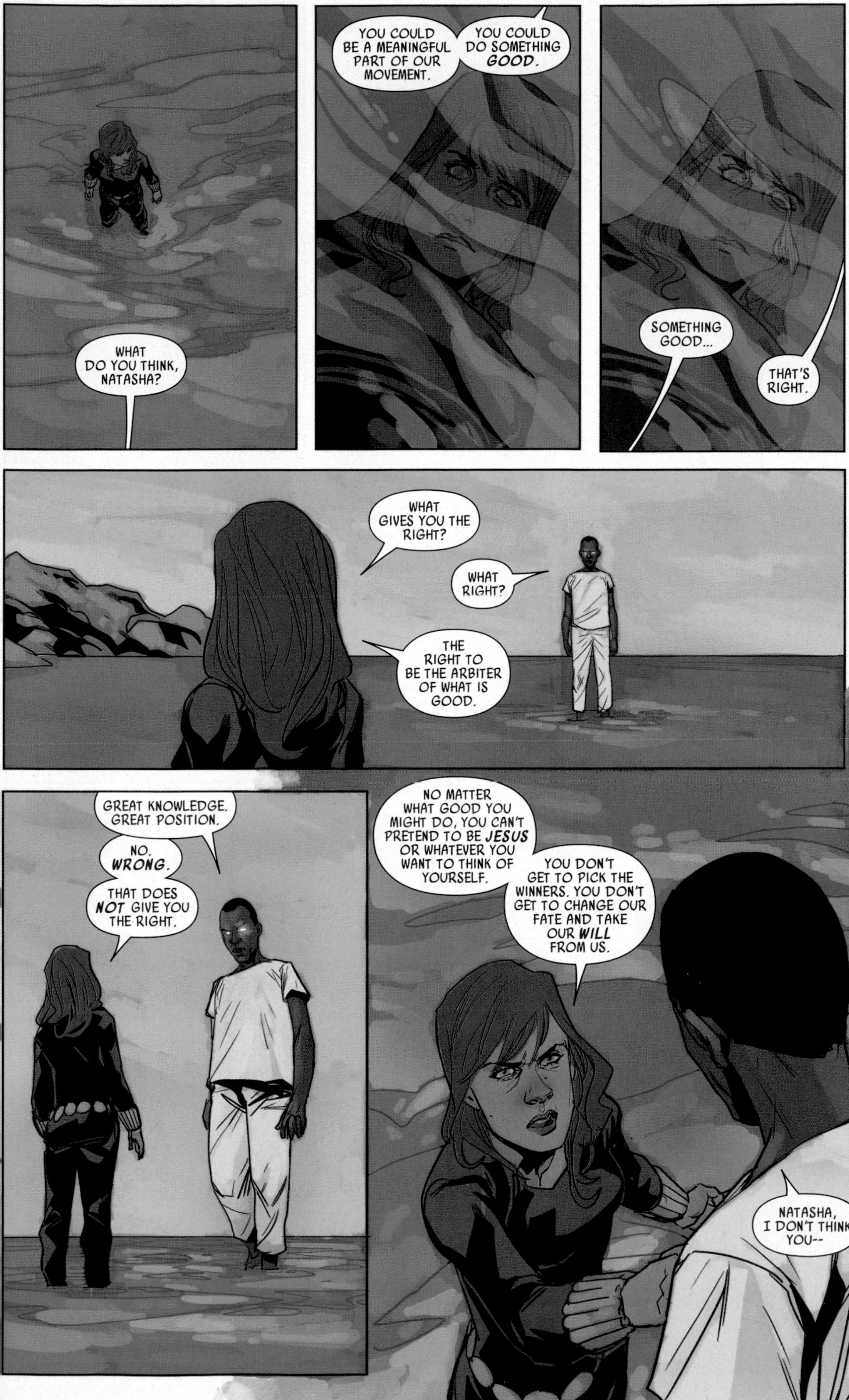
WHAT DO YOU THINK, NATASHA?
YOU COULD BE A MEANINGFUL PART OF OUR MOVEMENT.
YOU COULD DO SOMETHING GOOD.
SOMETHING GOOD...
THAT'S RIGHT.
WHAT GIVES YOU THE RIGHT?
WHAT RIGHT?
THE RIGHT TO BE THE ARBITER OF WHAT IS GOOD.
GREAT KNOWLEDGE. GREAT POSITION.
NO. WRONG.
THAT DOES NOT GIVE YOU THE RIGHT.
NO MATTER WHAT GOOD YOU MIGHT DO, YOU CAN'T PRETEND TO BE JESUS OR WHATEVER YOU WANT TO THINK OF YOURSELF.
YOU DON'T GET TO PICK THE WINNERS. YOU DON'T GET TO CHANGE OUR FATE AND TAKE OUR WILL FROM US.
NATASHA, I DON'T THINK YOU--

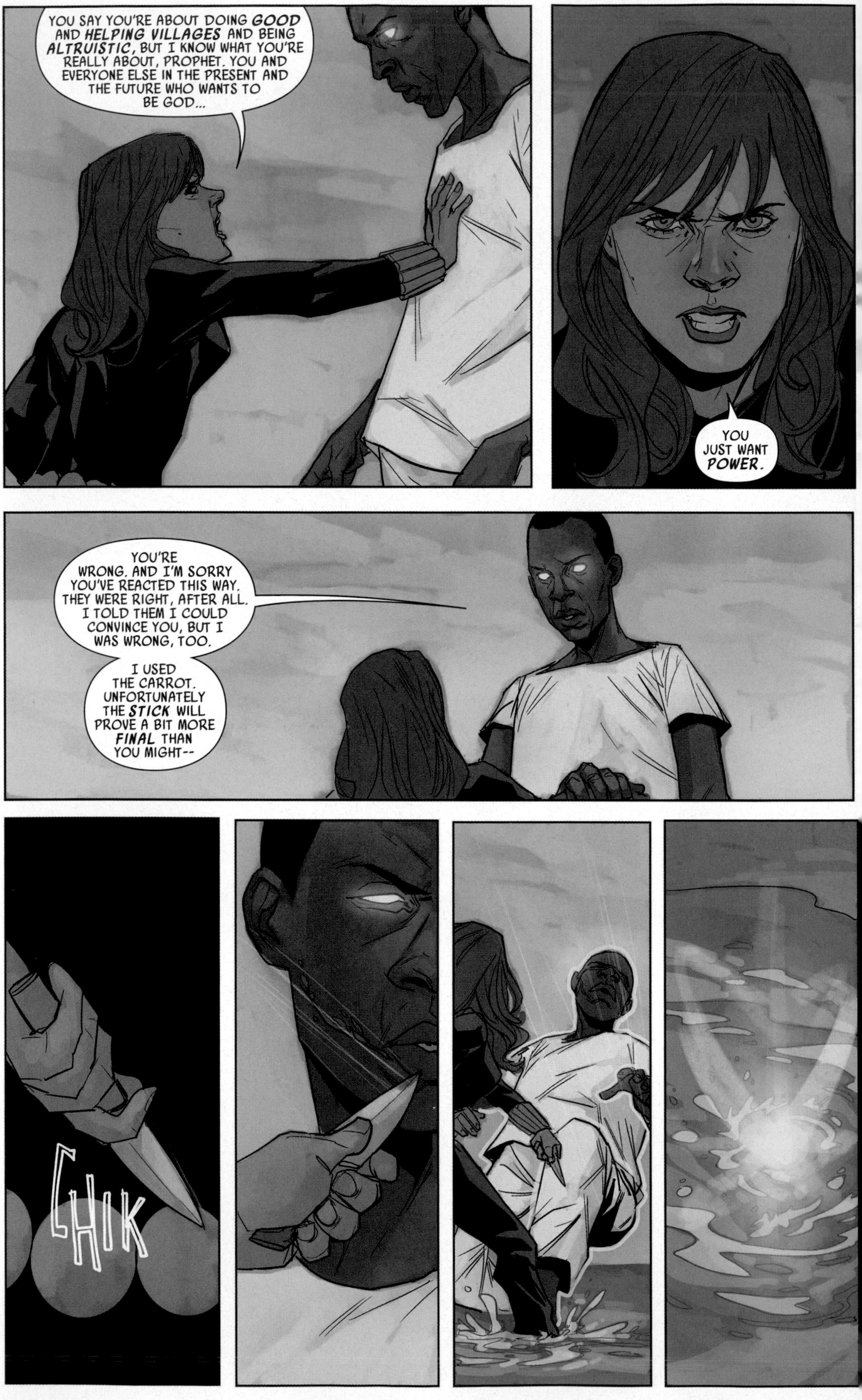
YOU SAY YOU'RE ABOUT DOING GOOD AND HELPING VILLAGES AND BEING ALTRUISTIC, BUT I KNOW WHAT YOU'RE REALLY ABOUT, PROPHET. YOU AND EVERYONE ELSE IN THE PRESENT AND THE FUTURE WHO WANTS TO BE GOD...
YOU JUST WANT POWER.
YOU'RE WRONG. AND I'M SORRY YOU'VE REACTED THIS WAY. THEY WERE RIGHT, AFTER ALL. I TOLD THEM I COULD CONVINCE YOU, BUT I WAS WRONG, TOO.
I USED THE CARROT. UNFORTUNATELY THE STICK WILL PROVE A BIT MORE FINAL THAN YOU MIGHT--
CHIK

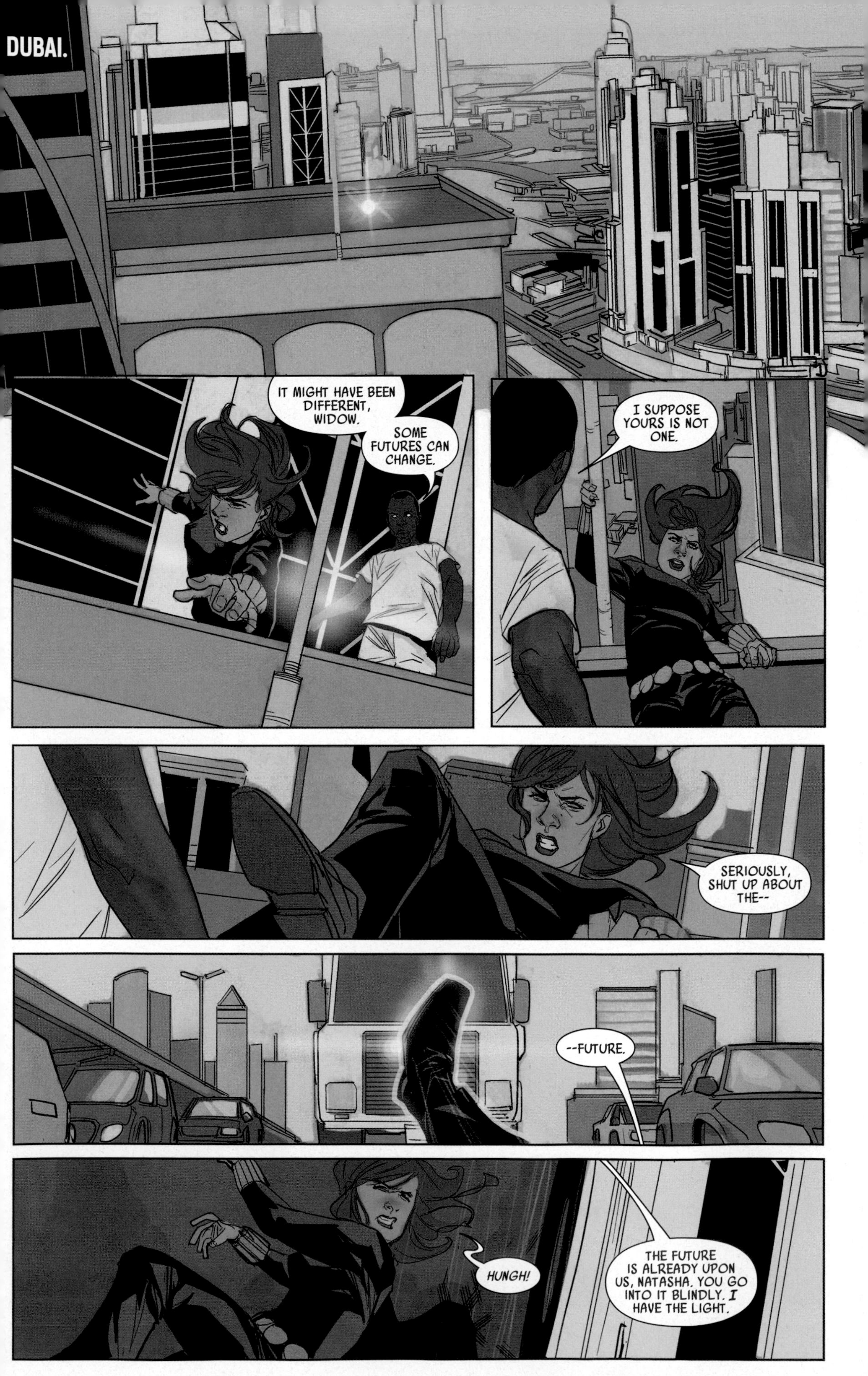
DUBAI.
IT MIGHT HAVE BEEN DIFFERENT, WIDOW.
SOME FUTURES CAN CHANGE.
I SUPPOSE YOURS IS NOT ONE.
SERIOUSLY, SHUT UP ABOUT THE--
--FUTURE.
HUNGH!
THE FUTURE IS ALREADY UPON US, NATASHA. YOU GO INTO IT BLINDLY. *I* HAVE THE LIGHT.

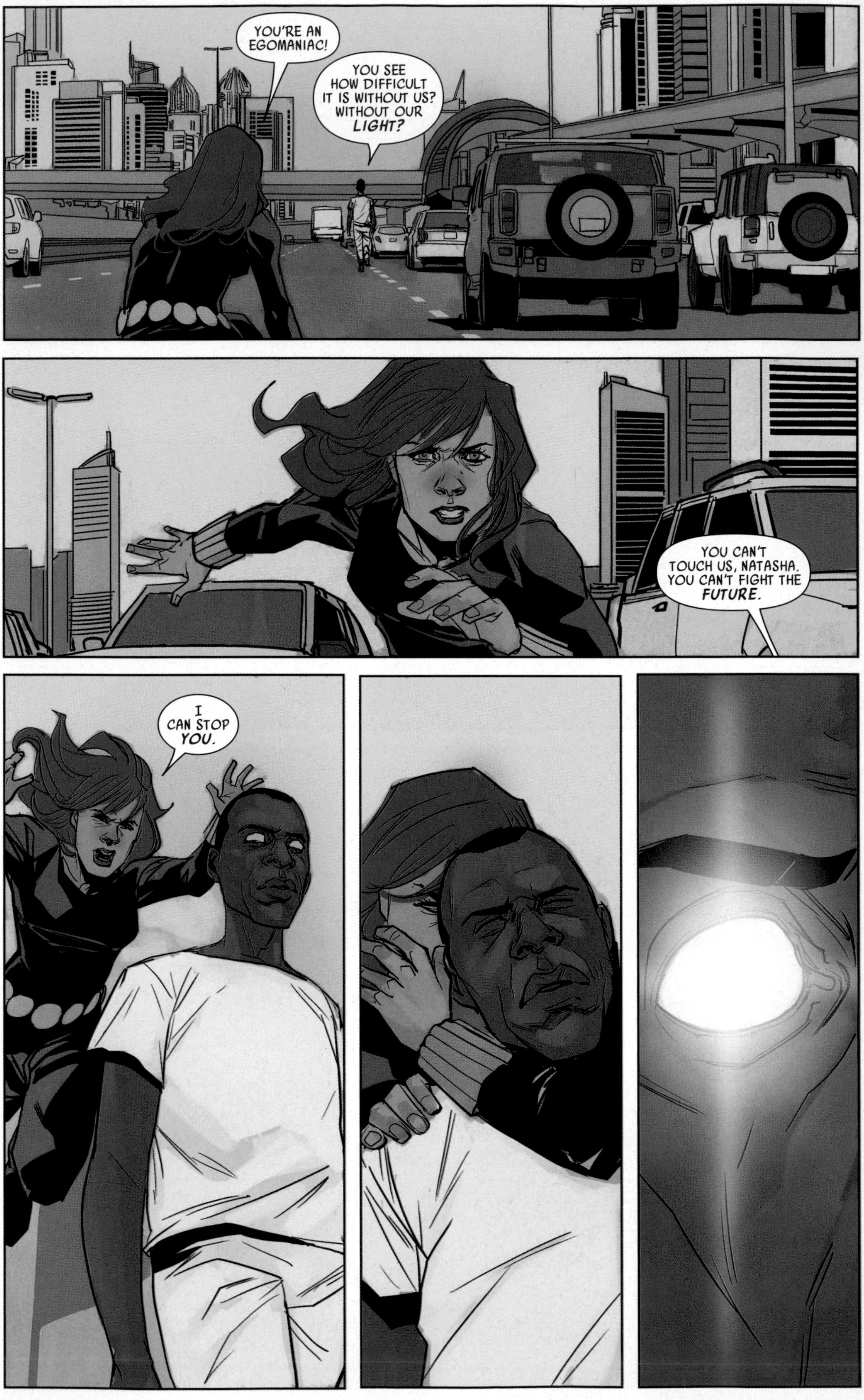
YOU'RE AN EGOMANIAC!
YOU SEE HOW DIFFICULT IT IS WITHOUT US? WITHOUT OUR LIGHT?
YOU CAN'T TOUCH US, NATASHA. YOU CAN'T FIGHT THE FUTURE.
I CAN STOP YOU.

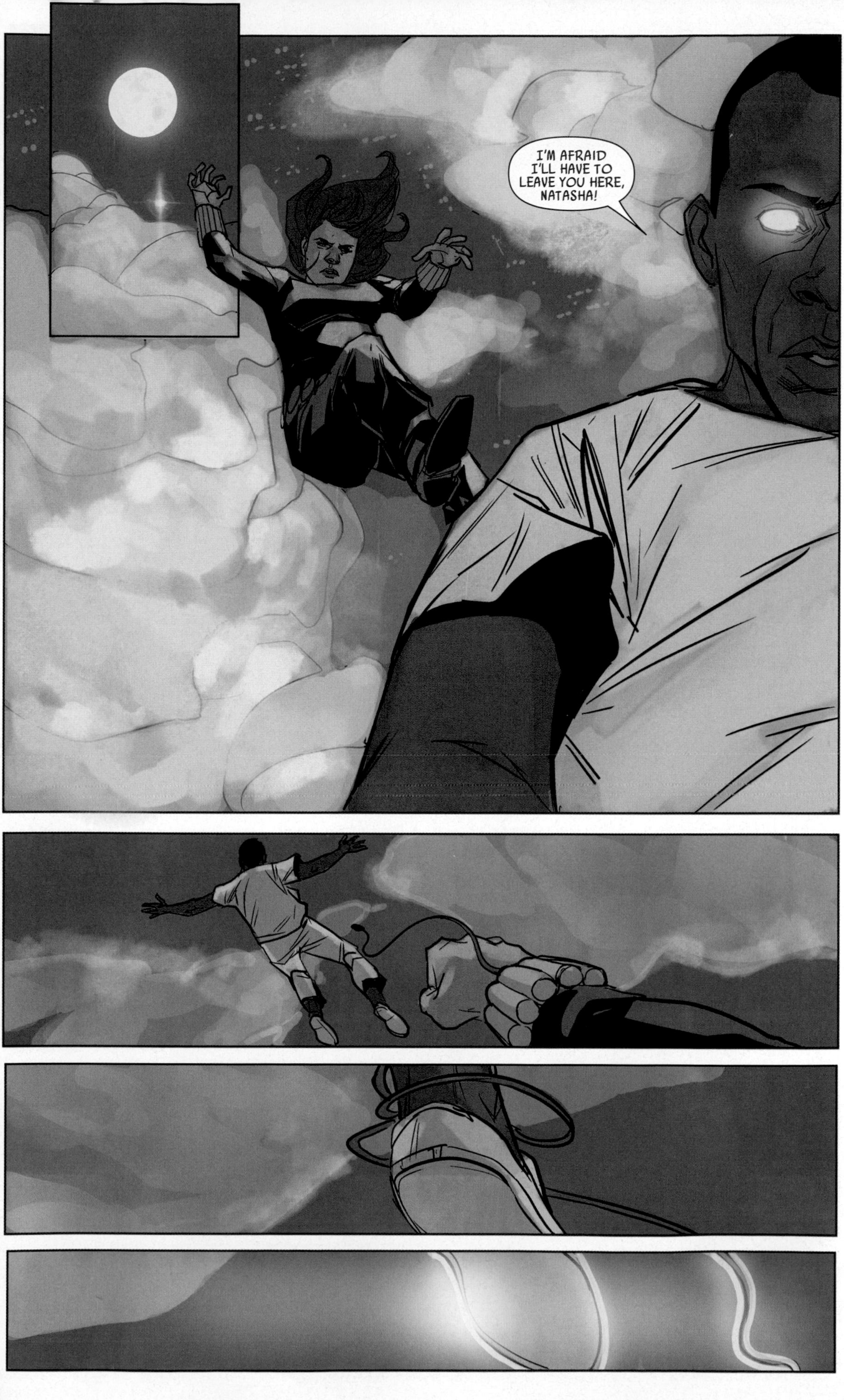
I'M AFRAID I'LL HAVE TO LEAVE YOU HERE, NATASHA!

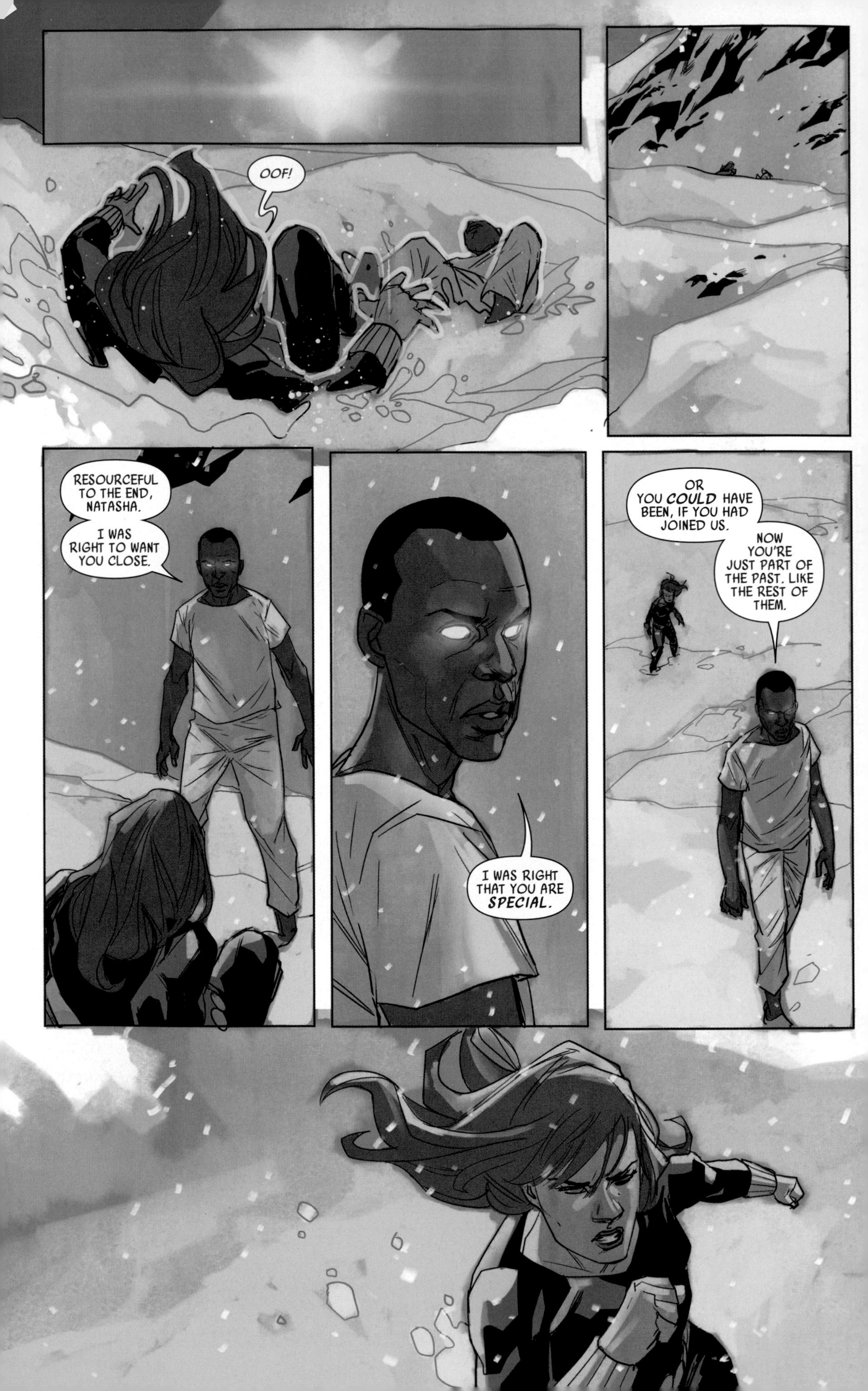
OOF!
RESOURCEFUL TO THE END, NATASHA.
I WAS RIGHT TO WANT YOU CLOSE.
I WAS RIGHT THAT YOU ARE SPECIAL.
OR YOU COULD HAVE BEEN, IF YOU HAD JOINED US.
NOW YOU'RE JUST PART OF THE PAST. LIKE THE REST OF THEM.

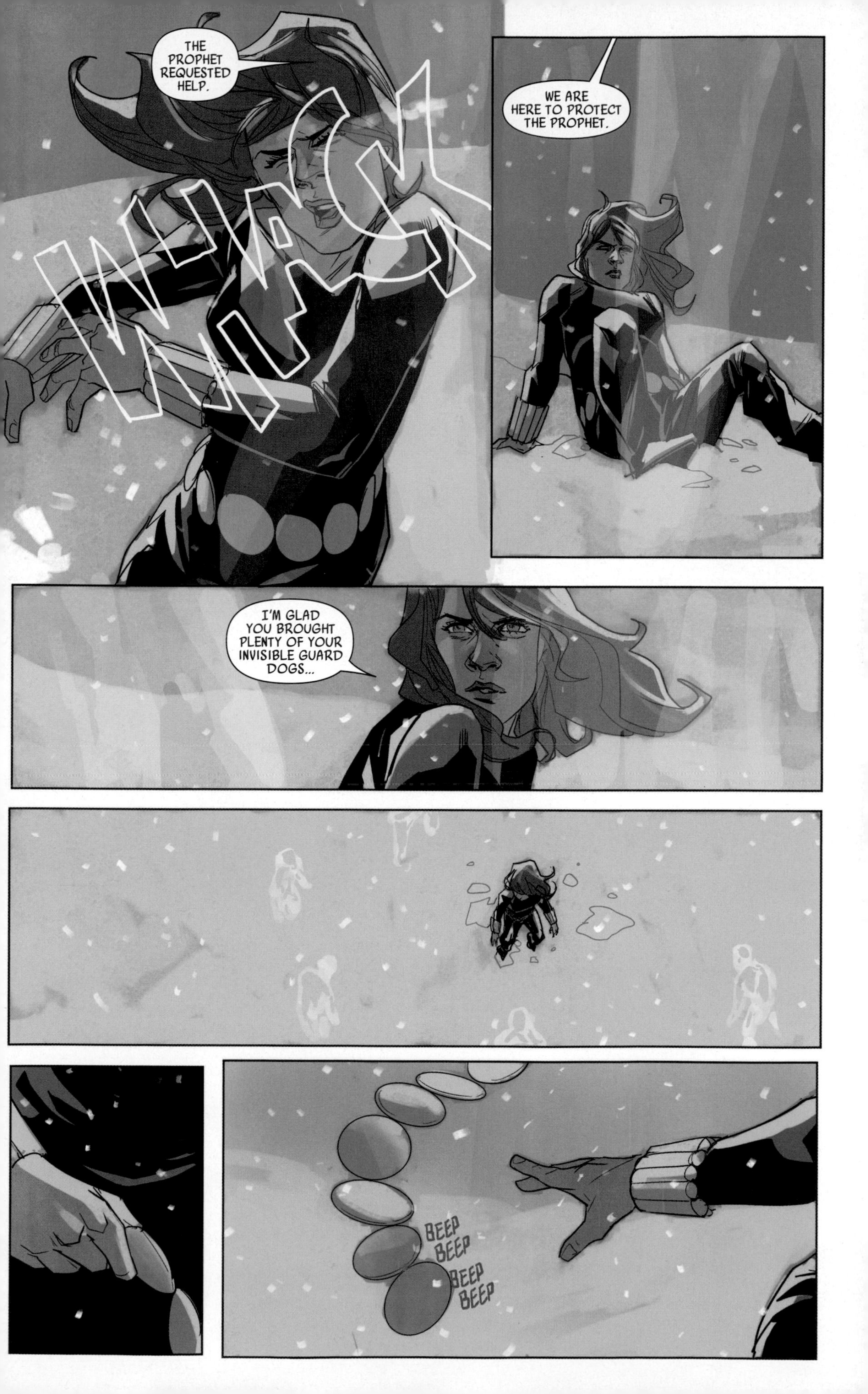
THE PROPHET REQUESTED HELP.
WHACK
WE ARE HERE TO PROTECT THE PROPHET.
I'M GLAD YOU BROUGHT PLENTY OF YOUR INVISIBLE GUARD DOGS...
BEEP BEEP BEEP BEEP

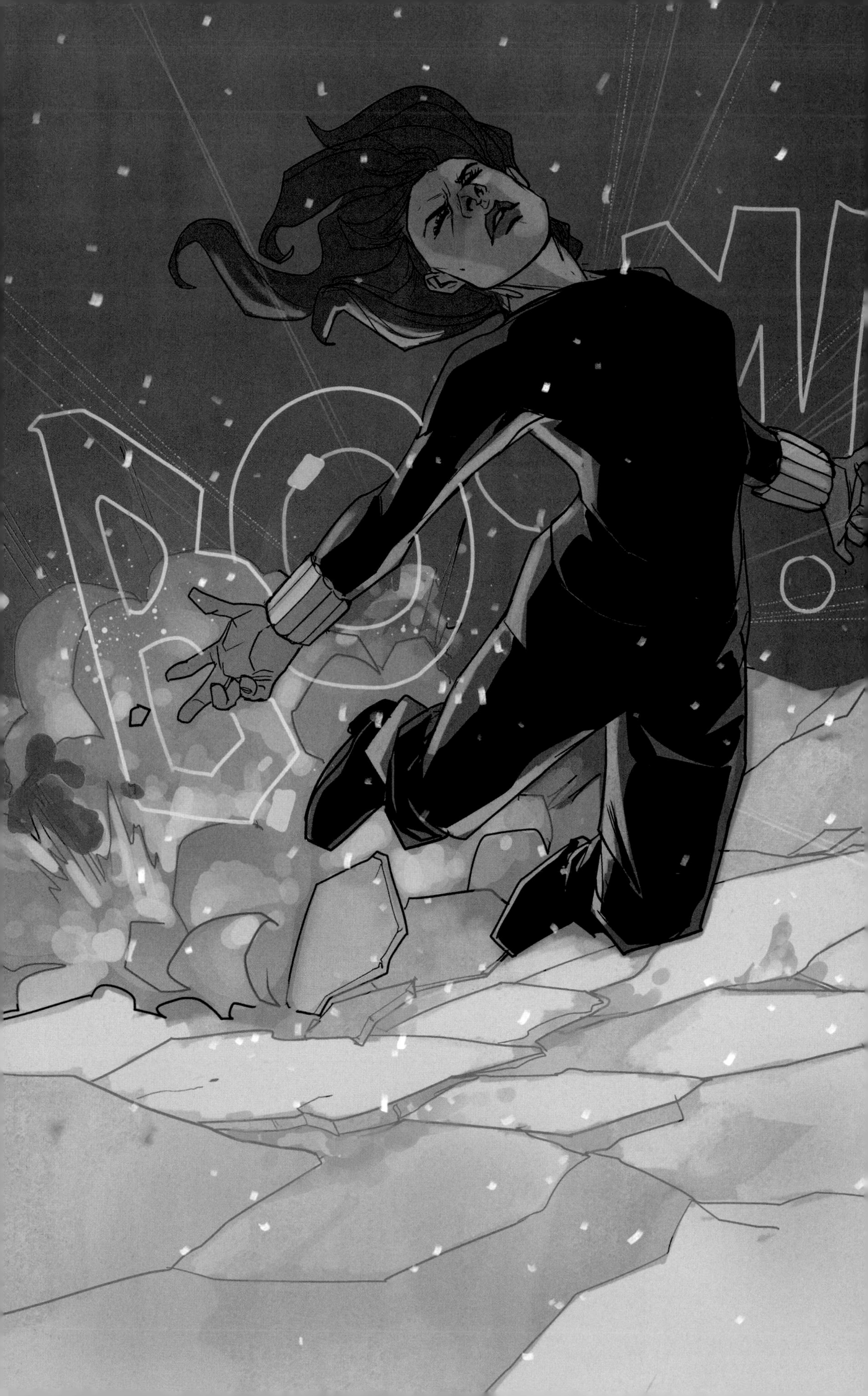

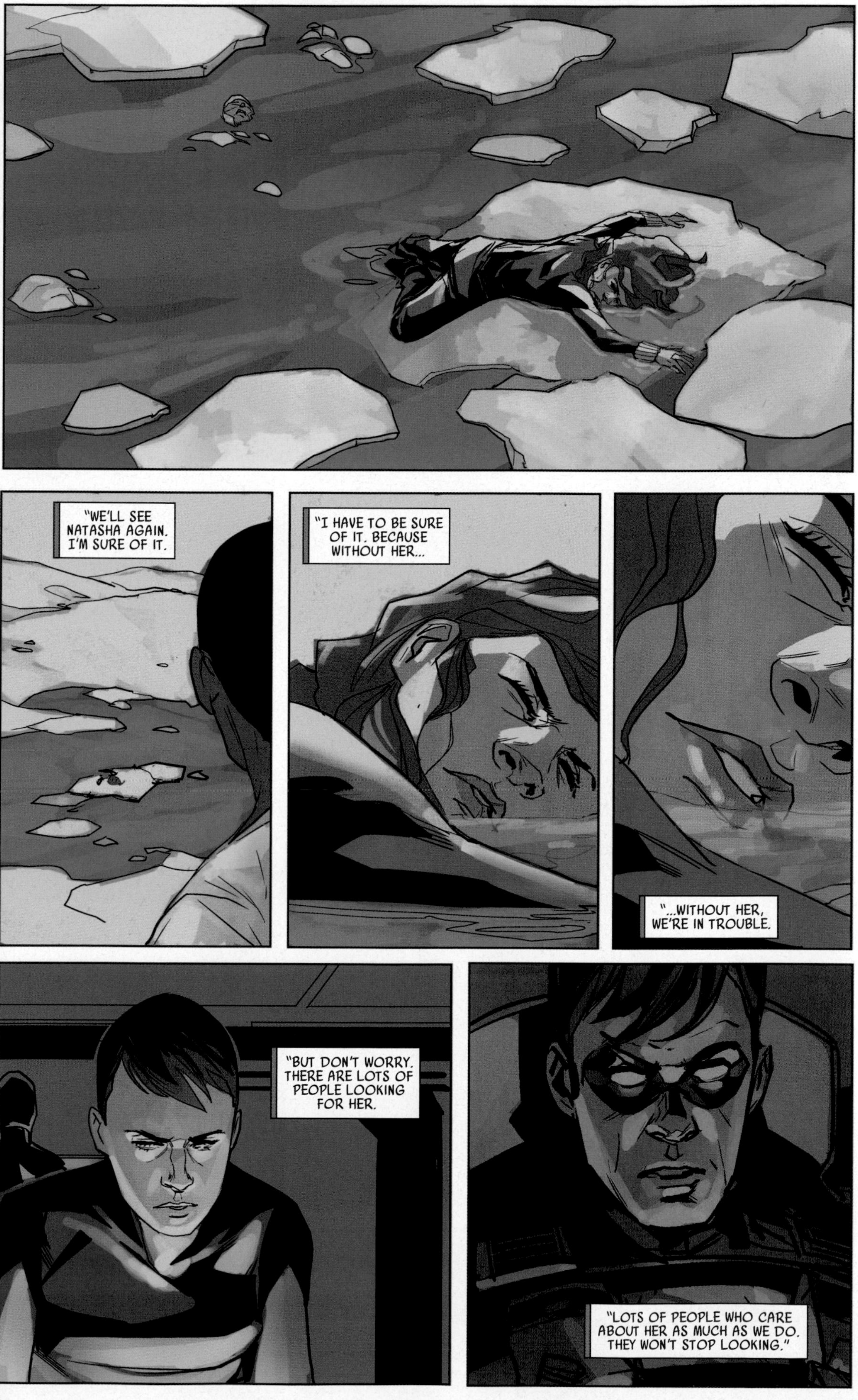
"WE'LL SEE NATASHA AGAIN. I'M SURE OF IT.
"I HAVE TO BE SURE OF IT. BECAUSE WITHOUT HER...
"...WITHOUT HER, WE'RE IN TROUBLE.
"BUT DON'T WORRY. THERE ARE LOTS OF PEOPLE LOOKING FOR HER.
"LOTS OF PEOPLE WHO CARE ABOUT HER AS MUCH AS WE DO. THEY WON'T STOP LOOKING."

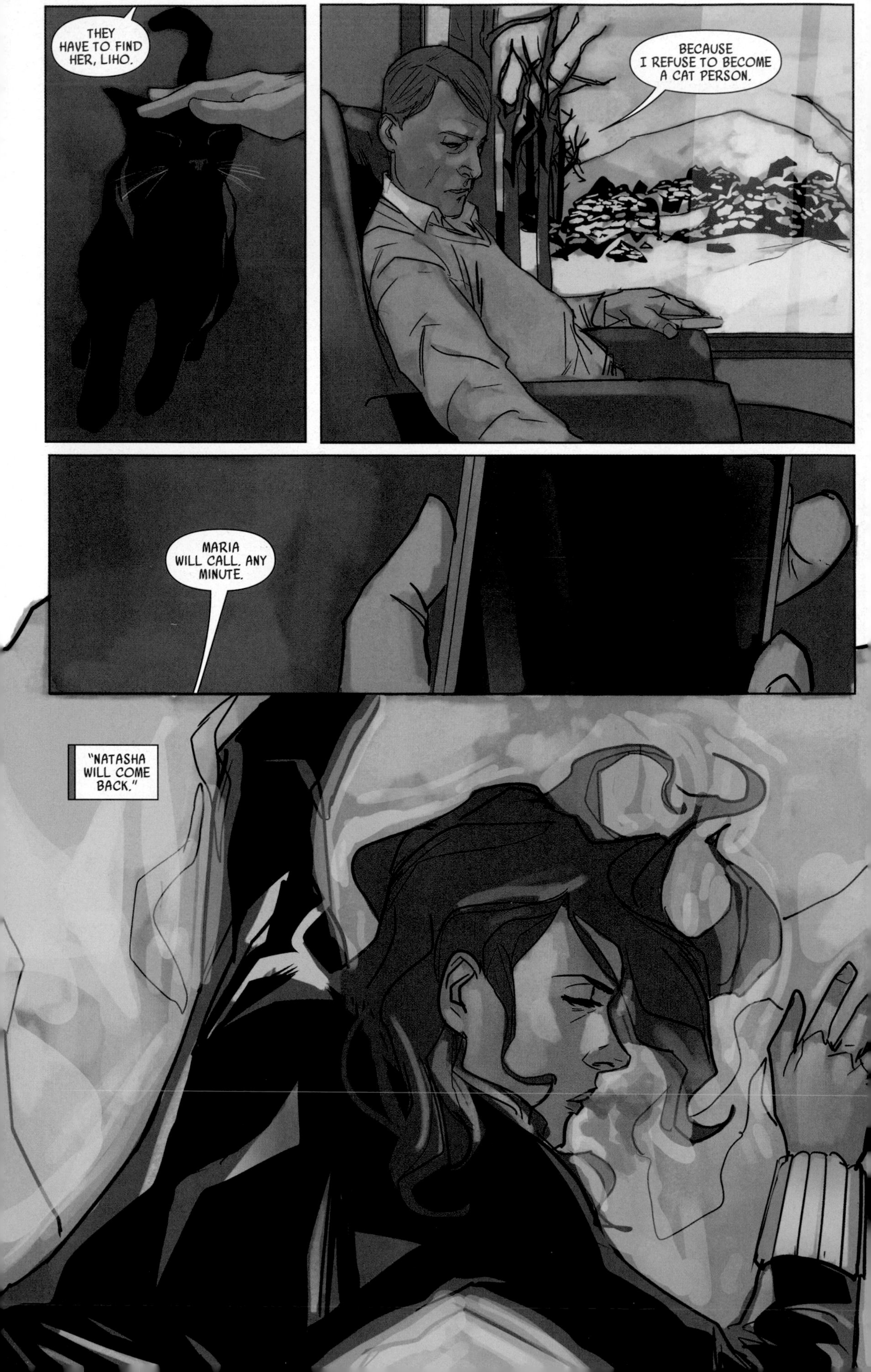
THEY HAVE TO FIND HER, LIHO.
BECAUSE I REFUSE TO BECOME A CAT PERSON.
MARIA WILL CALL. ANY MINUTE.
"NATASHA WILL COME BACK."

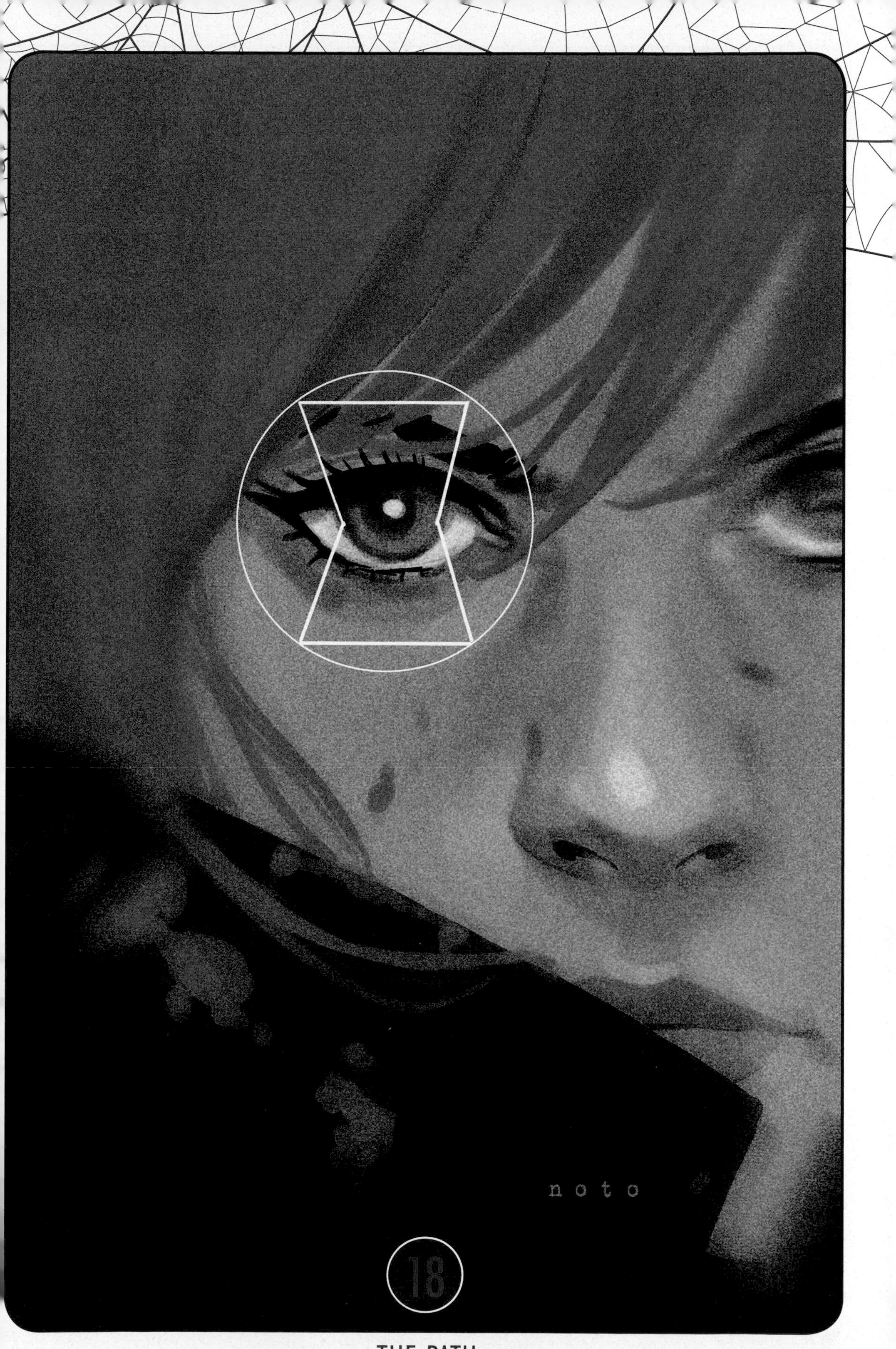
noto
18

THE PATH

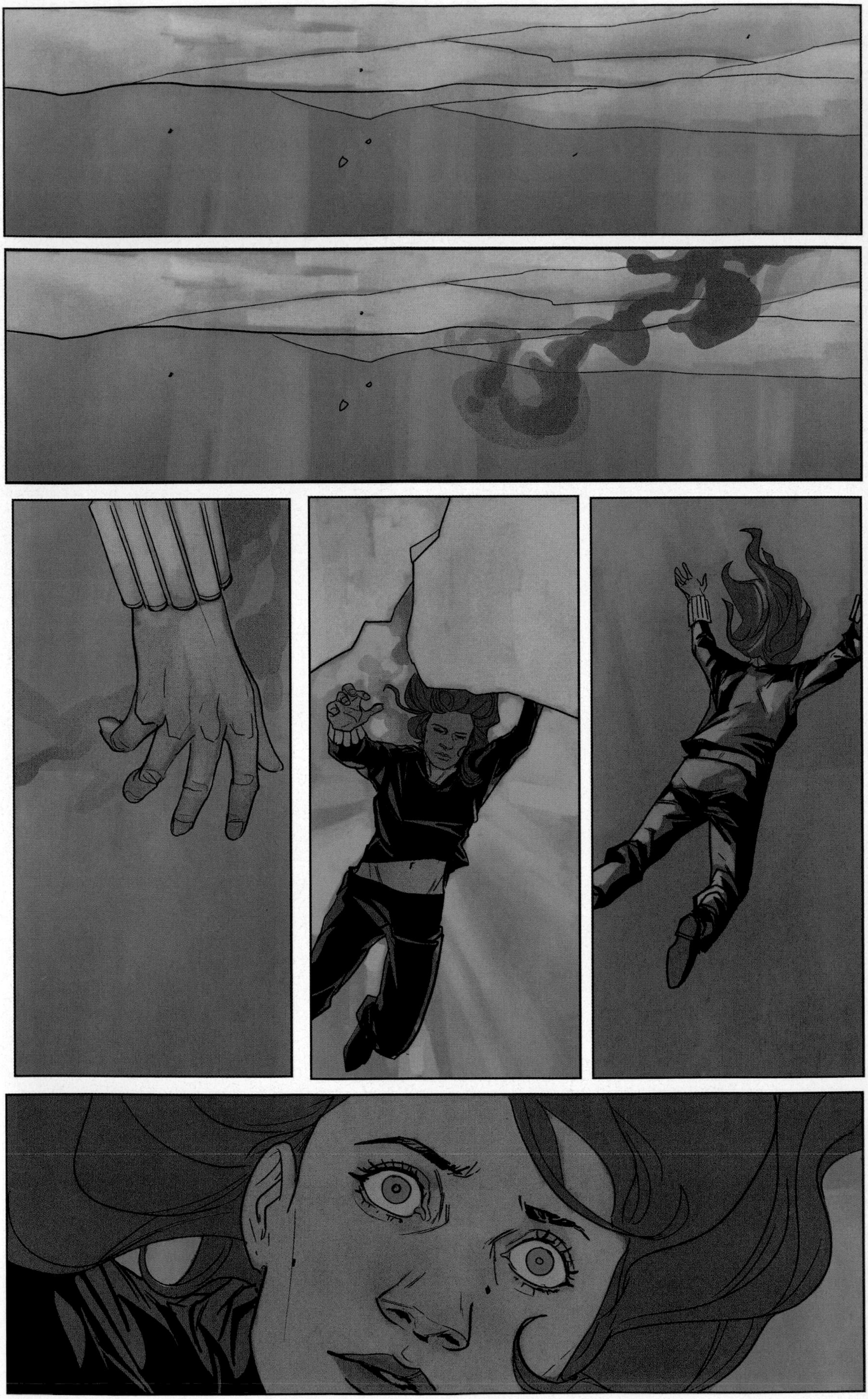

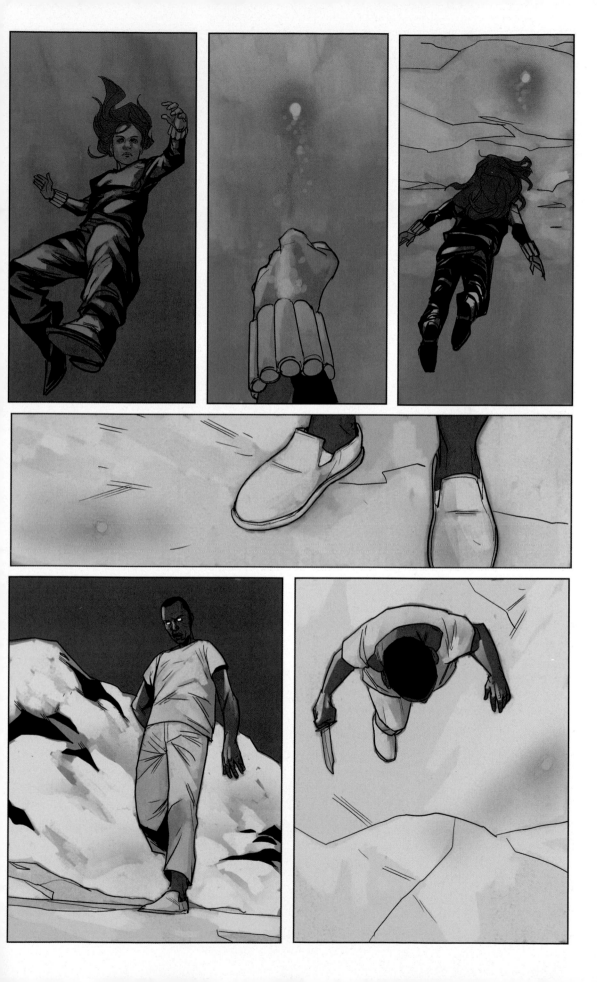

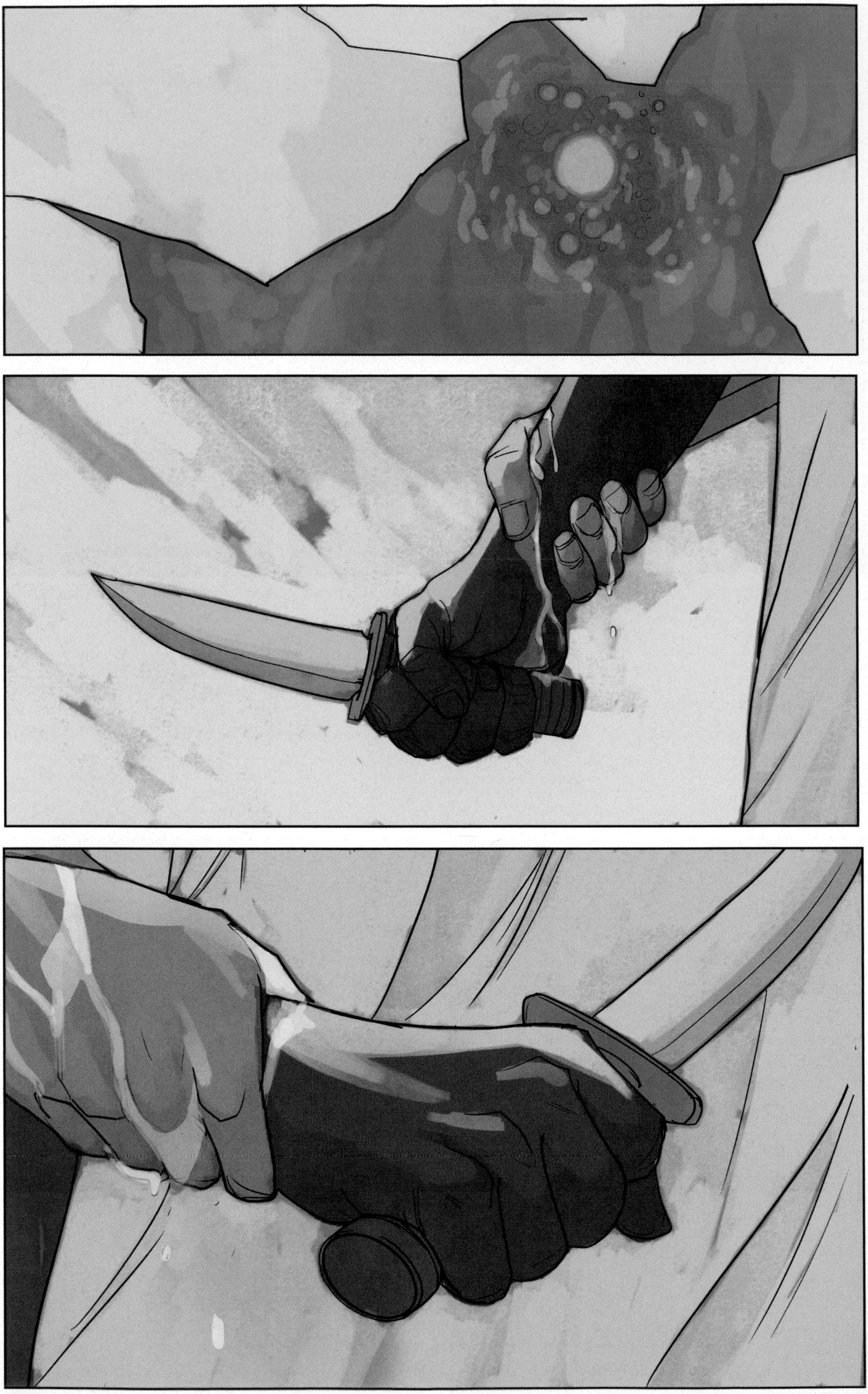

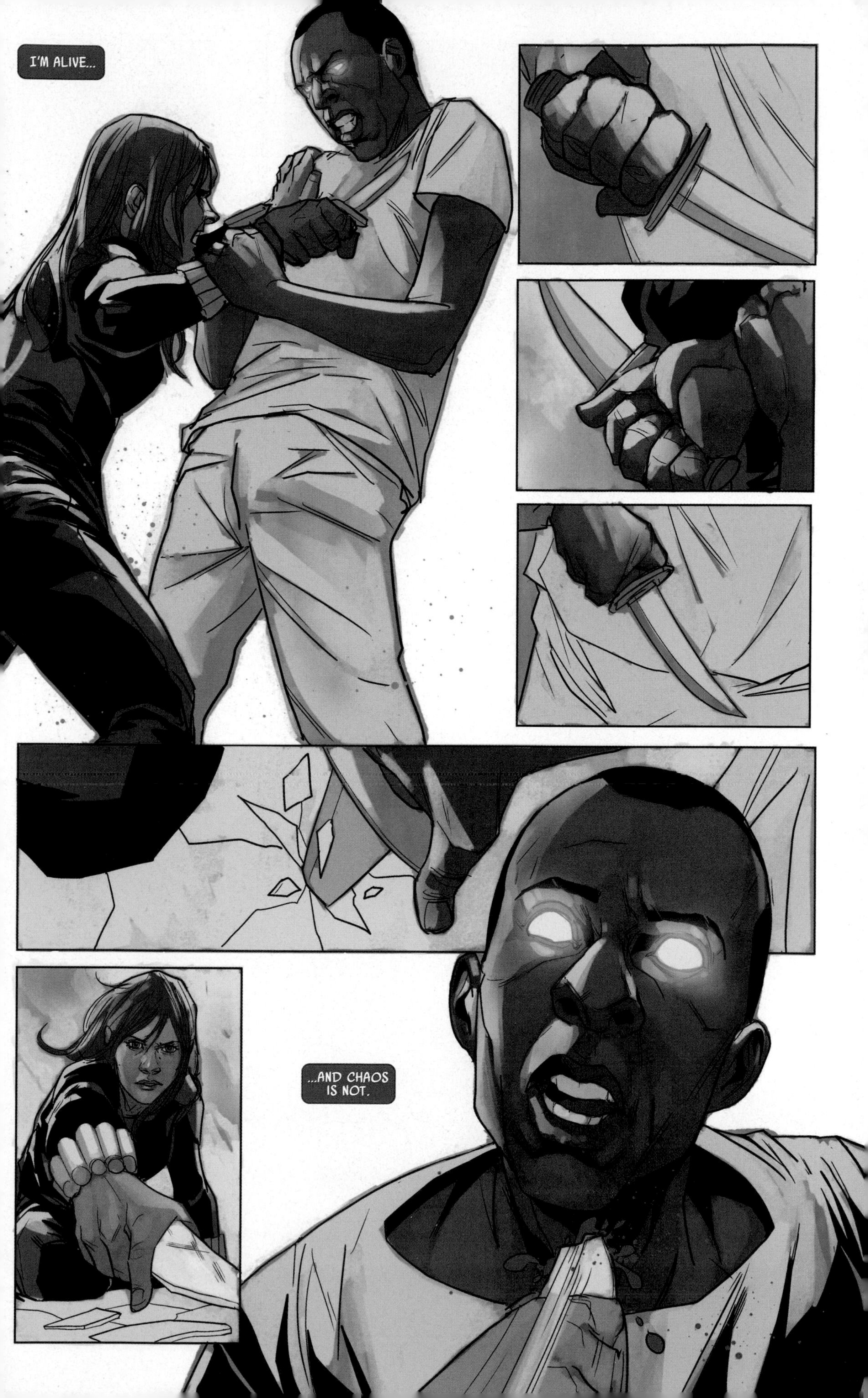
I'M ALIVE...
...AND CHAOS IS NOT.

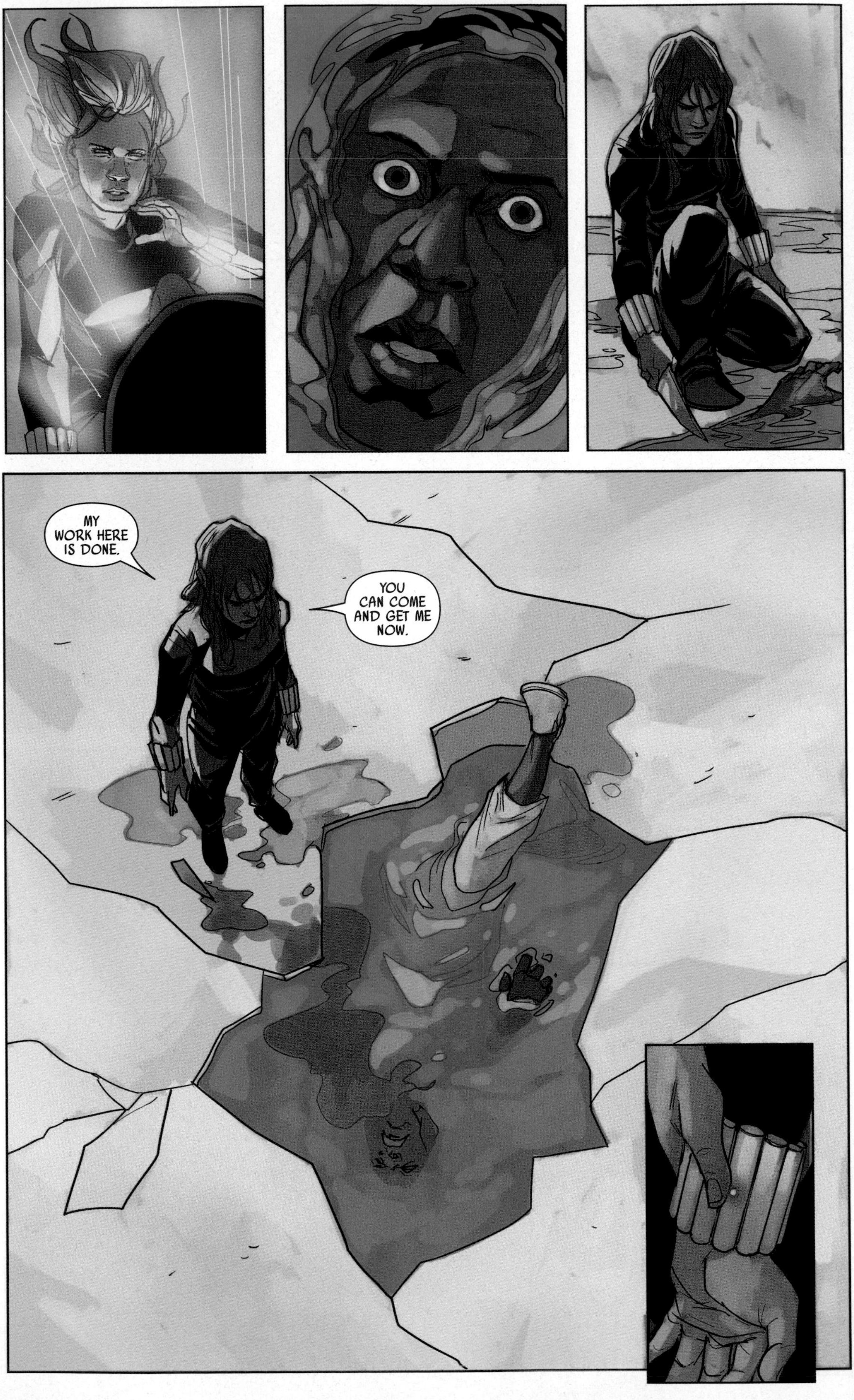

MY WORK HERE IS DONE.
YOU CAN COME AND GET ME NOW.

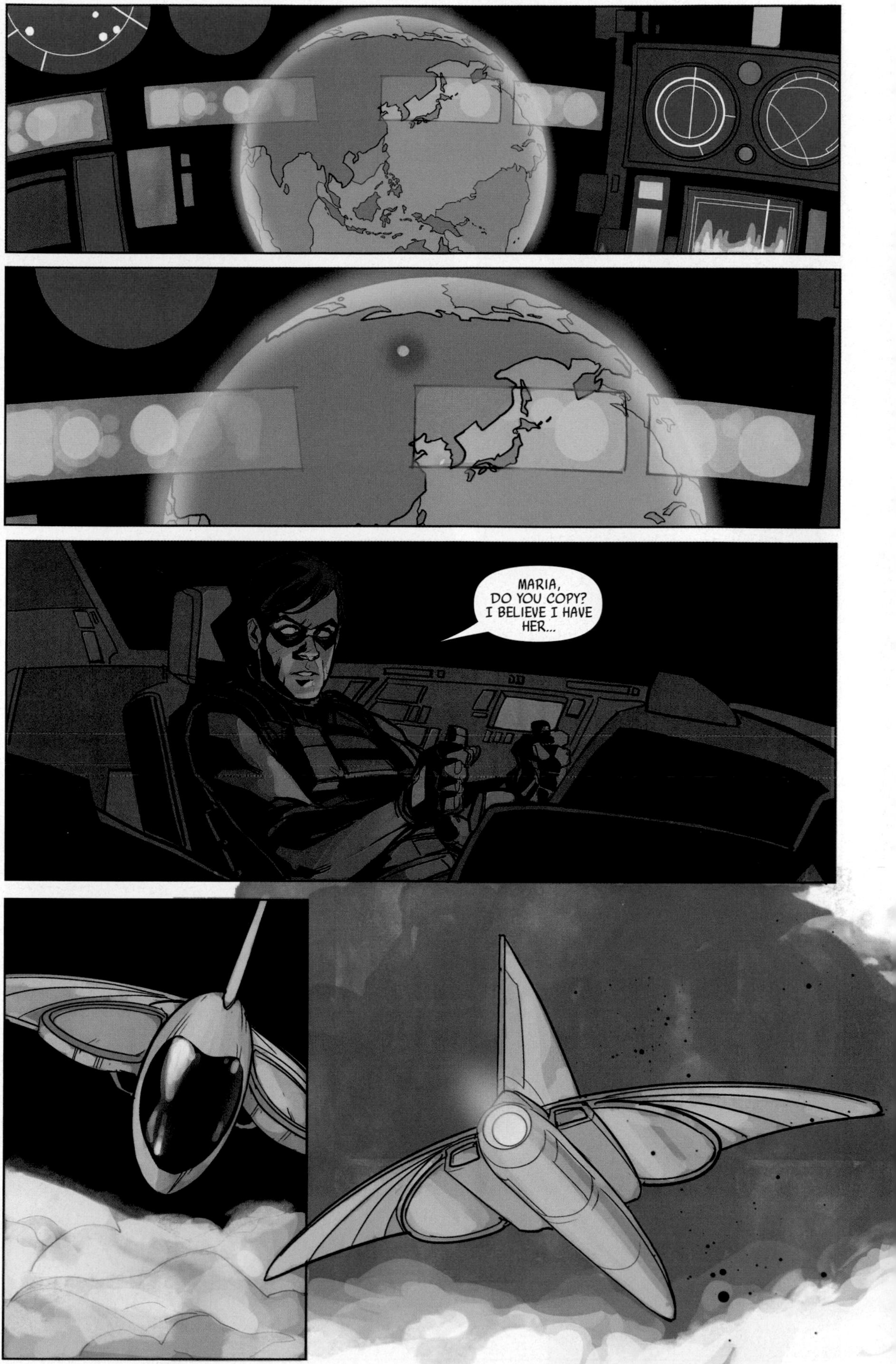
MARIA, DO YOU COPY? I BELIEVE I HAVE HER...

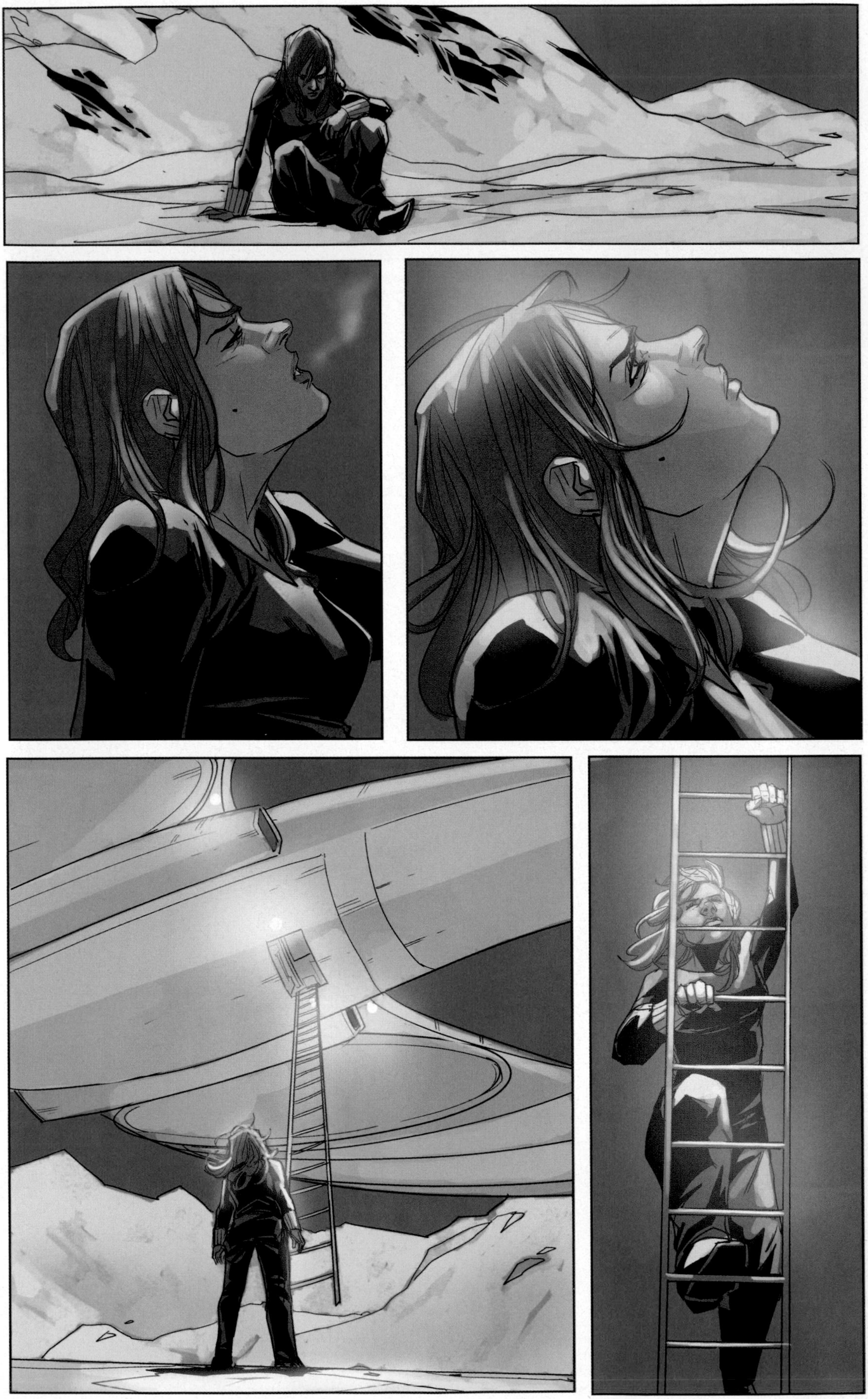

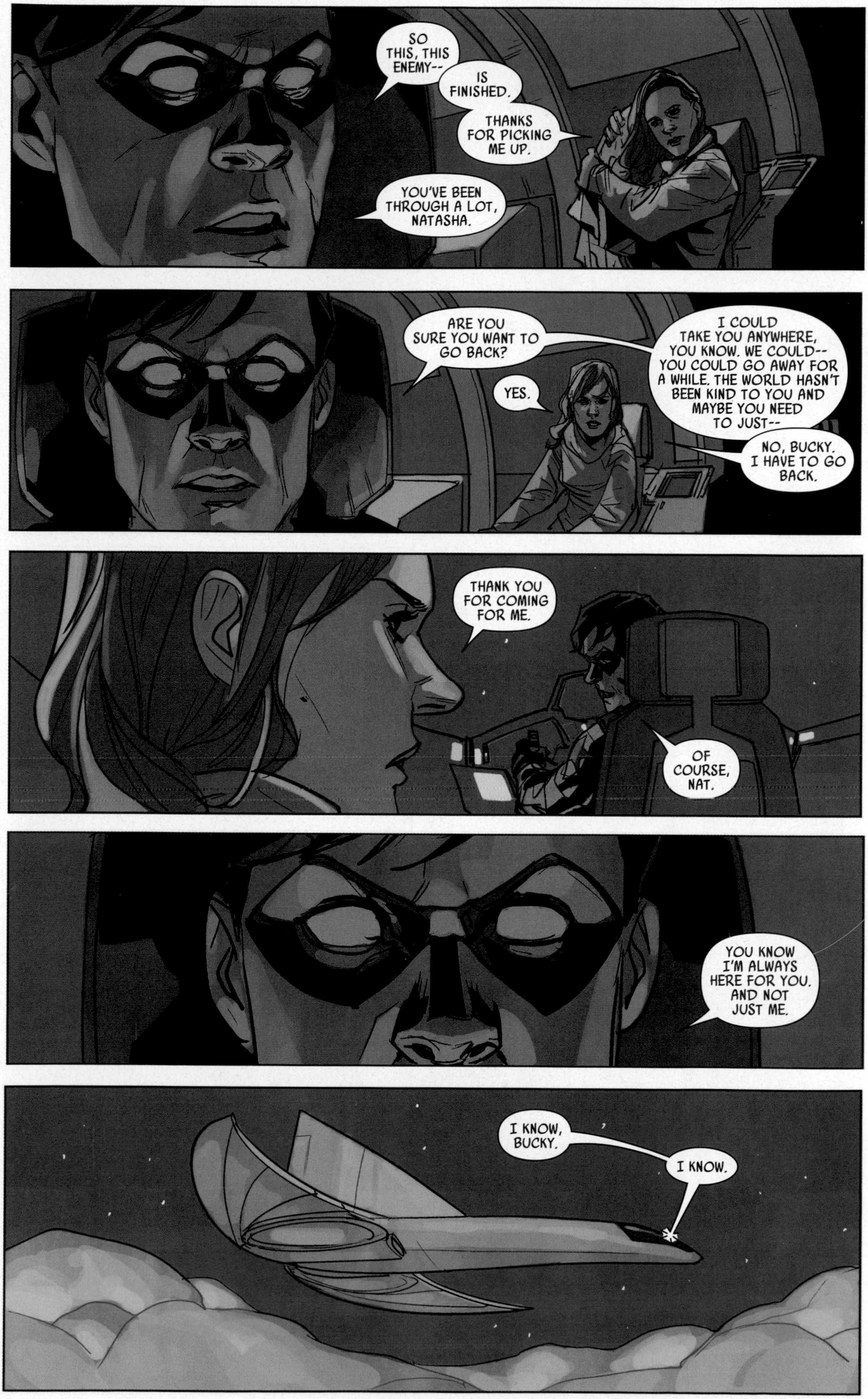
SO THIS, THIS ENEMY--
IS FINISHED.
THANKS FOR PICKING ME UP.
YOU'VE BEEN THROUGH A LOT, NATASHA.
ARE YOU SURE YOU WANT TO GO BACK?
YES.
I COULD TAKE YOU ANYWHERE, YOU KNOW. WE COULD-- YOU COULD GO AWAY FOR A WHILE. THE WORLD HASN'T BEEN KIND TO YOU AND MAYBE YOU NEED TO JUST--
NO, BUCKY. I HAVE TO GO BACK.
THANK YOU FOR COMING FOR ME.
OF COURSE, NAT.
YOU KNOW I'M ALWAYS HERE FOR YOU. AND NOT JUST ME.
I KNOW, BUCKY.
I KNOW.

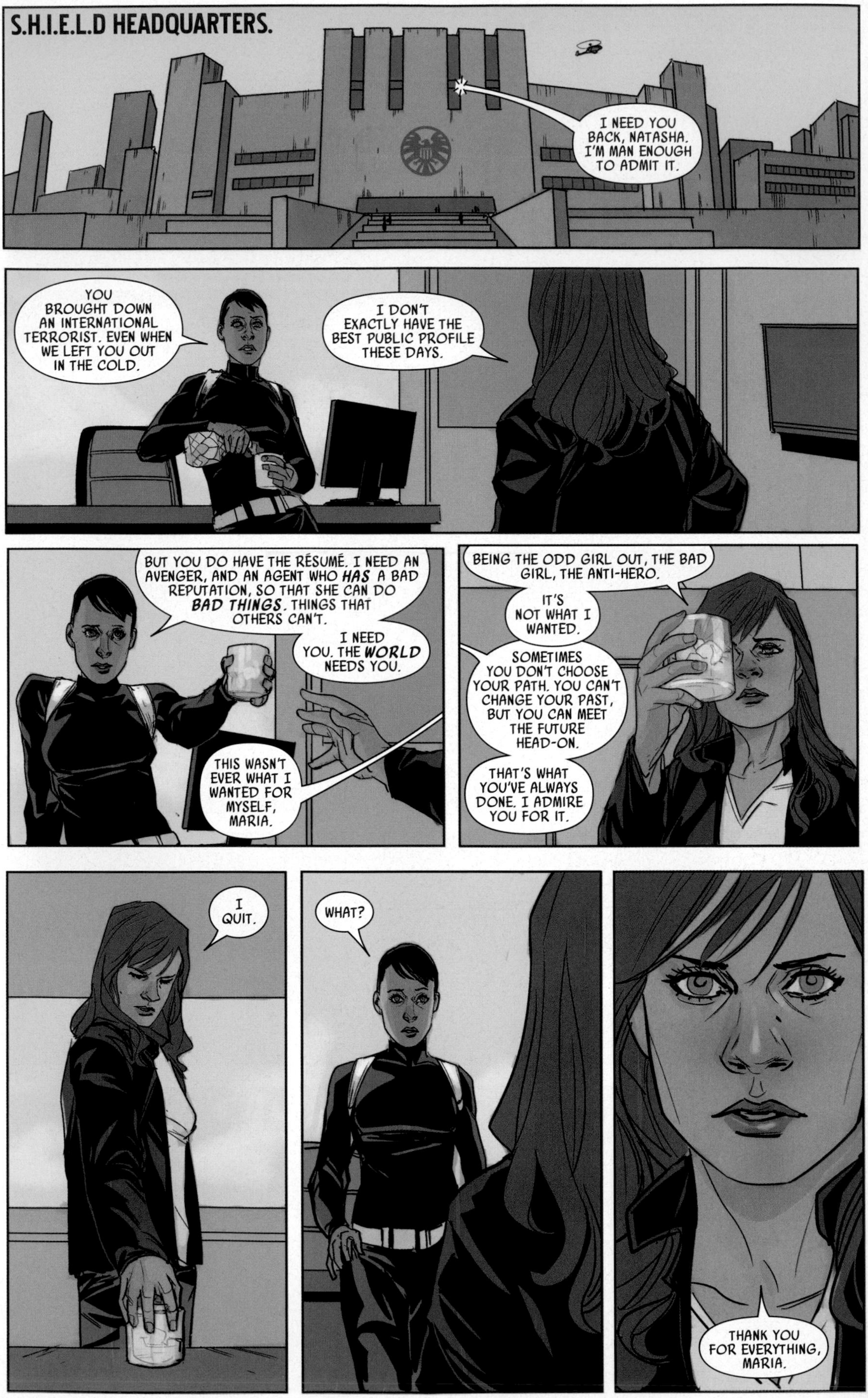
S.H.I.E.L.D HEADQUARTERS.
I NEED YOU BACK, NATASHA. I'M MAN ENOUGH TO ADMIT IT.
YOU BROUGHT DOWN AN INTERNATIONAL TERRORIST. EVEN WHEN WE LEFT YOU OUT IN THE COLD.
I DON'T EXACTLY HAVE THE BEST PUBLIC PROFILE THESE DAYS.
BUT YOU DO HAVE THE RÉSUMÉ. I NEED AN AVENGER, AND AN AGENT WHO HAS A BAD REPUTATION, SO THAT SHE CAN DO BAD THINGS. THINGS THAT OTHERS CAN'T.
I NEED YOU. THE WORLD NEEDS YOU.
THIS WASN'T EVER WHAT I WANTED FOR MYSELF, MARIA.
BEING THE ODD GIRL OUT, THE BAD GIRL, THE ANTI-HERO.
IT'S NOT WHAT I WANTED.
SOMETIMES YOU DON'T CHOOSE YOUR PATH. YOU CAN'T CHANGE YOUR PAST, BUT YOU CAN MEET THE FUTURE HEAD-ON.
THAT'S WHAT YOU'VE ALWAYS DONE. I ADMIRE YOU FOR IT.
I QUIT.
WHAT?
THANK YOU FOR EVERYTHING, MARIA.

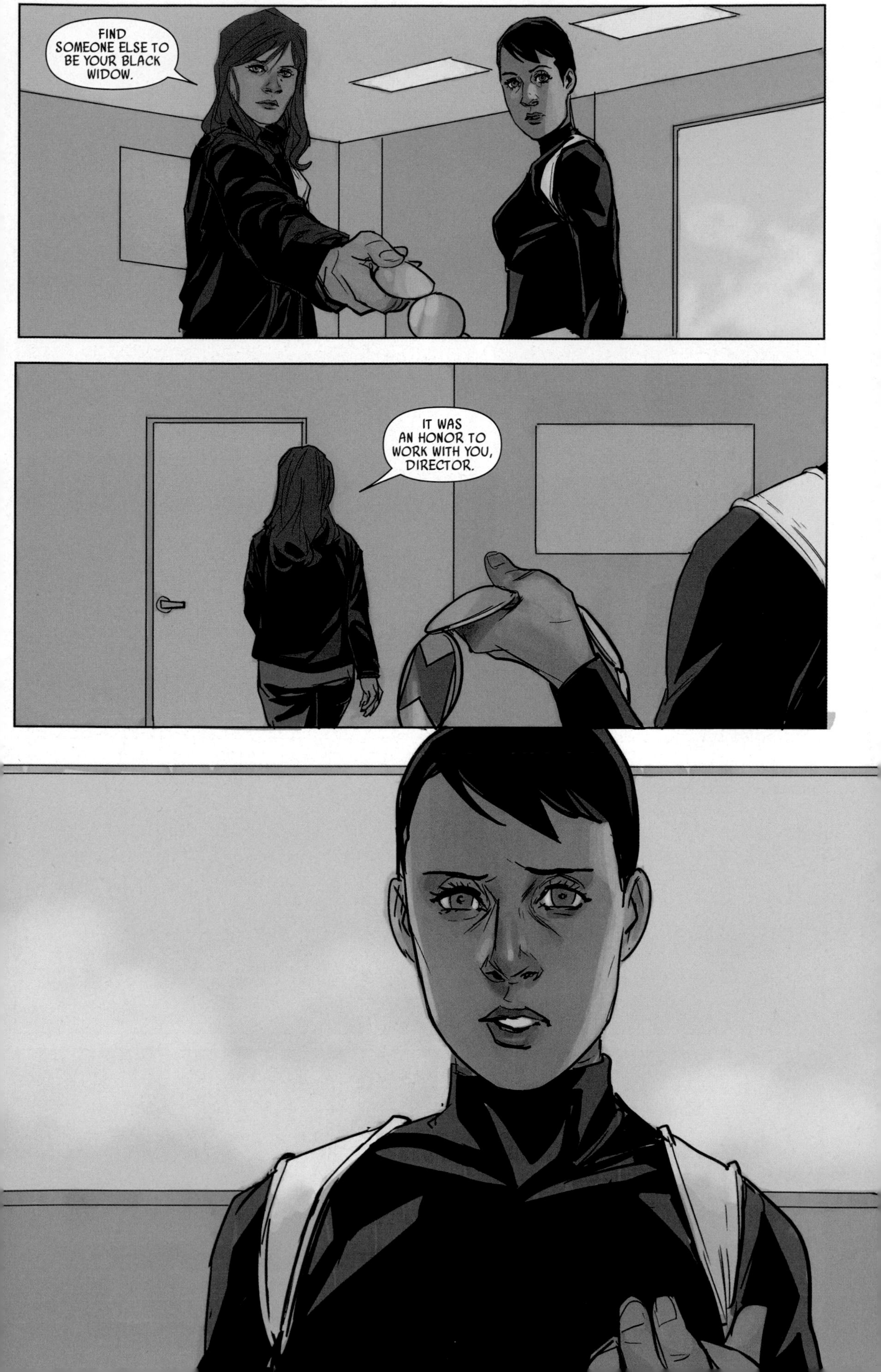
FIND SOMEONE ELSE TO BE YOUR BLACK WIDOW.
IT WAS AN HONOR TO WORK WITH YOU, DIRECTOR.

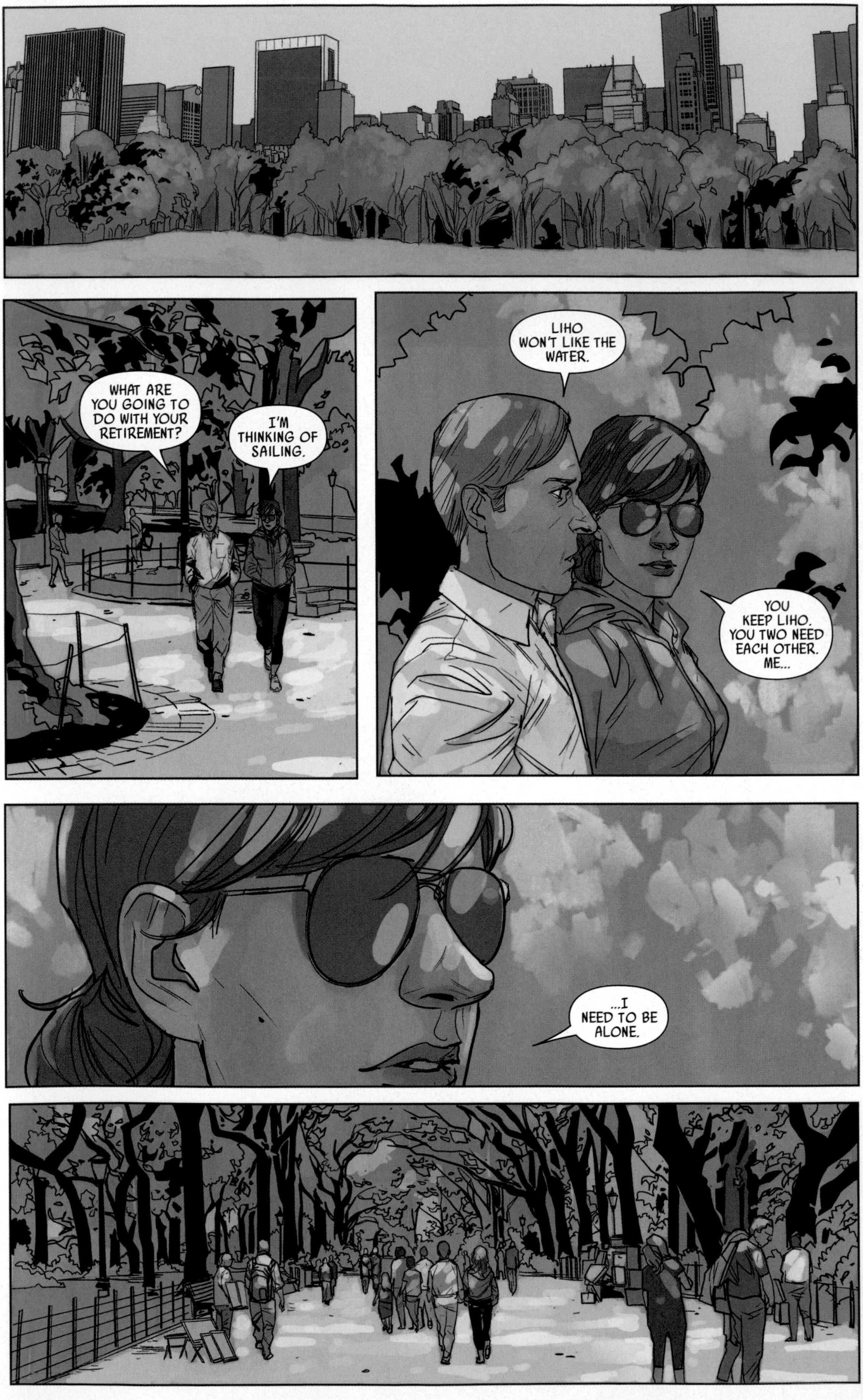
WHAT ARE YOU GOING TO DO WITH YOUR RETIREMENT?
I'M THINKING OF SAILING.
LIHO WON'T LIKE THE WATER.
YOU KEEP LIHO. YOU TWO NEED EACH OTHER. ME...
...I NEED TO BE ALONE.

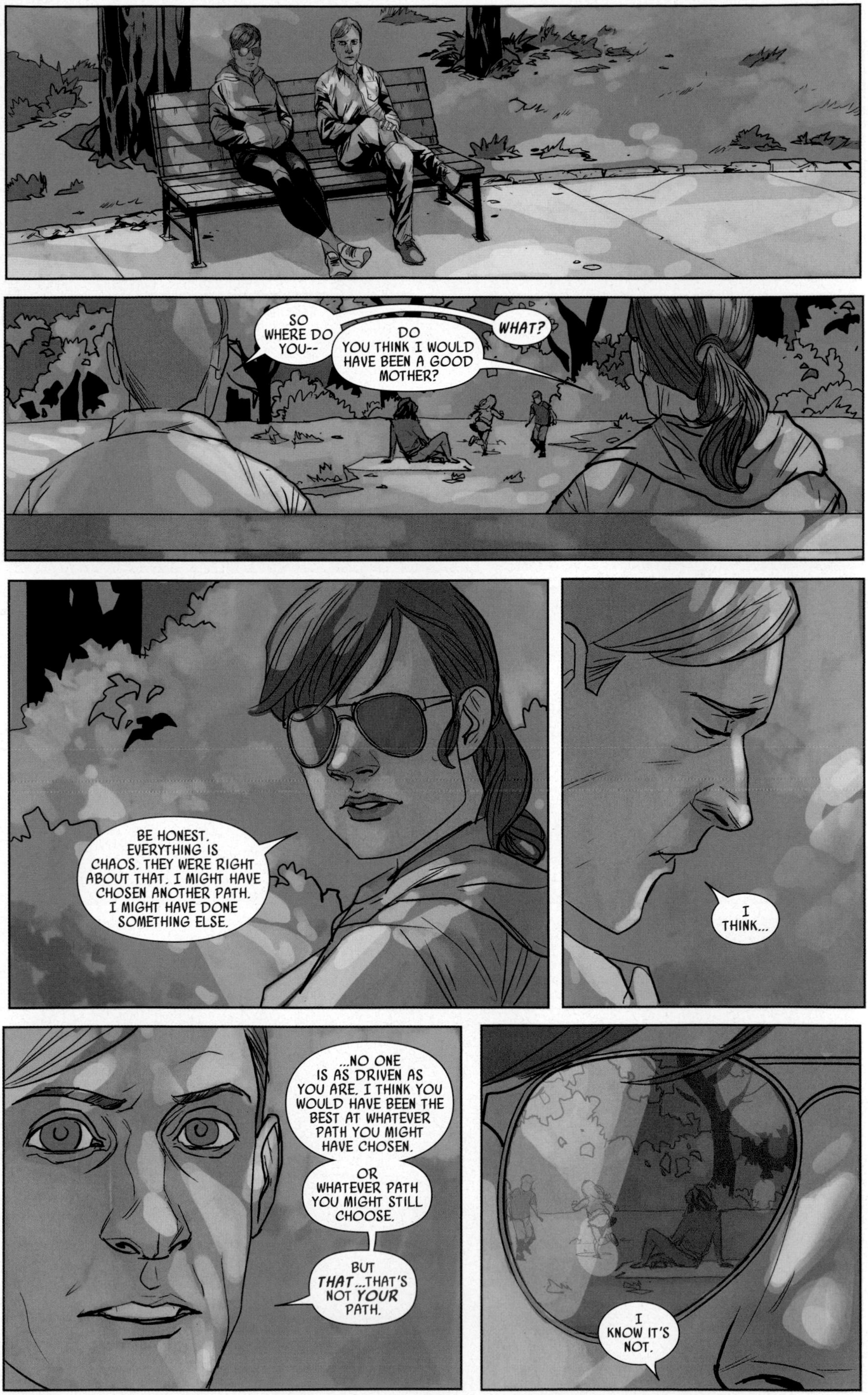

SO WHERE DO YOU--
DO YOU THINK I WOULD HAVE BEEN A GOOD MOTHER?
WHAT?
BE HONEST. EVERYTHING IS CHAOS. THEY WERE RIGHT ABOUT THAT. I MIGHT HAVE CHOSEN ANOTHER PATH. I MIGHT HAVE DONE SOMETHING ELSE.
I THINK...
...NO ONE IS AS DRIVEN AS YOU ARE. I THINK YOU WOULD HAVE BEEN THE BEST AT WHATEVER PATH YOU MIGHT HAVE CHOSEN.
OR WHATEVER PATH YOU MIGHT STILL CHOOSE.
BUT *THAT*...THAT'S NOT *YOUR* PATH.
I KNOW IT'S NOT.

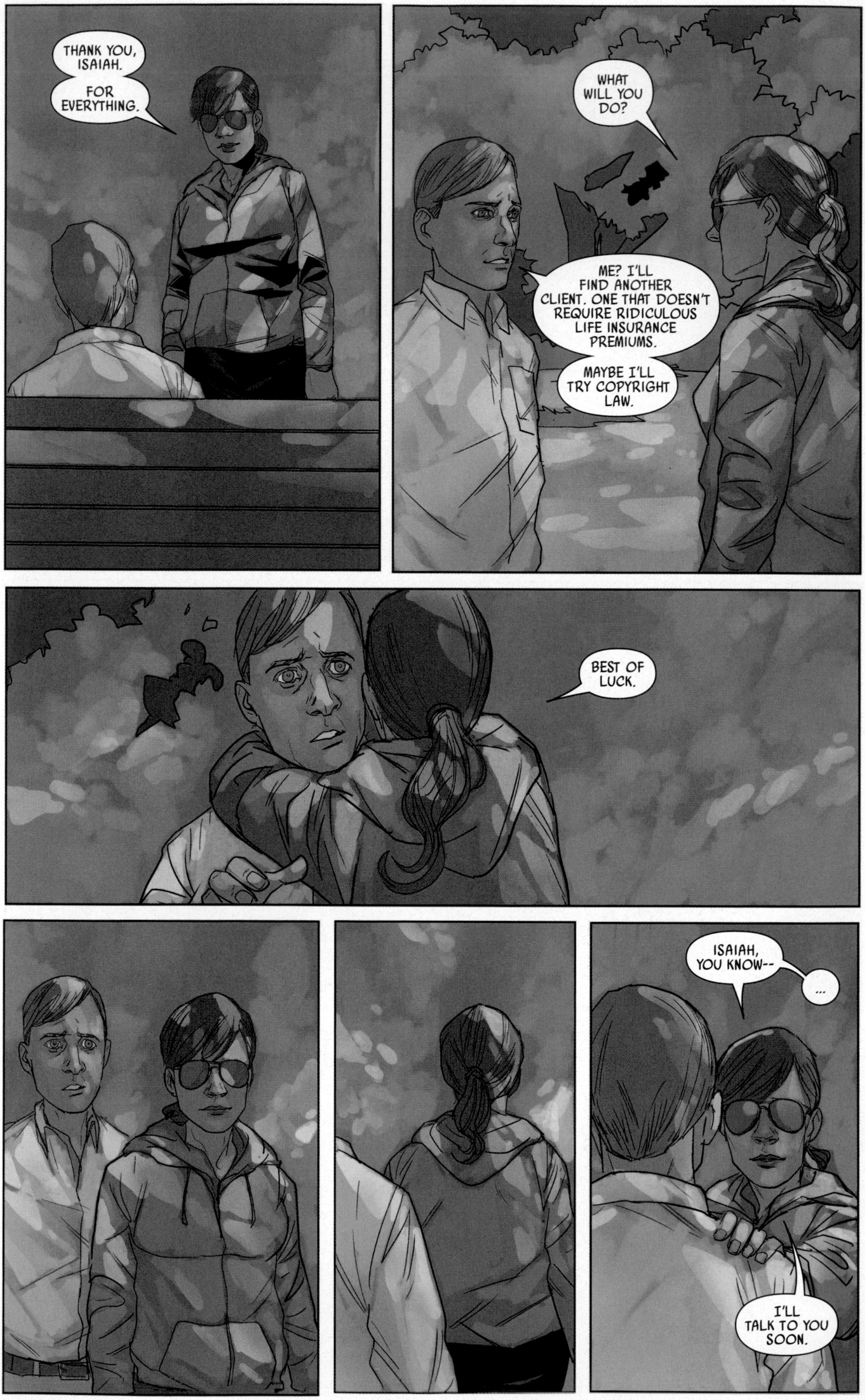
THANK YOU, ISAIAH.
FOR EVERYTHING.
WHAT WILL YOU DO?
ME? I'LL FIND ANOTHER CLIENT. ONE THAT DOESN'T REQUIRE RIDICULOUS LIFE INSURANCE PREMIUMS.
MAYBE I'LL TRY COPYRIGHT LAW.
BEST OF LUCK.
ISAIAH, YOU KNOW--
...
I'LL TALK TO YOU SOON.

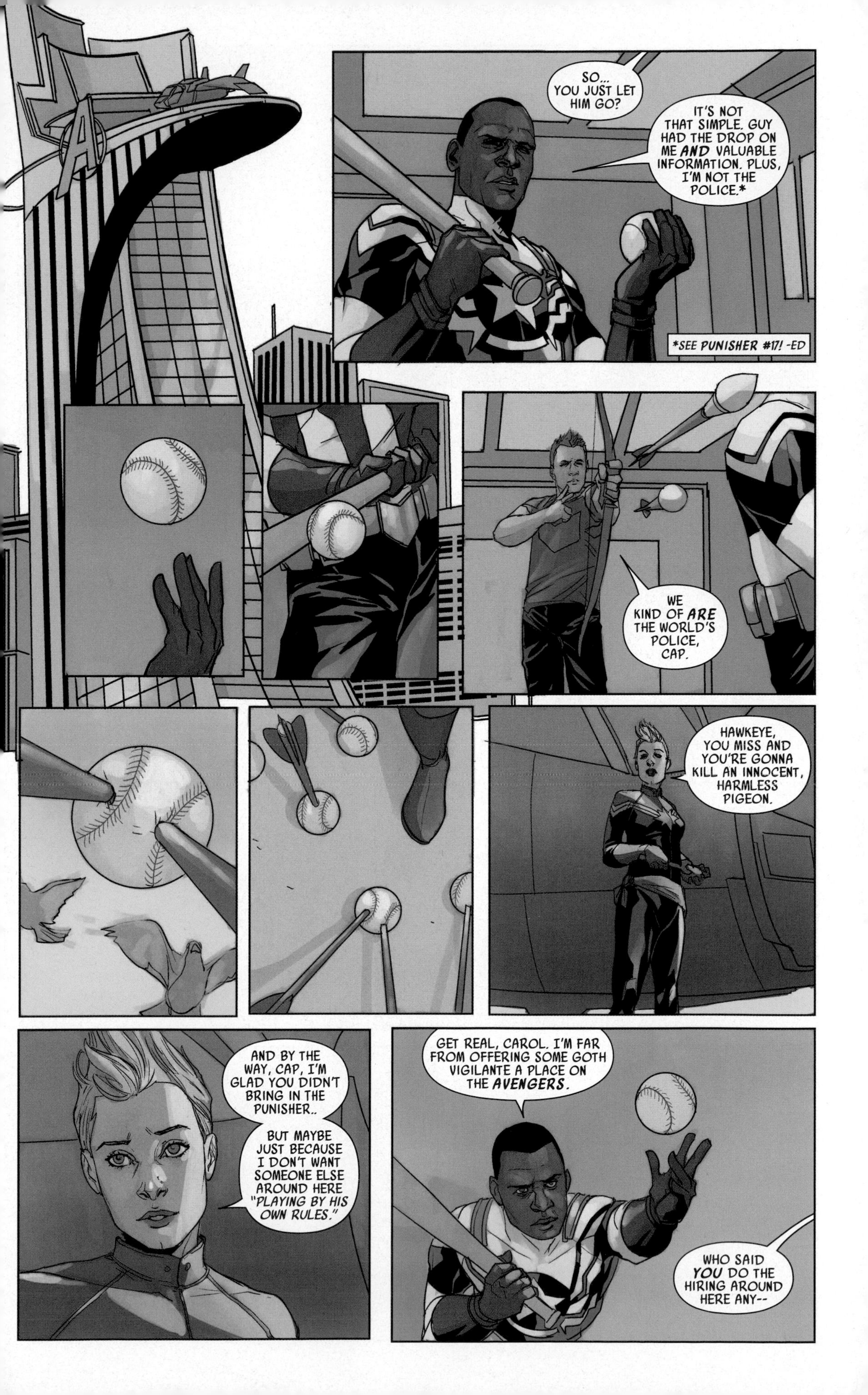
SO... YOU JUST LET HIM GO?
IT'S NOT THAT SIMPLE. GUY HAD THE DROP ON ME AND VALUABLE INFORMATION. PLUS, I'M NOT THE POLICE.*
*SEE PUNISHER #17! -ED
WE KIND OF ARE THE WORLD'S POLICE, CAP.
HAWKEYE, YOU MISS AND YOU'RE GONNA KILL AN INNOCENT, HARMLESS PIGEON.
AND BY THE WAY, CAP, I'M GLAD YOU DIDN'T BRING IN THE PUNISHER..
BUT MAYBE JUST BECAUSE I DON'T WANT SOMEONE ELSE AROUND HERE "PLAYING BY HIS OWN RULES."
GET REAL, CAROL. I'M FAR FROM OFFERING SOME GOTH VIGILANTE A PLACE ON THE AVENGERS.
WHO SAID YOU DO THE HIRING AROUND HERE ANY--

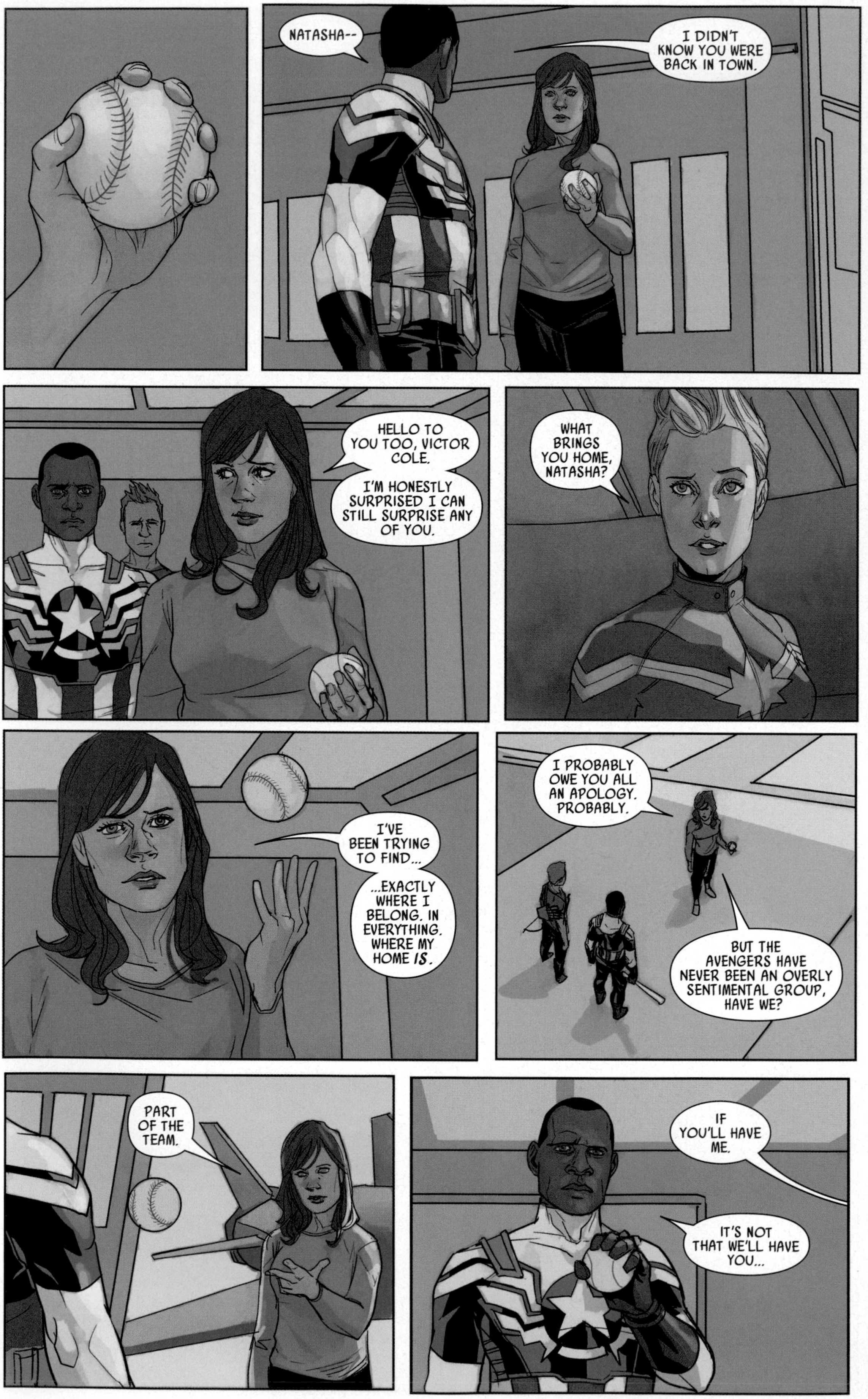
NATASHA--
I DIDN'T KNOW YOU WERE BACK IN TOWN.
HELLO TO YOU TOO, VICTOR COLE.
I'M HONESTLY SURPRISED I CAN STILL SURPRISE ANY OF YOU.
WHAT BRINGS YOU HOME, NATASHA?
I'VE BEEN TRYING TO FIND...
...EXACTLY WHERE I BELONG. IN EVERYTHING. WHERE MY HOME *IS*.
I PROBABLY OWE YOU ALL AN APOLOGY. PROBABLY.
BUT THE AVENGERS HAVE NEVER BEEN AN OVERLY SENTIMENTAL GROUP, HAVE WE?
PART OF THE TEAM.
IF YOU'LL HAVE ME.
IT'S NOT THAT WE'LL HAVE YOU...

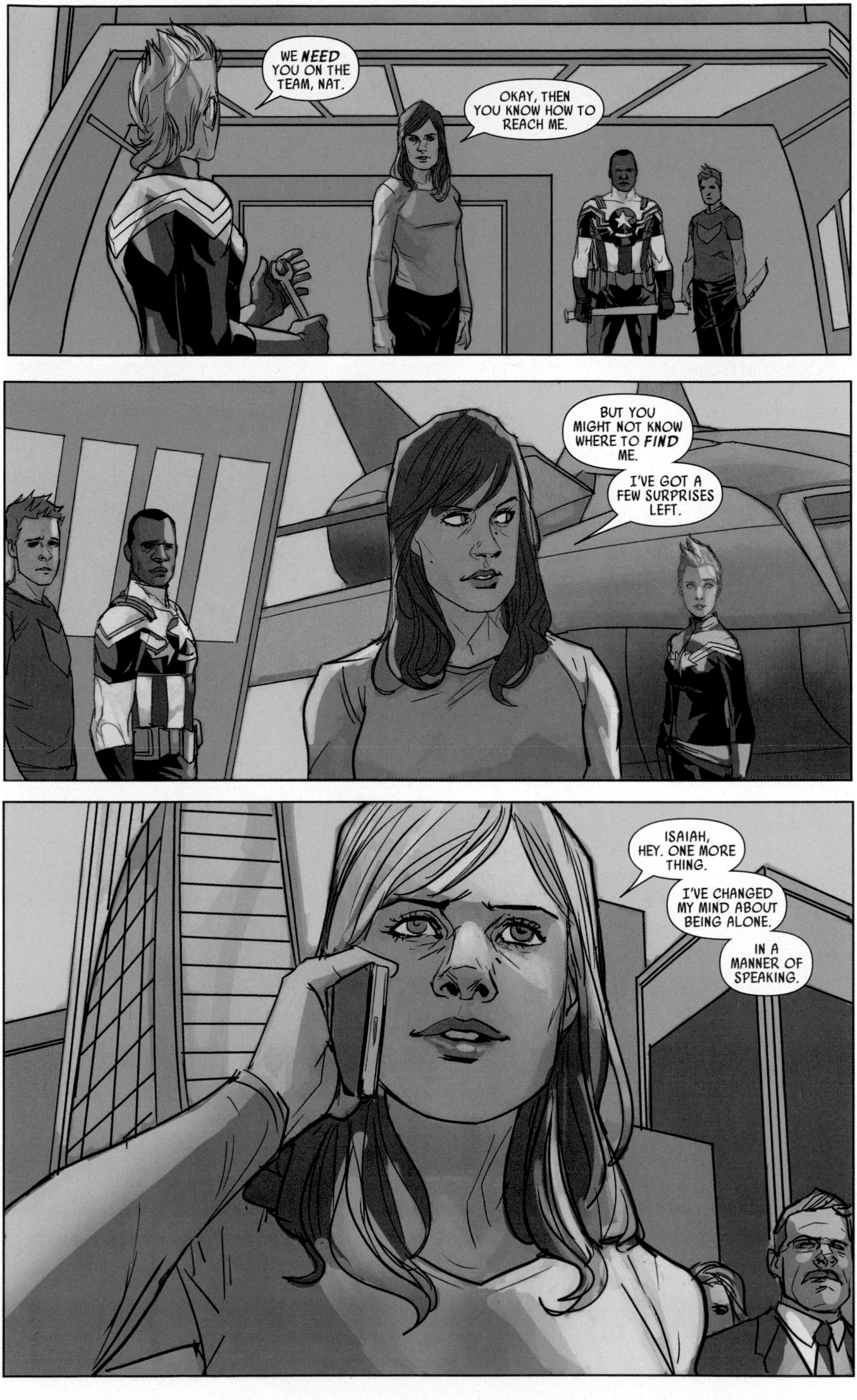
WE NEED YOU ON THE TEAM, NAT.
OKAY, THEN YOU KNOW HOW TO REACH ME.
BUT YOU MIGHT NOT KNOW WHERE TO FIND ME.
I'VE GOT A FEW SURPRISES LEFT.
ISAIAH, HEY. ONE MORE THING.
I'VE CHANGED MY MIND ABOUT BEING ALONE.
IN A MANNER OF SPEAKING.

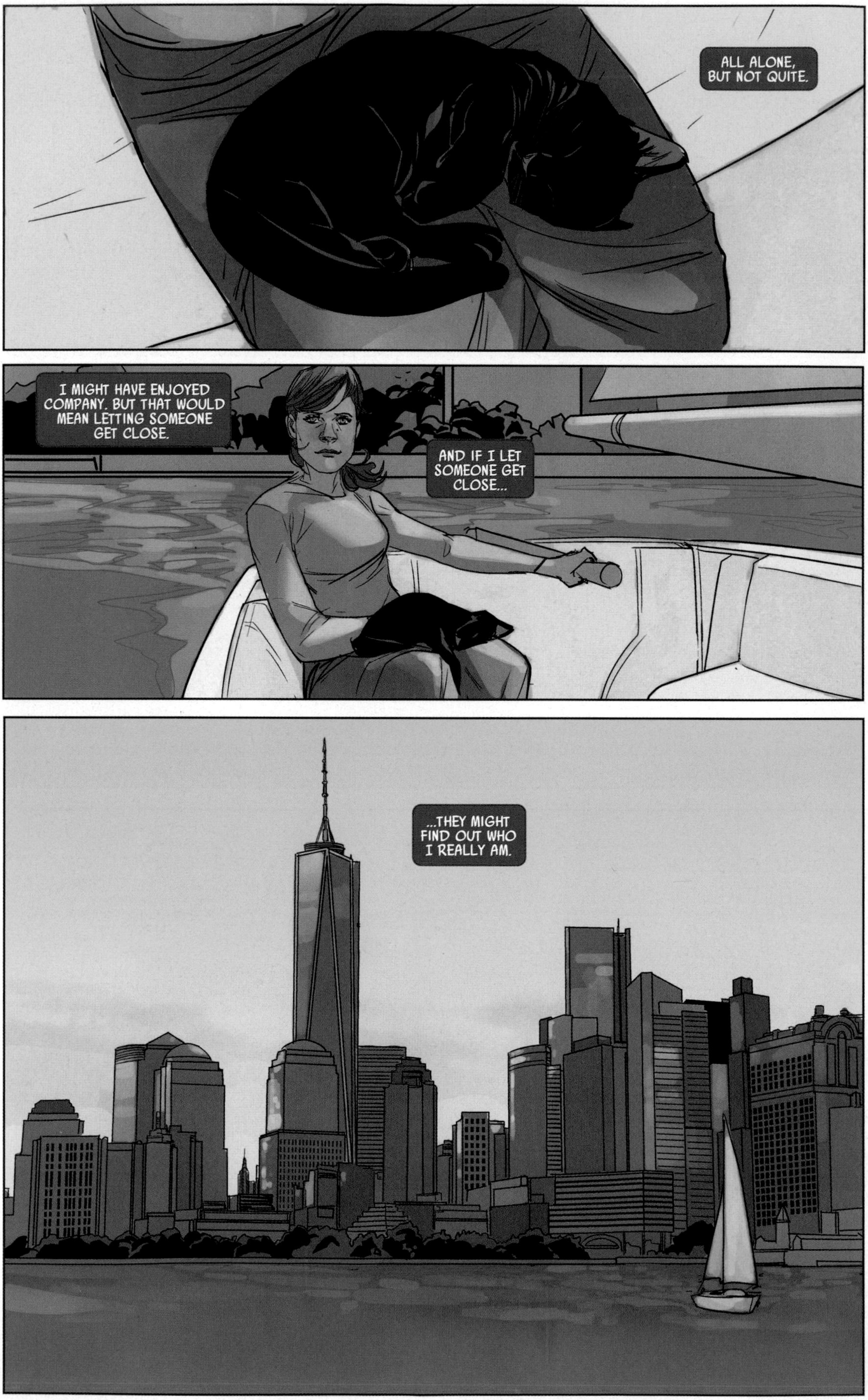
ALL ALONE, BUT NOT QUITE.
I MIGHT HAVE ENJOYED COMPANY. BUT THAT WOULD MEAN LETTING SOMEONE GET CLOSE.
AND IF I LET SOMEONE GET CLOSE...
...THEY MIGHT FIND OUT WHO I REALLY AM.

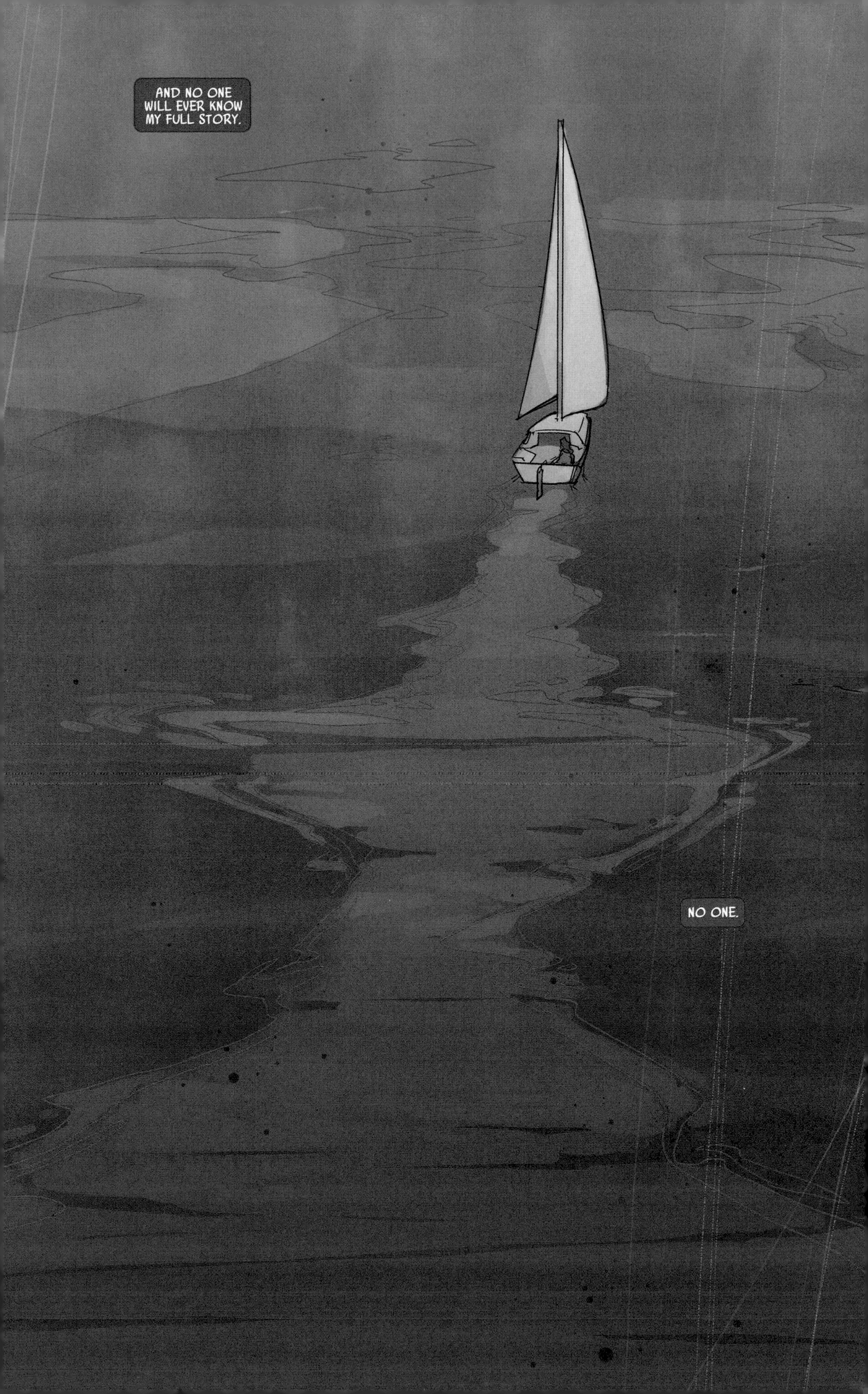
AND NO ONE WILL EVER KNOW MY FULL STORY.
NO ONE.

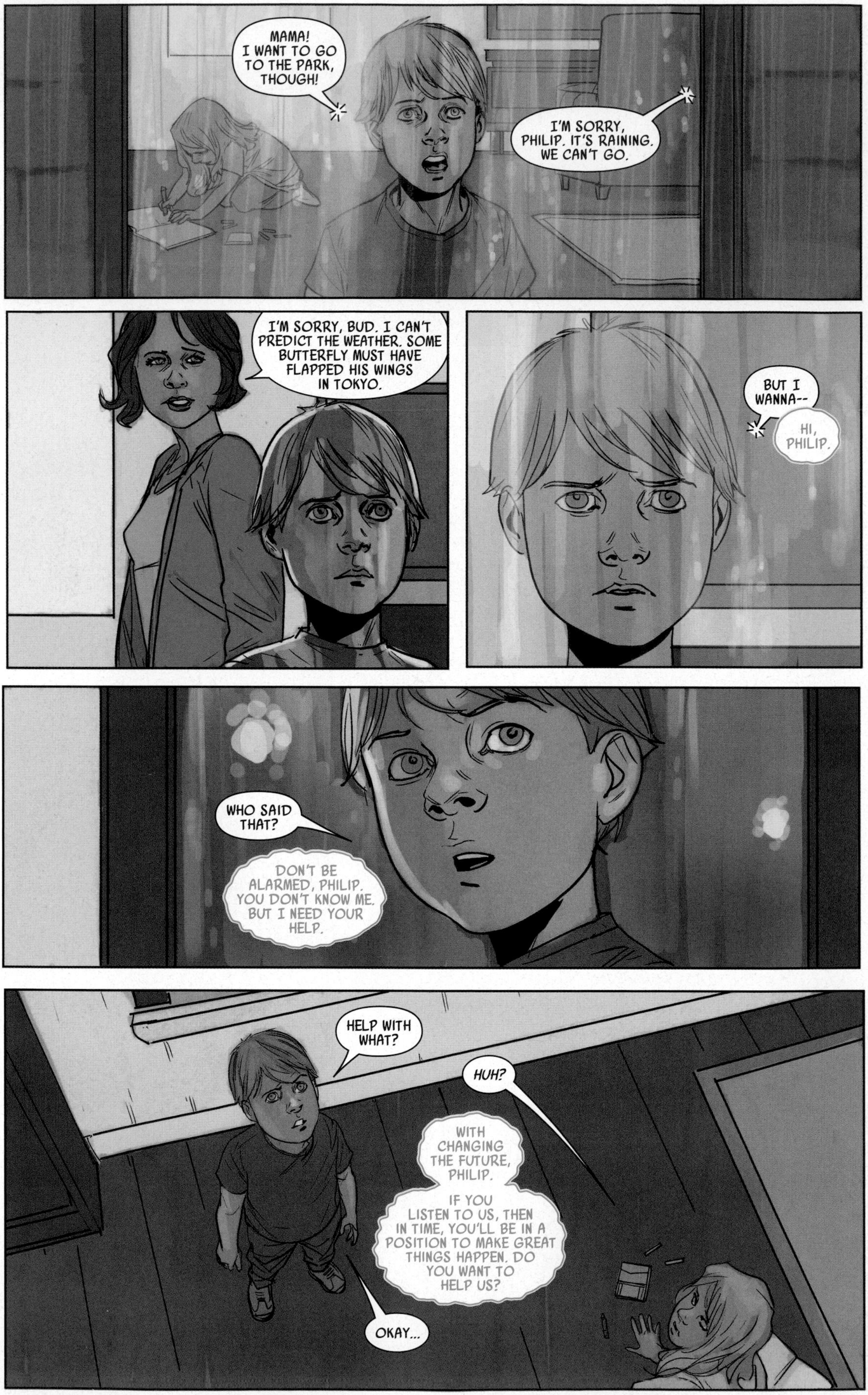
MAMA! I WANT TO GO TO THE PARK, THOUGH!
I'M SORRY, PHILIP. IT'S RAINING. WE CAN'T GO.
I'M SORRY, BUD. I CAN'T PREDICT THE WEATHER. SOME BUTTERFLY MUST HAVE FLAPPED HIS WINGS IN TOKYO.
BUT I WANNA--
HI, PHILIP.
WHO SAID THAT?
DON'T BE ALARMED, PHILIP. YOU DON'T KNOW ME. BUT I NEED YOUR HELP.
HELP WITH WHAT?
HUH?
WITH CHANGING THE FUTURE, PHILIP.
IF YOU LISTEN TO US, THEN IN TIME, YOU'LL BE IN A POSITION TO MAKE GREAT THINGS HAPPEN. DO YOU WANT TO HELP US?
OKAY...

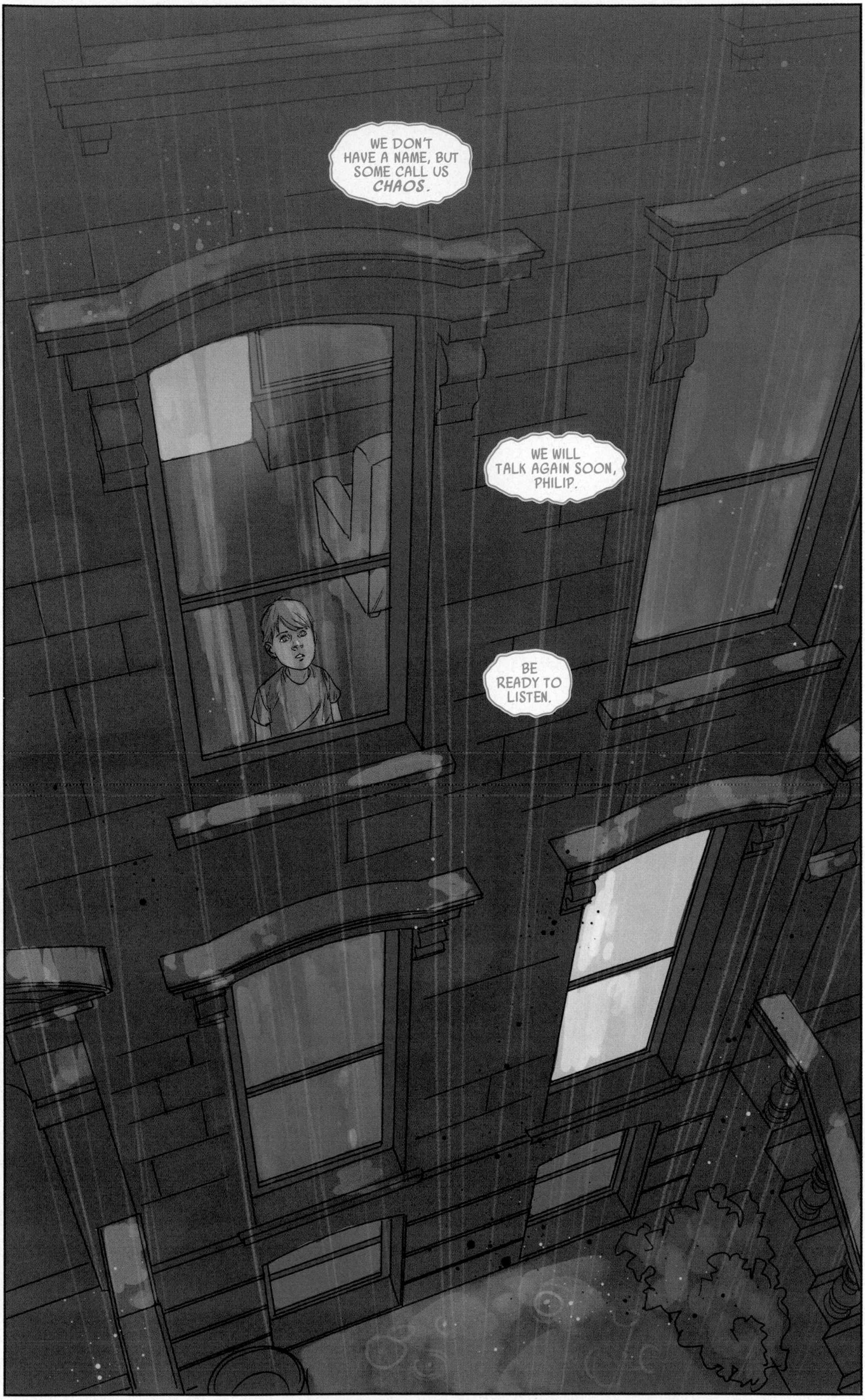
WE DON'T HAVE A NAME, BUT SOME CALL US *CHAOS*.
WE WILL TALK AGAIN SOON, PHILIP.
BE READY TO LISTEN.

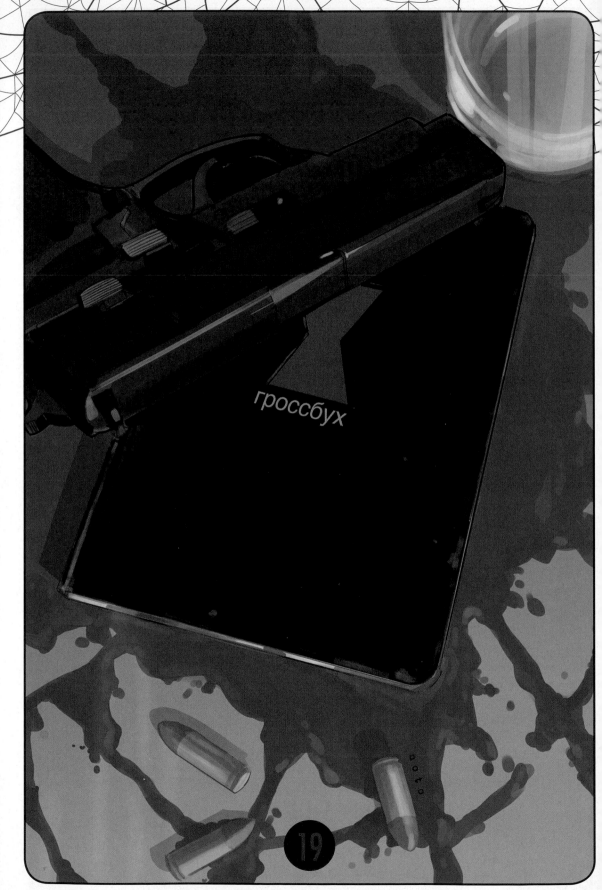

гроссбух

19

JANUARY: PART ONE

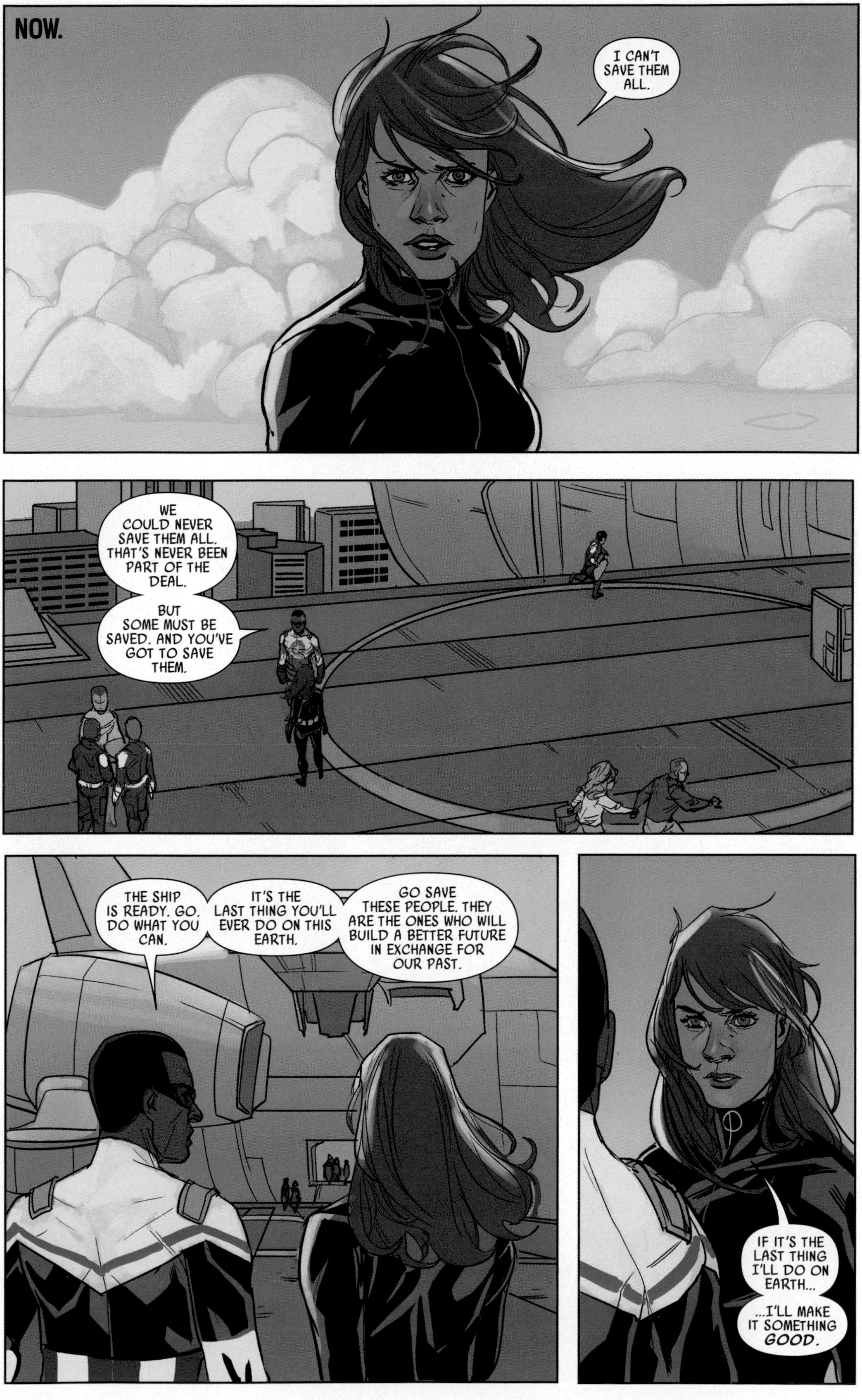
NOW.
I CAN'T SAVE THEM ALL.
WE COULD NEVER SAVE THEM ALL. THAT'S NEVER BEEN PART OF THE DEAL.
BUT SOME MUST BE SAVED. AND YOU'VE GOT TO SAVE THEM.
THE SHIP IS READY. GO. DO WHAT YOU CAN.
IT'S THE LAST THING YOU'LL EVER DO ON THIS EARTH.
GO SAVE THESE PEOPLE. THEY ARE THE ONES WHO WILL BUILD A BETTER FUTURE IN EXCHANGE FOR OUR PAST.
IF IT'S THE LAST THING I'LL DO ON EARTH...
...I'LL MAKE IT SOMETHING GOOD.

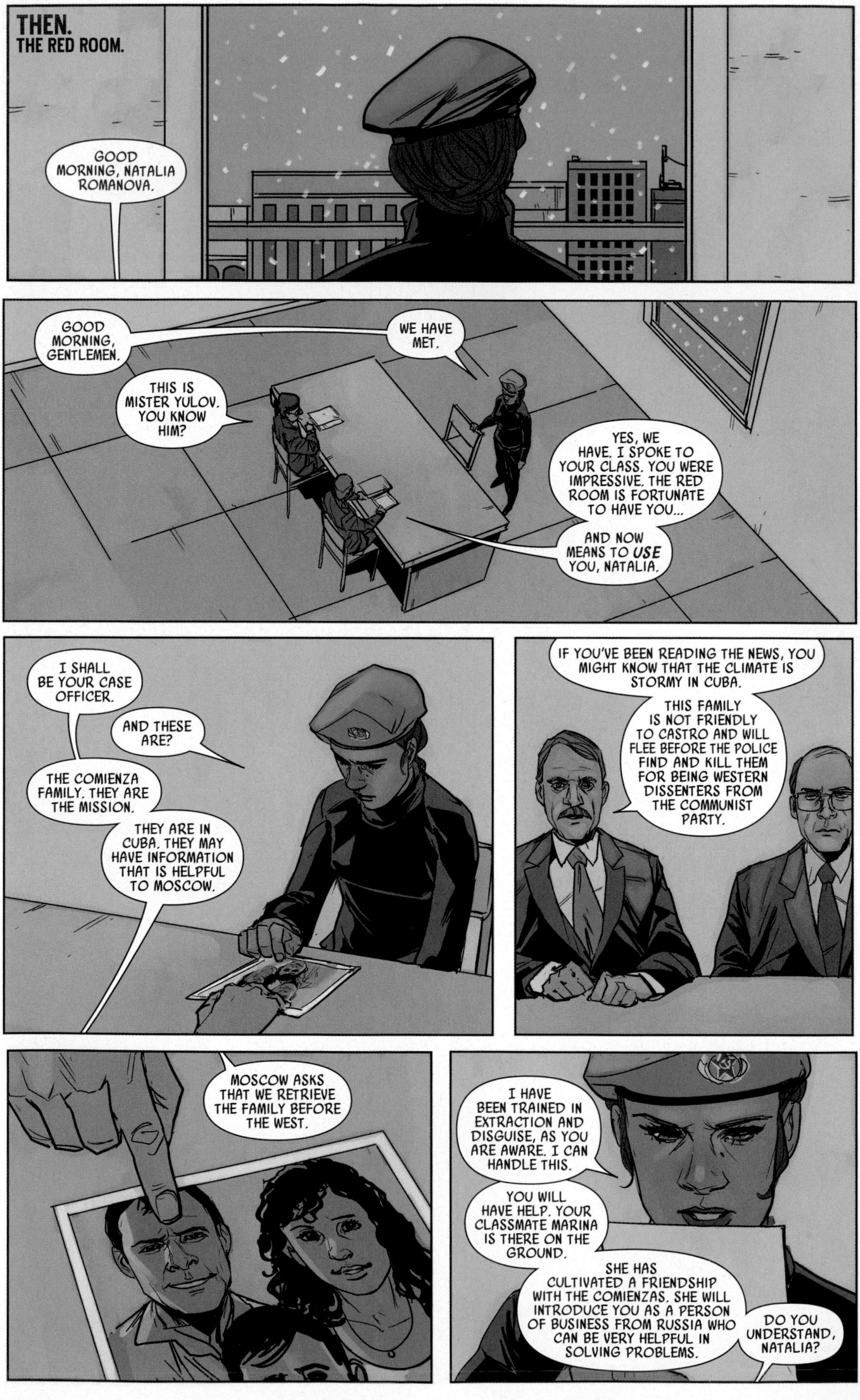
THEN.
THE RED ROOM.
GOOD MORNING, NATALIA ROMANOVA.
GOOD MORNING, GENTLEMEN.
WE HAVE MET.
THIS IS MISTER YULOV. YOU KNOW HIM?
YES, WE HAVE. I SPOKE TO YOUR CLASS. YOU WERE IMPRESSIVE. THE RED ROOM IS FORTUNATE TO HAVE YOU...
AND NOW MEANS TO USE YOU, NATALIA.
I SHALL BE YOUR CASE OFFICER.
AND THESE ARE?
THE COMIENZA FAMILY. THEY ARE THE MISSION.
THEY ARE IN CUBA. THEY MAY HAVE INFORMATION THAT IS HELPFUL TO MOSCOW.
IF YOU'VE BEEN READING THE NEWS, YOU MIGHT KNOW THAT THE CLIMATE IS STORMY IN CUBA.
THIS FAMILY IS NOT FRIENDLY TO CASTRO AND WILL FLEE BEFORE THE POLICE FIND AND KILL THEM FOR BEING WESTERN DISSENTERS FROM THE COMMUNIST PARTY.
MOSCOW ASKS THAT WE RETRIEVE THE FAMILY BEFORE THE WEST.
I HAVE BEEN TRAINED IN EXTRACTION AND DISGUISE, AS YOU ARE AWARE. I CAN HANDLE THIS.
YOU WILL HAVE HELP. YOUR CLASSMATE MARINA IS THERE ON THE GROUND.
SHE HAS CULTIVATED A FRIENDSHIP WITH THE COMIENZAS. SHE WILL INTRODUCE YOU AS A PERSON OF BUSINESS FROM RUSSIA WHO CAN BE VERY HELPFUL IN SOLVING PROBLEMS.
DO YOU UNDERSTAND, NATALIA?

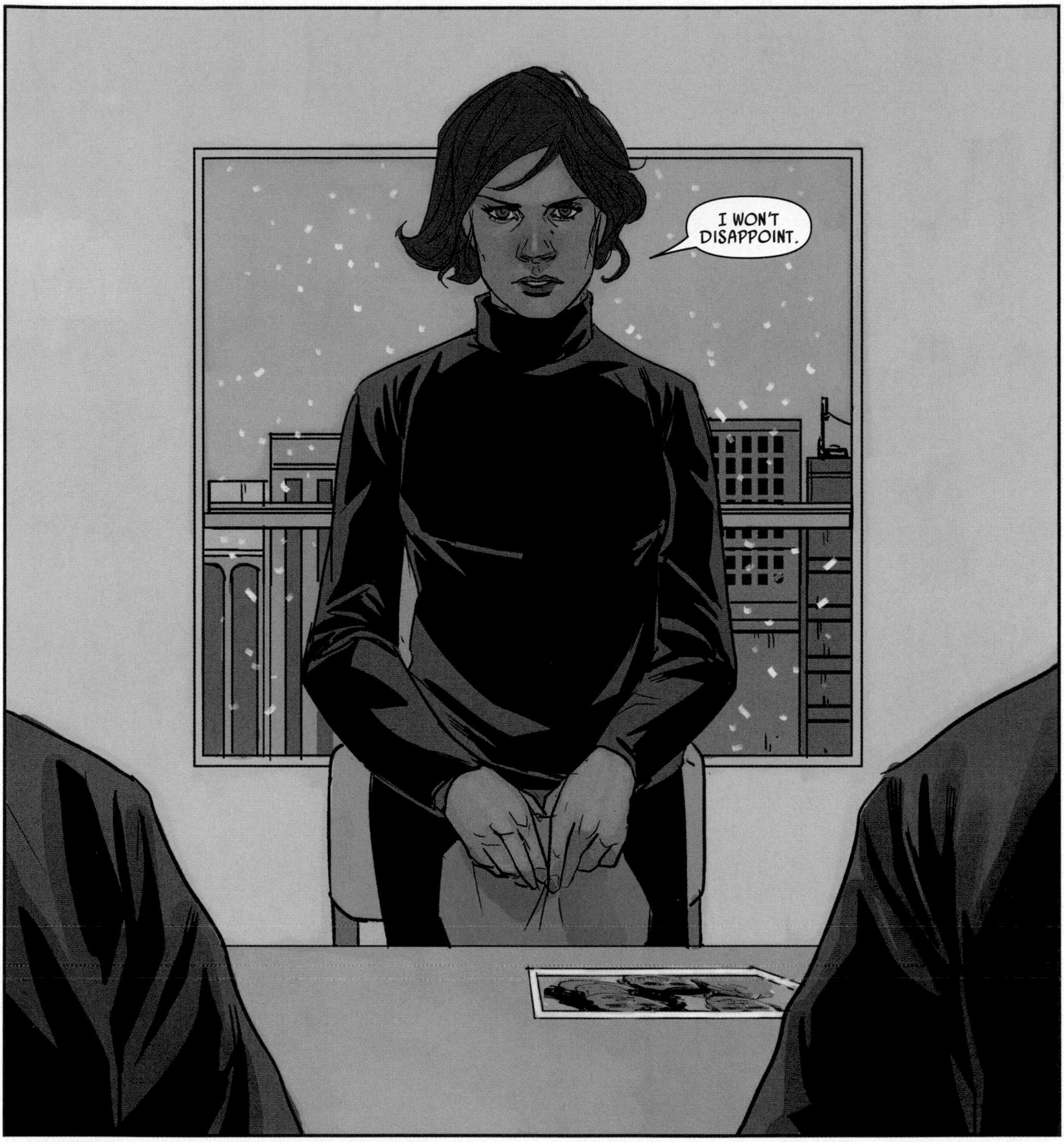
I WON'T DISAPPOINT.

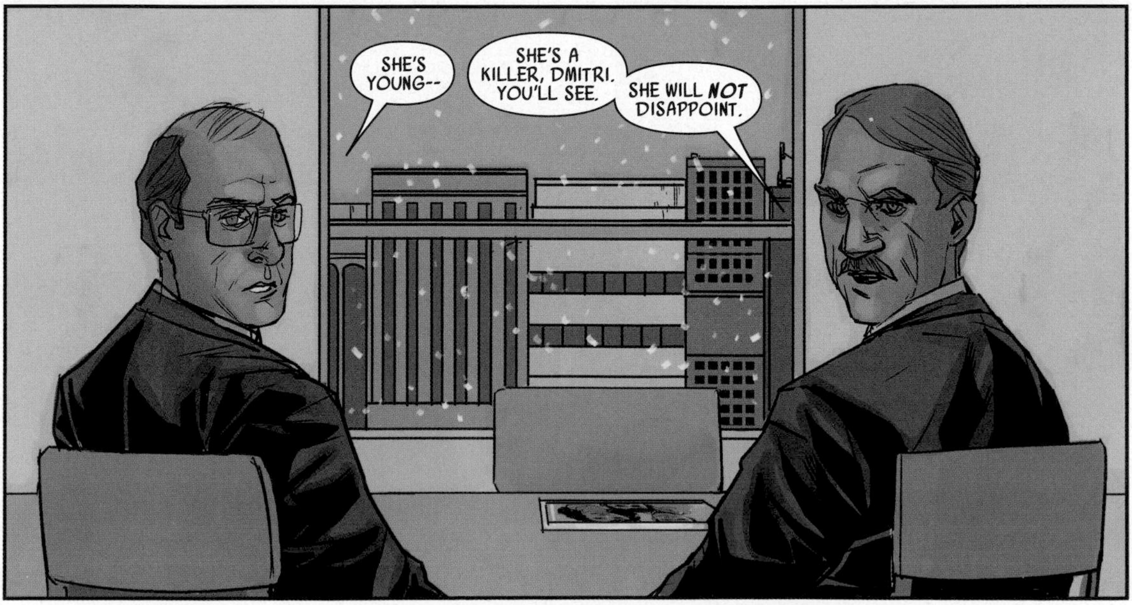
SHE'S YOUNG--
SHE'S A KILLER, DMITRI. YOU'LL SEE.
SHE WILL NOT DISAPPOINT.

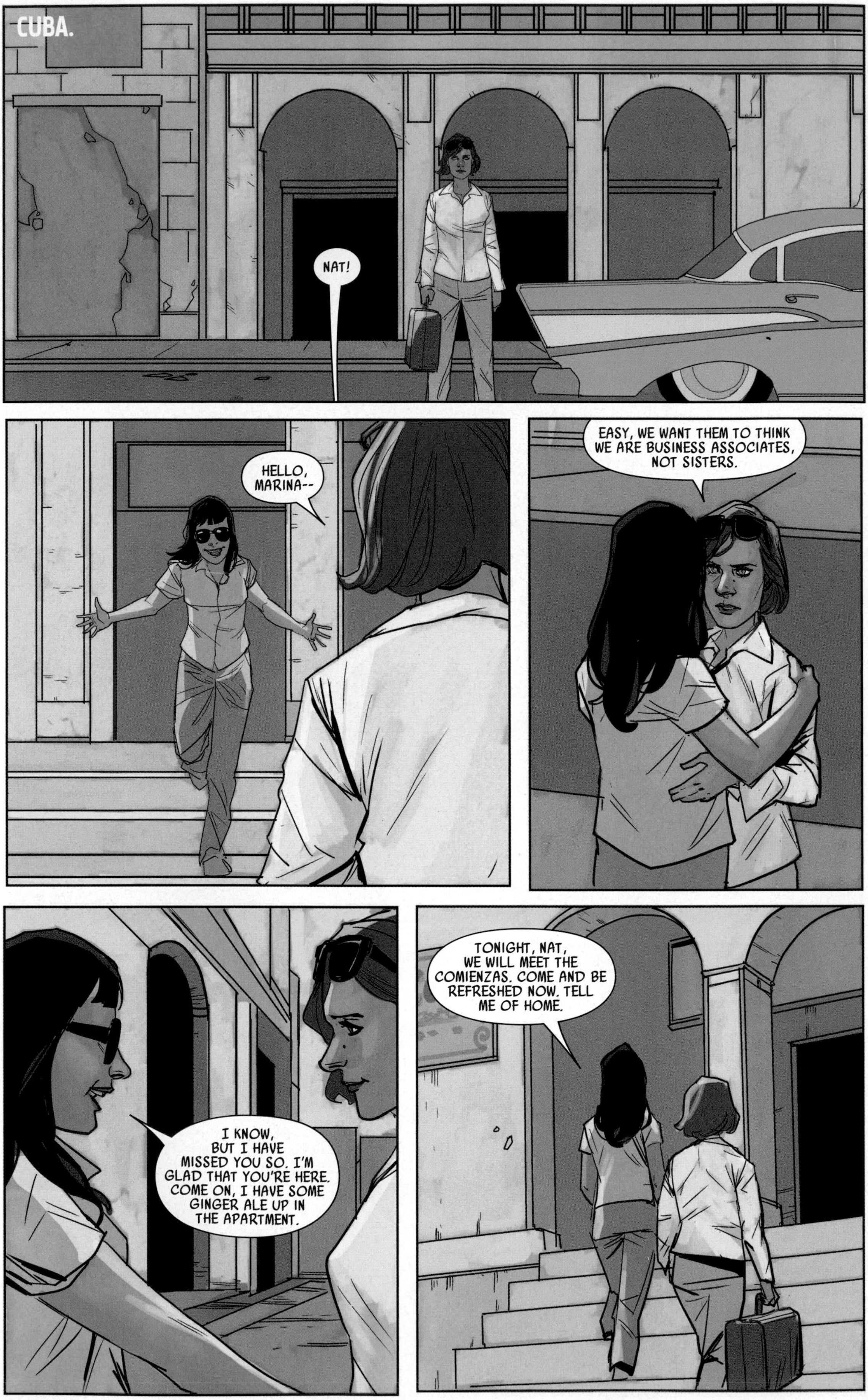
CUBA.
NAT!
HELLO, MARINA--
EASY, WE WANT THEM TO THINK WE ARE BUSINESS ASSOCIATES, NOT SISTERS.
I KNOW, BUT I HAVE MISSED YOU SO. I'M GLAD THAT YOU'RE HERE. COME ON, I HAVE SOME GINGER ALE UP IN THE APARTMENT.
TONIGHT, NAT, WE WILL MEET THE COMIENZAS. COME AND BE REFRESHED NOW. TELL ME OF HOME.

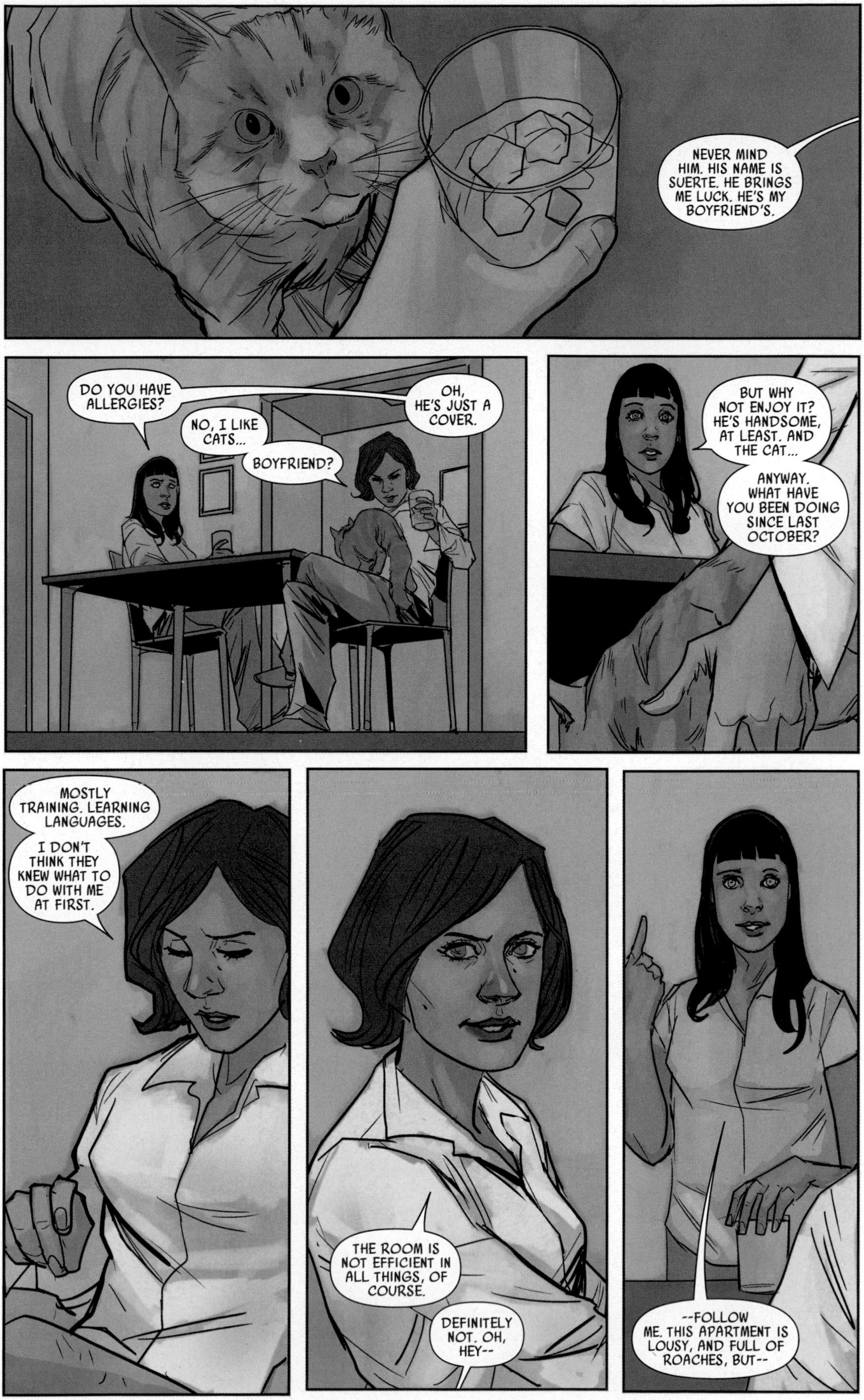
NEVER MIND HIM. HIS NAME IS SUERTE. HE BRINGS ME LUCK. HE'S MY BOYFRIEND'S.
DO YOU HAVE ALLERGIES?
NO, I LIKE CATS...
BOYFRIEND?
OH, HE'S JUST A COVER.
BUT WHY NOT ENJOY IT? HE'S HANDSOME, AT LEAST. AND THE CAT...
ANYWAY. WHAT HAVE YOU BEEN DOING SINCE LAST OCTOBER?
MOSTLY TRAINING. LEARNING LANGUAGES.
I DON'T THINK THEY KNEW WHAT TO DO WITH ME AT FIRST.
THE ROOM IS NOT EFFICIENT IN ALL THINGS, OF COURSE.
DEFINITELY NOT. OH, HEY--
--FOLLOW ME. THIS APARTMENT IS LOUSY, AND FULL OF ROACHES, BUT--

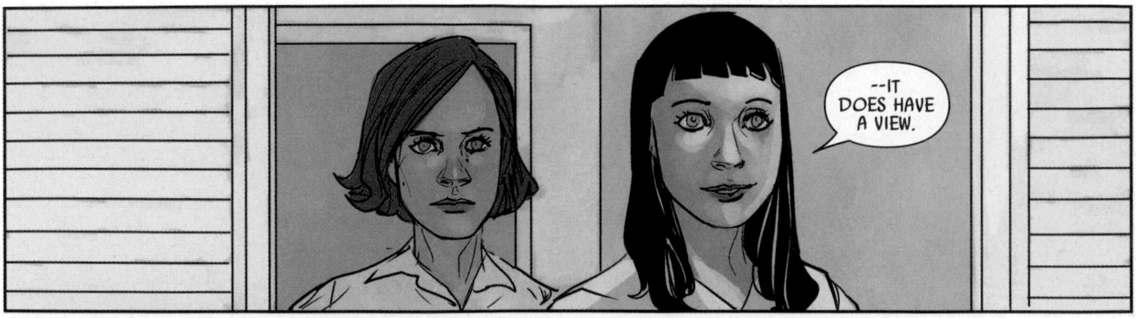
--IT DOES HAVE A VIEW.

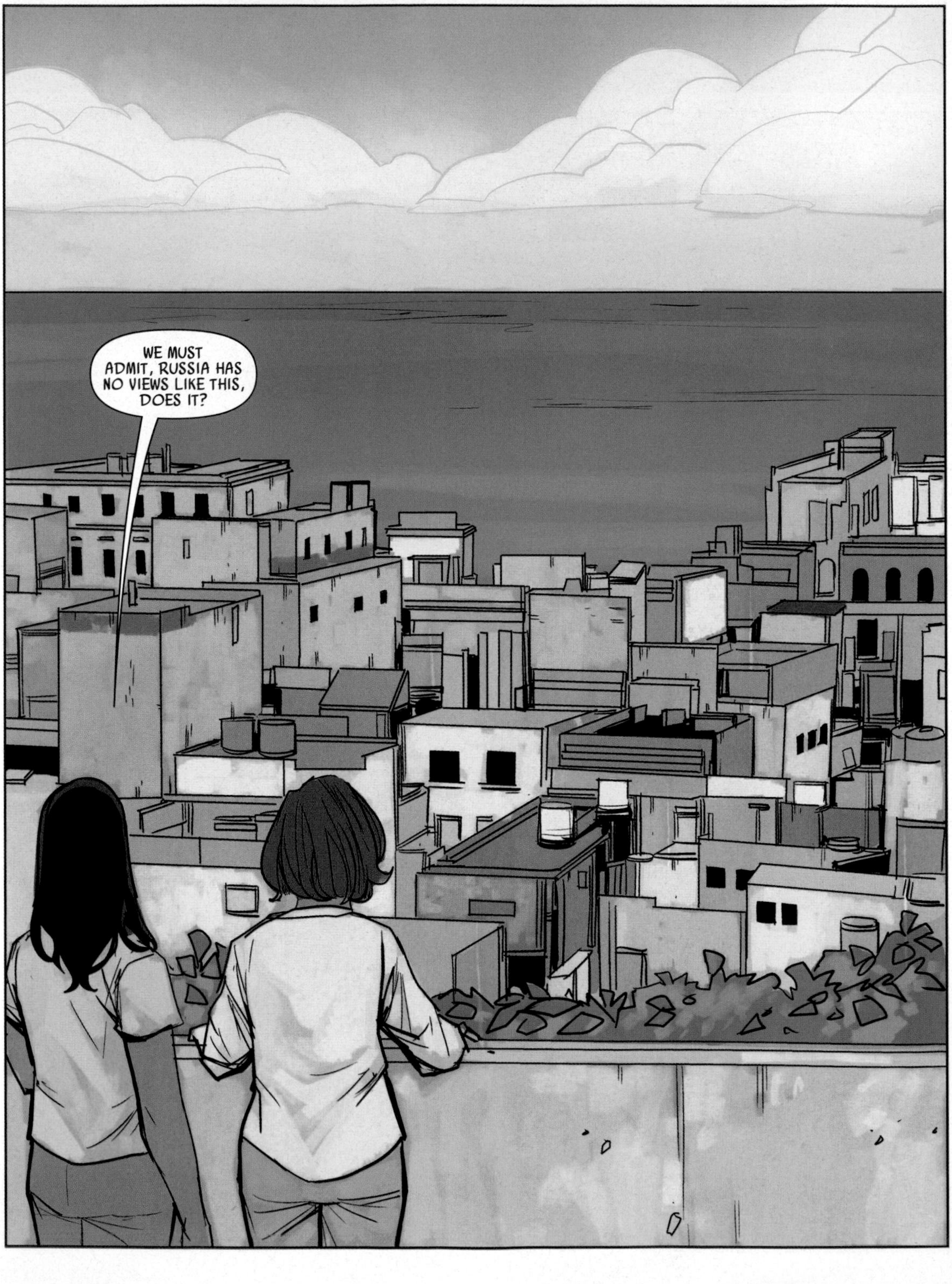
WE MUST ADMIT, RUSSIA HAS NO VIEWS LIKE THIS, DOES IT?

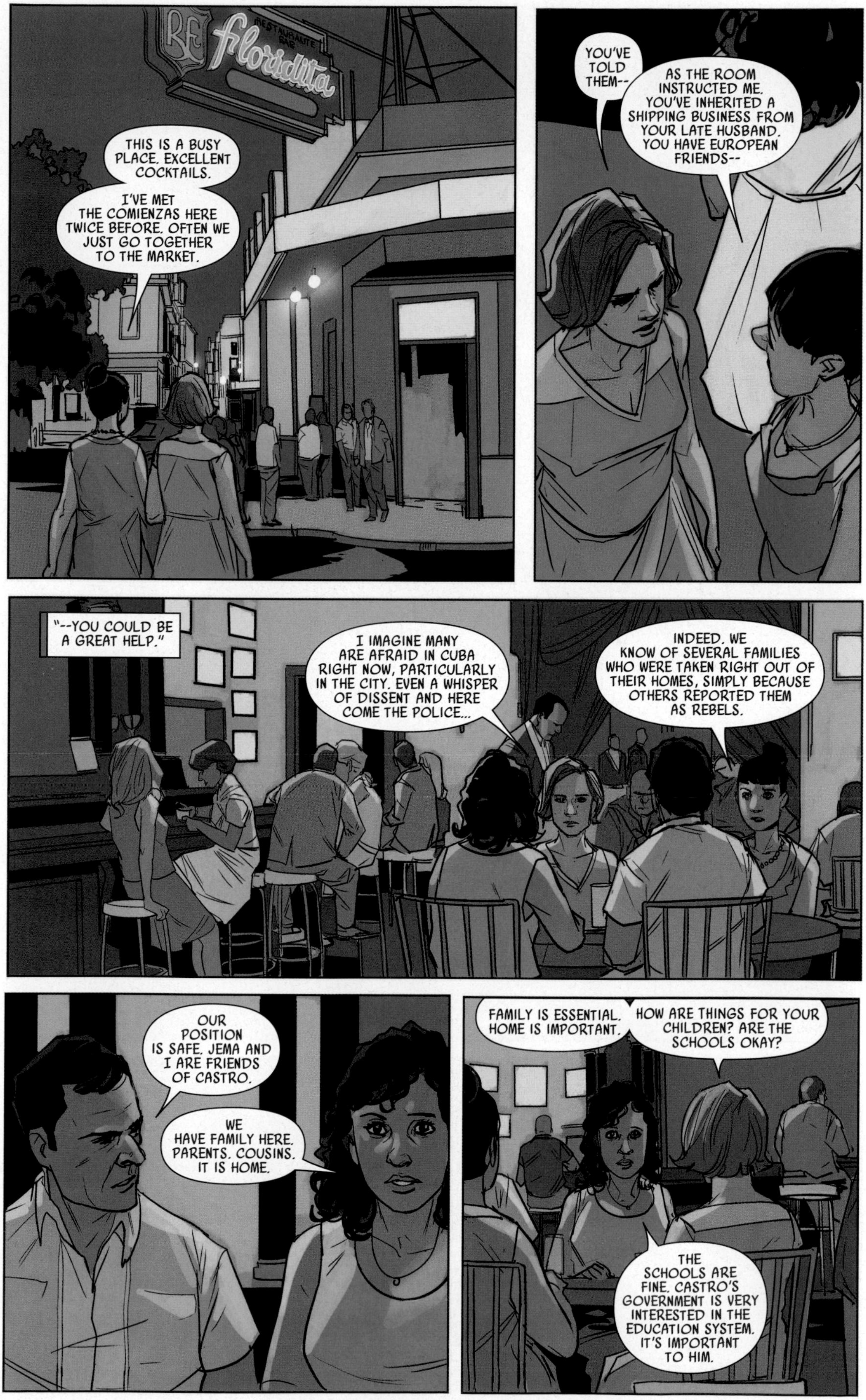
RESTAURANTE BAR
floridita
THIS IS A BUSY PLACE. EXCELLENT COCKTAILS.
I'VE MET THE COMIENZAS HERE TWICE BEFORE. OFTEN WE JUST GO TOGETHER TO THE MARKET.
YOU'VE TOLD THEM--
AS THE ROOM INSTRUCTED ME. YOU'VE INHERITED A SHIPPING BUSINESS FROM YOUR LATE HUSBAND. YOU HAVE EUROPEAN FRIENDS--
"--YOU COULD BE A GREAT HELP."
I IMAGINE MANY ARE AFRAID IN CUBA RIGHT NOW, PARTICULARLY IN THE CITY. EVEN A WHISPER OF DISSENT AND HERE COME THE POLICE...
INDEED. WE KNOW OF SEVERAL FAMILIES WHO WERE TAKEN RIGHT OUT OF THEIR HOMES, SIMPLY BECAUSE OTHERS REPORTED THEM AS REBELS.
OUR POSITION IS SAFE. JEMA AND I ARE FRIENDS OF CASTRO.
WE HAVE FAMILY HERE. PARENTS. COUSINS. IT IS HOME.
FAMILY IS ESSENTIAL. HOME IS IMPORTANT.
HOW ARE THINGS FOR YOUR CHILDREN? ARE THE SCHOOLS OKAY?
THE SCHOOLS ARE FINE. CASTRO'S GOVERNMENT IS VERY INTERESTED IN THE EDUCATION SYSTEM. IT'S IMPORTANT TO HIM.

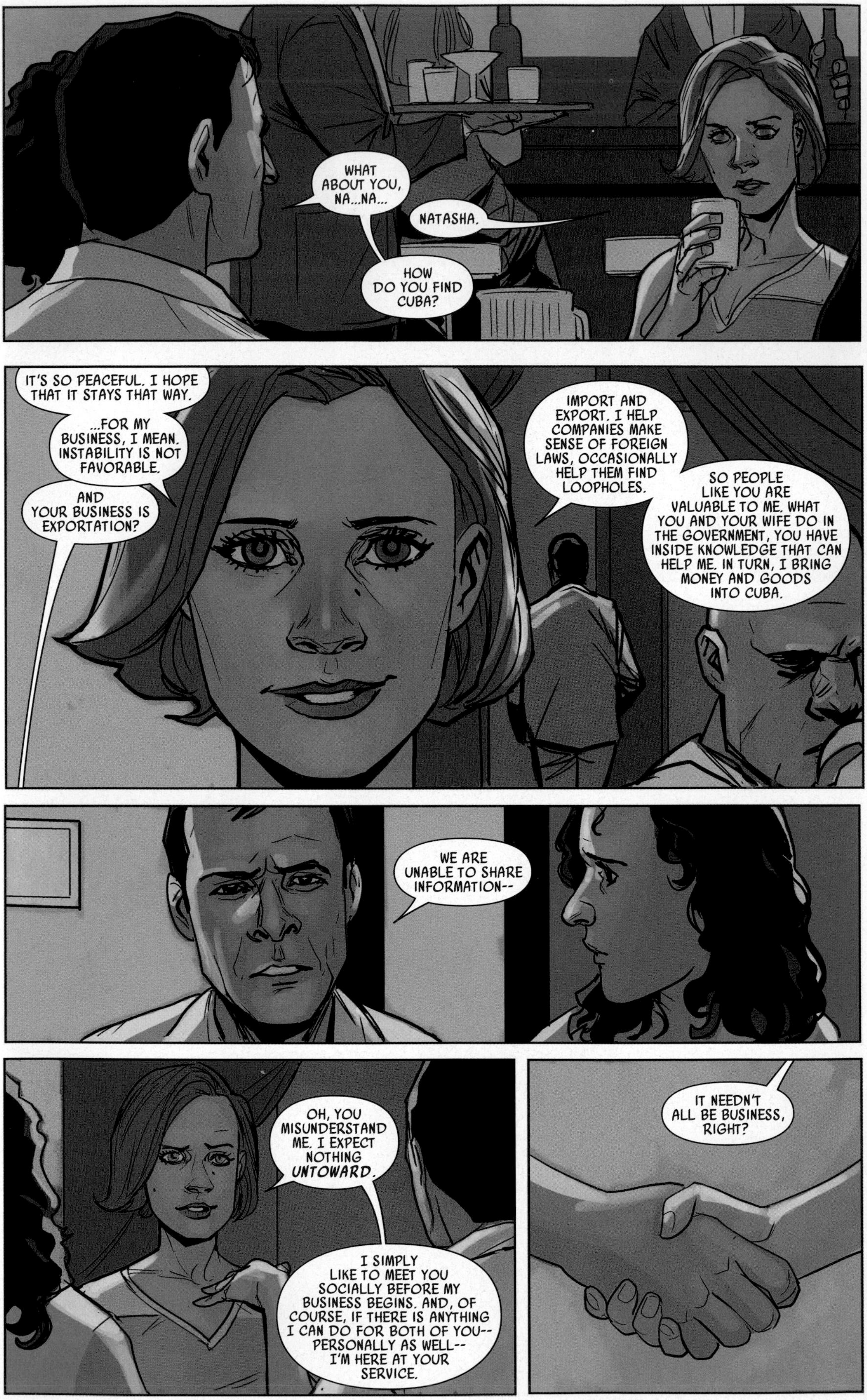
WHAT ABOUT YOU, NA...NA...
NATASHA.
HOW DO YOU FIND CUBA?
IT'S SO PEACEFUL. I HOPE THAT IT STAYS THAT WAY.
...FOR MY BUSINESS, I MEAN. INSTABILITY IS NOT FAVORABLE.
AND YOUR BUSINESS IS EXPORTATION?
IMPORT AND EXPORT. I HELP COMPANIES MAKE SENSE OF FOREIGN LAWS, OCCASIONALLY HELP THEM FIND LOOPHOLES.
SO PEOPLE LIKE YOU ARE VALUABLE TO ME. WHAT YOU AND YOUR WIFE DO IN THE GOVERNMENT, YOU HAVE INSIDE KNOWLEDGE THAT CAN HELP ME. IN TURN, I BRING MONEY AND GOODS INTO CUBA.
WE ARE UNABLE TO SHARE INFORMATION--
OH, YOU MISUNDERSTAND ME. I EXPECT NOTHING *UNTOWARD*.
I SIMPLY LIKE TO MEET YOU SOCIALLY BEFORE MY BUSINESS BEGINS. AND, OF COURSE, IF THERE IS ANYTHING I CAN DO FOR BOTH OF YOU-- PERSONALLY AS WELL-- I'M HERE AT YOUR SERVICE.
IT NEEDN'T ALL BE BUSINESS, RIGHT?

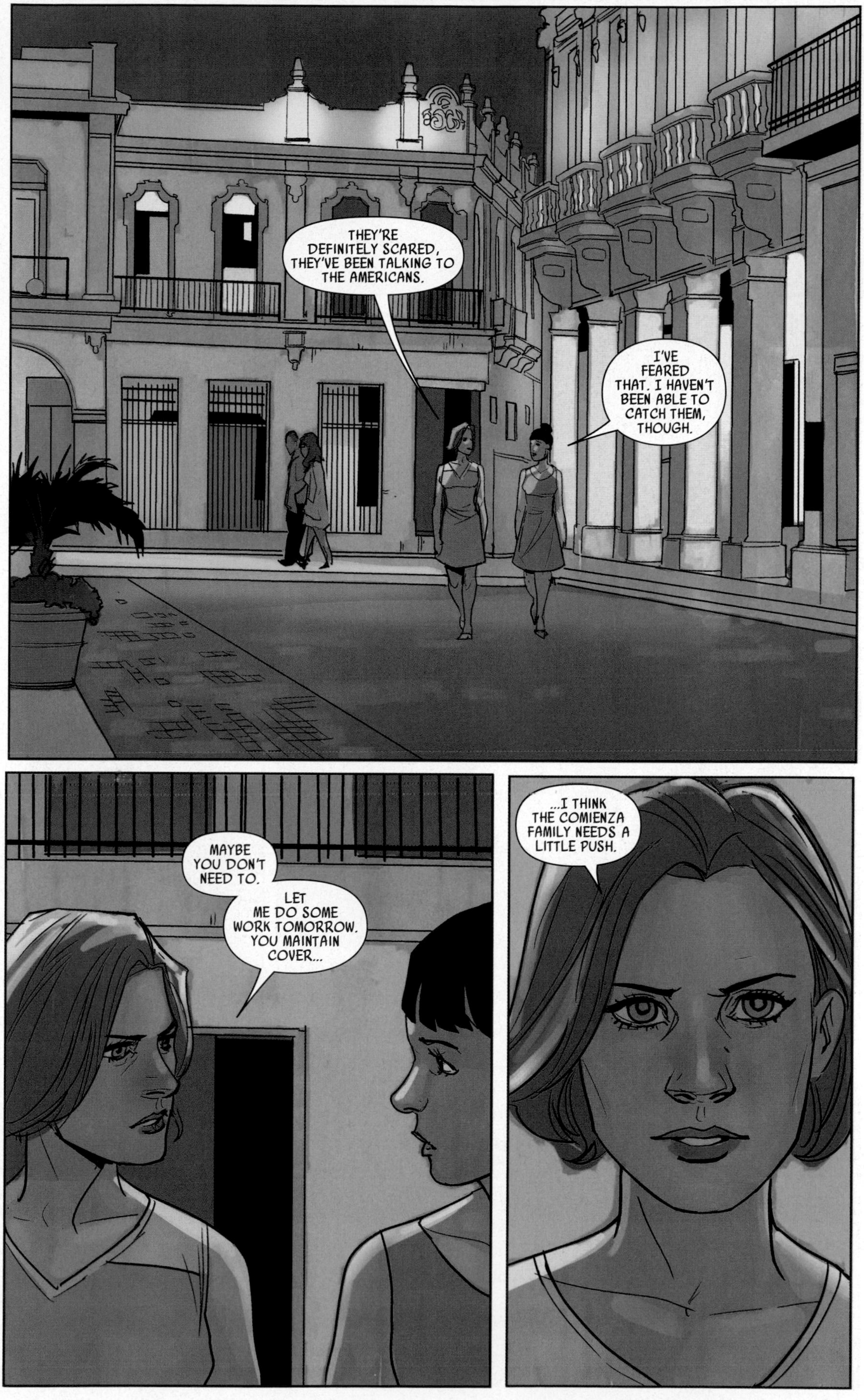
THEY'RE DEFINITELY SCARED, THEY'VE BEEN TALKING TO THE AMERICANS.
I'VE FEARED THAT. I HAVEN'T BEEN ABLE TO CATCH THEM, THOUGH.
MAYBE YOU DON'T NEED TO.
LET ME DO SOME WORK TOMORROW. YOU MAINTAIN COVER...
...I THINK THE COMIENZA FAMILY NEEDS A LITTLE PUSH.

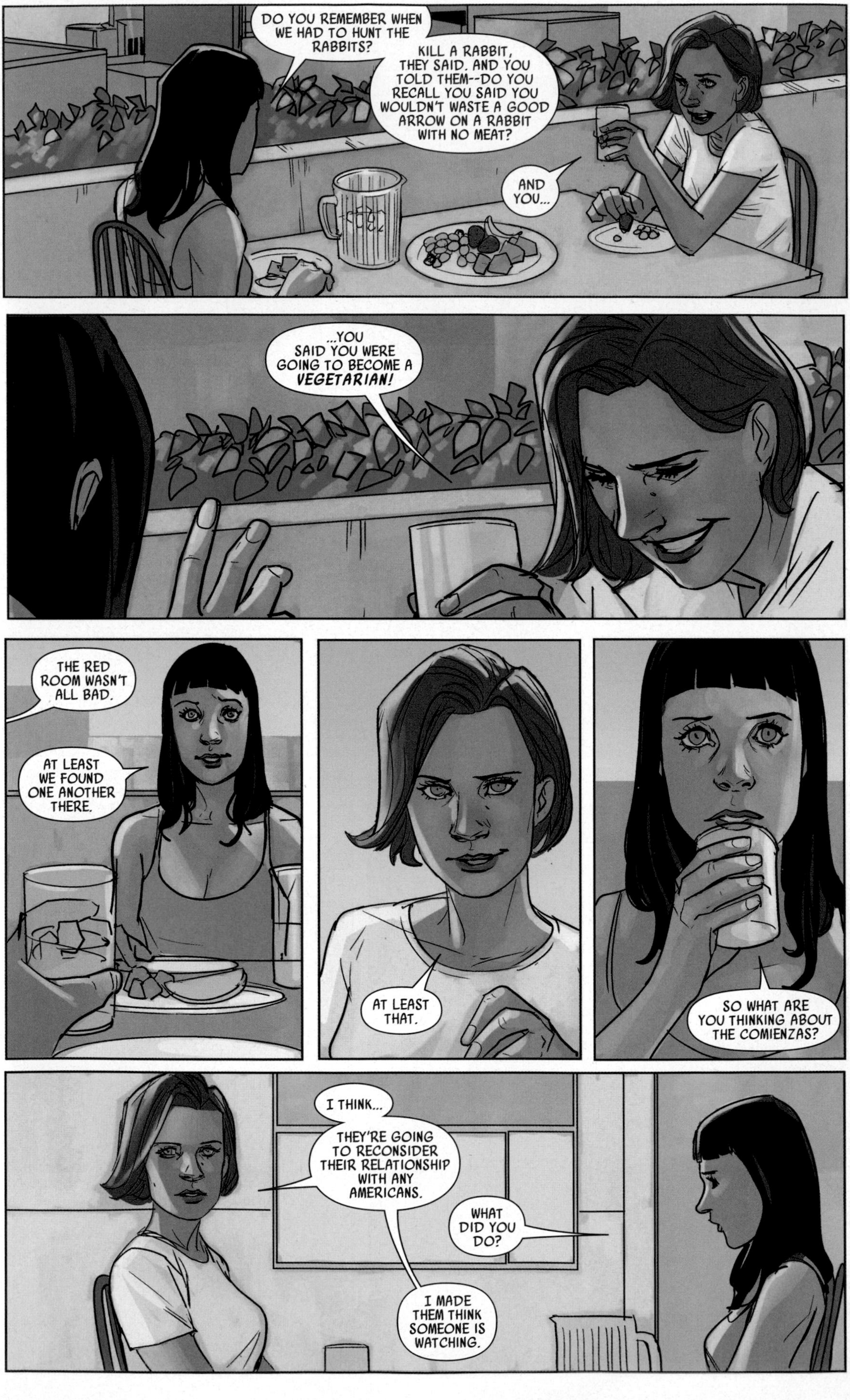
DO YOU REMEMBER WHEN WE HAD TO HUNT THE RABBITS?
KILL A RABBIT, THEY SAID. AND YOU TOLD THEM--DO YOU RECALL YOU SAID YOU WOULDN'T WASTE A GOOD ARROW ON A RABBIT WITH NO MEAT?
AND YOU...
...YOU SAID YOU WERE GOING TO BECOME A VEGETARIAN!
THE RED ROOM WASN'T ALL BAD.
AT LEAST WE FOUND ONE ANOTHER THERE.
AT LEAST THAT.
SO WHAT ARE YOU THINKING ABOUT THE COMIENZAS?
I THINK...
THEY'RE GOING TO RECONSIDER THEIR RELATIONSHIP WITH ANY AMERICANS.
WHAT DID YOU DO?
I MADE THEM THINK SOMEONE IS WATCHING.

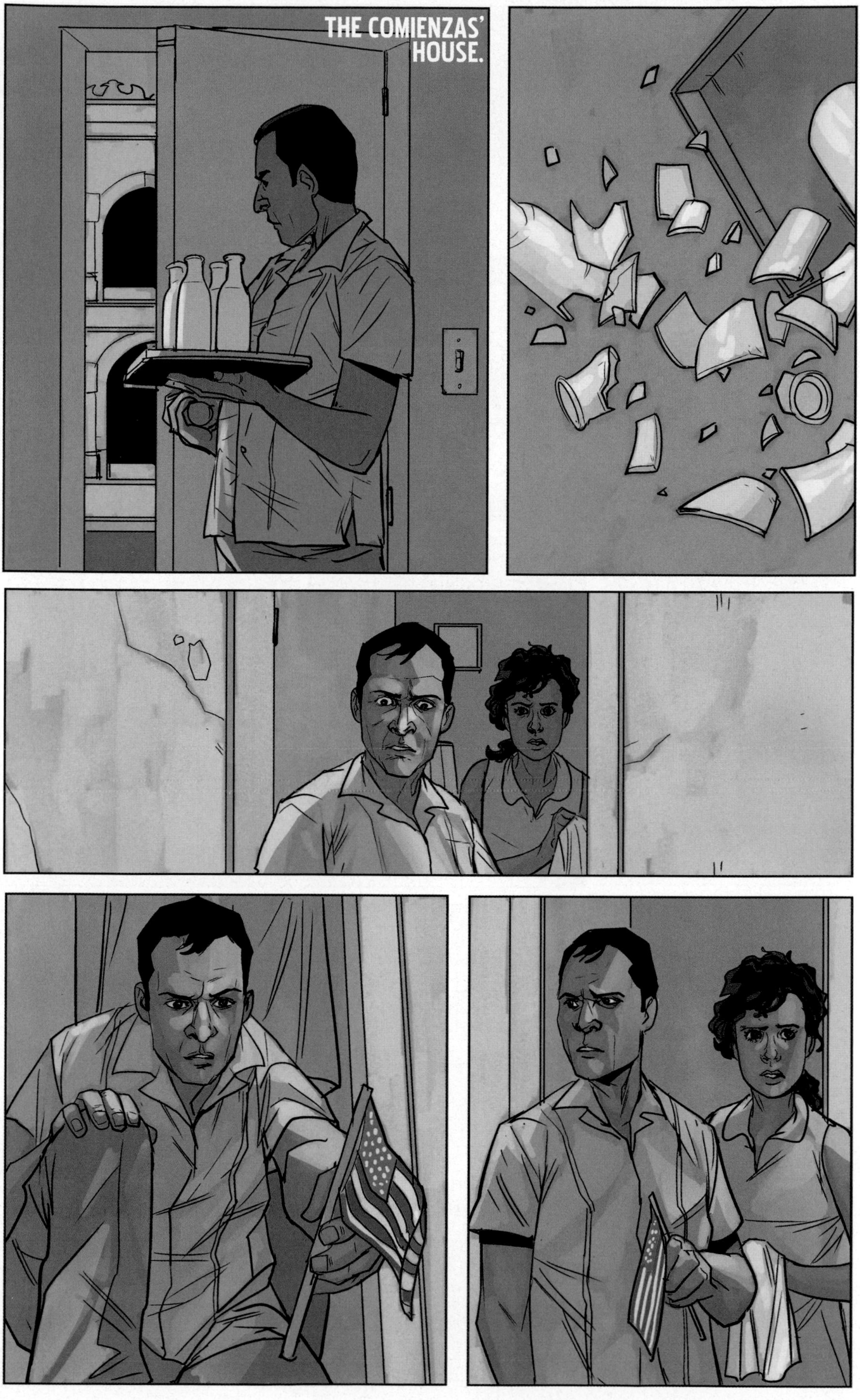
THE COMIENZAS' HOUSE.

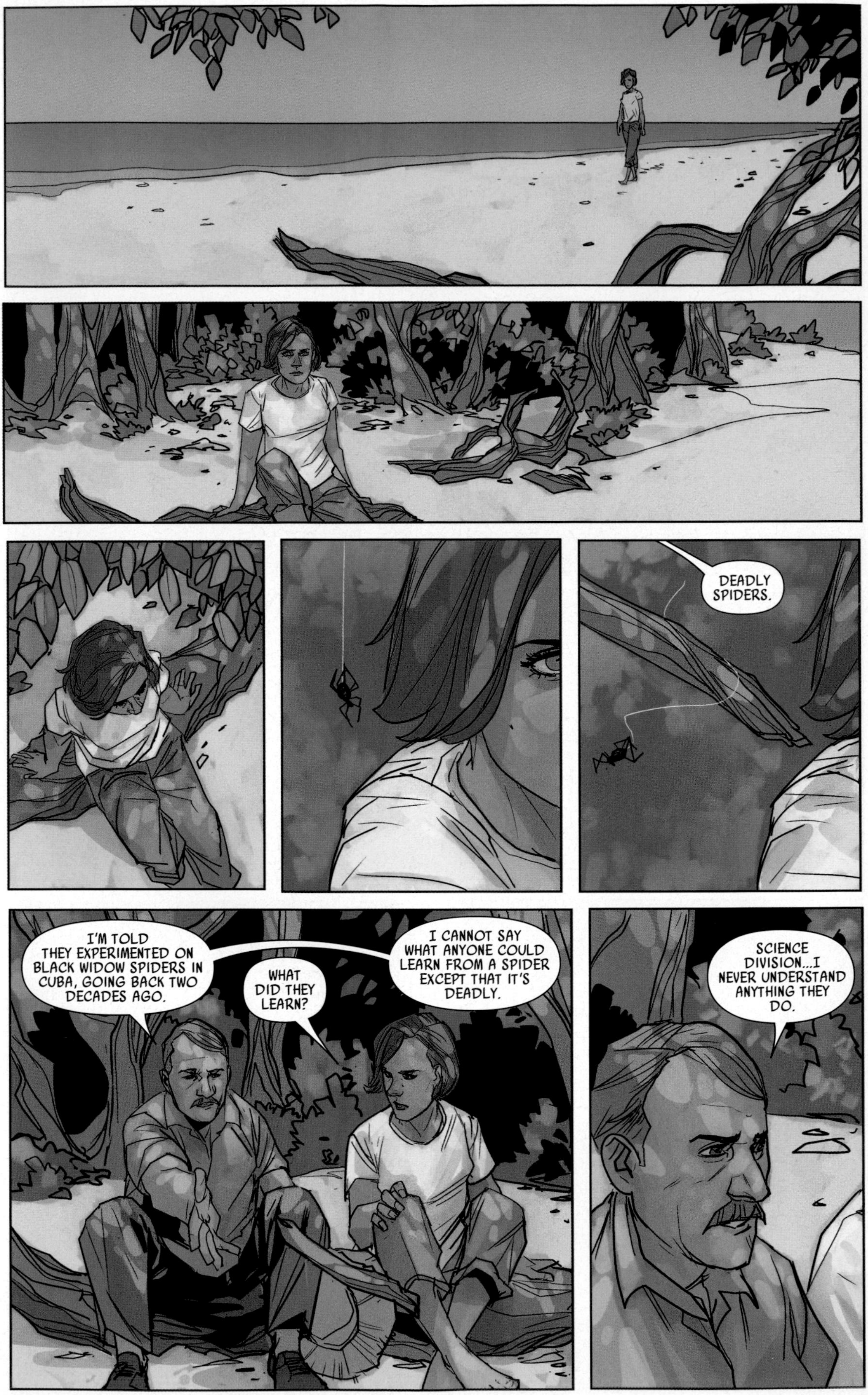
DEADLY SPIDERS.
I'M TOLD THEY EXPERIMENTED ON BLACK WIDOW SPIDERS IN CUBA, GOING BACK TWO DECADES AGO.
WHAT DID THEY LEARN?
I CANNOT SAY WHAT ANYONE COULD LEARN FROM A SPIDER EXCEPT THAT IT'S DEADLY.
SCIENCE DIVISION...I NEVER UNDERSTAND ANYTHING THEY DO.

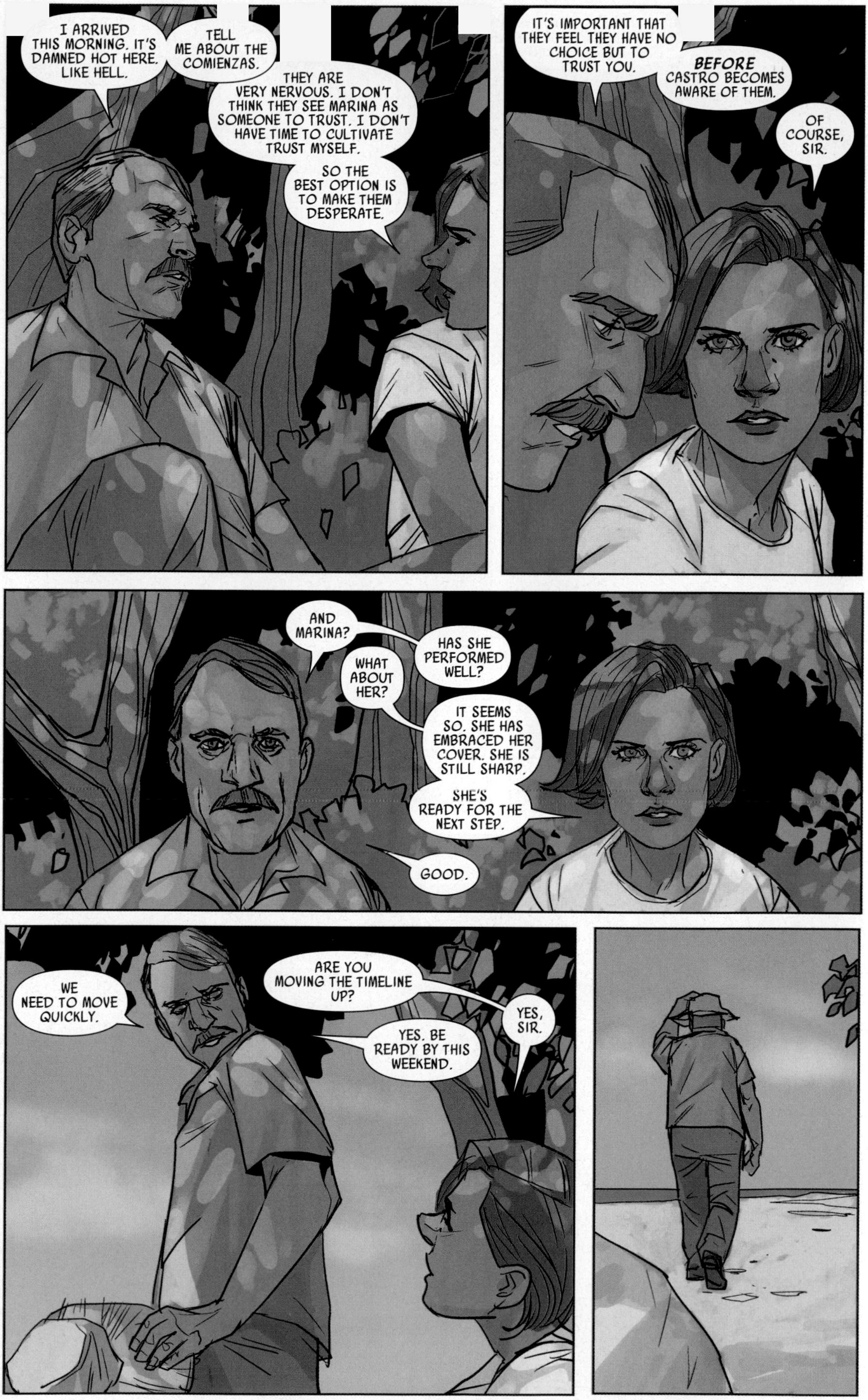
I ARRIVED THIS MORNING. IT'S DAMNED HOT HERE. LIKE HELL.
TELL ME ABOUT THE COMIENZAS.
THEY ARE VERY NERVOUS. I DON'T THINK THEY SEE MARINA AS SOMEONE TO TRUST. I DON'T HAVE TIME TO CULTIVATE TRUST MYSELF.
SO THE BEST OPTION IS TO MAKE THEM DESPERATE.
IT'S IMPORTANT THAT THEY FEEL THEY HAVE NO CHOICE BUT TO TRUST YOU.
BEFORE CASTRO BECOMES AWARE OF THEM.
OF COURSE, SIR.
AND MARINA?
HAS SHE PERFORMED WELL?
WHAT ABOUT HER?
IT SEEMS SO. SHE HAS EMBRACED HER COVER. SHE IS STILL SHARP.
SHE'S READY FOR THE NEXT STEP.
GOOD.
WE NEED TO MOVE QUICKLY.
ARE YOU MOVING THE TIMELINE UP?
YES. BE READY BY THIS WEEKEND.
YES, SIR.

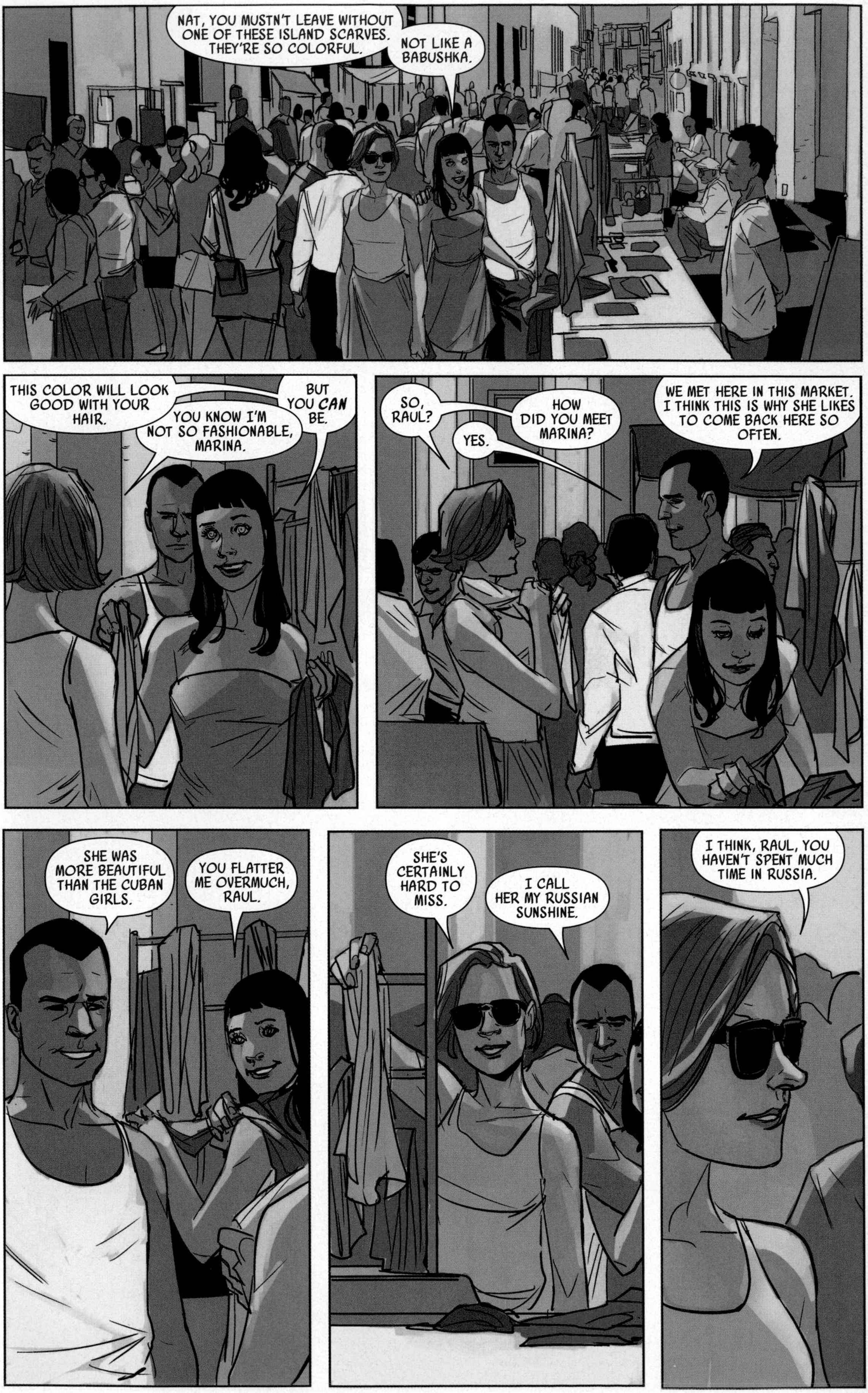
NAT, YOU MUSTN'T LEAVE WITHOUT ONE OF THESE ISLAND SCARVES. THEY'RE SO COLORFUL.
NOT LIKE A BABUSHKA.
THIS COLOR WILL LOOK GOOD WITH YOUR HAIR.
YOU KNOW I'M NOT SO FASHIONABLE, MARINA.
BUT YOU CAN BE.
SO, RAUL?
HOW DID YOU MEET MARINA?
YES.
WE MET HERE IN THIS MARKET. I THINK THIS IS WHY SHE LIKES TO COME BACK HERE SO OFTEN.
SHE WAS MORE BEAUTIFUL THAN THE CUBAN GIRLS.
YOU FLATTER ME OVERMUCH, RAUL.
SHE'S CERTAINLY HARD TO MISS.
I CALL HER MY RUSSIAN SUNSHINE.
I THINK, RAUL, YOU HAVEN'T SPENT MUCH TIME IN RUSSIA.

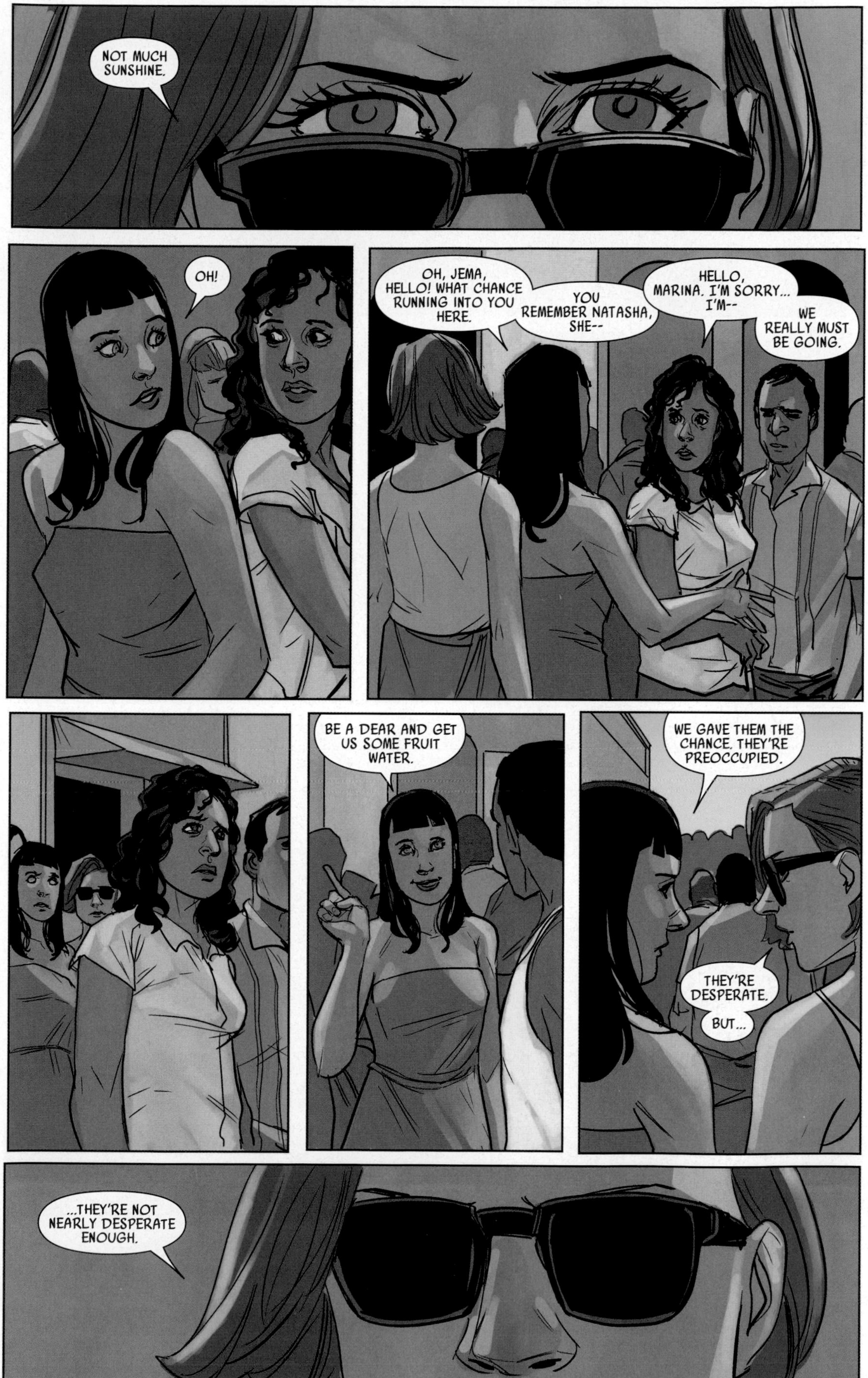
NOT MUCH SUNSHINE.
OH!
OH, JEMA, HELLO! WHAT CHANCE RUNNING INTO YOU HERE.
YOU REMEMBER NATASHA, SHE--
HELLO, MARINA. I'M SORRY... I'M--
WE REALLY MUST BE GOING.
BE A DEAR AND GET US SOME FRUIT WATER.
WE GAVE THEM THE CHANCE. THEY'RE PREOCCUPIED.
THEY'RE DESPERATE.
BUT...
...THEY'RE NOT NEARLY DESPERATE ENOUGH.

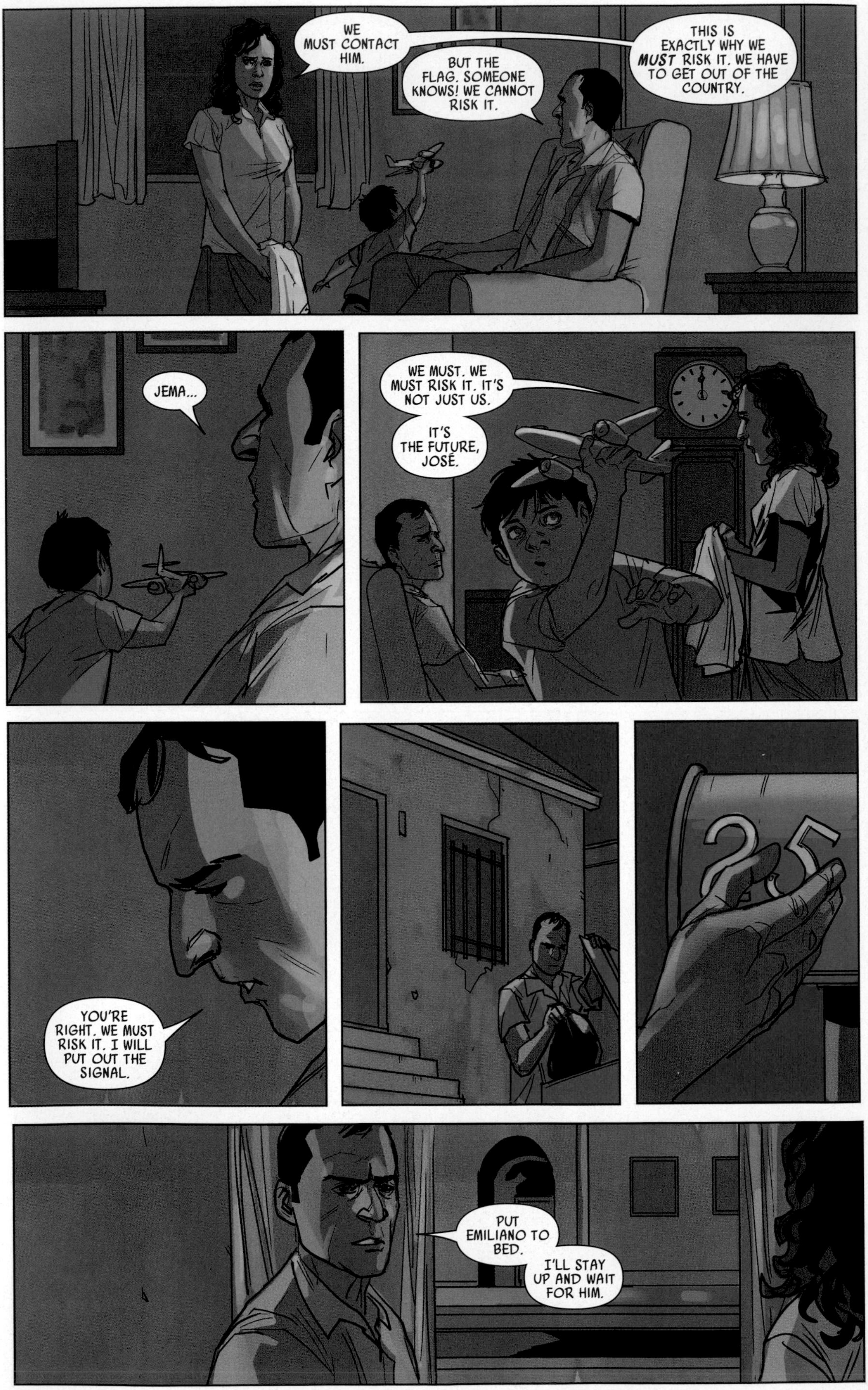
WE MUST CONTACT HIM.
BUT THE FLAG. SOMEONE KNOWS! WE CANNOT RISK IT.
THIS IS EXACTLY WHY WE *MUST* RISK IT. WE HAVE TO GET OUT OF THE COUNTRY.
JEMA...
WE MUST. WE MUST RISK IT. IT'S NOT JUST US.
IT'S THE FUTURE, JOSÉ.
YOU'RE RIGHT. WE MUST RISK IT. I WILL PUT OUT THE SIGNAL.
25
PUT EMILIANO TO BED.
I'LL STAY UP AND WAIT FOR HIM.

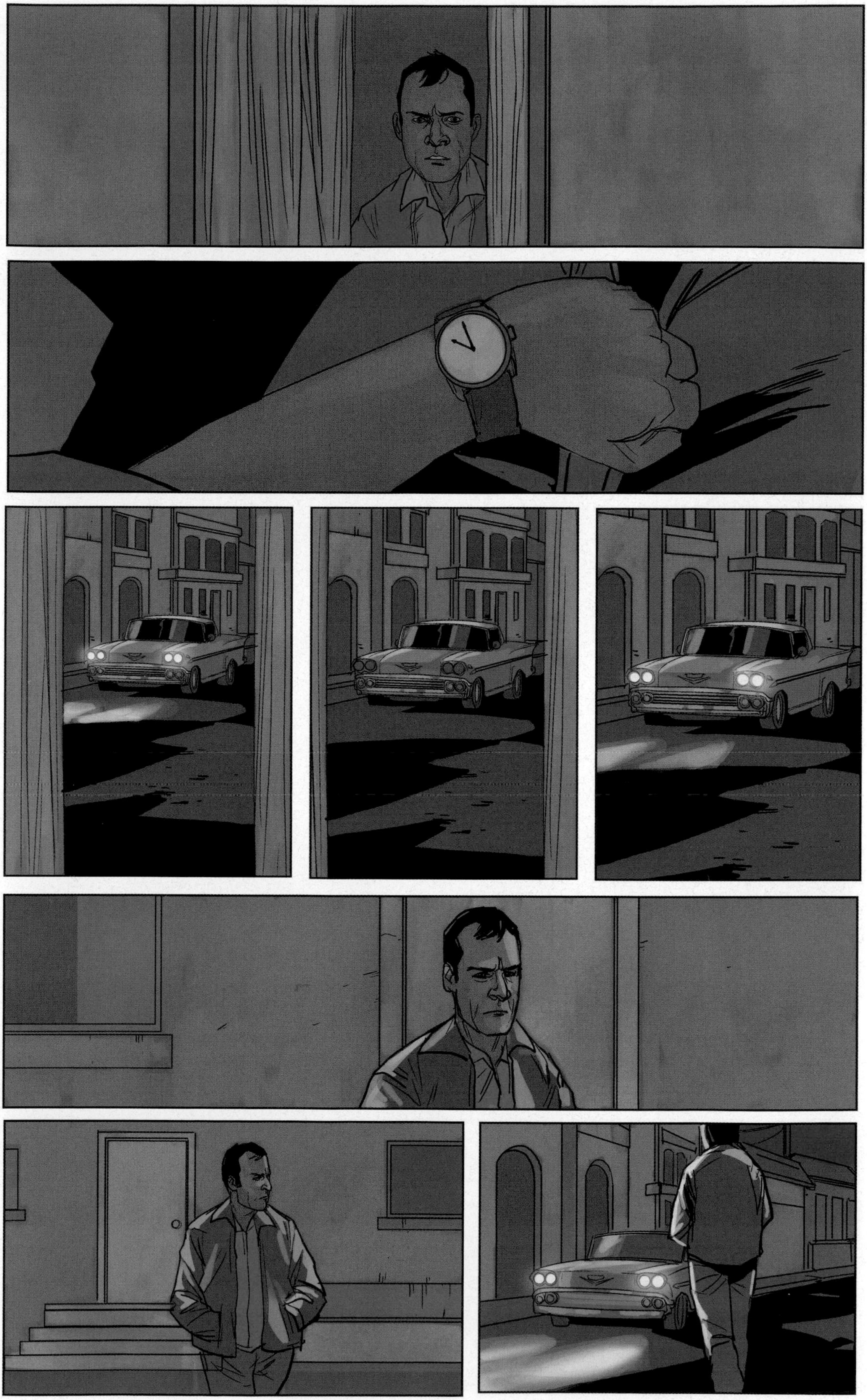

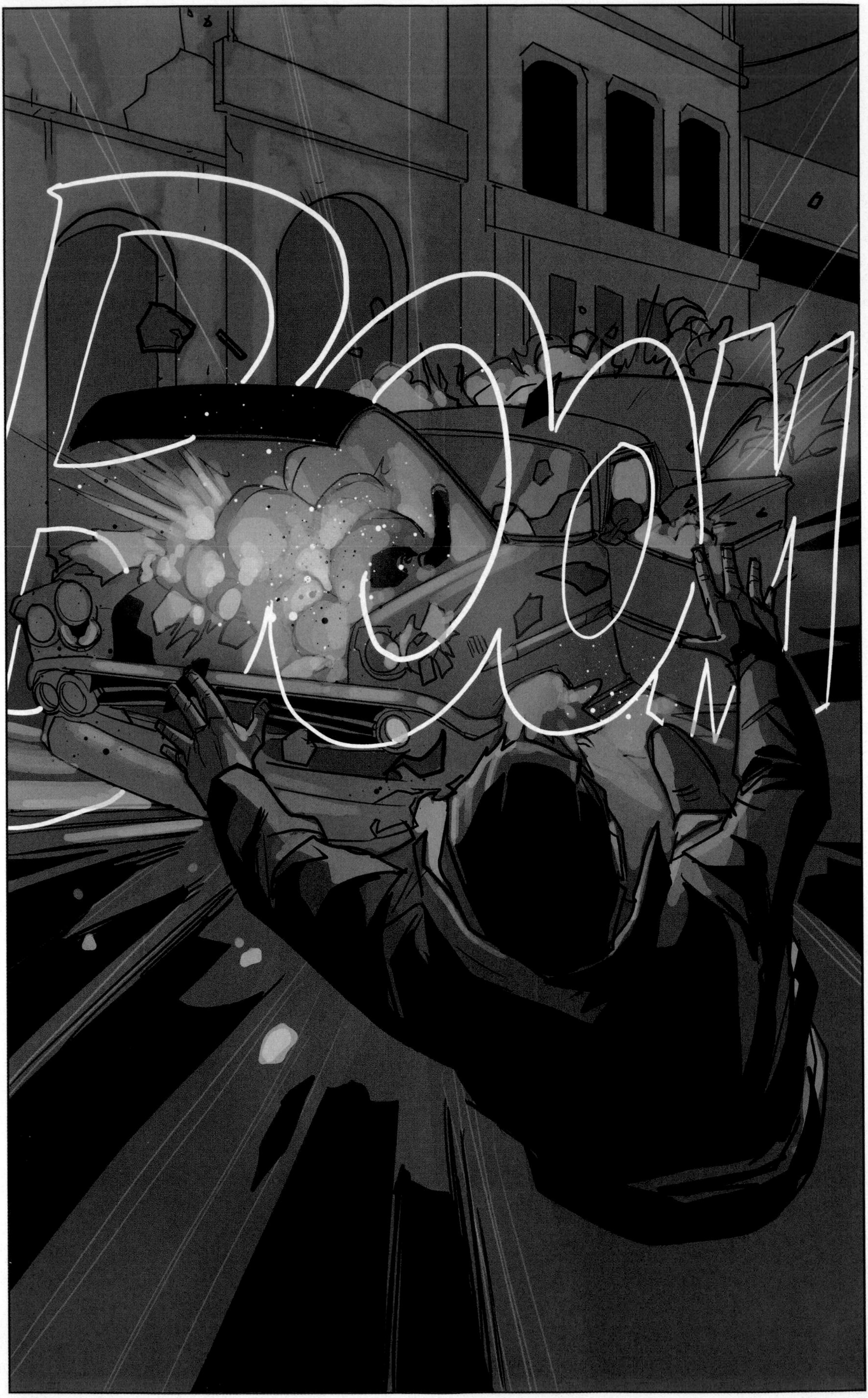
BOOM

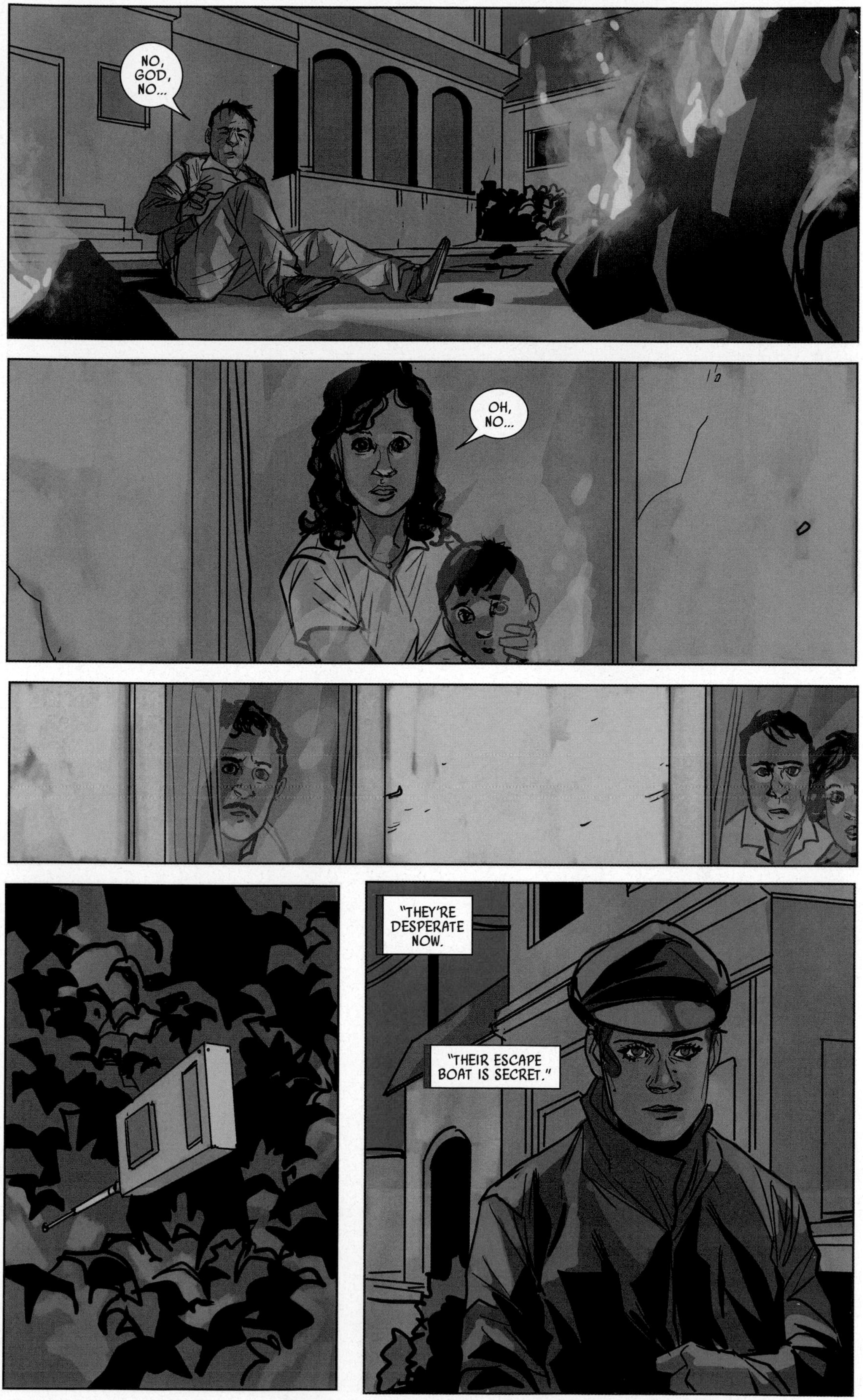
NO, GOD, NO...
OH, NO...
"THEY'RE DESPERATE NOW.
"THEIR ESCAPE BOAT IS SECRET."

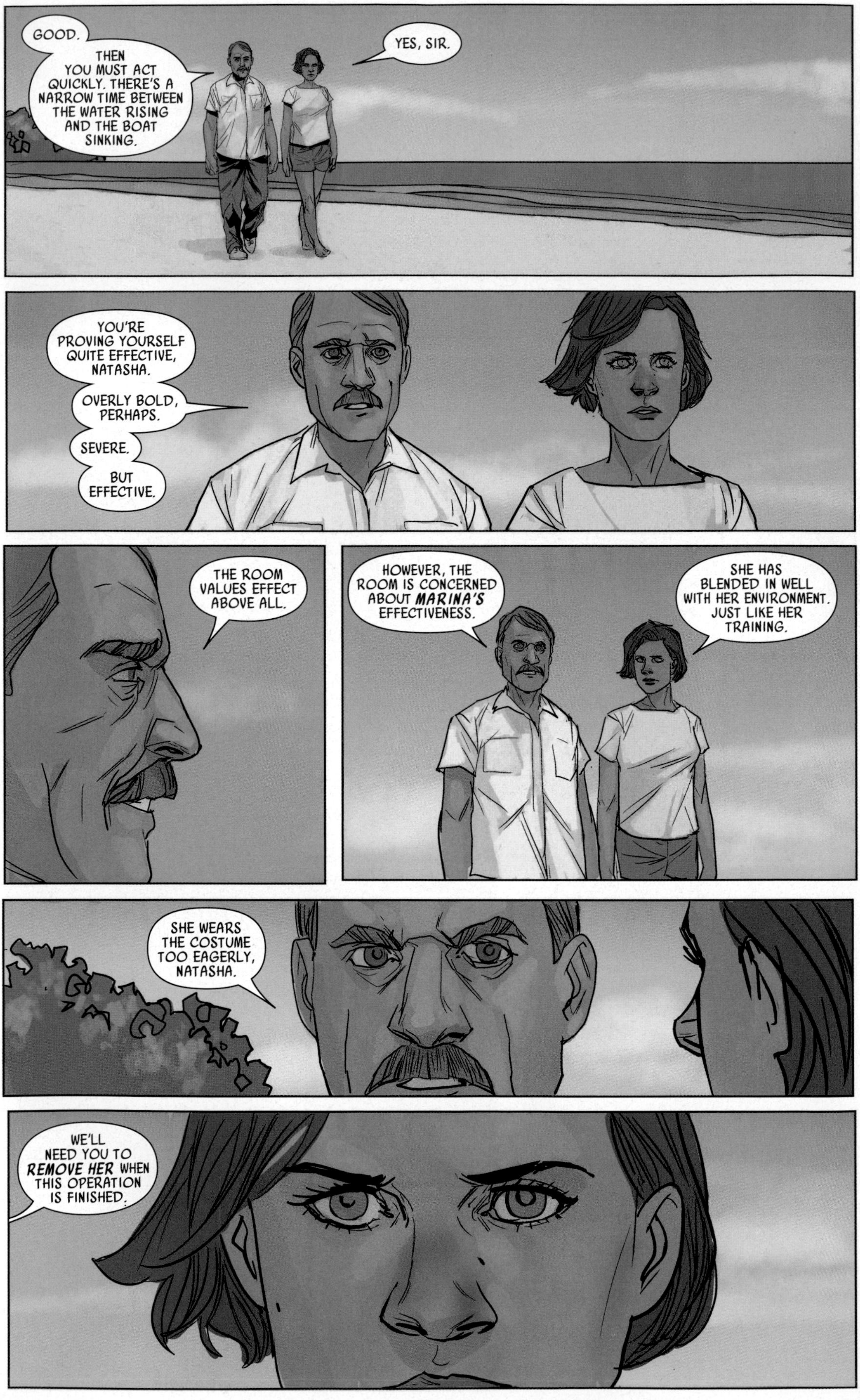
GOOD.
THEN YOU MUST ACT QUICKLY. THERE'S A NARROW TIME BETWEEN THE WATER RISING AND THE BOAT SINKING.
YES, SIR.
YOU'RE PROVING YOURSELF QUITE EFFECTIVE, NATASHA.
OVERLY BOLD, PERHAPS.
SEVERE.
BUT EFFECTIVE.
THE ROOM VALUES EFFECT ABOVE ALL.
HOWEVER, THE ROOM IS CONCERNED ABOUT MARINA'S EFFECTIVENESS.
SHE HAS BLENDED IN WELL WITH HER ENVIRONMENT. JUST LIKE HER TRAINING.
SHE WEARS THE COSTUME TOO EAGERLY, NATASHA.
WE'LL NEED YOU TO REMOVE HER WHEN THIS OPERATION IS FINISHED.

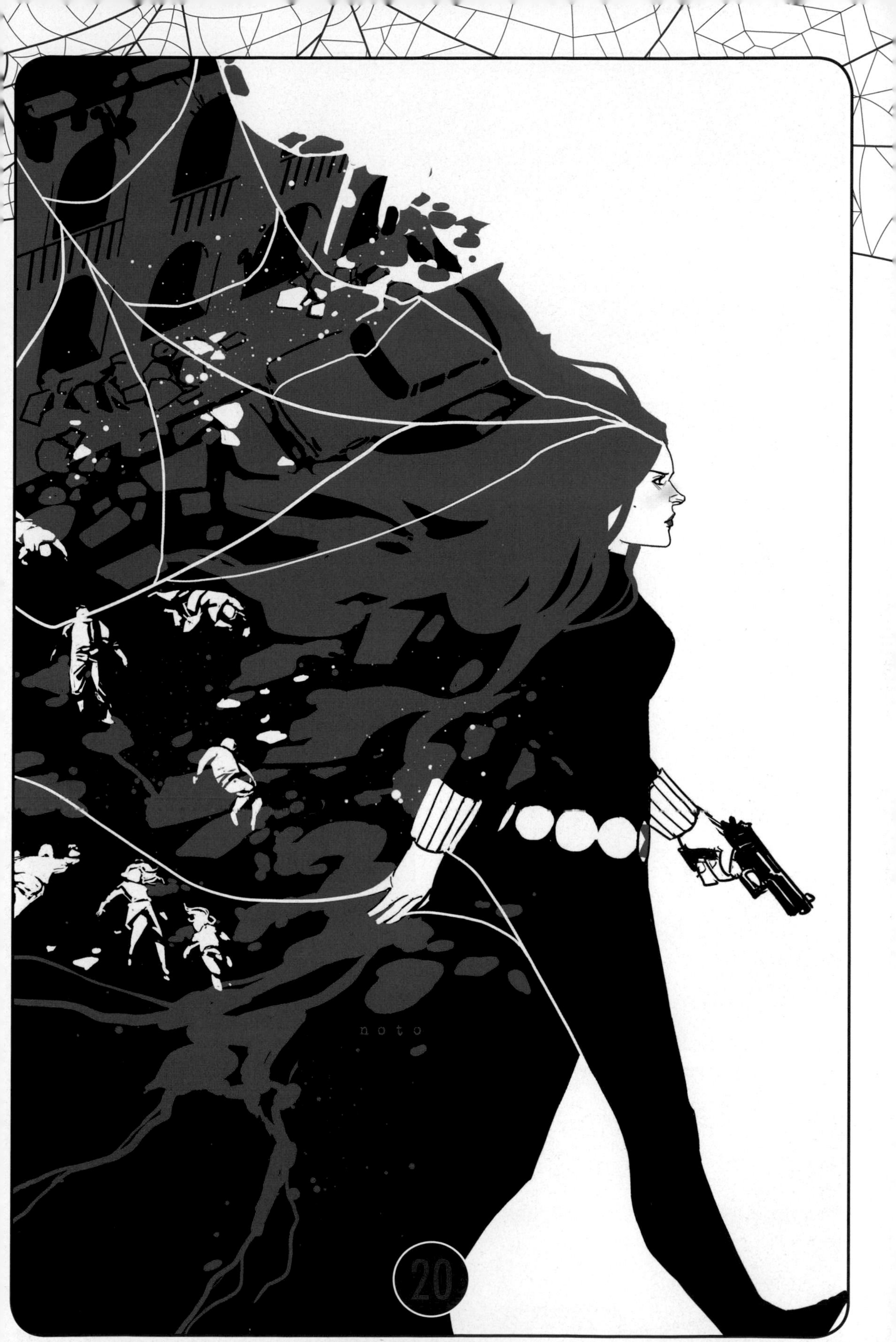
noto
20

JANUARY: PART TWO

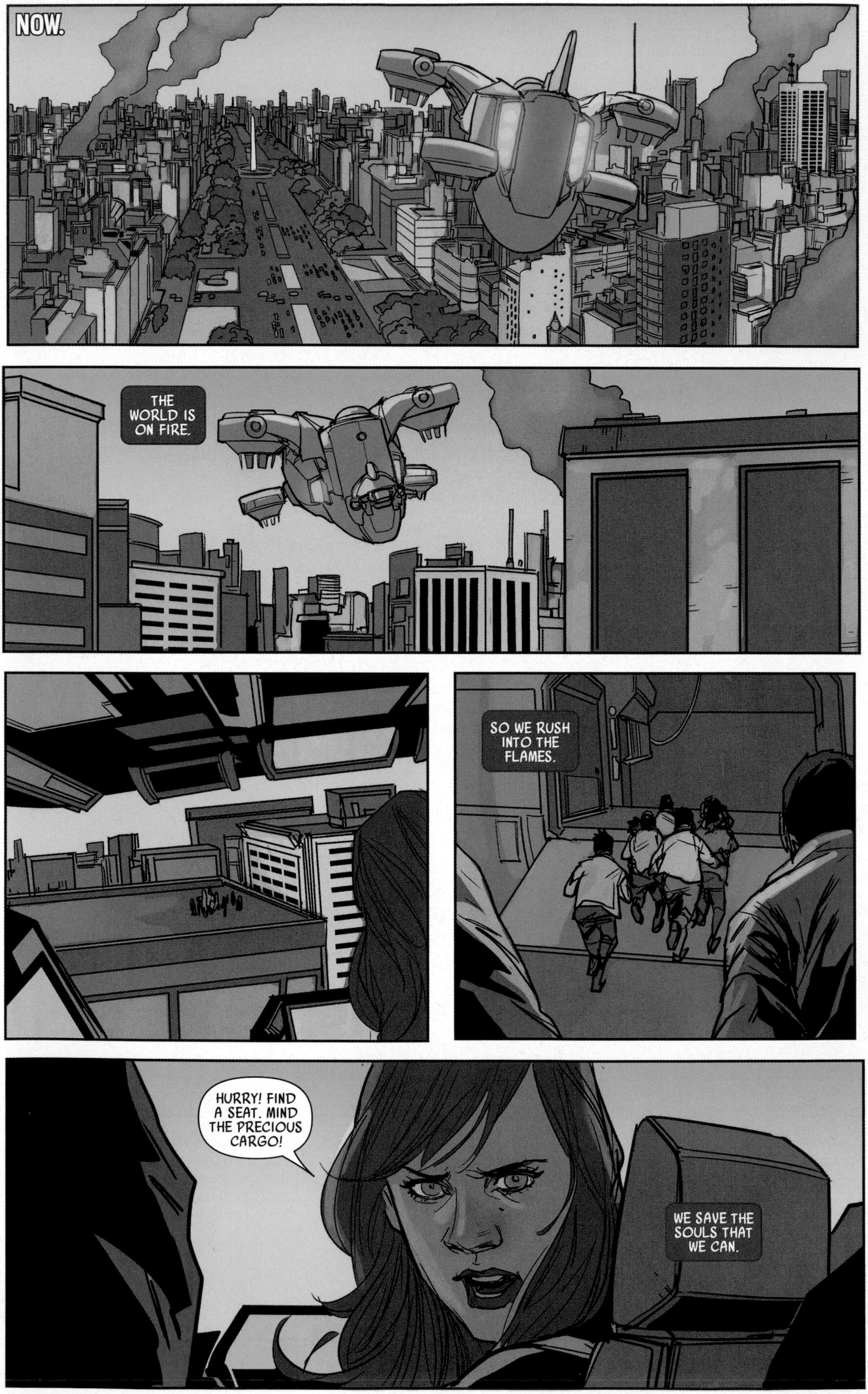
NOW.
THE WORLD IS ON FIRE.
SO WE RUSH INTO THE FLAMES.
HURRY! FIND A SEAT. MIND THE PRECIOUS CARGO!
WE SAVE THE SOULS THAT WE CAN.

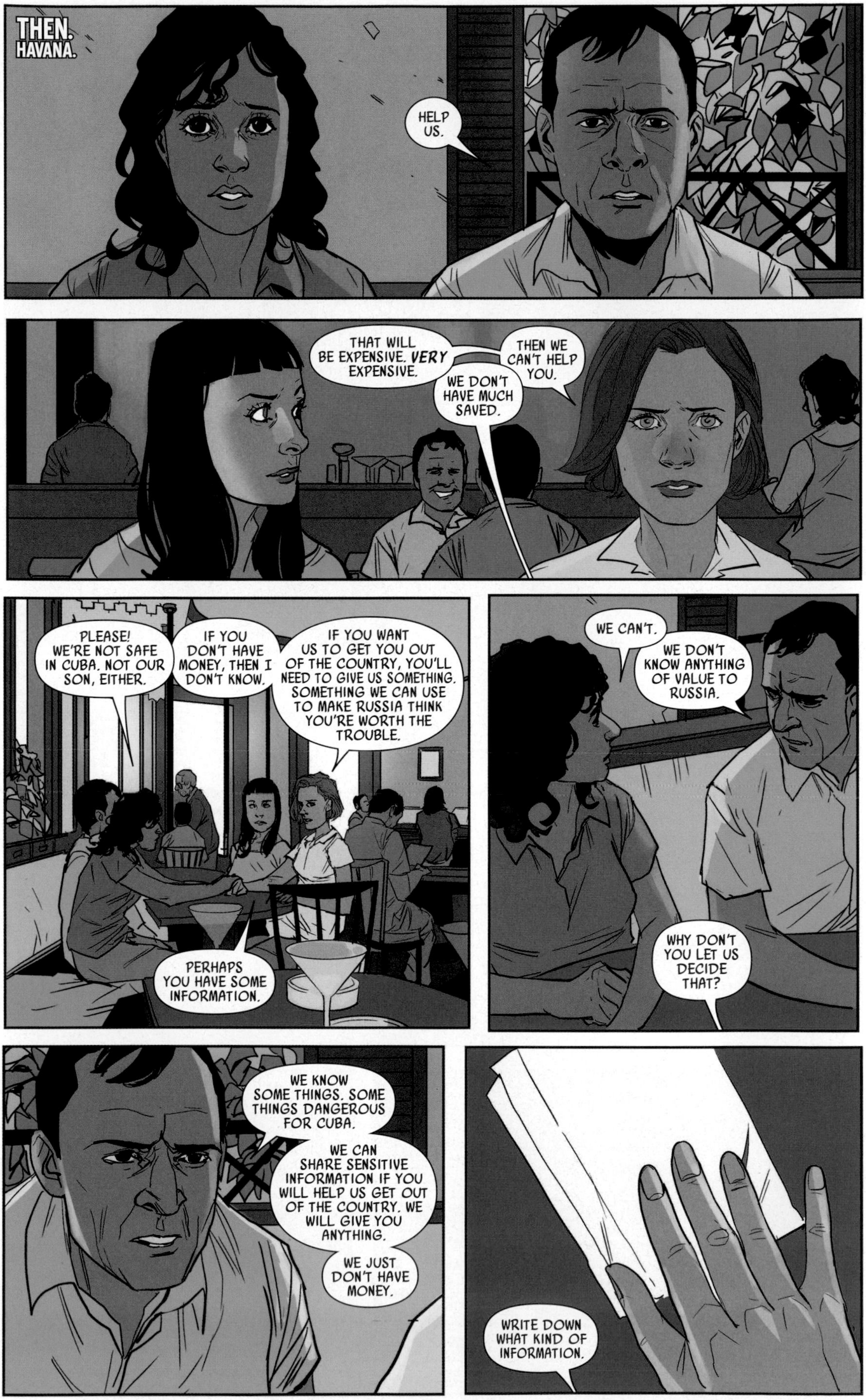
THEN. HAVANA.
HELP US.
THAT WILL BE EXPENSIVE. VERY EXPENSIVE.
THEN WE CAN'T HELP YOU.
WE DON'T HAVE MUCH SAVED.
PLEASE! WE'RE NOT SAFE IN CUBA. NOT OUR SON, EITHER.
IF YOU DON'T HAVE MONEY, THEN I DON'T KNOW.
IF YOU WANT US TO GET YOU OUT OF THE COUNTRY, YOU'LL NEED TO GIVE US SOMETHING. SOMETHING WE CAN USE TO MAKE RUSSIA THINK YOU'RE WORTH THE TROUBLE.
PERHAPS YOU HAVE SOME INFORMATION.
WE CAN'T.
WE DON'T KNOW ANYTHING OF VALUE TO RUSSIA.
WHY DON'T YOU LET US DECIDE THAT?
WE KNOW SOME THINGS. SOME THINGS DANGEROUS FOR CUBA.
WE CAN SHARE SENSITIVE INFORMATION IF YOU WILL HELP US GET OUT OF THE COUNTRY. WE WILL GIVE YOU ANYTHING.
WE JUST DON'T HAVE MONEY.
WRITE DOWN WHAT KIND OF INFORMATION.

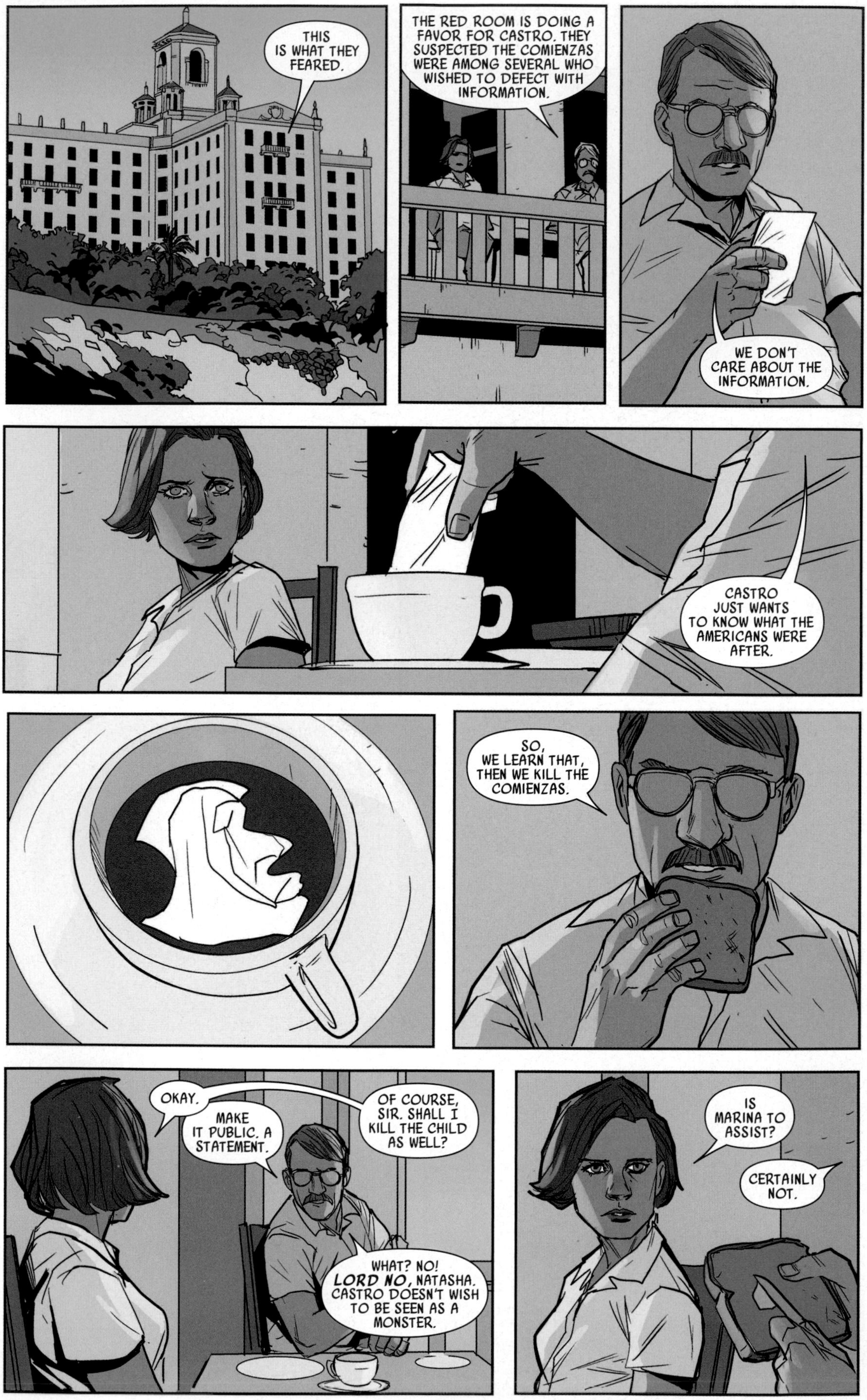

THIS IS WHAT THEY FEARED.
THE RED ROOM IS DOING A FAVOR FOR CASTRO. THEY SUSPECTED THE COMIENZAS WERE AMONG SEVERAL WHO WISHED TO DEFECT WITH INFORMATION.
WE DON'T CARE ABOUT THE INFORMATION.
CASTRO JUST WANTS TO KNOW WHAT THE AMERICANS WERE AFTER.
SO, WE LEARN THAT, THEN WE KILL THE COMIENZAS.
OKAY.
MAKE IT PUBLIC. A STATEMENT.
OF COURSE, SIR. SHALL I KILL THE CHILD AS WELL?
WHAT? NO! **LORD NO,** NATASHA. CASTRO DOESN'T WISH TO BE SEEN AS A MONSTER.
IS MARINA TO ASSIST?
CERTAINLY NOT.

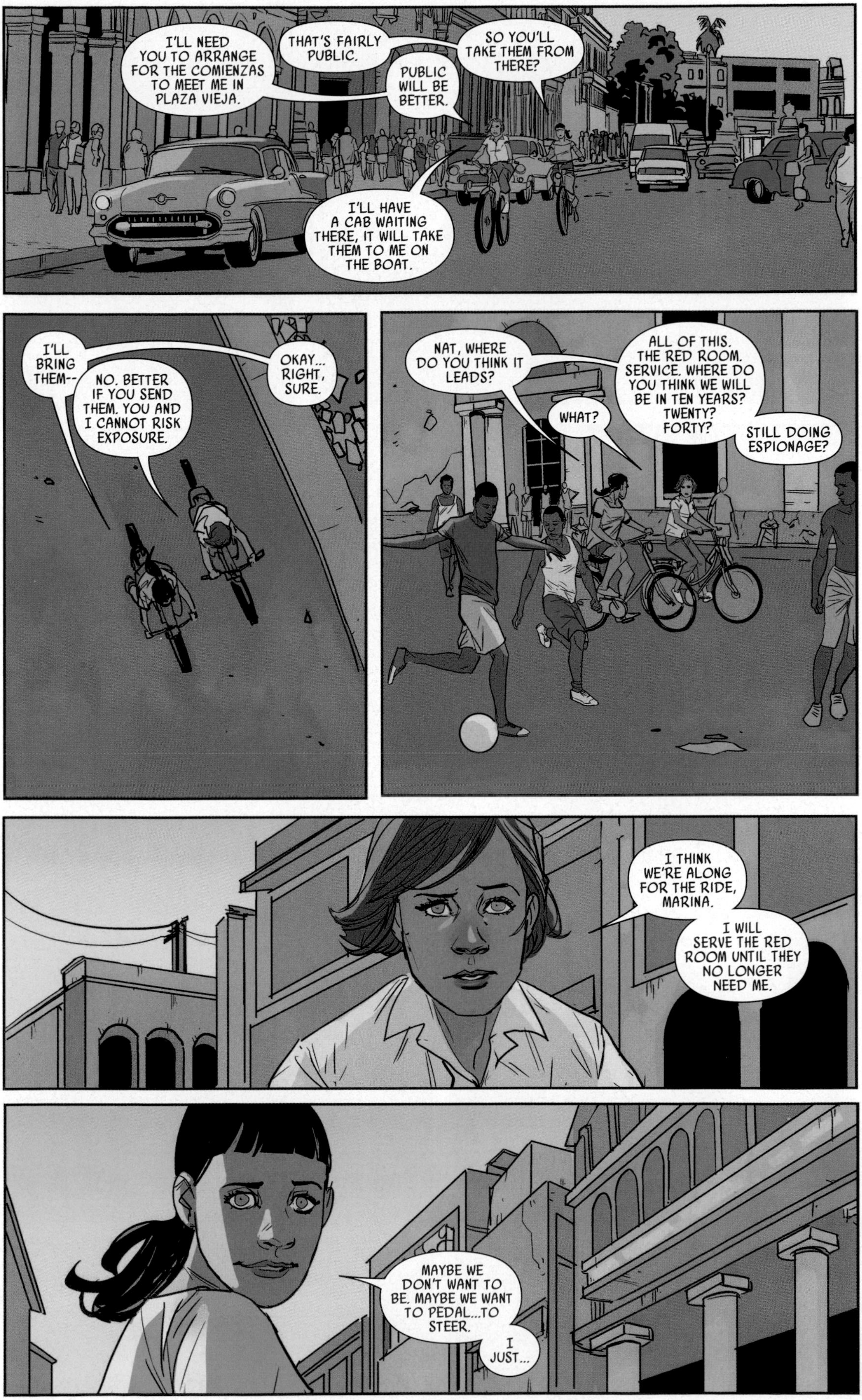
I'LL NEED YOU TO ARRANGE FOR THE COMIENZAS TO MEET ME IN PLAZA VIEJA.
THAT'S FAIRLY PUBLIC.
PUBLIC WILL BE BETTER.
SO YOU'LL TAKE THEM FROM THERE?
I'LL HAVE A CAB WAITING THERE, IT WILL TAKE THEM TO ME ON THE BOAT.
I'LL BRING THEM--
NO. BETTER IF YOU SEND THEM. YOU AND I CANNOT RISK EXPOSURE.
OKAY... RIGHT, SURE.
NAT, WHERE DO YOU THINK IT LEADS?
WHAT?
ALL OF THIS. THE RED ROOM. SERVICE. WHERE DO YOU THINK WE WILL BE IN TEN YEARS? TWENTY? FORTY?
STILL DOING ESPIONAGE?
I THINK WE'RE ALONG FOR THE RIDE, MARINA.
I WILL SERVE THE RED ROOM UNTIL THEY NO LONGER NEED ME.
MAYBE WE DON'T WANT TO BE. MAYBE WE WANT TO PEDAL...TO STEER.
I JUST...

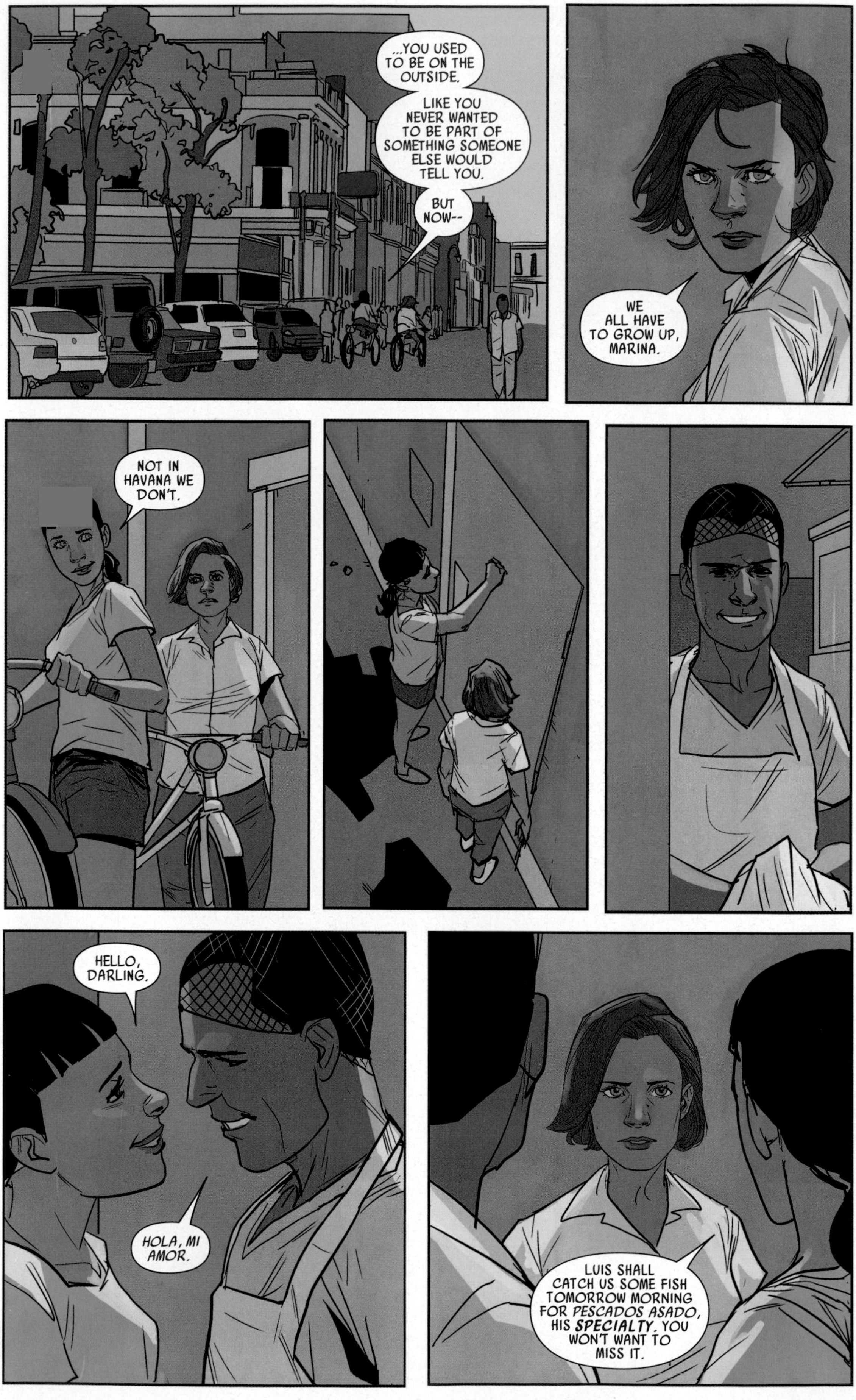
...YOU USED TO BE ON THE OUTSIDE.
LIKE YOU NEVER WANTED TO BE PART OF SOMETHING SOMEONE ELSE WOULD TELL YOU.
BUT NOW--
WE ALL HAVE TO GROW UP, MARINA.
NOT IN HAVANA WE DON'T.
HELLO, DARLING.
HOLA, MI AMOR.
LUIS SHALL CATCH US SOME FISH TOMORROW MORNING FOR *PESCADOS ASADO*, HIS **SPECIALTY**. YOU WON'T WANT TO MISS IT.

LATER.

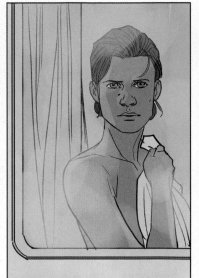

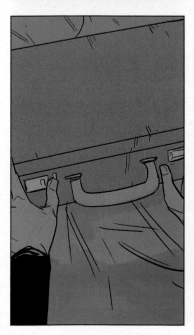

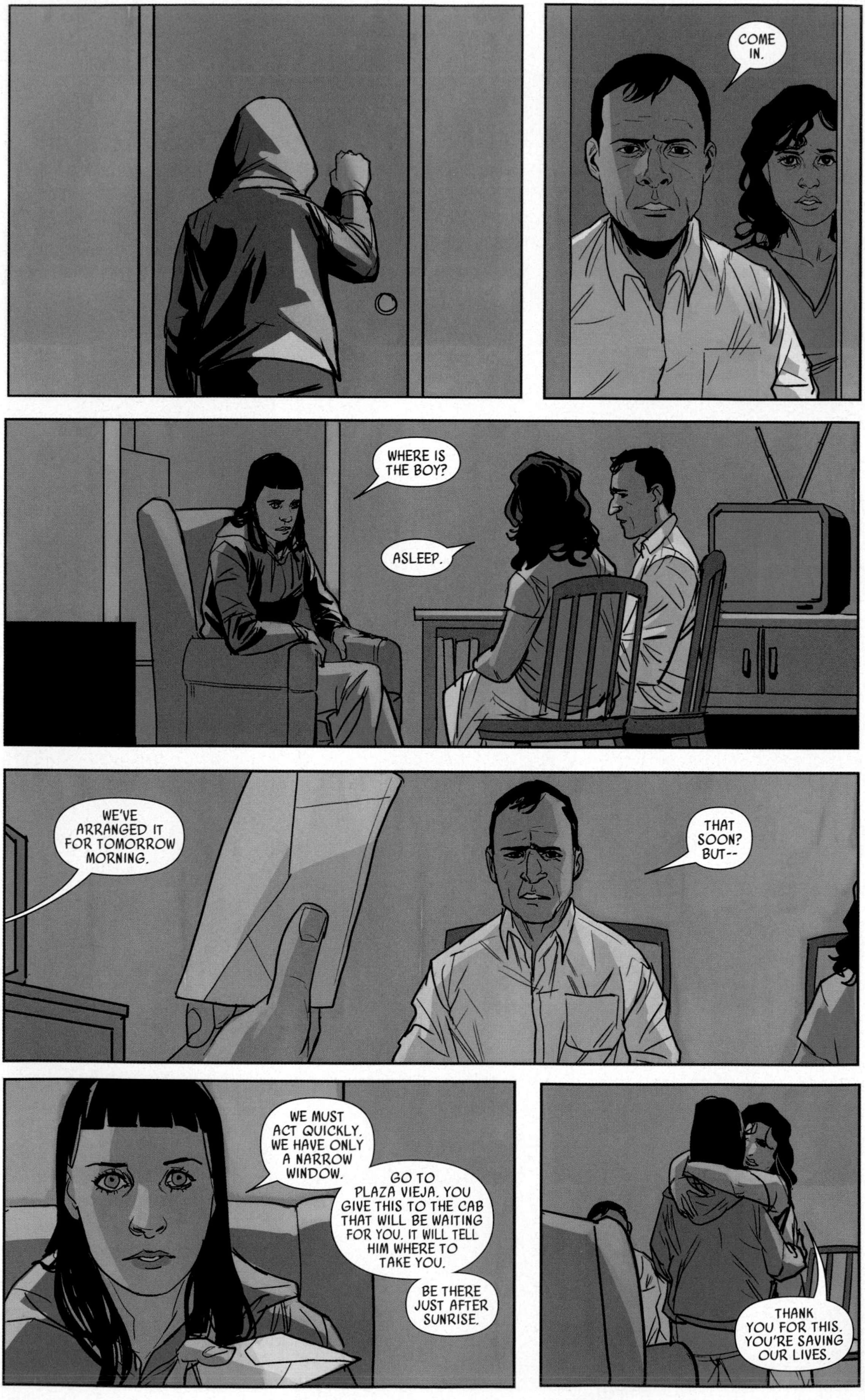
COME IN.
WHERE IS THE BOY?
ASLEEP.
WE'VE ARRANGED IT FOR TOMORROW MORNING.
THAT SOON? BUT--
WE MUST ACT QUICKLY. WE HAVE ONLY A NARROW WINDOW.
GO TO PLAZA VIEJA. YOU GIVE THIS TO THE CAB THAT WILL BE WAITING FOR YOU. IT WILL TELL HIM WHERE TO TAKE YOU.
BE THERE JUST AFTER SUNRISE.
THANK YOU FOR THIS. YOU'RE SAVING OUR LIVES.

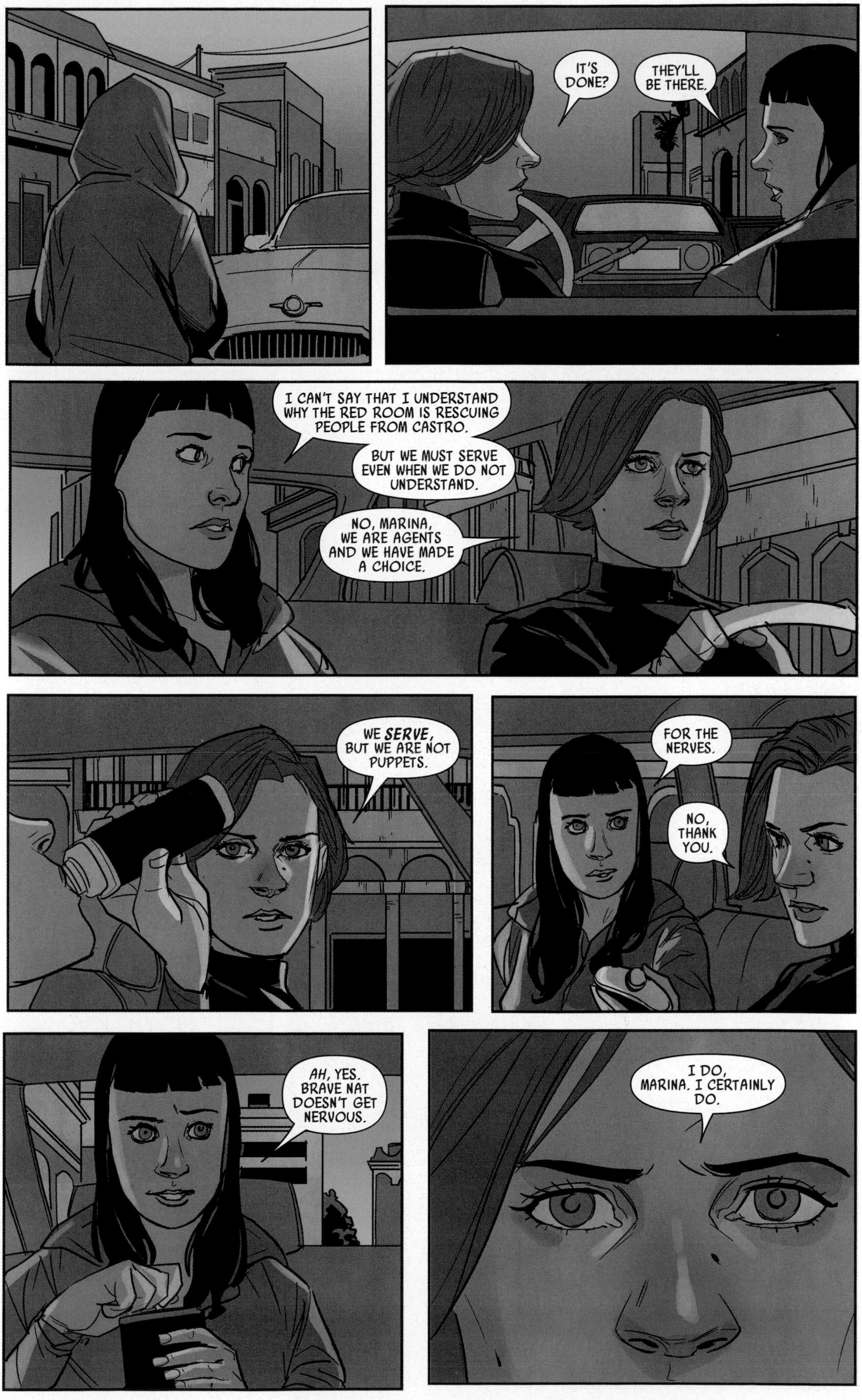
IT'S DONE?
THEY'LL BE THERE.
I CAN'T SAY THAT I UNDERSTAND WHY THE RED ROOM IS RESCUING PEOPLE FROM CASTRO.
BUT WE MUST SERVE EVEN WHEN WE DO NOT UNDERSTAND.
NO, MARINA, WE ARE AGENTS AND WE HAVE MADE A CHOICE.
WE *SERVE*, BUT WE ARE NOT PUPPETS.
FOR THE NERVES.
NO, THANK YOU.
AH, YES. BRAVE NAT DOESN'T GET NERVOUS.
I DO, MARINA. I CERTAINLY DO.

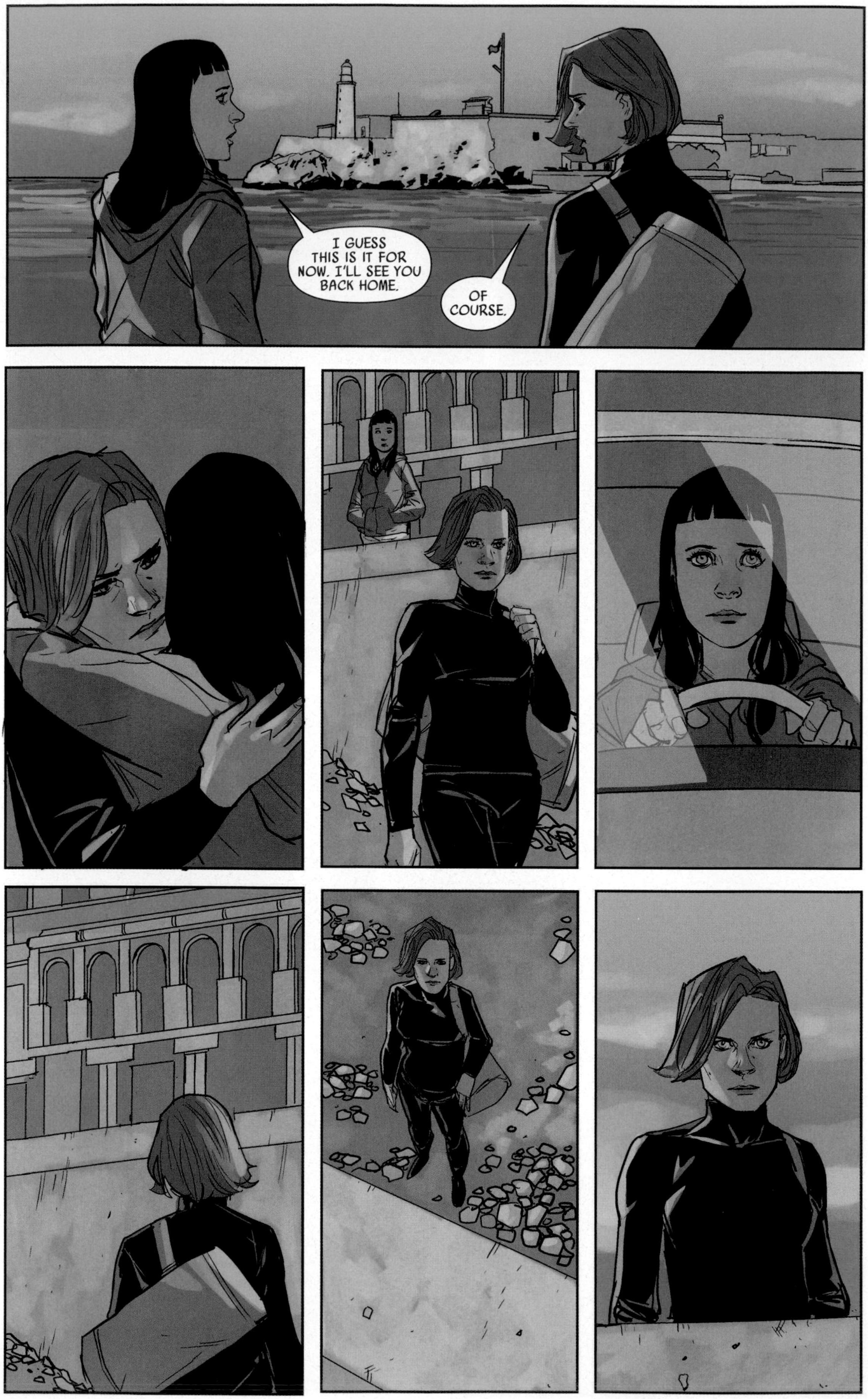
I GUESS THIS IS IT FOR NOW. I'LL SEE YOU BACK HOME.
OF COURSE.

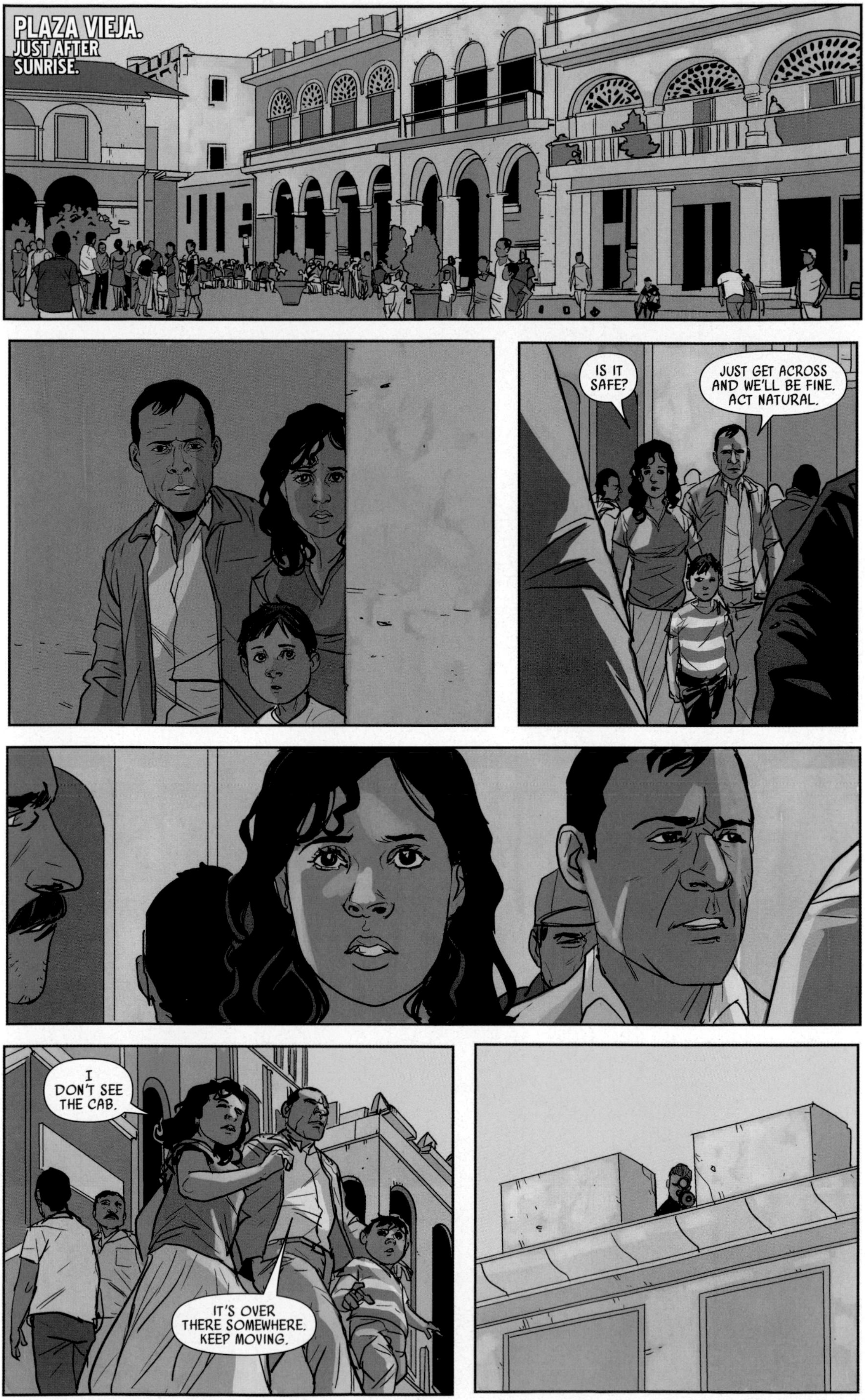
PLAZA VIEJA. JUST AFTER SUNRISE.
IS IT SAFE?
JUST GET ACROSS AND WE'LL BE FINE. ACT NATURAL.
I DON'T SEE THE CAB.
IT'S OVER THERE SOMEWHERE. KEEP MOVING.

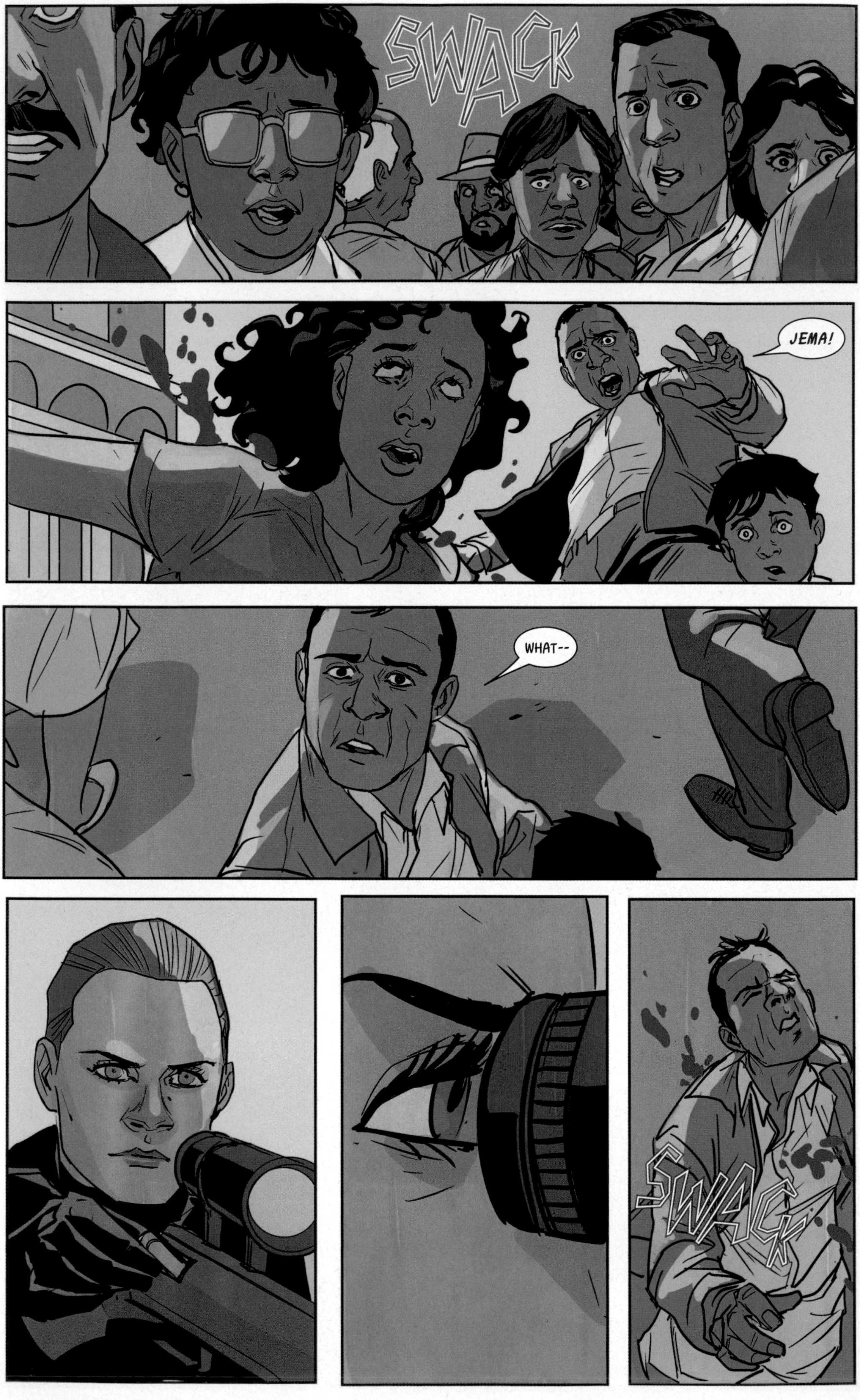
SWACK
JEMA!
WHAT--
SWACK

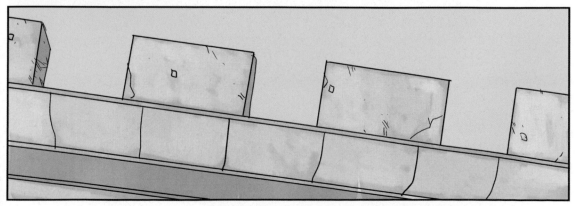

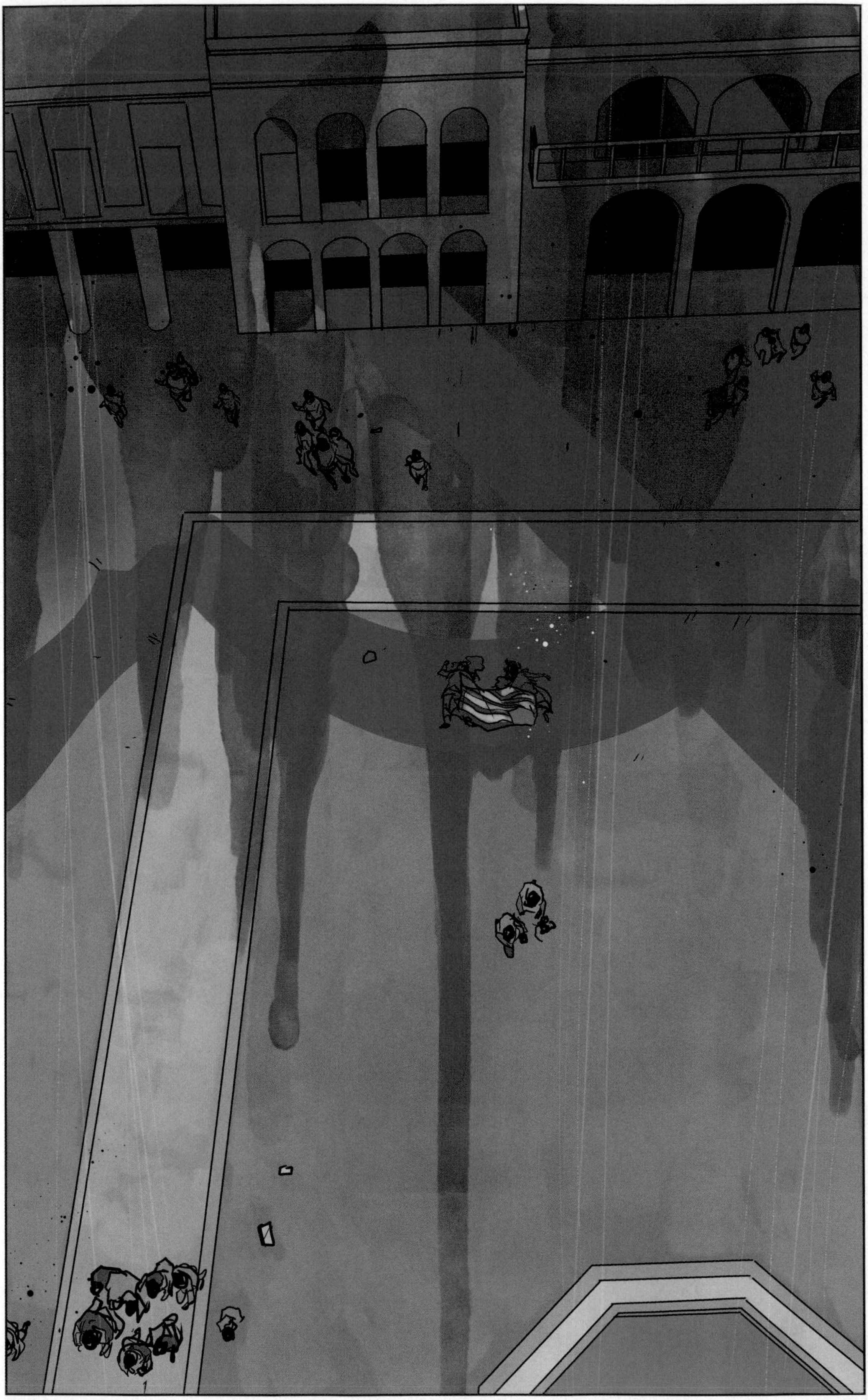

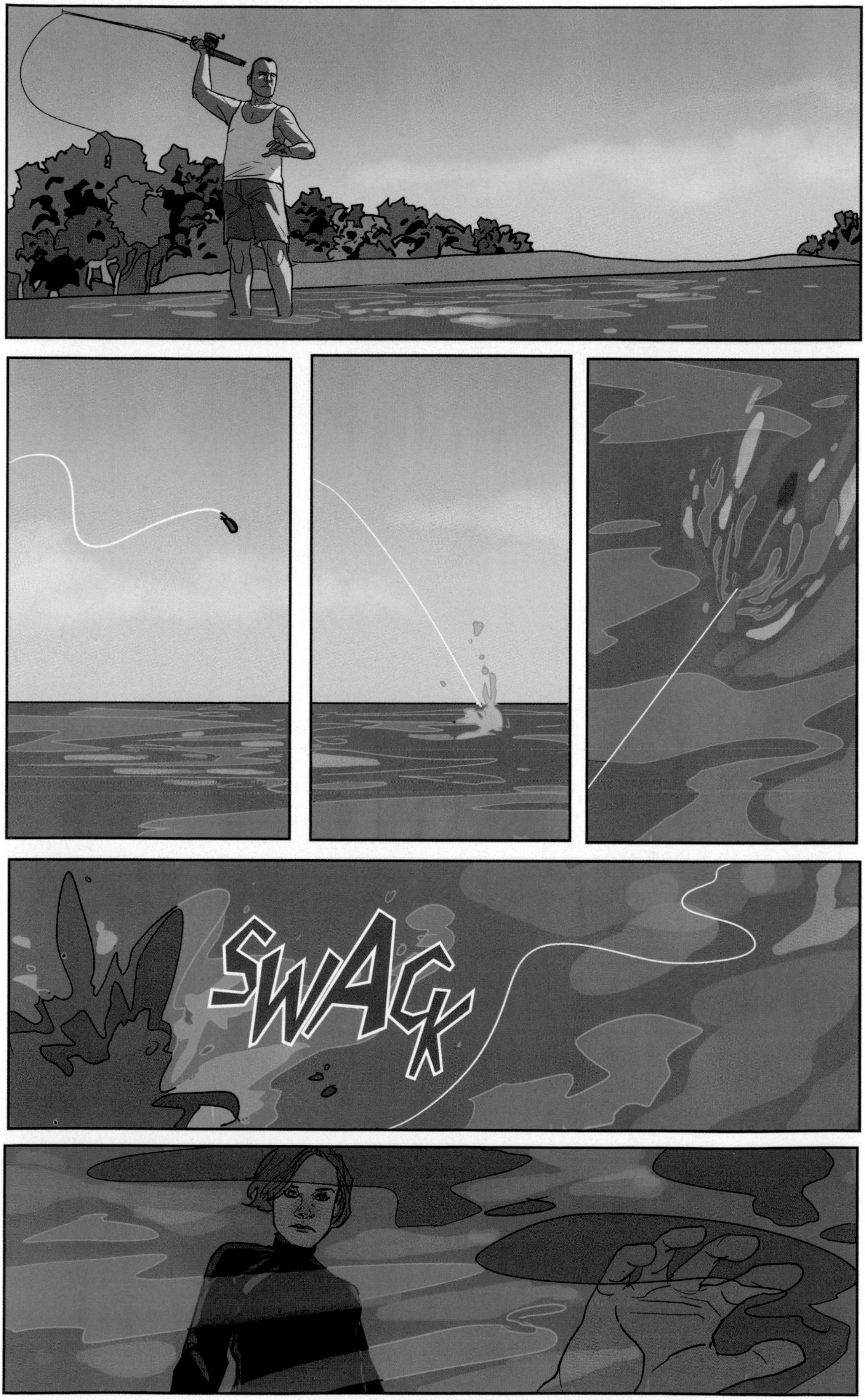
SWACK

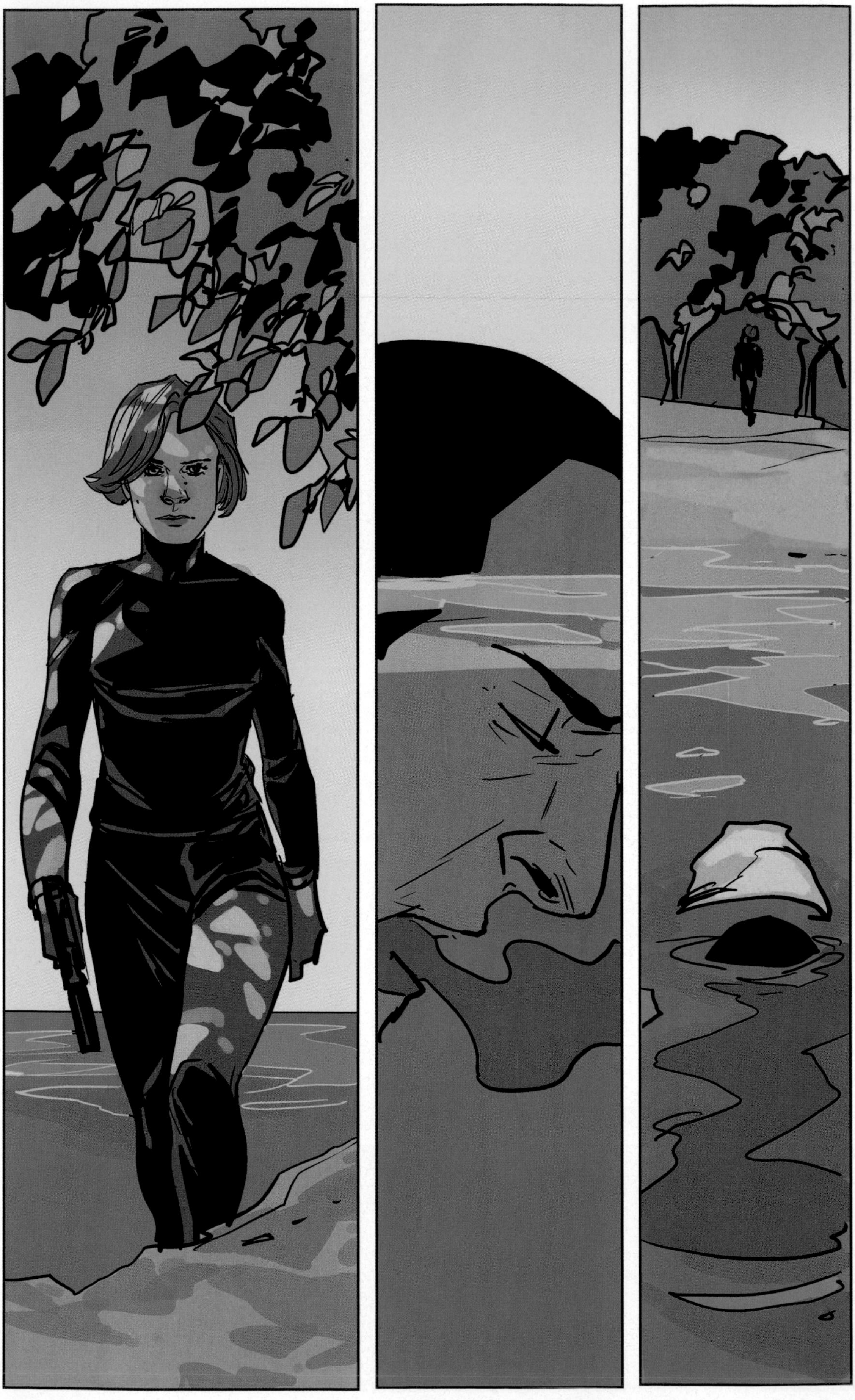

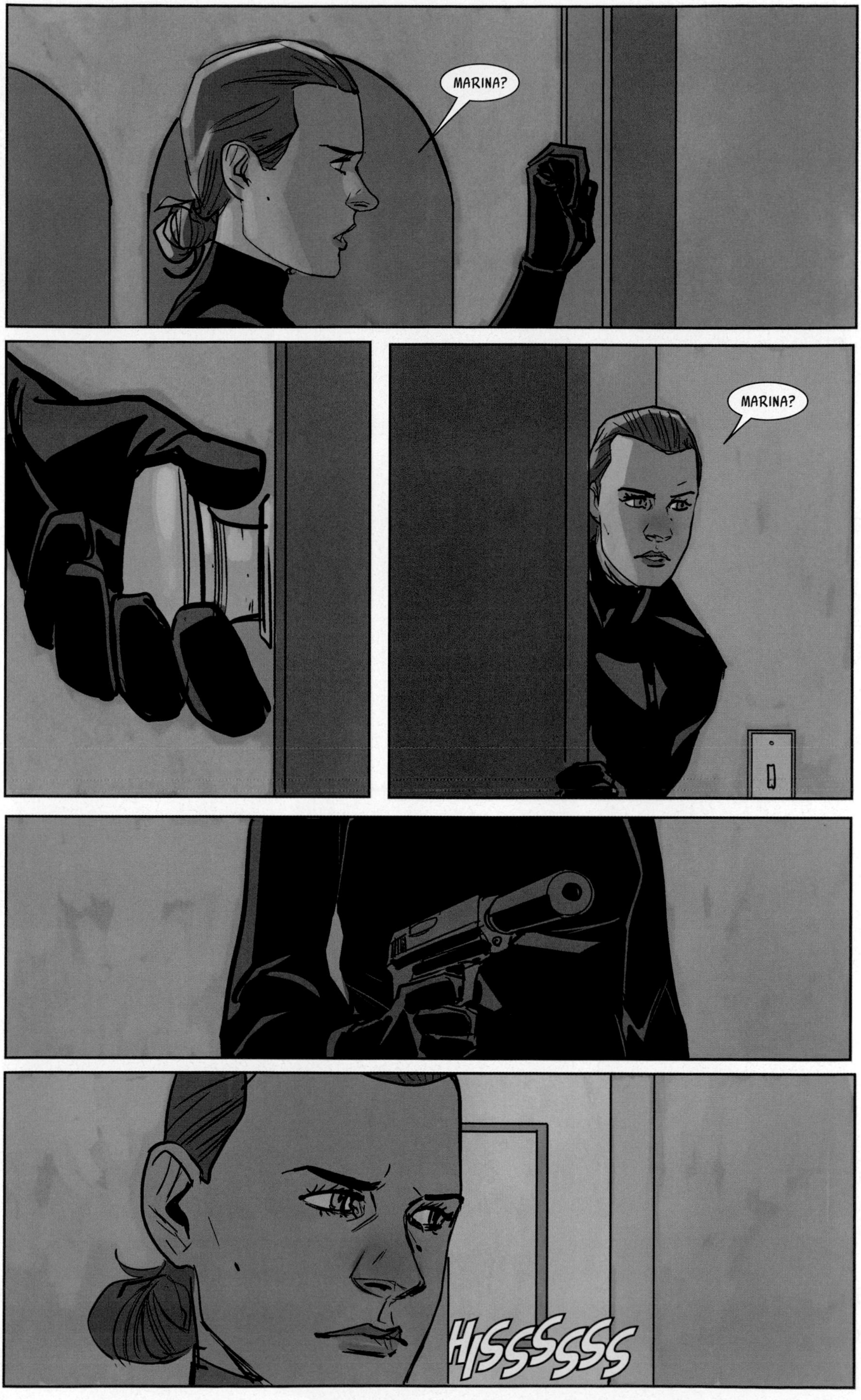
MARINA?
MARINA?
HISSSSSS

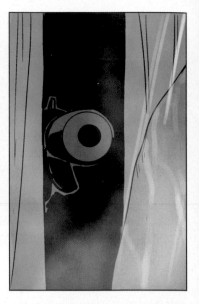

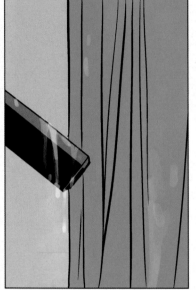

SWACK

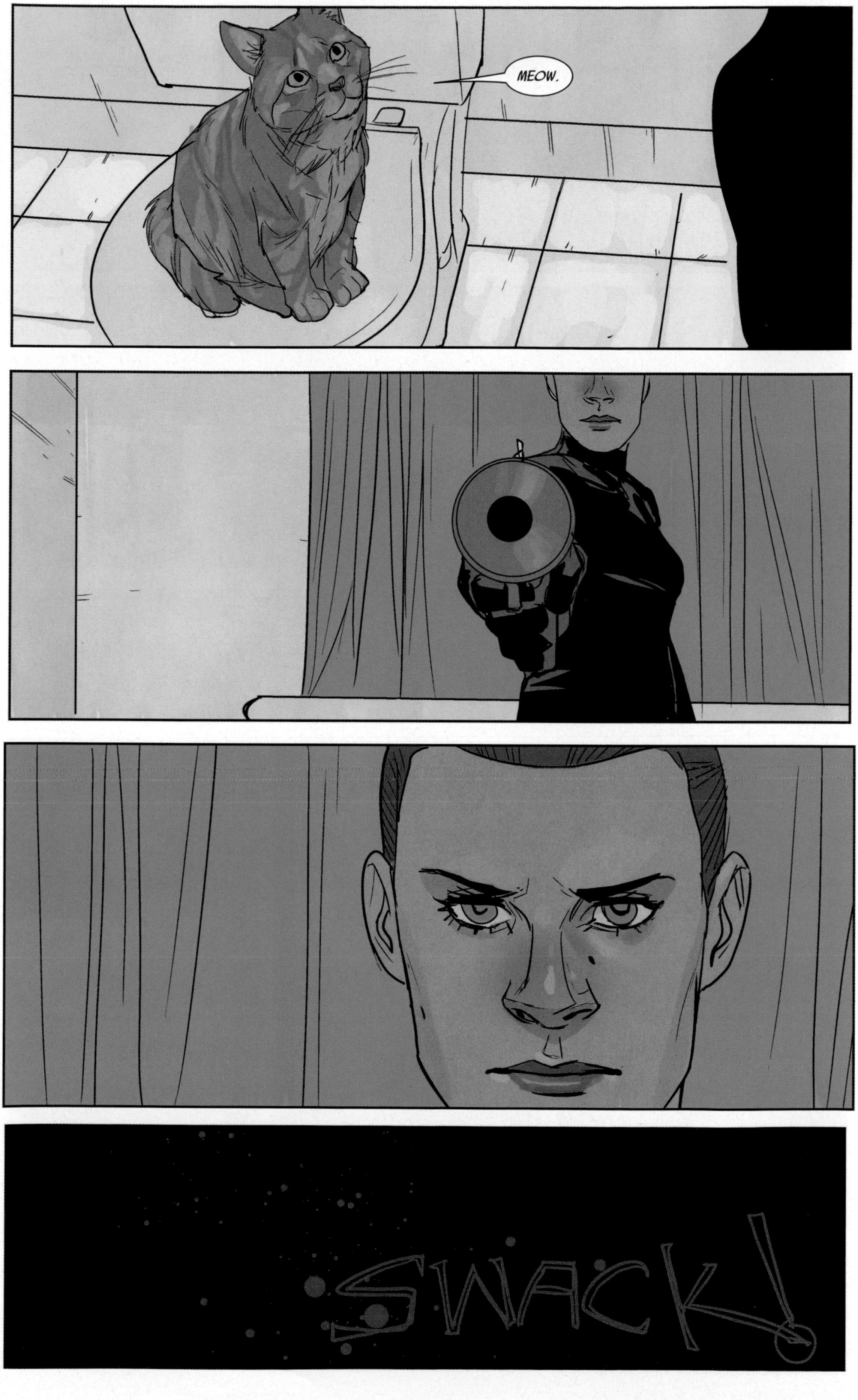
MEOW.
SWACK!

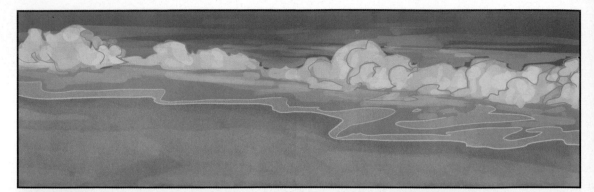

TIME TO LEAVE.

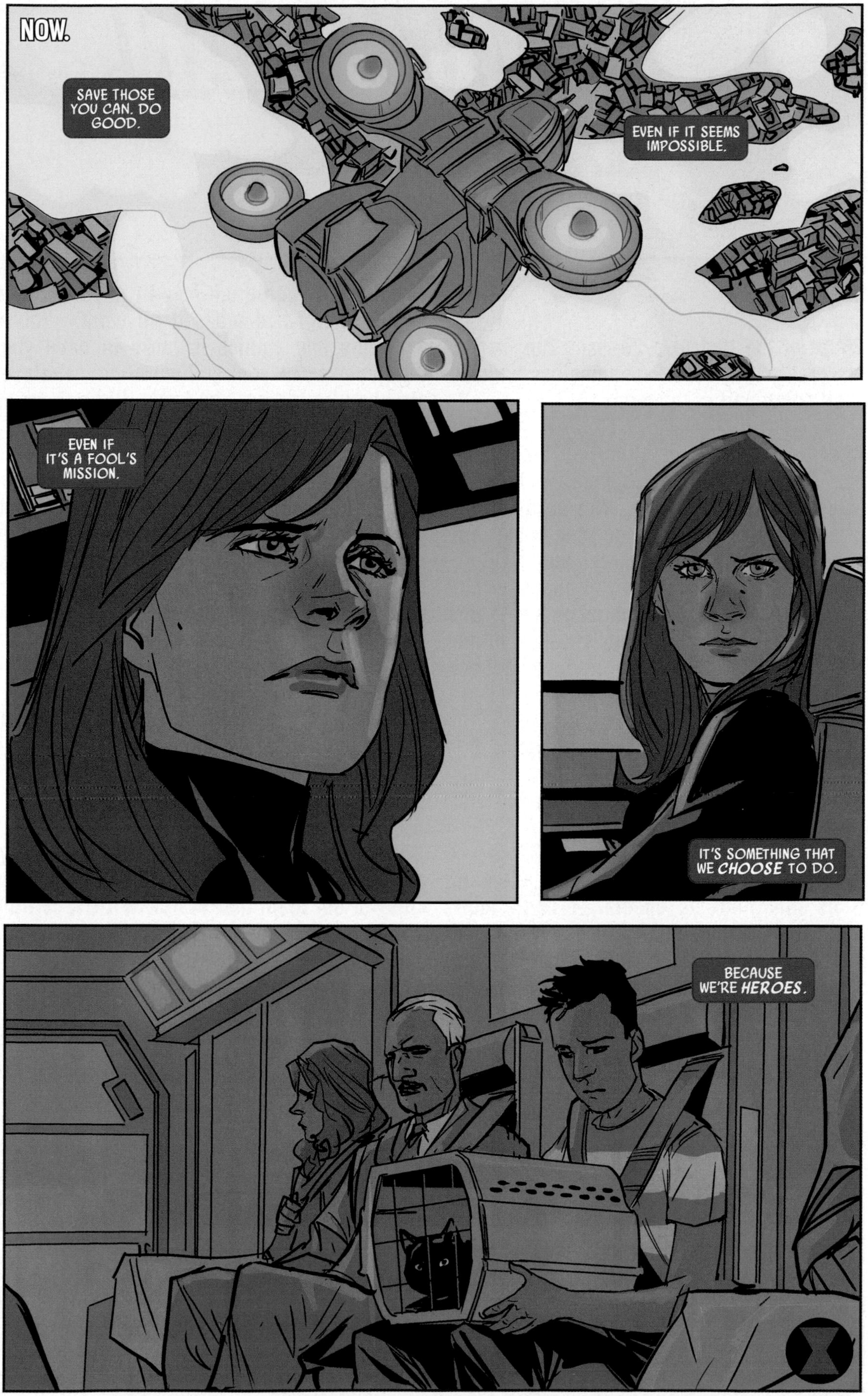
NOW.
SAVE THOSE YOU CAN. DO GOOD.
EVEN IF IT SEEMS IMPOSSIBLE.
EVEN IF IT'S A FOOL'S MISSION.
IT'S SOMETHING THAT WE CHOOSE TO DO.
BECAUSE WE'RE HEROES.

TO RUSSIAN, WITH LOVE...

DEAR READERS!

We're at the end of a 20-issue run, and it feels great, but it's all meaningless without you all being part of the team.

At Marvel they keep telling me that we've done something really special, which is always a surprise to hear. Not because I'm not extraordinarily proud of the book, not because it hasn't been a real and thrilling adventure and not because I'm unaware that we've offered real story and character to the Marvel Comics canon. Simply because for me I just showed up to work and tried my best not to screw it up.

Still, it's hard to ignore the tweets, the cosplay, the blog posts, the accidental Iggy Azalea Google Alerts. And this resonated with our team at Marvel.

When those at Marvel and our readership tell us this book is special, I don't think they're just talking about title longevity and sales numbers. I think we're talking about an experience we've shared with Natasha, all of us together. I know she's affected me. I've identified with her journey and I've been inspired by her strength. Everyone who's cracked these books is captivated by the art, and literally drawn into her secrets and trials by Phil's visceral art, in which we've all found something we treasure.

Speaking of Phil, let me say: brother, it's been a real and inspiring pleasure. I know we were perfect together on this book because we didn't have to discuss process for the entirety of 20 issues. We shared story ideas, then you knew how to make the best of what I wrote and I figured out how little you needed in descriptions to make it all work. You're a genius and comics is lucky to have you. Whatever book you're illustrating, whatever story you're telling, you know I'll be there as your biggest fan.

One kid, two houses and over two years ago, Axel called with this arranged marriage and he correctly, I think, foresaw the opportunity for great chemistry on this book. He's the first of four editors who were appropriately hands-off to the whole endeavor to allow Phil and me room to tell the story we saw in our heads. And yet, starting with the wonderfully visionary Ellie Pyle, and then guided by foxhole brother Jake Thomas, all under the "That makes NO sense at all" purview of Tom Brevoort, and not forgetting our letterer supreme, Clayton Cowles, this was undeniably a team effort.

Twenty issues of anything is a real victory, and you, our readers, have made irrefutably clear to our team that BLACK WIDOW is truly special.

Let's be clear: this isn't a breakup letter. None of us on Team Nat wants for this lovely relationship we've built with you to end. In fact, we want to take it to the next level. So let's try some new books together.

But if we've learned anything from Natasha in these 20 issues, it's that we can't be afraid to move on. So let's move on, and I'll see you on the other side, with another character between us.

Best regards from L.A.
Nathan

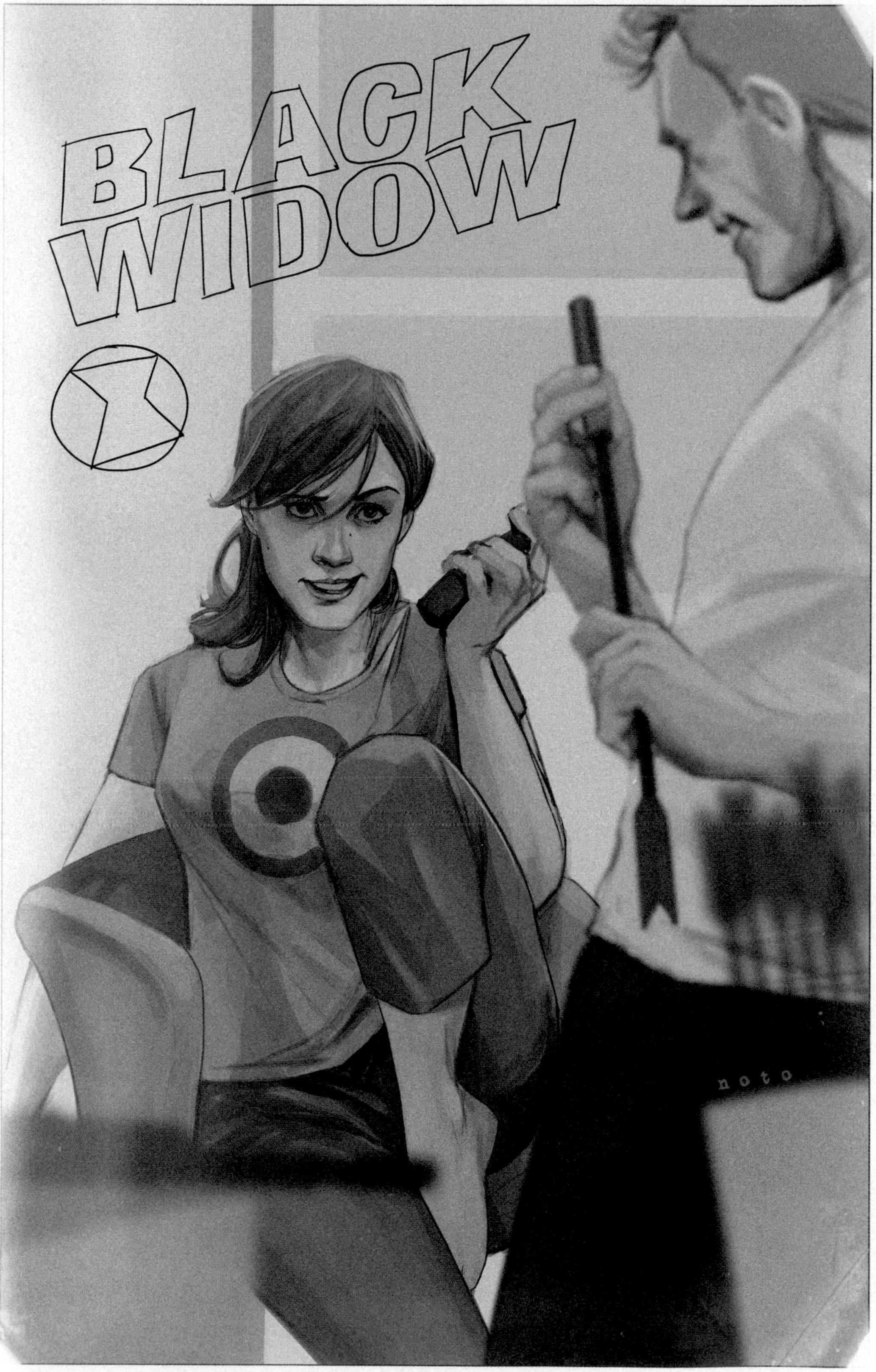
BLACK WIDOW
noto

#15 VARIANT BY PHIL NOTO

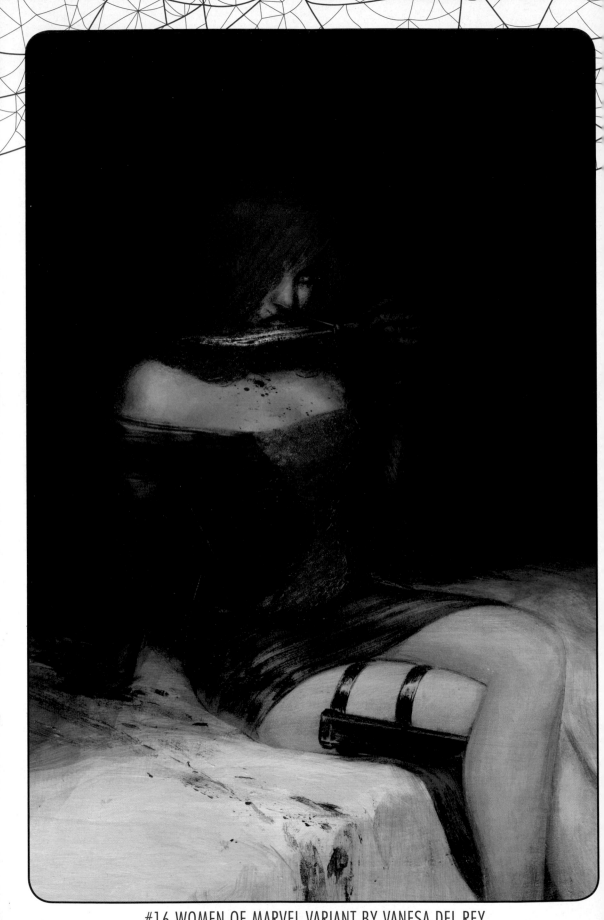

#16 WOMEN OF MARVEL VARIANT BY VANESA DEL REY

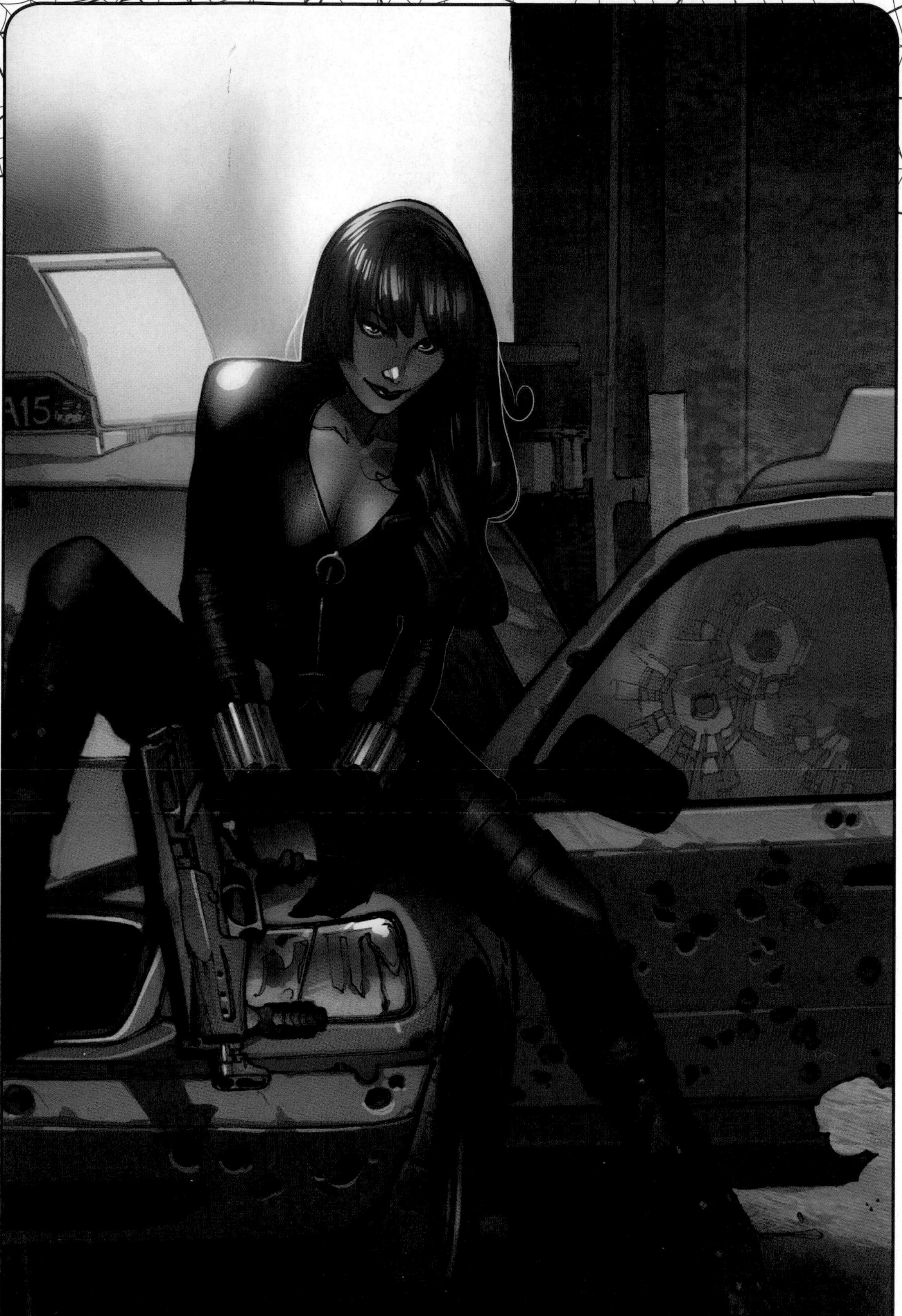
A15

#18 NYC VARIANT BY OLIVIER COIPEL & MARTE GRACIA

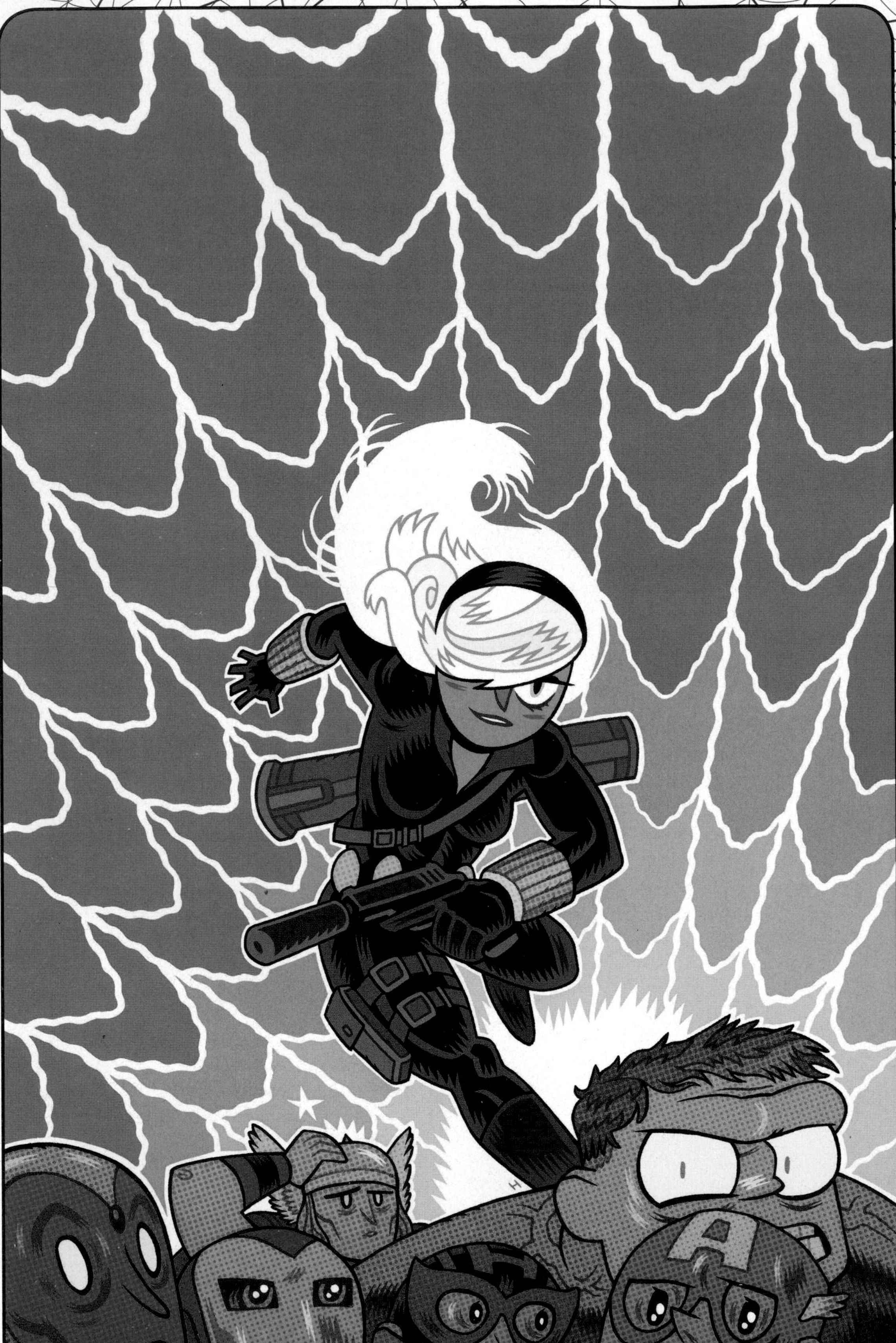

#19 GWEN VARIANT BY DAN HIPP